PETER BROOK

BY THE SAME AUTHOR

The Book of US
Tank
One in Four
theatre@risk

PETER BROOK

A Biography

Michael Kustow

BLOOMSBURY

First published in Great Britain 2005

Copyright © by Michael Kustow 2005

The right of Michael Kustow to be identified as author
of this work has been asserted by him in accordance with
the Copyright, Designs and Patents Act 1988

Every reasonable effort has been made to contact holders of copyright
material reproduced in this book, but if any have inadvertently been overlooked
the publishers world be glad to hear from them and to make good in future
editions any errors or omissions brought to their attention.

Bloomsbury Publishing Plc, 38 Soho Square, London W1D 3HB

A CIP catalogue record for this book
is available from the British Library

ISBN 0 7475 7646 7

10 9 8 7 6 5 4 3 2 1

Typeset by Hewer Text Ltd., Edinburgh
Printed in Great Britain by Clays Ltd, St Ives plc

All papers used by Bloomsbury Publishing are natural, recyclable
products made from wood grown in well-managed forests.
The manufacturing processes conform to the environmental
regulations of the country of origin.

To Jane

Beliefs are the rungs of the ladder. We need them, but as we grasp them, something tells us they are not as solid as they seem.

Peter Brook

Contents

Thanks

My thanks of course are to Peter Brook, for giving his time over the past three years to answer searching questions, to free-associate, call up memories, point me to documents and interviewees. At our meetings, he invariably switched right into our work, despite being in the throes of rehearsing – a revival of *Happy Days* – and the research and travel for his new theatre piece. This is an authorised biography and I received what would be the equivalent of critical notes to an actor, but notes which rarely felt like constraints, and I would expect no less from as fearless a questioner as he. It was an encouragement, too, to see him visibly becoming more involved in the emotions of the book.

I owe an immense debt to Nina Soufy, Peter Brook's assistant and life-organiser. From her office at the Bouffes du Nord, crammed with scripts, photographs, editions, videos, she was tireless in tracking down crucial elements and chronologies. Even when under the greatest pressure, she always made me feel welcomed and at home, and I realised what a centre she provides for Brook's many-faceted life and work.

I interviewed scores of Brook's associates – actors, writers, designers, critics, producers, in England, France, America – and I thank them for their memories and vivid insights. Even when their words have not been quoted in the text, their contributions have coloured and influenced it. Special thanks are due to Robert Facey, a friend of Peter's since prep school, who, in the Canadian suburb where he now lives, opened up his cache of a lifetime's correspondence with Peter.

A travel fellowship from the Leverhulme Trust enabled me to make such journeys. The tapes of my interviews were faithfully transcribed by Sherry Baines, and Rebecca Pilbeam brought a keen passion for theatre to the later stages of tracking and clearing sources and photographs.

At Bloomsbury, in Bill Swainson I have been blessed with an editor of contained enthusiasm and fierce concentration, who has helped me dig the book out from too many words, and made me feel, as a theatre enthusiast himself, that the book and its subject would matter to those who love theatre and could speak to those who may not. His assistant Sarah Marcus has cheerfully guided the book towards production. Picking my way through narrow book-lined landings above Soho Square has made each trip to Bloomsbury an excitement. Liz Calder has been calmly encouraging.

My agent David Godwin's endless enthusiasm and belief sustained me along the way. Simon Callow, John Goodwin and John Barton, former theatre colleagues and friends, have at key points lifted me back into the main current of the book. Their pointed, even their critical comments have been priceless. My French translator Marie-Thérèse Weal, working on a text that seemed to shift under her gaze, asked sharp and pertinent questions. David Bradby and Royal Holloway University of London kindly awarded me a fellowship, and David's interest and knowledge of French theatre has continually refreshed me.

Acknowledgements

For permission to reprint copyright material the author and publishers gratefully acknowledge the following:

Copyright (© 1998) from *Threads of Time* by Peter Brook. Reproduced by permission of Methuen Publishing Ltd. Copyright (© 1988) from *The Shifting Point* by Peter Brook. Reproduced by permission of Methuen Publishing Ltd. Copyright (© 1987) from *The Mahabharata* by Jean-Claude Carrière, translated by Peter Brook. Reproduced by permission of Methuen Publishing Ltd. Copyright (© 1992) from *Peter Brook – A Theatrical Casebook* by David Williams. Reproduced by permission of Methuen Publishing Ltd. Copyright (© 1972) from *Orghast at Persepolis* by Anthony Smith. Reproduced by permission of Methuen Publishing Ltd.

Extracts from *The Empty Space* reprinted by permission of HarperCollins Publishers Ltd. © Peter Brook, 1968.

Extracts from *Peter Brook – Directors in Perspective* by Albert Hunt and Geoffrey Reeves © Cambridge University Press (1995) reproduced with permission of Cambridge University Press, Albert Hunt and Geoffrey Reeves.

Copyright (© 1990) from *Burnt Bridges: A Souvenir of the Swinging Sixties and Beyond* by Charles Marowitz. Reproduced by permission of Hodder & Stoughton.

Copyright (© 1991) from *Peter Brook and the Mahabharata: Critical Perspectives* by David Williams. Reproduced by permission of Routledge/ Taylor & Francis Books, Inc.

List of Illustrations with Credits

Peter Brook, aged twelve, curious about film. (Peter Brook)

Peter Brook aged twenty-one in 1946. (Peter Brook)

Brook at twenty-one celebrated by *Vogue*. (Clifford Coffin/Vogue © The Condé Nast Publications Ltd)

Brook directing *A Sentimental Journey* at Oxford, 1944. (Robert Facey)

Brook with John Gielgud and Anthony Quayle at the Shakespeare Memorial Theatre, 1950. (popperfoto.com)

Brook and Natasha Parry at the time of their marriage, 1950s. (Peter Brook)

Alec Guinness, distraught, in Sartre's *Vicious Circle*, 1946. © Victoria and Albert Theatre Museum Images)

Captivating post-war elegance: *Ring Round the Moon*, 1950. (Houston Rogers, © Victoria and Albert Theatre Museum Images)

Peter Brook and Natasha Parry with Fidel Castro, Cuba, 1953. (Peter Brook)

Paul Scofield as a mould-breaking King Lear, Stratford, 1962. (Photo © Zoe Dominic)

Paul Scofield as Lear in the film, 1969. (British Film Institute)

Descent into savagery, *Lord of the Flies*, 1963. (British Film Institute)

The inmates of Charenton asylum in the pit, The *Marat/Sade*, 1968. (Photo © Maurice Newcombe)

At work on the Vietnam War material for *US*, 1966. (Photo © Maurice Newcombe)

Model of Sally Jacobs' design for *A Midsummer Night's Dream*, 1970. (Theatre Museum)

Snug the Joiner frightening the 'mechanicals' in *A Midsummer Night's Dream*, 1970. (Photo © Maurice Newcombe)

INTRODUCTION

Peter Brook is arguably the greatest living theatre director, although 'theatre director' is an inadequate term. It implies a specialist craft, and many of his contemporaries could match him skill for skill. But more than a stager of shows, Brook is the radical spirit of contemporary theatre. Over a career of more than sixty years, he has shaken and re-shaped modern theatre no less deeply than its pioneers, Stanislavski, Craig, Meyerhold, Artaud or Grotowski. He has changed its rituals, made it ask harder questions, probed its links to language, culture, myth and the brain.

His productions in every kind and genre, from the most showbizzy to the most spiritual, provided a richly eclectic theatre experience for his later distilled experiments. His writing about the theatre, his interrogation of its very nature, notably in his book *The Empty Space*, have re-energised theatre-makers. His cross-cultural work over the past thirty years has taken drama into the heart of our attempts to understand a society of tradition and modernity, ourselves and the Other.

But parallel to his work in theatre is his lifelong work on himself. Brook's life has become a relentless pursuit of authenticity, a search to make sense of the glimpses of 'something else' he experienced as a child. This 'something else' gives him a detachment about theatre, an awareness of dimensions beyond the stage. Yet he continues to pursue and refine theatre, for 'the way of theatre' can become another kind of discipline, in which great truths can be grounded, through playing and storytelling and communicating truthfully with an audience.

If many of the qualities of theatre now – its spectrum of formal and informal spaces, its physicality, its drive towards a greater, more naked theatricality – can be traced to Peter Brook's example, it is sobering to recall how different and distant from us was the theatre in which he began. Post-war British theatre was the *divertissement* of a wounded nation, seeking comfort and elegance after the privations of war, a theatre of style over substance. Brook had no scruples about becoming one of its foremost stylists, then darting out to scale the peaks of English classical culture. Always he preserved his keen sense of what was dead or conventional; this led him to bolder acts of seeing afresh. They were greeted either as outrage, or as the frisson-inducing iconoclasm of the prodigal son.

More than half a century later, now based in Paris, he practises another way of making theatre. It goes beyond the reflexes and specifics of British, or indeed, French, culture. It is a way of working at which he has arrived through determination, ruthless clarity and a sensitivity to the full human span.

Brook's work with his 'inter-cultural' group, as it has been labelled by the academics, is not a swap-shop of skills and techniques, but, as he once suggested in an aside, culture like yoghurt, culture as fermentation. His Bouffes du Nord theatre has housed a mixed group unafraid to descend into disorder to surface with forms of performance that are nuanced, direct and – using a word Brook likes – transparent. This theatre does not belong to any single culture. It has no homeland, and no abroad. It is extra-territorial.

At the same time, in countless, often almost imperceptible ways, Brook's work and thinking have exemplified another of his keywords: 'elimination'. Indeed, his whole curve of work in the theatre, from the glitter and glamour of his spectacular days in the fifties to the serene simplicity of *Tierno Bokar*, can be seen as a process of casting away, of distillation. Paring away can lead to a void or to a womb, and the secret of Peter Brook – the author of an essay 'There Are No Secrets' – doesn't lie in any clear-the-stage formula but in the example of a director unafraid to question most where he has most succeeded, and a man who has guided his own profusion to a rich simplicity.

PART ONE

LIGHTING THE FIRE

1

SONS AND FATHERS

1925–39

'If you close your eyes and try to think what the world looks like, what do you find?' Peter Brook asked a group of young actors in London in 1992. 'As I was born in Turnham Green, my first impression of a universe went in one direction as far as Richmond Park and when my mother took me to Kew Gardens, the world was all sweetness and light. But when we needed pâté or salami in the home, my father would take me in the opposite direction, along the Goldhawk Road, to the other end of the world, all the way to Mr Eisner's delicatessen in a mysterious zone of dark excitement called Shepherd's Bush.'

Peter Brook was born on 21 March 1925 to parents who were Russian-Jewish émigrés from Latvia, then part of the Russian Empire, finding their feet in the London suburb of Chiswick in the 1920s. He grew up in comparative comfort, interrupted by the occasional crisis, like the economic crash of 1929. His dynamic father, an entrepreneur as much as an electrical engineer, left an especially deep impression on his younger son. The Russia which Simon and Ida Brook had left behind them in 1914 still permeated the house where Peter was born.

In his frank yet masked memoir *Threads of Time* he decodes the topography of the family house at 27 Fairfax Road, its 'green front door with a brass knocker and the number in shining brass'; its cellar, 'a complete underworld of coal and cobwebs and grime'. But this 'place of blackness', he writes, had its own light, warmth and security, and 'when the war came . . .

became our shelter from the bombs'. As he showed later in his work and his journeying into hidden worlds, there is no negative that is wholly negative, no black that does not make light more radiant. 'My mother later swore that the happiest time of her life was holding her family close to her in this deep womb.'

Dvinsk, where Peter Brook's grandfather Matthew was born, was a centre of both Russian and Jewish life. His father, Simon, fifth child of non-observant-minded parents, was born in Dvinsk in 1888, and grew up in a liberal atmosphere. At sixteen, showing a radical temperament and a determination to join in the mainstream of Russian political life, Simon joined the Mensheviks. They were the moderate faction of the Russian Social Democrat Party, led by an intellectual from Odessa, born Julius Cedarbaum but taking the conspiratorial nickname Martov. The Mensheviks were in continual conflict with the Bolsheviks. They supported Alexander Kerensky, Russia's first post-revolutionary prime minister, who was then deposed by the Bolsheviks. The Mensheviks, in constant cut-throat dispute with the Bolsheviks, gave the young Simon Brook a spring-board for his social fervour and political ideas. A rebellious young man, he earned a scant living by selling newspapers. 'It was probably a double rebellion,' his son Alexis, Peter's older brother, told me, 'political, and against his strict, authoritarian father.' Simon Brook was arrested and jailed for two months for making inflammatory political speeches, before securing his bail through family connections and setting out for Belgium. He catapulted himself out of his native place, as many did in this period of upheaval.

After leaving Russia, Simon Brook settled in Liège where he joined the university to read physics, mathematics and electrical engineering. The family name underwent its first metamorphosis, courtesy of frontier officials. From the letters БРУК, it was transliterated by a Belgian official to Brouck. In London it would be transformed again into Brook. Ida Judson, his future wife, who he had met in Russia, joined him in Liège. She studied chemistry, and wanted to be a doctor but she gave this up because any country she settled in would have required extensive retraining. They got married in 1914, while on holiday in Germany; she with an excellent degree as Doctor of Science, he with a reasonable one as an electrical engineer.

As the Great War threatened to engulf Belgium in early 1914, the young couple caught the last train to Brussels, where the local students were digging trenches, and then the very last train from Brussels to Ostend, where, with a group of Russian engineers, they travelled to England, arriving with one English pound in their pockets. Simon Brook found his first job in England, with a London firm making field telephones; by the end of the war he had become works manager. His wife (who features less vividly in Brook's memoir than her husband) worked for a firm making antidotes to poison gases.

Brook was a rotund baby, already with the sharp gaze that is one of his defining features. His father was beginning to make his way, starting an electrical engineering company and acting as the English representative of a German engineering firm. But he lost his business as a result of the crash of 1929. With the help of his wife, and her chemistry degree, he switched tracks and started a manufacturing pharmaceutical firm, Westminster Laboratories. The company patented and marketed several successful brands of the time – a stomach powder called Magtriz, a form of aspirin, and a best-selling laxative called Brooklax, no less. When Peter started out in theatre, some English actors and technicians were less than kind to this small, irrepressible director, and made jokes in the pub about 'the little shit'.

Outwardly, Brook grew up as a cultivated, well-heeled middle-class English boy. 'My parents,' said Alexis, 'always spoke Russian between themselves, particularly anything Peter and I were not supposed to understand.' Their mother came from that part of Latvia which was strongly influenced by Germanic culture. Theirs was already a household through which different cultures flowed. As the fortunes of 'Papa Brook' (his family nickname) looked up, the family were able to afford a servant, who combined cooking and cleaning. A key figure in Brook's childhood was his piano-teacher, a Russian, Mrs Biek, whose son Leo became one of Peter's boyhood friends. In a moving passage of his memoir, he reveals that it was Mrs Biek who taught him the essential artistic lesson of rhythm, and an even more vital sense that 'there was no such thing as preparation; you have to be fully prepared each time'.

There may have been many painful moments in childhood which I have put to one side. But essentially, everything was exciting. And if it wasn't that, I was looking for excitement, which meant the inexhaustible excitement of this strange unknown thing called life, all around, on every level. I can't look back on any painful experiences. I suppose I have a mechanism that puts them out of the way, so I would say very simply that for the first segment of my life – twenty or thirty years – every single response I had was so totally involved and engaged in the world, my world, that I never turned introspective. I had nothing to connect with the phrase 'inner life'. What was 'inner life'? There was life. Everything was one hundred per cent extravert.

This untroubled focus of consciousness was a great gift, and one Brook would expand. To the young Brook, the taste of life was grounded in a sense of wellbeing in which there was no fissure between inner and outer worlds. It came from an utter confidence and trust in the support of his father. In *Threads of Time*, Brook describes the security provided by his father's gaze and concern: 'I adored my father and never knew the tragic rejection of the father-figure that is so much part of our time.' More recently, he gives an even warmer picture:

My father was very proud of his adaptability, the fact that he had made many changes in his life, that he had gone through the Depression, so from the stories that he would tell – and he was always telling stories – I obviously saw there a line that taught adaptability. Within that, he had natural wide ambitions for his children. He would have liked me at a certain point to go into his business, but was delighted when I didn't want to. In wanting his children not to be like him but to go beyond him, it was clear to him that he should encourage, give the means and in no way hedge anything in. That can be boiled down to one word: constant encouragement. That was very fundamental. One of the things he would repeat was, 'If one day you commit a murder, and everyone in the world is against you, you know that your father will stand by you.'

Papa Brook was all the things the young Brook wanted him to be – playful, reliable, solid, clever – and physically lax. 'My father was absolutely there,' says Brook, in the documentary film *Brook par Brook* made by his son

Simon in 2001. 'He was present. Loving. He transmitted the highest standards, yet he never imposed anything.' It was an enviable start in life.

By the time he was ten, Brook had been given his own movie camera, a 9.5 mm Bolex. He was already devouring photography magazines, thrilled by their talk of lenses, film-stock, tricks of shooting and printing. Seeing home movie footage of Papa Brook at play in *Brook par Brook*, you observe a bright, animated man juggle, puff at cigarettes, caress his sober-faced wife, perform conjuring tricks for Peter's camera. For Peter was already trying the magic of trick photography: Simon waves his arms and his sons appear. He waves them again, and they're gone.

Simon Brook looks like a man who was confident himself, enjoyed and understood his younger son, and was wise enough to make space for his determined and distinctive development. Peter was treated like a young man, not a small creature to be bent to his father's will. The presence of this unconditionally loving father fed Peter's self-belief. As his psychiatrist brother Alexis notes: 'Peter identified with Simon's drive and mastery. Simon saw some of his unacted hopes and achievements fulfilled through Peter.'

After the war, Brook's parents began to argue. His mother Ida was, in Brook's words, 'both stubborn and afraid. She had loyally followed my father to a science-orientated university without a medical school and renounced her deep wish to be a doctor. Because of this she never lost a sense of deep disappointment with herself in a life which gave no outlet to the special talents she had begun to develop. When guests came to the house, my mother would panic and hide in the bathroom, leaving my father to organise every detail of the evening.'

In the interplay between parable and documentation which makes *Threads of Time* such a moving but teasing read, Brook soothes out the strife of mother and father and its effect on their sons. In his writing, the disputes between parents become a wise balance, a see-saw of opposites: 'the unremitting struggle between energy, impulsiveness and determination opposed by a need for yielding, for balance, for reconciliation'. These were the two forces at work in Brook from early on: his father's forcefulness, his wish to conquer and control the real world, his mother's equilibrium, her withdrawal, and, perhaps, her resignation. It is noteworthy that Peter doesn't give such a vivid image of his mother as of his father, but what she had been through shouldn't be discounted: she had given up her profession for her husband, and had wound up in a culture that didn't accept that women should work.

> She was very frustrated, and this became a focus of their quarrels. My father would be coming home from work at a quarter to six, and on the way he would meet my mother rushing out because she'd forgotten to buy butter. This became a coat-peg on which so much of the friction was displaced.

Meanwhile, his father was planning jobs for his sons, not wanting them to lack status in their new country. Papa Brook, like many émigrés, determined that his boys would have a better life than he'd managed. With so much insecurity following the 1929 crash, he wanted to ensure that both his sons were professionals: 'my son the lawyer and his brother the doctor'. From the age of fifteen, Alexis moved towards medicine, but Peter showed little interest in the law. By the time he was seven or eight, he was already a precocious play-maker. He had become enraptured by a Pollock's Toy Theatre, an enchanted miniaturised version of a traditional, nineteenth-century, gilt-and-velvet Victorian theatre. Pollocks supplied cut-out move-able scenery which a child could hand colour and scene-shift, and tiny cardboard actors striking heroic poses, which could be manipulated. Peter began to do both. (In his autobiographical film *Fanny and Alexander*, Ingmar Bergman traces his passion for theatre to a similar toy playhouse, and his love of film to a domestic projector, which in Brook's house also opened pre-television windows on the world.)

Alexis was very interested in photography, 'but not with the same degree of passion,' he says. 'My father played with both of us much more than my mother. In the family, playing was always with Dad. Caring was from them both, though more from her. It wasn't an integrated family.'

Brook has an often-told story about staging *Hamlet* in the family draw-ing-room for an initially entertained and eventually sorely tried audience of his parents and their friends. The title page of his script was inscribed

'*Hamlet*, by William Shakespeare and Peter Brook'. He divided the drawing-room in half with a scarlet curtain, making a proscenium and an auditorium, cut the play, made the puppets, pulled their strings and spoke everyone's lines. Having got to the end, and exhausted his family, the excited Peter wanted to start all over again with a different version of the play. He had to be dissuaded, thanked and sent to bed; an early precursor of his hunger to get to the bottom of a piece of work in every way.

Aged ten, Brook was happy with his toys. 'I had my camera and my puppet theatre, I was passionate about photography. It simply never occurred to me that after school you could do these things as proper jobs.' At his preparatory school, St George's, he played only minor parts in school plays. The school magazine gave 'the talkative Brook – will he never stop his chatter?' his first review, as the Governor of Harfleur in *Henry V*: 'The best acting was by Brook, who has the power of almost changing his personality.'

Brook detested his prep school, and all the bullying, toadying, philistine, xenophobic qualities which it ground into its pupils. As a clever, lively, not-altogether-English boy, he was the butt of bullying by the more powerful boys in the school's rigid hierarchy. The teaching staff did not approve of his reluctance to join in school games, to wave the flag for his 'house' and follow the 'team spirit'. 'School', he wrote, 'was the smell of latrines, sweat, unkindness, and boredom; it was boxing, with blood streaming down the face; it was never being left alone; it was being bullied.' It drove him inwards, made him a stranger to the group, to common pursuits.

When he first arrived at Westminster School, he recalls being accosted by an archetypal master-race prefect called 'Brown' – and when he tells the story, he stretches the syllable out so it's halfway between a drawl and a yawn – who pronounced the Pirandellian sentence, 'You're my shadow; I'm your substance.' In addition to being a fag, obliged to carry out any menial task for Brown, Brook junior had to trek around in the senior's footsteps, aping him, learning the customs of the school. Full of ideas and bright chatter, Brook did not seem to fit the role very well, so one day he was summoned to a kind of kangaroo court run by the seniors. 'You're getting too big for your boots,' announced Brown. 'We have to take you down a peg or two.' (It's a phrase which Brook still considers an index of English resentment.) The punishment could have been worse; they made him stand on a table and sing a funny song and pull faces, and they all fell about.

But the cumulative structures and attitudes of Westminster School, which he calls 'fascistic', took their toll on him. At the age of eleven, Peter had developed tubercular boils in his neck, an illness of the bovine gland. 'At that time, the conventional treatment was to cut such glands out, but my parents were against this, and preferred the other approach, fresh air and sun, to let it heal.' Peter was first sent to stay in Broadstairs with two spinster ladies called 'The Aunties' who took in children as paying guests. Then his father decided that Peter and his mother should go away to Switzerland.

It took him nearly twenty years, with his film *Lord of the Flies*, to settle his scores with the English school system – and even longer before his dislike of the English class system, and the negative and disparaging attitudes it planted in the English psyche through its schools, played their part in his decision to quit the country. But his journey to Switzerland in 1938, which stretched from the six weeks prescribed at first to more than a year, was the start of the making of him.

It was a great, if sometimes lonely, liberation. He was thrown back on his own resources and the occasional tutor. He had done well at school, winning prizes for English, French, German, instrumental music. He had addressed the school Camera Club with a talk on 'Faking the Picture'. And he was benefiting from the zest and the push of his father. Attending a school meeting in 1936, Simon Brook was impatient with the polite parents of other boys, and cut through their gentle questions to the teachers. Alexis remembers:

My father wanted to know from the school whether 'my boys are doing well'. Not physically, that didn't count. At a parents' meeting at school, after much talk about how the boys were doing in football, my father couldn't contain himself: 'That's enough about their feet; what about their heads?' When he was in his eighties, someone met him and said to him, 'You look very well. You must do a lot of exercise.' My father replied, 'Look at that tree. It's two hundred years old. Has it moved?'

Early on, Simon Brook instilled in his younger son a love of travel. He had, says Brook, a belief that travel was as educational as any university, and that one of the great traditions of the England he had adopted was 'the sense of England being a place from which you travelled. The fleet, the navy, colonisation across the world was not only to throw the bad elements out of the country – to Australia, for example – but a sign that every Englishman was potentially at least, a sailor, a globetrotter. But, although some Englishmen settled abroad, he believed they always came back to the home country. It's like Peer Gynt, that endless movement of departure and return.'

Peter remembers his father taking him, aged ten, and Alexis on their first adventurous motoring holiday, driving the Austin across the North Sea on the ferry and travelling across Norway into Sweden – 'it was a big adventure at the time, driving a whole day without seeing a petrol pump' – to meet their mother in Stockholm. 'She'd been to Latvia, where there was a mud treatment, for her rheumatism and arthritis,' says Brook.

Both for holidays and for the trip to Switzerland for his son's health, Simon Brook took every opportunity 'to travel a great a great deal', wrote Brook, 'and this planted in me very early a restlessness that has never gone away.' Brook's restlessness is something that recurs continually: it's an inward as well as an outward impatience, an urgency about his art as well as his life; it has the dissatisfaction of a search, a hunger to discover, a quest.

For a boy who had been restless, lonely, frustrated and furious at school, falling ill with a tubercular growth that whisked him abroad was an accident or a consummation devoutly to be wished. In a succession of pensions and hotels, in a country alive with French, German, Italian and various mongrel dialects, Brook pursued his apprenticeship of 'abroad'. Meanwhile, Papa Brook had begun to paste cuttings and documents about his son into the first of many leather-bound albums, starting with stories and reports from the school magazine. In Brook's office at the Bouffes du Nord today, among the scripts and videos, the African masks and the CDs, there are thirty-eight bound volumes of his father's labour of love, from the 1930s to the 1970s: reviews, news stories, profiles and articles from school magazines and polyglot press-cuttings services, trimmed, pasted, annotated, indexed, cross-referenced. And much re-read.

*   *   *

Switzerland's space, light and air opened the young Brook's senses and blitzed his glandular carbuncle (you can, however, still see its scar on his neck). He spread his wings. A thirteen-year-old with a head full of impulses, sensations and appetites, he started to concoct his vision of the world. His closest friend was Robert Facey, whom he had met at his prep school. They shared a keen interest in science and swapped diagrams and theories. From his teens until today, Brook maintained this friendship. His letters to Facey from around the world record excitements, confessions, opinions on films and books, and give Facey advice about his girlfriends, his health and his career. Facey, today a retired health-care physicist in the suburbs of Toronto, has kept every letter.

Writing from Switzerland, Brook began their correspondence by recalling his arrival at the dark, Dickensian Westminster School:

School starting at 9.30 a.m, at ten to nine on the first day of term a small but fat youth with a colossal umbrella and gleaming top hat (he spent half the night polishing it) approached the main gate of the Westminster School, paused a moment, turned a little white, then, taking a deep breath, plunged into the general room of the first and second year boys. It's ¾s the size of our Drawing Room. Very darkened, gloomy. At the top are some heavily barred windows.

He depicts himself as an outsider credited by his credulous schoolmates with hypnotic powers: 'My father was a professional hypnotist – I was expelled from St George's for hypnotising a dog – at my last school I hypnotised all the boys and masters, and could not wake them, so the school promptly had to cease to exist – etc!'

He moved with his mother into a *pension de famille* in Montana, a brighter place, where the space and sun and openness come jostling in:

11 March 38 Villa Jeanne d'Arc, Montana, Switzerland
You say that the maid told you I was ill. I was not ill, only I came here to finally (what a dreadful split infinitive) get rid of my glands. I suppose the maid hissed, all in one breath – 'Master Brook is ill and 'as gone to Switzerland till March and good bye – CRASH' and slammed down the receiver.

As regards the Mikado we read in Remnants class in the days of voluntary drawing . . . I was 'Pooh-Bah – it was said to suit me, though I cannot see why!'

He signed off the letter 'Pooh' as he did with all his letters to Facey. Was it Pooh-Bah's large egg-shape, or his sense of self-importance, that made his mocking schoolmates pick this nickname? He goes on a long walk and tries his hand at descriptive prose:

The lakes have remained covered with thin iced snow until about two days ago. Then a melting wind (it froze me) set in, and within four hours the whole lake was watery, I mean, just like in summer. The lake used to be safe to walk across, but one day, while doing so, I went in up to my middle. The worst of it is that I was wearing large Wellingtons, so they were filled to the brim with icy water which absolutely numbed my feet – I say, don't laugh, I assure you it was a very tragic matter. Good Heavens! I started to tell you about the peasant villages and have ended with myself sitting in bed with a hot water bottle by my toes.

He began to share his discoveries, in film, photography and reading. He recommends Priestley (*The Good Companions* and *Angel Pavement*) and 'the most beautifully written book I have ever read, *The Garden of Allah* by Robert Hichens. It is about the desert. It was filmed in colour with Marlene Dietrich and Charles Boyer about a year and a half ago.' And he praises a political Penguin, *Mussolini's Roman Empire* – 'for only 6d. It is not dry at all.'

Already he was filming in Dufay colour, reading the equipment adverts in the film magazines as well as the reviews. 'The light is terribly tricky here in the winter with the reflection from the snow, especially for colour films as they have almost no exposure latitude . . .' Then he discusses recording sound on disc. It's clear that by the time he was sixteen, he had collected a good deal of film know-how, and could back up his critical assessment of films with a technical knowledge. He reads the *Observer*'s criticisms closely, and wonders whether the new invention of television will be able to match the cinema's pictorial values.

In May 1939, his parents brought him back to England, and sent him to Gresham's, the school in Holt, Norfolk, where W. H. Auden and Benjamin Britten had been pupils. It was a school which prided itself on its open-minded staff and flexible schedule, its ability to rise to the needs of particular pupils. But it looked a bit glum to Brook, with the sunrays and iced air of Switzerland still in his head. He quoted Byron's mock-despairing verses as his epigraph:

28.6.39
Through life's road so dim and dirty
I have dragged to two and thirty
What have these years left to me?
Nothing – except thirty three.

I had better begin with the school. I must pass through photography to politics – stopping at J. Dunne's *Experiment with Time*. I've only got a quarter of an hour before prep, now. And I have so little free time. What with photography, music . . . I don't know whether I like this place immensely or detest it infinitely! My emotions are in some far extreme. What a lot of nonsense I am writing! It must be because I am in a bad mood again.

War was moving closer. He had opened his mind and senses in Switzerland, his first long absence from Britain, and now he was back in the country of his birth, upon which he already cocked a slightly alien eye. His emotions 'are in some far extreme', pressing at the limits of the school, where he felt at home, yet not fully of the place. He was celebrating his new finds – the poetry of T. S. Eliot, the piano he was beginning to master, now with his school music-teacher after his apprenticeship with Mrs Biek. Photography had dropped down the ladder of enthusiasms; cinema and music were topping it. By the end of the summer term 1939 he had found his own gang of bright, talkative boys:

As a matter of fact, I had pretty well closed down photography, but will restart. At school I am in what amounts to an intellectual clique: 'In the room the women (scholars) come and go / Talking of Michelangelo' – but there is

hardly time both to talk about Michelangelo and take his photo. I am afraid I
have completely lost touch with science. I am sure I would recapture the same
old thrill overnight.

A couple of days before they sent out a circular saying that they considered
Holt a safe area, but now it is strongly suspected that the school has been
commandeered by the military. Anyhow, in a frantic hurry we were all packed
off home while the school began to consider evacuation . . .

Gone With The Wind: I was most impressed. Firstly, as an adaptation of an
excellent novel. It stuck word for word (that is the pretext on which it got so
much sordid and risqué material past the Hays office and the Lord Chamberlain), and it picturised the characters almost perfectly, without destroying
any illusions. Heroine Vivien Leigh acts most beautifully in a difficult and
unpleasant role. Technicolor surpasses itself even outdoing Turner's imagination! Best bit is where in Civil War the whole town blazes away at night, and
heroine rides away, very sexy. Very horribly realistic war scenes. Whole film
most harrowing.

He wanted, he told Facey, to make a film based on T. S. Eliot's poem
'Rhapsody on a Windy Night'. But he fears he will never be a writer. 'I am
most unprolific,' he wrote, 'and produce about one piece of prose or verse
every three months. Attached a piece of prose – please please return it. I will
make it appear within the school literary mag. The war is becoming more
and more depressing. I try not to think about it.'

That summer of 1939, holidaying in Biarritz, Papa Brook had taken the
family across the border into Spain on an excursion. They must have
motored past the long straggling lines of defeated refugees – in all, half a
million fled Franco's Spain across the Pyrenees into France. The fourteen-
year-old watched the victims and victors of modern Europe's bitter war
between Fascists and Republicans. He was both moved and detached.

We crossed the frontier at La Hendaye. The first impression of Spain is of the
great number of young soldiers, shabbily dressed in dirty open-neck shirts and
ragged breeches, who lounge about in small groups doing absolutely nothing.

There are a lot of refugees returning to Spain. I saw two of these soldiers
having their little suitcases searched at the Customs House. A Spanish soldier

tried to prevent me looking, but I saw the guard rip up the lining of the case
and take out a slip of paper, which he perused carefully. The young soldier,
not yet 18, went pale and watched him nervously. I did not see any more.

We were escorted by an especially official Army Guide in special style state
charabancs. The guide – a very nice young fellow – wore the party costume: –
black jacket, tie, and breeches, red (!!) beret. He looked so honest that I think
he must believe all that he was saying against the reds. That the Reds
murdered, that the Reds pillaged churches, that the Reds used dum-dum
bullets, etc. etc. When we passed through Irun and saw streets of houses in
ruins that the Reds, he said, dynamited in retreating – 'Franco only bombed
military objectives – never civilians!!!'

Later, he unleashes his teenage sarcasm on the religion that bathed the whole
town of Lourdes, taking care, however, not to offend Bob Facey, whose
father was a clergyman:

I do not want to drop any bricks, nor offend your family profession, but
Lourdes has left me more confused than ever. I cannot find anything to
contradict my agnosticism (I go no further than that). You see, although my
credulousness urges me to accept the authenticity of the miracles quoted in the
guide-book, and to close my eyes on the underlying commerciality, the fat,
sleek priests, the countless shops making fortunes out of pseudo-relics and
candles ('the larger the candle, the quicker the cure'), every ounce of common-
sense in my body cries out at the idea of a deity using such devious methods –
like appearing to a peasant girl aged fourteen (the papers were recently full of
young girls leading a repressed, humdrum existence, who self-inflict serious
wounds, and tell of men with 'glaring eyes') in the form of a white lady (Iris?
Retina? Optical nerve? Protoplasm?) and with a flower on each foot, saying 'I
am the Immaculate Conception'.

In the *Daily Express*, he saw a photo of a man in a hospital masquerading as
Chamberlain. And then, on 23 August 1939, ten days before war finally
begins, in an unfinished letter, this fourteen-year-old quotes *Mein Kampf* to
argue Facey out of believing that Hitler can be trusted, while conceding that,
in the light of the Nazi-Soviet pact which Stalin had just signed, all his

certainties about politics have been shaken. The letter trails off with an acid Jewish joke about Italian servility to Hitler:

> Do you know the story of the Italian going for a walk in a park in Rome one beautiful morning who sees Musso in a fur-coat, all wrapped up and crouching on a bench. 'What, Duce,' says the Italian. 'Why are you so warmly dressed on such a lovely morning?' Mussolini looked up gloomily. 'Hush Hush!' he said, 'Don't you know it's snowing in Berlin.'

Soon after the war began, the family moved, from Berkhamsted to Beaconsfield, after Peter's father's office had burnt down. Brook chattily keeps his news flowing to Facey; he has become a surrealist, he writes, and his enthusiasm for new cinema inventions continues apace: 'Saw in *Sight and Sound* that the Russians have perfected three-dimensional spectacles (black-and-white or colour!) which have been installed in main Moscow cinema. Have you heard of Fantasound? If not, it is a treat to come.'

In his letters from Spain, his voice had been 'very precise, without abbreviating any words and carefully articulating every syllable'. This was the way he had described how he spoke during his time at Gresham's school, in a confused but revealing story, 'L'Après-midi d'un faune', which appeared in 1939 in the school magazine, *The Grasshopper*.

The protagonist is a teacher, torn between his analytical intelligence and his artistic yearnings, symbolised by the elusive faun of the title. Like Brook's father must have been in 1914, he is uneasily aware that his schoolmates find his name not quite normal, perhaps not quite English. 'Out of the corner of his eye he caught sight of a freckled finger pointing at him, but he tried to ignore this, and pretended not to hear the boys making the usual pun about his name.' Maybe Peter was already having to get used to mocks and jibes about the laxative Brooklax.

Peter's double in the story is given to big pronouncements: 'Art must be alive and vibrant, it must appeal to the violence of the soul, and not to the aloofness of the dissecting mind!' He throws off his clothes, plays unearthly music on the school organ. The character displays an erotic interest in a slim, dark-haired beauty, the gypsy boy who haunts him the way a slim dark-haired Italian girl had attracted Peter in Switzerland.

What the story, with its almost numbed sadness, doesn't stress but which Brook remembers vividly, is his rebellious sense of freedom, his refusal to be pushed around or dragooned into a collective mythology:

> My drama at school consisted in every teacher trying to explain to me, in a Tony Blair way, what it means to be part of a community. 'You're part of the school group, you must be rooting for the school.' Everything I did was the opposite; I wanted to be an individual, all the time I was against the idea of supporting the school in a cricket match, I was endlessly saying, 'Why should I? Support the house? No.' 'But you're part of it.' 'I don't feel part of it.' I had trouble with the headmaster and the teachers and the prefects.

The faun of Brook's story was also an image of his sexual stirrings, which were swiftly rebuked, much to the teenage Brook's fury:

> When I was about fifteen, I had a sort of love affair – it didn't go much beyond going for walks and holding hands – with a boy who was twelve or thirteen, a junior. A romantic friendship – I didn't even know that homosexuality existed as such until I was about nineteen. At my first job in films, I remember a woman saying, 'He's queer', and I said, 'What's queer? What does it mean?' and they all sniggered. The boy was told he wasn't to see me. I was banned from seeing him, and him me. You can't imagine my fury. Absolute fury. They wouldn't explain it as such. I could only see it as an incredible violation of independent rights by an aged establishment which I didn't believe in. Myself I believed in more.

Much more mysterious and prophetic of things to come is 'Yogi', the story he published in *The Grasshopper* in January 1940. Its storyline is literally a rebirth – the resurgence of Noah and humanity after the Flood recounted in the Book of Genesis. But Brook explores his tale with an inwardness, and varies its action with such subtlety that it becomes a story of consciousness, of the conflict between wishing to go out into the world and reluctance to leave the dazed intensity of the inner life.

> Monotonously it rose and swelled, or drooped and bowed at the caprice of the wave. It seemed strange to Noah sitting in the bow that there should still be

forces left to act of their own accord. For in the passionate serenity of the endless still waters, fascinating by the immobile rapture of their colours, a rich, almost dripping, beauty was squeezed by the sun from the inert and colourless waters as the cherished rare drops are crushed from a sterile orange.

This is like a Baudelairean reverie, a tone-poem by Debussy. It has the same synaesthesia, reading one sense in terms of another. 'He heard the colours sounding for the first time, he heard the brazen burnished blue trumpets and the cold redness of the drums.'

But Noah loses his grip; he cannot hold together his mind, 'split like a violin whose strings lie scattered on the cold marble floor'. The symphony of senses that has sustained him on his journey now peaks in 'the crescendo of a death knell'. And then the fifteen-year-old Brook brings in the violent intrusion of the outside world. 'With painful suddenness, a sickly yellow screech [from a pig being killed for the noonday meal] drove a wedge into his consciousness and threw him shuddering into an awareness of life. He looked about him, and saw the tawdry ragged awning, and the greasy coils of rope on the un-swept boards.' The ship sails on, lands, and Noah is carried ashore and placed on the bank of a clear still stream. There he sits all day, staring into the sun. 'At length he attained the power of banishing all thoughts from his mind other than of the one glowing reality.' He has become a yogi, empty of thought but suffused with contemplation.

At fifteen, Brook was foreseeing his future dedication to the workings of the mind and the truths of the East, which he would find through travels to Afghanistan, India and Iran, to the wisdom of Sufism and esoteric religion, and which he would materialise in productions of great beauty and inner tension – *The Conference of the Birds, The Mahabharata, Tierno Bokar.*

2

ENTERING ENGLAND

1940–45

'Linked to the fact of having Russian parents, I feel myself at once very English and not English at all,' said Peter Brook in 2001. 'All kinds of influences coming from different sources are therefore able to pass through me and influence me.' In 1940 he was about to be immersed into Englishness, first as an apprentice in a jobbing film studio – among cameramen, recordists, sparks who fixed the lights, and gaffers who shifted the sets; then as an Oxford undergraduate within that enclave of heritage Englishness: scholars' gowns, college servants, chapel, refectory, tall spires and tolling bells.

He had agreed with his father that after leaving school he could spread his wings for a year and explore his talents before going up to Oxford. In 1941 he went off to the Merton Park Film Studios in south London. An industrial hangar had been converted ten years before into a film and sound-recording studio. It had begun by handling overflow work from Twickenham film studios; this was the era of a busy British film industry, with small studios scattered across the country. As war approached, Merton Park was requisitioned by the Crown Film Unit for propaganda, promotional and cheer-up films.

The sixteen-year-old intern hung around, did the things a 'go-fer' does on a film-set ('go fer a coffee, go fer the star's coat') and watched and absorbed everything – shooting, scene-painting, scripting, processing, editing. He followed conversations between producers and directors, befriended cameramen and screenwriters. When a screenwriter fell ill, Peter wrote his first scenario. While at Merton Park, he rehearsed a group of friends in *The Duchess of Malfi* in a cellar, a kind of 'fringe theatre' *avant la lettre*. Even though it never saw the light of day, he later noted that it was always helpful to have even an unfinished production under one's belt; it meant that the new production was not one's first, and that inspired confidence.

At work in the studio, he was beginning to show elements of the resourcefulness and adaptability he had inherited from his father. But he began also to realise that his resourcefulness and drive went hand in hand with a blithe unawareness of the consequences of his actions. It was as if he defined a task, achieved it, and then cut himself off:

> The director of a film on which I was working as fourth assistant said, 'Tomorrow we need a globe of the world.' Within a few hours, I'd found the Canadian embassy, got through to the secretary of the ambassador, found he had a globe of the world in his office, pleaded very hard – 'This is the Crown Film Unit, government outfit, war work,' got the studio transport department to collect it – all this in a few hours. The globe's brought down to the set, powdered to take the shine off it, filmed triumphantly the next day.
>
> A week later (I was sixteen) comes a furious call from the Canadian embassy saying, This is disgusting, we responded to your request, no care was taken of our globe, it came back dirty and dented. I hadn't thought that was part of my responsibility; I'd obtained it. No thought of following through. These are the sort of shocks I went through.

While he was learning the nitty-gritty of film production, he was still in love with the cinema. 'The Long Voyage Home: have you seen it, you must!', he wrote to Facey. 'Directed by John Ford, its greatest part is the photography. It is an arty affair of moving shadows, ripples of moon on the water, puddles of light on the wet cobblestones, silhouettes of ropes, etc, but all perfectly in place. And as a literary effort, it gives a genuine, if somewhat story-less slice of life, a chronicle not of an individual but of any typical merchant ship's crew. It is Russian-realistic, it does not glamorise, it is sincere.'

The Crown Film Unit, where Brook worked for a few months, when Crown moved to Pinewood, was the new name for the GPO (General Post Office) Film Unit, which during the thirties, inspired by John Grierson, had

spearheaded the British documentary tradition. It looked at the changing
face of modern Britain – at its miners, North Sea fishermen and famously, in
Night Mail, with music by Benjamin Britten and a verse narration by W. H.
Auden, at its postal workers. The Ministry of Information had taken over
the GPO Unit as part of the war effort, and offered Brook a job there. It
gathered together many talents, including Humphrey Jennings and Dylan
Thomas. But Brook wasn't around to meet them; he was off to keep his
appointment with Oxford University, as he'd promised his father.

Excused from military service because of his childhood illness, Peter went up to
Magdalen College, Oxford, in 1942, at the age of seventeen. He had the
confidence of having served – albeit in a minor capacity – in professional film-
making. He was due to read medieval French and German; in addition, he
elected to study Russian. His parents now and then had used the language at
home, to hide things they didn't want their children to know. Now he began to
study it with a Professor Konchalovsky. 'By the time I left Oxford,' he told me,
'I had read Tolstoy and Dostoevsky in the original. As usual at the university, I
was not allowed to read a "modern" language by itself, so I had to learn Old
Church Slavonic. Which was interesting.' He also developed a taste for the
German romantics, especially the fantastic tales of E. T. A. Hoffmann.
   Kenneth Tynan, one of Brook's contemporaries in wartime Oxford,
described his arrival whimsically: 'It was as if he'd come up by public
request. Rather like a high-pressure executive arriving to take over a dying
business.' With the energy and radical questioning he had inherited from his
father, Brook now confronted the self-deprecating but nonetheless real
power of Oxford University, one of the pinnacles of the English establishment. Oxford wore its learning lightly and disguised its seriousness with self-
mockery. While Cambridge excelled in the sciences, Oxford prided itself on
its achievements in the humanities – literature, languages, history and
philosophy. The college system essentially had not changed much for half
a millennium. 'Scouts', seasoned servants, served their young 'masters' with
hot water for ablutions, made their beds and spied on their bedmates. It was
a society of sexual imbalance: even during the war, when young Englishmen
went off to fight, male students outnumbered women by a considerable
ratio, and there was great competition for girls. At the same time, there was a

far from secret homosexual culture and a high-camp sensibility, later to be caught by Evelyn Waugh in *Brideshead Revisited* and by the caricaturist and wit, Max Beerbohm, who noted of undergraduates that 'the nonsense which was knocked out of them at school is all put gently back at Oxford.' But Oxford was also a home of radical dissent: it had recently passed a motion at the Oxford Union, its debating society, that it 'would not fight for King and Country'.

Oxford, theatrical in its style, its architecture and open spaces, also nourished a proliferating theatrical activity. To this day, it remains a distinctive feature of both Oxford and Cambridge that many leading actors and directors in British theatre took their first steps in student drama at these two ancient universities. Plays, from classics to cabarets, were mounted not only in theatres and halls, but in the gardens of the centuries-old colleges. London critics, some ex-Oxford students themselves, came up to review these productions. Just as the Oxford Union was a showcase for aspirant politicians, so productions by OUDS (the Oxford University Dramatic Society) and ETC (the Experimental Theatre Club) were a showcase for actors and directors. And for critics – the bustling Oxford scene gave Kenneth Tynan his first shot of adrenalin, as he began to write his showy and perceptive reviews.

But wartime Oxford was intensely competitive. Brook looked around at the university drama scene. He played a couple of walk-on parts. He was front-of-house manager for Professor Neville Coghill's production of *A Midsummer Night's Dream*, in Magdalen College Grove, and managed to bestow the curtain-call bouquet on the wrong woman. Deciding that Oxford drama was in the hands of careerists and conservatives, he fixed his ambition on two targets, beyond the dreams of most undergraduates: away from the university he would stage Marlowe's *Doctor Faustus* and take command of the University Film Society to make a film of Laurence Sterne's *A Sentimental Journey*. A letter from September 1942 to Robert Facey, now chief assistant on the project, reveals some of the pressures Brook was handling, as he prepared his *Doctor Faustus* cast to perform in the Torch, a tiny fringe stage near Hyde Park Corner in London. The letter is festooned with drawings for the stage carpenter, and written in scribbled pencil during a lecture.

Dreadful catastrophe. Brian, with some two days notice, has been called up. And here I am just about to go off for a godforsaken milesfromanywhere camp when I don't return until ten days before the play, having had all Brian's duties thrown in my face.

- Go ahead with rehearsals. BUT NOTE, WE CAN'T AFFORD ANY IN THE TORCH THEATRE UNTIL I ARRIVE. Thank God for your father's schoolrooms.

- Stanley Waldman – Please phone him, get him to rehearsal or somehow meet him (I've never done so) and find out if he is good enough for part of the Pope – if that is your opinion CLINCH ON THE SPOT – make him the Pope and sack Churton – only gently – say he hasn't time to change etc – 'cause he MUST be Lucifer.

- Re Costumes:

I am sorry. I must be firm definite final. No Modern Dress. Please don't think I haven't thought over your idea. It was a very good one. After the last rehearsal it attracted me greatly. Since then I've considered it from all angles and finally decided 'No.' Obviously I can't explain now. Only please trust me and accept this. I'll of course love to argue it when I see you again but this is the DECISION. So for Christ's sake order the costumes at once.

Believe me, Bob, I thank God for your existence. The sooner you start props of course the better.

Yours, sigh of reliefingly,

Pooh.

They sold tickets for *Doctor Faustus* door to door for its three performances, with proceeds going to the Aid to Russia Fund. It was Brook's first experience of directing and galvanising a cast. An unsigned editorial in *Sight and Sound* noted that 'to anyone who appreciates the difficulties of staging Elizabethan plays, and who was lucky enough to see this performance, it was a remarkable achievement'. The *Daily Telegraph* commented: 'Here was a producer not afraid to let his reach exceed his grasp.' It's also noteworthy that the play Brook chose for his debut is one of the most alarming plays in the repertoire, with its smell of brimstone and its magical invocations. Mephistopheles played all the Seven Deadly Sins, and in an anticipation of his later interest in shamans, spellbinders and esoteric teachings, Brook tracked down the magus and 'black magician' Aleister Crowley, smuggled him into his college rooms and into rehearsal, to instruct the cast in performing the mysteries which summoned up spirits.

It wasn't all hard work; there was a busy social scene. At the Oxford Union, Brook proposed with Noel Coward the motion that 'the community owes a duty to the artist rather than the artist to the community'. An excitable letter just before work began on Peter's other major undertaking, the film of Laurence Sterne's *A Sentimental Journey*, gives a glimpse of him and of his room-mate, Gavin Lambert, who went on to become a novelist and leading Hollywood screenwriter. An ever-so-slightly camp note enters Brook's letters:

> Gavin Lambert – Publicity. He is what you would call 'one of my queer Magdalen friends'; a dear boy, with remarkable personal devotion, also a very Wardour Street commercial brain, a sense of publicity (he writes the most beautiful letters to the critics) and much efficiency.
>
> Oxford is terribly thrilled. Everyone knows about the film. Rumours circulate madly! Gossip has it that I was seen going round New College the other day, followed by 20 people taking down my remarks in their note-books.
>
> Delicious news: Gavin and I decided to have a party a couple of nights ago, and to give it an original flavour we asked along Aleister! The old devil came like a shot and was in fine form. I can't tell you what he did now; let one anecdote suffice. I was doing Schools [a university examination], and Gavin went to meet him. We took him to tea at the Randolph. Now nearly everyone who has tea there is a resident, so when the waiter came up to him and asks him his number, '666!' I replied, and Aleister in a loud voice confirms . . .

In his own memoir, *Mainly About Lindsay Anderson*, Lambert confirms that he and Brook had a sexual relationship. It is entirely in character that this authoritative, voluble, voracious young man, as eager as Faust to plumb new knowledge, new experiences, should explore every aspect of sex. Looking back, Brook is down to earth about his sexual adventures. He speaks of his

freedom to capture more and more in every direction – intellectually, physically. When I was at Oxford, girls were remote, there were only two colleges
for girls. So the first thing I did was to plunge into every homosexual affair I
could. Yet whenever I saw a girl I wanted to pick her up, and I could not accept
for a moment that there was a definition – 'homosexual' – that precluded me
liking girls as well as boys. The choice came about by a process of natural
selection: having been in bed with creatures of all sorts, I began to find a
natural preference for the female organs rather than the male.

Gavin Lambert was a keen film-buff, and would go on after the war to
become a polemical film critic and the editor of the British Film Institute's
committed magazine *Sight and Sound*. They saw as many films as they
could. Brook loved the anarchy of *Hellzapoppin* ('I have seen it – to my
eternal joy!', he wrote to Facey in Cambridge), and kept an acute and critical
eye on the man then regarded as the most gifted film director working,
Orson Welles, whose *The Magnificent Ambersons* had just been released:

Actual estimate of film – as a whole it is rather worthless. Its story is rather
tripey, but the significant thing is not that Welles' technique gets it across but
rather hinders its getting across. So many of his effects divorced from their
context become irritating and distracting, and the story would have been far
more acceptable if the technique had been at its level. The whole art of stage
production, and also that of filming existing material like a novel is in
adapting one's technique to each work, and not in bringing a rigid, insensitive,
ah-but-personal style to bear on it.

This is a young would-be film-maker eyeing up the competition, weighing
up a cinematic master just ten years older than him, judging Welles' stylistic
virtuosity against the interaction of form and content.

Half a century later, Brook conjures up a portrait of himself as a febrile
youth, fizzing with energy:

I was what today would be called 'hyper-active', and my hyper-activity
expressed itself more than anything else in talking. If one asked, what was
my greatest capacity, it was to talk. When I was small and adolescent, I talked

and talked and talked. I suddenly remember that soon after Oxford, there were two girls I'd picked up, I took them out to dinner in Shepherd's Bush, and being a great show-off, I talked non-stop about this and that, doing one thing and the other. And I felt that I'd seduced them both. And next day, a friend told me they were both terrified and never wanted to meet this alarming person again!

A Sentimental Journey, an offshoot of Laurence Sterne's wayward co-medic masterpiece *The Life and Opinions of Tristram Shandy*, is a peripatetic journey from England into France and Italy, with all manner of comic, picaresque and mildly erotic adventures. Brook took a 1936 French film, Sacha Guitry's *Le roman d'un tricheur* (*The Story of a Cheat*), as a model for his first, very low-budget production. It was a film that François Truffaut was to consider one of the French cinema's masterpieces. He praised it for a startling innovation: the use of a novel-like 'voice over' instead of dialogue. Guitry, who was growing a little tired of filmed plays in the cinema, conceived something which would have the form of a filmed novel. 'The character on screen won't say, "I'm unhappy today" – no, he'll say nothing. He'll just look unhappy, and the narrator's voice will say, "I was unhappy that day." With this decision, Sacha Guitry invented the "play-back", even if he wasn't aware of doing so, three years before *Citizen Kane*. The direction (*la mise-en-scene*) is guided by a *mise-en-sons* (a sound-treatment).' It was this technique Brook planned to use for his Sterne film, partly for budgetary reasons and partly because he thought that such French flair went well with Sterne's tale of an innocent abroad.

Making the film of *A Sentimental Journey* in 1943 demanded ingenuity and initiative from Brook and his team. It was wartime, and film-stock was confined to the war effort. 'A four months' search was necessary before we could bring together enough strips of film to start shooting,' wrote Brook in a programme note. He called up former colleagues at the Merton Park studio, asking for roll-ends, old pre-war stock, each roll with a different chemical reaction. As President of the Oxford Film Society (Bob Facey completed the *coup d'état* by becoming vice president), Brook was able to earmark some of its £250 budget to his film; family and friends contributed

the balance. The recorded narration would be set to a soundtrack of period
music – Bach, Byrd, Couperin, Corelli.

Frederic Hurdis, the actor who had been Brook's Faustus, played Sterne's
alter ego, Yorick. Real people from Oxford and its surroundings played the
characters whom the hero meets on his travels, in courtyards in Banbury, in
the marketplace in Abingdon. On the shoot in Woodstock, the crew was
attacked by local bystanders for skiving off from army service. Brook's
cameraman was Leo Biek, the son of his former piano-teacher. The en-
terprising young director, coasting on chutzpah, thrust his way in to meet
John Gielgud, who was appearing in *Love for Love* at the Haymarket
Theatre, and with his fluent charm and enthusiasm, obtained the use of
costumes for his shoot, of the stage set and the theatre itself for some interior
scenes. Meeting Gielgud was the beginning of a fruitful collaboration
between an actor of prodigious mental and vocal agility and the young,
mercurial director.

In August 1943, in the middle of his shoot, catastrophe struck. Brook was
found to have infringed Magdalen College regulations by having a friend
stay in college after closing time. He was fined, and when his payment for the
fine failed to appear, he was told he would be 'sent down' – expelled from
the university. Had this expulsion from Oxford's Olympian heights actually
happened – and it was chiefly because of Simon Brook's stalwart defence of
his son that it didn't – it would have been a blot on Peter's reputation and
career. Even though it didn't come to that, the Magdalen College archive
reveals the petty and prejudiced face of the Englishness which Simon Brook
wished his sons to join.

The correspondence begins with a letter from Magdalen's Dean of the
Arts to Peter on 30 July 1943:

> Dear Brook, Doctor Sutton and I have seen the President who entirely agrees
> with the action that we have taken in fining you £3 and requesting you to leave
> Oxford tomorrow for the rest of the vacation. The principle is a clear one: if a
> stranger is in the rooms of a member of the College after the College has
> closed, he is the guest of the man to whom those rooms have been allotted . . .
> May I remind you that both fines (there was a fine of £2 outstanding) must be

paid from one week from the date of this letter? Yours sincerely, H.M. Sinclair, Senior Dean of Arts.

Brook went to see the College President, and explained he was in the middle of pre-production on his film, and that he had contracted numerous financial obligations. At worst, he needed more time to organise the postponement of the filming. Could he at least request a delay of his date of departure from Oxford? The President granted him two further days in college. Brook moved out on 2 August 1943, renting a room in the Blenheim Hotel, Woodstock, outside the Oxford boundaries. Since he was not allowed back into the town, he gave a cheque for £5 to his friend Gavin Lambert, who deposited it at the Porter's Lodge of Magdalen College. Peter assumed this put an end to the affair.

It was therefore with some shock that he received this letter from the vice president, K. B. MacFarlane, written like a judge passing sentence:

14 August 1943
Dear Mr. Brook,

   I am informed by the Junior Dean of Arts that more than a week ago he told you that if you did not pay a fine within seven days he would advise the President to send you down. In the absence of the President I have now received that advice and have decided to act upon it. Your name will be removed from the books of the College at the end of this month. Meanwhile, if you have anything to say I shall be willing to hear it. Your scout tells me that a rope fire-escape has disappeared from your room during his absence on holiday. I presume you are responsible: will you kindly return it at once?

The verdict was crushing for Peter, and he burned with the injustice of the decision: 'Your letter has caused me much astonishment,' he replied to the Vice President, 'in view of the fact that it is now a week since I sent my cheque to the Dean. I am very pained that it should be necessary to take such drastic action without my being so much as informed that the cheque had not been received.' He offered to send a replacement cheque, which was acknowledged by the Vice President who, in signing off the letter, crossed out 'Yours sincerely' and substituted 'Yours truly'. Uppity students must be addressed icily. Three days later, the Vice President returned to the fray, saying no sign could be found of Brook's first letter and cheque: 'I am still open to conviction but I am beginning to grow impatient.'

Peter replies that he's not surprised that the letter may have been mislaid at the Porter's Lodge: he has had many experiences of telephone messages mislaid, mail not forwarded, even his wartime ration book not being sent on to him. 'I expected my explanation – and I am not a liar – to be accepted. I have no wish to be sent down over such a misunderstanding, especially as I am perfectly clear in my own conscience that I did all that was ever required. You have informed me that to clear myself I have to prove that the cheque was delivered. If you will be so good as to let me know what it is you still expect me to prove, I will do everything in my power to do so.'

A new factor now enters this fusillade of point and counterpoint: was Peter actually warned by the Junior Dean that if he did not pay his fine within a week, he would be sent down? Brook *fils* was in no doubt about the matter: 'At no time was it even so much as suggested to me by the Junior Dean or anyone else that I might be sent down.'

Simon Brook came down to see MacFarlane on Saturday 4 September 1943. It's clear that he had fastened on to the lack of evidence that his son had been given due warning. After the interview, Macfarlane wrote to the Junior Dean of Arts.

> I had a very disagreeable hour and a half with Senior, who had indeed found the one weak link in our case, especially as I had not known of its existence. In your absence and without a copy of the essential document I was bound to accept his story that your letter contained no word about sending down. That surely does make a difference? If it is not true, my letter is so worded as to allow me to revoke my decision. So let me know if it is not. Otherwise the incident is closed. Ruthlessness never pays unless it can be easily defended.

With that sublime piece of realpolitik, Mr MacFarlane withdraws the sentence of expulsion. MacFarlane then wrote to Peter, still unable to shed his tone of rebuke, and making his clemency conditional on an undertaking by the headstrong student, preoccupied with making a film rather than following the rules of his college:

Your father was here with me this afternoon and presented your case as fully as possible – and, may I add, much more ably than you have done yourself? It is not, in my opinion, a strong case. At the best you have behaved very carelessly, and I am far from sure that it is possible to put the best interpretation on all your actions. I am not prepared to admit that there would be any miscarriage of justice if you were to suffer the extreme penalty of having your career here cut short. But there does seem to be an *outside* chance that you were too preoccupied at the time to realise that you would be sent down if your fine was not punctually paid. This was not explicitly stated in the Junior Dean's letter to you, although it was, I think, implicit in that letter and was unquestionably said *viva voce* by the Junior Dean in his interview with you earlier.

But because it was not repeated in writing in so many words, it was just possible for you to think that it no longer held good. That being so it seems to me that you should be given the benefit of the doubt. You have, therefore, my permission to return into residence next term in order to qualify for a war degree. It must be understood, however, that you are here to work. Your father assured me that you would not be engaged upon any dramatic or film production in the Michaelmas term and I am afraid that I must make that a condition of your being allowed to come up.

A letter to Simon Brook informing him of his decision ends with fulsome sententiousness: '[I hope] that I shall live to be told by my colleagues that I have done the right thing.'

There were to be no more theatrical or cinematic pranks for Master Brook. There are, however, some footnotes to this sorry business. Leslie Sutton, the Junior Dean of Arts, writes to MacFarlane from his holiday in Devon, commiserating with him about 'such an unpleasant and difficult job over the Brook', and concludes, 'The excuses made and their variation, seem to show clearly the character of father and son.'

It's hard not to interpret these words as either xenophobic or anti-Semitic, or both, though they are couched in the nudge-and-a-wink style of English upper-class prejudice. Small wonder that the present-day Master of Magdalen told me sadly, when I asked to see the 'Peter Brook dossier', 'I'm afraid that no one comes out of this well.'

It was, however, Simon Brook's capable hands that provided a rousing finale to the affair. On 11 September 1943, magnanimous in victory, he wrote to MacFarlane, thanking him for making the right decision. He then lists in a four-page letter all the points of the case that he had discussed at his meeting with the Vice President, and the effect they had had on his son.

> My son became most alarmed. He was in the midst of producing a film, had responsibility for money entrusted to him, for a cast of 20 people, costumes, furniture, expensive apparatus, etc. His problem was how to remove all these, what to do next, how to discharge his responsibility towards so many interested parties.
>
> I fully accept your view that my son did not present his case quite ably, but after all he is only 18, has not had any legal or business training nor previous occasion to defend himself in such a situation. The Junior Dean, more experienced in such matters, evidently presented the offences to the President and yourself in such a way that at the time you considered the fines justified. I conclude this from the fact that when full details were put before you, you agreed that the offences were only of a technical nature. Surely not deserving of the punishment imposed.

He deals a strong blow in relation to the Junior Dean's failing to spell out the expulsion threat: 'How can one explain why the Junior Dean, who insists that young men must be particular about minor details, is so careless in a matter which may involve the whole future of a young man?'

He magisterially dismisses a further charge which had been adduced by the College to show that Peter was, as they might have put it, 'a bad egg':

> You stated that it is on account of my son's being often late for breakfast. My son had the misfortune to develop a bovine gland in his infancy which necessitated his staying for two years in Switzerland. The Medical Board recently examined him for military service and declined to grade him, and under doctor's instructions he must rest in the daytime and not get up too early. Had the Junior Dean shown more sympathy and understanding and listened to my son's explanation instead of resorting to punishments, he would soon have discovered that his late rising was for health reasons and not out of disrespect to the College authorities.

MacFarlane replied in stinging terms to Simon Brook's rebuttal and defence of his son:

> You would be very wrong if, however, you supposed that I accepted your record of events, or the interpretations you chose to put upon them. Now that I have reached a decision – and I am sure an over-lenient one – I am no longer obliged to listen to you. Your letter of the 11 of September will therefore be ignored. If you are dissatisfied with the College and think that your son would do better elsewhere, by all means take him away. Nothing would please us more.

This is not a letter any parent would expect to receive from an Oxford college, given the rather trivial circumstances of the offence. It cannot have endeared Brook to English conduct, culture and institutions.

After his final term, in which he worked for and obtained his war degree, Brook left Oxford at the end of 1943. Since he had been graded IV at his army medical, he returned to the Ministry of Information, and was sent to the documentary section of Gaumont British, a Wardour Street company chaired by J. Arthur Rank, making training and instructional films for the Ministry of Information, the Admiralty and the War Office. He worked as a scriptwriter and director, and prepared the premiere of *A Sentimental Journey*.

It opened in January 1944 at the Torch Theatre in Knightsbridge, where *Doctor Faustus* had played. Brook and Gavin Lambert managed to get it reviewed by the national press, who were lenient about its shortcomings in view of its spirit and intelligence. The *Guardian* set the tone: 'It has passages of tedium, poor direction, worse lighting, extremely amateur acting and very bad photography, but it escapes stupidity . . . Hollywood has been known to do worse at many times that sum.' The *Observer*'s film critic C. A. Lejeune, commenting on Brook's youth, wrote, 'It is all to the good that these young people have tried to do an honest job of work instead of largely criticising the work of others.' The review that must have caused most merriment came from the *Outfitter*, a tailoring monthly. 'Those who remember the novel will be glad to hear that the incident of the black silk tights is handled well. Clothing is authentic throughout.'

After his run-in with the authorities, Brook left Oxford on his guard; fuelled by his father's wanderlust, he ached to get out of England. While in Switzerland with his mother he'd enlarged his horizons with a day trip to Milan. 'We were in a big motor-coach, and it was full of Germans. Pumped up as I was by news of the war, I leapt up, ran over to a fascist-looking German and shouted at him, in German, *Verflugte Nazi!* (Damned Nazi!). My mother was appalled.' His last trip before the war had been to Paris to see his father's sister, who had emigrated there. He remembers being taken to the Opéra Comique for a miserable production of *Carmen*: 'the procession in the last act consisted of one poor toreador on a pathetic horse.' From Paris, the family had gone south to Biarritz, where he was impressed to see a sign pointing to 'The Russian Orthodox Church', but disappointed when this turned out to be a placard on an apartment block, 'Russian Church, Third Floor, Right'.

He was, he says, 'drenched with this double sense of the meaning of travel: the English common-sensical view of taking a journey to get somewhere and the much more worldly Continental sense of the educational value of travel in general.' The moment the war ended, he travelled by boat to Belfast, the first place he could get to, and from there he went to Dublin and Cork. Later, as currency restrictions were eased, he went to Lisbon – 'where I visited my first brothel' – and from Lisbon he discovered he could get a boat to Tangier, and thus set foot in Africa for the first time. The release was exhilarating: 'We'd been cooped up in this island for four years, the need to go out was enormous.'

He wanted to see the world, he told his father, who proposed a worldwide trip, to be paid for by Westminster Laboratories, to visit and report on all the company export agents. Simon Brook planned a six-month itinerary for his son, drew maps and made schedules. Peter began by going to Brussels, where he discovered that the local agent, who did his best to butter up the boss's son, was a Nazi sympathiser. But the plans came to a halt after that trip, because real work claimed him.

Now he was out in the world, at home in French, German and Russian, having poured his film-making skills and leadership drive into one rough-hewn costume-drama film. With *Doctor Faustus*, he had shown he could lead a cast with as much authority as he had staged his puppet-theatre

Hamlet as a child. From schooldays to the end of his student career at Oxford, he had shown a fierce dislike of settled authority. Everything, for the nineteen-year-old Brook, was up for question; nothing – no artistic reputation, no accepted moral touchstone, no holder of office, no time-honoured tradition – could be taken at face value. He was fluent, quick-thinking, unpredictable, that steady blue gaze arresting to both men and women. He had already been noticed by some theatre and film people as a name to watch. He was full of ambition and projects, ready to make his professional entrance. Where would he begin?

3

SIGNS OF A CALLING
1945–50

At first, Brook took off stutteringly. A play in a London suburban 'fringe'. Another on tour for the British army overseas. But within three years, through a combination of luck, ambition, shrewdness and a fountainhead of talent that could not be suppressed, he had staged three plays in a major repertory theatre, and begun a long and close working relationship with Paul Scofield, who would become one of the great actors of the age. He'd mounted Jean-Paul Sartre at the Arts Theatre, Shakespeare at Stratford-upon-Avon, and, at the age of twenty-three, been named Director of Productions at the Royal Opera House, Covent Garden. He learned much from his actors, who were often older and more experienced than him. Yet he shaped their performances and gave direction with a confidence that came from more than just keen wits. There were unmistakable signs in his work of a creative independence, a sense of vocation.

The West End set the tone of the London theatre in 1945 with audience-pleasing plays by Noel Coward, Terence Rattigan, Emlyn Williams and Daphne du Maurier, and star-studded seasons of Shakespeare and popular classics. Edith Evans, John Gielgud and Robert Morley were among the stars of the time; Cecil Beaton and Oliver Messel devised luxurious designs for audiences whose senses had been starved by wartime austerity. The Old Vic and the Shakespeare Memorial Theatre at Stratford-upon-Avon upheld a theatre of public purpose, as did key repertory theatres outside London. Joan Littlewood's Theatre Workshop was struggling on the road, often in one-night stands, to combine the movement teaching of Rudolf Laban, the epic drama of Bertolt Brecht, and its own brand of song-studded socialism. With these exceptions, the post-war British theatre in which Brook took his first steps as a professional was a reflection of British society: backward-looking, nostalgic, still under the spell of the glories of empire, untested by enemy occupation, nannyish, childish.

In Kensington Brook found a tiny theatre, the Chanticleer, and persuaded its director, Greta Douglas, who was trying to sustain an ensemble of actors, to let him stage *La Machine Infernale* (*The Infernal Machine*), Jean Cocteau's spiky, mannered rewrite of the Oedipus story. Brook shot across to Paris to see Cocteau in his flat in the Palais Royal, meeting the great actor Louis Jouvet, gulping down productions and sharpening his ideas on the whetstone of the French language. His production of Cocteau's play was a counter-statement of French elegance and imagination against British common-sensical culture. He knew about the moral compromises, the anti-Semitism, the heroism and the fierce internecine battles which had torn Occupied France apart. Their society had been tested in a way British society had not, and consequently they came out of the war with sharper minds and senses.

He turned up on the first day of rehearsal at the Chanticleer with every move and lighting cue strictly plotted, too insecure to dispense with this directorial crutch. But he seems to have got away with it. 'Peter Brook,' wrote the *Spectator*, 'is an intelligent and tactful young man who obviously has his whole heart in it. The play was done with the passionate intensity of youth, and yet with none of its gaucheries.' The *Observer* admired 'the fantastic ingenuity of Mr Peter Brook's direction. He has done nobly on his two-by-four stage with a play which needs all the patterns of theatrical effect.' In the audience was a man who would have a decisive influence on Brook's early career, the impresario of the West End – indeed, many called him its velvet-lined dictator – Hugh 'Binkie' Beaumont.

Brook found another fringe venue, the Q Theatre at Kew Bridge, for his next production, *The Barretts of Wimpole Street*, a tear jerker about the love affair between the poet Robert Browning and the ailing Elizabeth Barrett. This had the merit at least of leading him on to his following production. Mary Grew, an actress who had become a friend, saw *Barretts* and recommended Brook to ENSA to do a production of Shaw's *Pygmalion* in which she, though somewhat too old for the part, would star. ENSA, the Entertainments National Service Association, had been set up to provide amusement for troops at the front. Headquartered in some chaos at Drury Lane Theatre, and affectionately known as 'Every Night Something Awful' to millions of service men and women, it specialised in variety, with showbiz singers and comics such as Gracie Fields, George Formby and Vera Lynn, the 'forces' sweetheart' singing in barracks, mess halls and from the back of military trucks. It continued to function after the war. Brook's *Pygmalion* would add a classic comedy to ENSA'S playbill.

The veteran director William Armstrong, one of the cultivated homosexual men who gave the British theatre its style in these post-war years came to an early run-through of the play. 'A very refined, elderly gentleman, whose bald head dropped sadly onto one shoulder,' wrote Brook of Armstrong. 'He took me by the arm, walked me up and down between the stalls.' Armstrong was complimentary, and undertook to recommend Brook to his friends.

One of them was Sir Barry Jackson, a pioneer of 'art theatre' in England, a friend of Shaw and Granville Barker. Jackson invited Brook to direct no fewer than three plays – Shaw's *Man and Superman*, Shakespeare's *King John* and Ibsen's *The Lady From The Sea* – at his Birmingham Repertory Theatre. Birmingham Rep was a cornerstone of England's independent theatres, seeking, Jackson said, 'to serve an art instead of making that art serve a social purpose'. Jackson had founded the theatre in 1913, helped by a bequest from his father. The theatre staged innovative modern-dress Shakespeare, Greek tragedy, Chekhov, Strindberg, Ernst Toller and a succession of George Bernard Shaw premieres, leavened by Eden Phillpott's Devon comedies whenever the bank balance flagged. Brook found Jackson 'an essentially simple, direct man, an English gentleman of a kind that is now virtually extinct. He was kind, formal, impeccably courteous.'

Barry Jackson also founded and ran the Malvern Festival, presenting Shaw's plays in a theatre set in one of England's most uplifting landscapes. The polarity of the natural lyricism of Malvern, where Jackson lived, and the industrial enterprise and engineering genius of Birmingham, stirred Brook. It is perhaps an early template of the dichotomy between high and low, spirit and body, beauty and force, which lies deep in him. In Birmingham, Jackson who, at sixty-five was forty years Brook's senior, took him under his wing, confiding in the younger man during daily lunches at the Station Hotel, where Brook lodged. Jackson was another refined homosexual in the British theatre; the silken ladder of Peter Brook's early ascent was manned, as Peter Hall remarks, by some notable 'great ladies' of the theatre. The prevalence of gay men and women in this world, the imagined conspiracy which W. H. Auden sent up as 'The Homintern', was an index of the sexual constraints of British society. In the theatre, a place of transgression and transformation, gay people could find a haven. In France, where Cocteau strutted his homosexuality flamboyantly in many art forms, there was, it seemed to Brook, a greater acceptance of love and sex in all their diversity.

It was at the Repertory Theatre that the twenty-year-old Brook met Paul Scofield, the actor who was to become a muse and inspiration. It was an elective affinity for both of them, two strong and complex characters, each following his own daemon. Scofield recalls:

> When I first met Peter, I was Sir Barry Jackson's leading male actor at the Birmingham Repertory Theatre in Station Street. I was accustomed to working with very experienced, even elderly, directors. Peter and I confronted each other for the first time in Sir Barry's office. I think he saw me as something of an enigma. I felt the same about him. We were different from each other, I a few years older and simply an actor, he an intellectual who was also an artist. I remember that I felt that for him an actor was not very interesting.
>
> But as we progressed with his three productions, *King John, Man and Superman*, and *The Lady From the Sea*, there was a change. Perhaps the daily experience of working with a company of actors and actresses in developing his interpretations of the plays, as opposed to following a pre-prepared scheme of action, fundamentally altered his vision. Now he seemed to be looking outward rather than into himself. Certainly the ice-blue eyes seemed to express a new excitement. The productions were well-received and successful – something was in the air. Looking back, I see that Peter and I began a partnership of mutual and tacit understanding.

Scofield brought his penetrating intelligence, dazzling good looks and great charm to Shaw's John Tanner in *Man and Superman*; his hooded mystery to Ibsen's Doctor Wangel; his vigorous attack to the iconoclastic bastard Falconbridge in *King John*. Brook deployed squads of monks, shifted speeches, and in *King John* updated Shakespeare's word 'commodity', which had changed meaning since Elizabethan times, to the comprehensible 'expediency'. He justified the change in *The Sunday Times*: 'I feel most strongly that one is entitled to alter a line only when every other resource of acting and production fails to bring it to life.' Brook's impulsiveness and instinctive rebellion against 'old guard' attitudes brought him into lively conflict with the Rep's stage management, as did the disconcerting tomato-coloured suit he always wore. But with Paul Scofield, it was a story of elective affinity and mutual enchantment.

'We began to have an almost instinctive knowledge of each other's working development,' says Scofield. 'I think that, as I did, he started a project with no preconceptions, no strategic plan, but allowed the impressions of a play to steal up on him, to trust those impressions, and to follow them until a conception was achieved. And since this was my own way of working it is my belief that in this lay the basis of our partnership. We came to perceive each other's methods, whereby we reached together a shape and pattern of thought and feeling which would finally materialise as performance.'

Scofield was struck by Brook's apparent lack of concern for the usual signs of success, and his equanimity before a first night. 'Peter is not interested in rules, in tried and tested formulae for success; and if the criterion for success is whether or not it works, he will treat that stricture with calm disregard. His qualities are mysterious, he is the servant of the "idea", of the "word", and of his kaleidoscopic imagination. The impetus of his work is entirely independent of its reception. There is never, before a production reaches out to the public, the impression that "he hopes they'll like it"; rather an enviable serenity, as of one who, if he likes what he sees and others don't, then that's too bad.'

Looking back over fifty years at the age of eighty, Scofield summed up a long creative relationship:

Our work together, particularly in its latter years, has been inter-dependent, a gradual progress from the meeting of two people who seemed to have nothing in common, to an extraordinary working relationship which finally became a mutual and perhaps almost telepathic understanding of each other as artists and also as human beings. I have felt a rare sense of freedom and trust. A liberation of my thinking, a certainty that I am free to follow my own path. I know too that he was aware of my trust, which in itself offered him also a certain freedom. Peter was sometimes caustic, though open to the development of instinctive interpretation; sharp in disagreement but aware of a potential benefit in another means of approach. Flexibility and openness to what each day could contribute is one of his gifts.

With Peter I made the discovery of the need for 'dialogue' with a director, and one not necessarily of words; rather a communication between actor and director which did not entail simply following his directions, though mostly I did, or of being blindly obedient to his conception of a play; but somehow sensing the direction in which he was moving. It was a shared gift, an intuitive knowing; perhaps, in him, the most potent secret of his mastery of his craft.

Barry Jackson called Brook 'the youngest earthquake I've known', and in 1946, when he was asked to run the Shakespeare Memorial Theatre at Stratford-upon-Avon, he brought Brook and Scofield and other Birmingham Rep actors with him. Jackson invited Brook to walk round the theatre with him for an initial assessment of what lay ahead. They found a building in near-ruin backstage, with an outdated switchboard, piles of unidentified scenery and hampers of rotting costumes. Standing in the auditorium amid torn seats and carpets, Jackson turned to Brook and said with a twinkle, 'Well, I think we could turn this into another Salzburg, don't you?'

From its beginning in 1769 as the site of a Shakespeare Jubilee festival mounted by David Garrick, England's leading actor of the day, Stratford-upon-Avon had been in decline and become a combination of Bardolatry and tourism. In the 1930s, some great actors had stamped themselves on the leading roles and there had been one or two productions, notably by the Russian director Kommisarjevky, that probed Shakespeare's depths. But by 1946, the theatre had become a bit of a sinecure for yesterday's men and women, on and off stage. Brook's *Love's Labour's Lost*, following an operatic but unrevealing *Tempest* and a dull *Cymbeline*, was anticipated as the flagship of the new regime.

When his production of the then comparatively unfamiliar play opened on 26 April 1946, it was greeted with delight. The critics in this cold post-war world relished the dance of love's infatuations and illusions, in a setting inspired by Watteau's graceful painting *L'Embarquement pour l'Ile de Cythère*, conceived by Brook and executed by Reginald Leefe, one of the theatre's traditional scene designers. Brook found in Watteau, who was at that time his favourite painter, the flight of the imagination, the gift of stopping time in an ever-present Arcadia. Watteau's silks and satins lifted Shakespeare's dukes and princesses into an idealised world; its hazy sunset ending promised a departure to enchanted destinations. Brook's command of a glowing imaginative world, in all its French beauty, was self-assured. Yet audiences and critics also went for the incongruous Britishness of the low-life characters – Constable Dull, a Crazy Gang policeman with a truncheon, Don Armado (Scofield) a touching village-schoolmasterly pedant out of *Don Quixote*. Brook conjured up a paradisal retreat, which could also embrace that quintessentially British entertainment, the pantomime.

Even making allowances for the honeyed prose of the period, you can feel the critics' excitement: 'It is a recipe compounded of many simples, allusive, reminiscent or fleeting, but always lovely – Goldoni, Watteau, *commedia dell'arte*, Fragonard, Shakespeare and harlequinade. Yes, harlequinade – this *Love's Labour's Lost* has a Constable Dull who produced a string of sausages from his pleasant, pale blue tunic and was still inside the picture.'

They shivered at Brook's *coup de théâtre* when Death irrupted into the playground of the young lovers. 'You will find at Mercadé's entrance a pause and a moment that resolves all the tumult, as might a solemn break in a symphony introduce some tremendous and severing chord that sets the new mood,' continued Phillip Hope-Wallace in the *Manchester Guardian*. 'It makes tender, human sense of all the little that remains to be said. Nothing could be farther from gay glitter or the crackling of thorns.' The *Observer* added, 'At its close, after the mazes are trod, Mr Brook finely expresses that fall of frost on the summer night, when Mercadé enters upon the rout of the worthies and death brings to the masquing court the realities of life.'

As *The Times* summed up, 'Brook's presentment of the play as a masque of youthful affectations shows a remarkably complete grasp of its somewhat elusive values, and is, from first to last, consistent with itself. He has given its movement on the stage a puff-ball lightness, imaginative expertness, and once or twice succeeds in fading out a scene in such a way that colour and grouping summarise and heighten its significance.' A young Peter Hall went to see the production: 'I first saw it, in a school party from Cambridge. I was fifteen and I was transported. I was also furious, that someone so young could be directing. It was a misty, romantic vision – that post-war romanticism, exquisite and ever so slightly camp.'

Brook spent the rest of the year in London, directing Dostoevsky's *The Brothers Karamazov* and Sartre's *Huis clos* (*Vicious Circle*), plays by two authors more obviously attuned to the harsh spirit of the times. Here too he was fortunate to find talented and powerful actors to work with: Alec Guinness, who appeared in both, and adapted the Dostoevsky, and the veteran actor Ernest Milton. *Karamazov* was presented at the Lyric Hammersmith by The Company of Four, an offshoot of H. M. Tennent Ltd, 'Binkie' Beaumont's powerful commercial production company, modelled on Jacques Copeau's *Compagnie des Quinze* in France. Its aim was to present plays which were more innovative than the West End could take. Brook made clear his intention to *épater le bourgeois* in *Karamazov* by shocking them out of their seats with the loudest pistol fusillade the gilt-and-ginger auditorium had ever witnessed.

The Arts Theatre, where he did *Huis clos*, was a members-only club theatre. This was doubtless because of the lesbian undercurrents of Sartre's philosophical melodrama, in which two women and a man are trapped together for eternity, inflicting the utmost pain, of an emotional rather than a physical kind, on each other. 'Hell is other people' as the play's most famous line put it. Brook fed his imagination by going to Paris whenever he could; the Paris not only of Sartre but also of many other artists who nourished his mind and senses and would lead to future work in both London and Paris: Roland Petit's ballet troupe with their jazzy despair, Jean Anouilh's trenchant comedies, Jean-Louis Barrault's ventures into Claudel's epic theatre.

At the Arts Theatre, Brook had teamed up with a voluble, inventive designer, Rolf Gerard, who designed an austere Second Empire room for

Huis clos. Alec Guinness was a haunted hero; Beatrix Lehmann and Betty Ann Davies tormented each other and him. Brook liked Gerard's affable, inventive and very European energy; he had a cabaret quickness. They would go on to work together on Shakespeare, operas and musicals. Gerard was a friend of Sartre's agent, Jan van Loewen (originally a German, Hans Loewen, who changed his name to a Dutch-sounding version to avoid disagreeable German connotations). Brook had met him at the Arts Theatre, and soon found himself taken up for late-night dinners at the Savoy Grill by these gregarious 'Continentals'.

Brook was beginning to step out into London society: profiled by Tynan, photographed for *Vogue*. An adulatory piece by Paul Kalina in the April 1946 edition of *Illustrated* brandishes alliterations to make Brook sound like Noel Coward: 'He is fond of good food, of bright tweeds and flashy dressing-gowns; touchy about trivial things like ties and toothpastes. Apart from the theatre and cinema, he likes skiing and skating, music and playing the piano, cats and compliments.' The social whirl was fun, though he couldn't take it too seriously.

He found himself writing about ballet for the *Observer*. Its editor, Ivor Brown, who had praised Brook's work from the start, realised that there was something like a golden age of ballet in London, which should be covered in his pages. He asked the arts editor, J. C. Trewin, to call Brook about the idea of writing, and Brook accepted. It was a tight brief: to cover all ballet premieres in no more than 150 words, since the *Observer* was still constrained by paper restrictions. 'Ideally,' wrote Trewin, 'each sentence, in the Hazlitt manner, had to smoulder like touchwood and next to catch fire by attrition.' Brook's enthusiasm went deeper than simple pleasure at having another platform for his talent: he admired the purity and demanding disciplines of ballet; he had already been called a 'balletic' director, for his spare use of space and his elegant groupings. He knew that ballet had a noble past, including a great Russian legacy, but there was an urgency in him that demanded change in this revered, Apollonian art. And he was voraciously building up a visual and kinetic store of stage images, movement and grouping, for future use.

Reviewing an amateur dance troupe from the Chinese embassy, Brook praised its economy and minimalism, qualities of oriental theatre he would later draw into his own work. 'It was evident that this style of theatre has an extraordinary imaginative power, and that within the circle of its formal scene the actor can evoke his cloud-capped towers with a freedom unknown in the West' [26 January 1947]. Reviewing Leonid Massine's choreography of *The Three Cornered Hat*, he relished the Hispanic fire drawn from the reserved personality of Margot Fonteyn.

> Hard, fierce and burning, a triumph of the anti-romantic vein, set in the glaring angularity of the Picasso arena, led by the beats, clashes, stamps and hand-claps that strike sparks off the de Falla score, this ballet is conceived to express neither picture nor posture, but simply the spontaneous urge to movement that any rhythm dictates. Margot Fonteyn has not the temperament for the part; but she has attempted the impossible and comes very close to succeeding. [9 February 1947]

At Covent Garden, a performance of Massine's *La Boutique fantasque* brings out Brook's romanticism, which, he says, is not a luxury, but a vital recovery experience from the trauma of war. 'It is a revival from another world, and of another world; of that childhood kingdom, through-the-looking-glass and topsy-turvy, where dolls delight while mortals sleep; a world of music, movements and colour, where Massine's choreography gallops apace and Derain's costumes make the darkness full of light . . . To visit Covent Garden is to have the mind awakened and the eye entranced, the ear enchanted, the spirit quickened, and the imagination set a-whirl; and to step back from that pool of civilisation into the encircling gloom is suddenly to realise not only the function of ballet but its present necessity.' [3 March 1947]

Two months later he is shocked awake by the sexy, syncopated slouch of Roland Petit's ballet *Le Jeune homme et la mort*, designed by Georges Wakhevitch, a Russian scenic artist with whom he would work:

> It was rehearsed to jazz rhythms, but it is danced to a passacaglia by Bach. Wakhevitch's carefully arranged décor makes an extraordinary effect. Here is an attic set to end attic sets. Dark, damp and crumbling, with an iron bed that expresses the horror of all the iron beds of all the top floors of the world. The

choreography by Roland Petit toys with realism and totters on the brink of the
ridiculous. Yet it emerges triumphant, for in its kicking and biting, in its
slouching and its clambering over tables and its sucking at cigarettes, it
manages to find not naturalism but poetry, not the dance-destroying movement of the commonplace but the great line of real dancing.

In August 1947 *The Fire Bird* rouses him to compare its primal Russian
qualities, which Brook calls 'Byzantine', with the puritan simplicity of the
English theatrical imagination:

> The theatre in England suffers from a general reluctance to let itself go;
> barrenness is too often confused with sincerity, and simplicity with style. At
> Covent Garden *The Fire Bird* has now risen triumphantly from its ashes, and
> this hot wind of the Byzantine in ballet serves as a reminder that magnificence
> is not necessarily an unwelcome quality. Stravinsky's music is still almost
> unbearably exciting – a great tribute when one considers that there is hardly a
> device or discord in it that has not long become a film-score cliché.

The following year, 1947, Brook returned to Stratford-upon-Avon to stage
Romeo and Juliet. After a summer of preparation in Portugal and Tangier,
he fleshed out a directorial concept based on a key line of the play: 'These
hot days is the mad blood stirring'. He and Rolf Gerard decided to capitalise
on the big space of the Stratford-upon-Avon stage: before a vast, pulsating
cyclorama they set the skylines and rooftop and the low crenellated wall
delimiting the city of Verona. Brook aimed to remove the sweetly sentimental and replace it, he said, with 'the violence, the passion and the
excitement of the stinking crowds, the feuds and the intrigues. To recapture
the poetry and the beauty that arise from the Veronese sewer.' Brook's
language here has the swagger of a film producer pitching a film of dramatic
extremes. At ease with handling crowds, he staged the street fights, the duels
and brawls with balletic flair. He cast an eighteen-year-old, Daphne Slater,
as Juliet, the scarcely older Laurence Payne as Romeo, and Paul Scofield as
Mercutio. Scofield found a mysterious night-poetry in the Queen Mab
speech, catching visions emerging out of sleep, lying on the ground dreaming
out loud like a half-conscious poet.

For Peter Hall, seeing the production as a teenager, 'Brook's *Romeo and Juliet* had no lyricism, because the leading actors couldn't hack it. It was hot; that was its thing. But the atmosphere was not strong enough to hide the flaws.'

The production brought Brook his first bad notices, reams of them. The nastiness of some outraged critics recalls the laborious sarcasm of Brook's mentors at Magdalen College. The *Observer* wrote:

> This play, one must, at risk of platitude, advise him, is one of the finest helpings of verbal noise in a language and literature notably rich in such aural provender. Here is a lyric love indeed, and, if the poetry is slurred, if the matchless wedding of melody and moonshine be dissolved, then the horrified listener may contemplate a leap into the Avon, now torrential. Fortunately, the riparian dining-rooms are open again and so comfortably victualled as to deflect the suicidal impulse.

The two young actors playing Romeo and Juliet, 'were wrongly cast, worse directed, and nonsensically en-scened'.

But there was a counter-punch from a young playwright and actor called Peter Ustinov. He opened his review in *New Theatre* by giving Brook some ironic tips on How To Conserve Shakespeare As Traditionally Understood. First, don't have a Spanish composer (Brook had chosen Roberto Gerhard) and a full orchestra. Second, avoid brilliant colours and vast open spaces. Third, don't have clear-cut characterisations, 'when there are so many excellent, experienced ladies and gentleman whose sense of characterisation is discreetly confined to their beards and wimples'. Fourth, don't make the mistake of treating the play as a complete action and adventure instead of a string of literary gems. 'To deny a celebrated speech its aura, to embark on a passage of such fame that it has been too often divorced from its context by school exams and the like, without that slight pause for coughing and mental readjustment beforehand, is unthinkable. The heresies in this production are manifold, but the general misconception can perhaps be best suggested by the lamentable fact that the play had no feeling at all of being a revival. Without being too cruel, it is necessary also to record the alarming fact that there was hardly a dull moment all evening.'

Ustinov adored the vast blue cyclorama, 'a glorious background, not only for the passionate riot of colour, but also for the rusting imagination'; Ivor Brown had seen it as 'a few megaliths and air-raid ruins which have been blown into the stratosphere and have somehow stuck there'.

For one member of the audience at least, the production met Brook's criterion for a real theatre experience – that it etch a lasting image on the mind. Decades later Clive Barnes, a pugnacious critic in London and later in New York, still remembered and saluted Brook's radicalism: 'Not much liked by the critics of the day, Peter Brook's *Romeo and Juliet* was, I suspect, a turning point in the history of the British theatre. It approached Shakespeare with few preconceptions; it tried to treat the extraordinary as if it were living theatre, and proved in the process that it was. The production had little style, but the fight scenes were magnificent, and the actors did not speak Shakespeare as if they wanted to spit the plum-stones out . . . If we ever get a national theatre, I will always think of Brook's *Romeo* as its first production.'

Another keen pair of eyes, from another artistic institution in need of renewal, became aware of Brook. David Webster was general manager of the Royal Opera House, Covent Garden. In the autumn of 1947 he received a letter from the twenty-two-year-old Brook suggesting that the opera house needed a 'Director of Productions' to raise its production standards and bring it into the world of theatrical innovation and design. Brook talked his way into Webster's office, and Webster impulsively promised him the job, removed the name of the existing 'production consultant', the distinguished choreographer Frederick Ashton, from the playbills, had second thoughts, then got his board to endorse the move. He told them that Brook had a 'first-class musical mind', though the truth was that this went little further than the lessons he had received as a boy from Mrs Biek.

Brook's duties would be not only to direct his own productions, but to maintain the standards, preserve the integrity of the original production, and not let it subside into the morass of traditional 'business' that afflicted so many operatic revivals. His arrival did not please the traditionalists, who included Music Director Karl Rankl.

Brook began with his own production of Mussorgsky's *Boris Godunov*, in the composer's original version. Working with the Russian-born designer

Georges Wakhevitch, who he had pursued after seeing his work for the Roland Petit company, Brook took particular pleasure in directing the chorus of the Russian people:

> It is essential to remember that they are not actors in fancy dress, but the Russian people. The Russians are essentially the same in behaviour, whatever the period. We have tried to represent them in a way that makes them more like a present-day crowd. The same idea in the representation of the crowd was at the bottom of my production of *Romeo and Juliet* at Stratford. The universality of the crowd must be appreciated by the audience, who will compare them with displaced persons, the starving common people of today.

Already there were signs that the conservative opera connoisseurs and fastidious critics saw the confident young Brook as a marauder; inside the Opera House he had to learn to fight battles against obstruction. The *Observer*'s critic, Charles Stuart, objected to 'numbers and sumptuousness for their own sake' in Brook's *Boris*. But he capitulated at the climax of the opera, the death of Boris. Using the Covent Garden flying system, Wakhevitch and Brook sent the tragic Russian tyrant spinning downstage through a corridor of silently shutting doors, like the closing iris of a camera lens. The final door bore a vast image of a Byzantine Christ, with piercing eyes.

Creatively, Brook had advanced further along his path towards an almost kinetic function of stage design, 'a set', as he put it, 'that was able to undergo modification, clarify points and sharpen the stage action'. In terms of his relations with the backstage staff, things were not so good. Norman Lebrecht's mischievous history of Covent Garden tells the tale. 'He ran up against the rock of reality in the shape of "Bogey" Ballard, the wing-collared, octogenarian backstage boss who ruled the bowels of the house. Brook ordered a change of scenery for *La Bohème*; Ballard insisted on doing things the way Mr Puccini had instructed him. Brook went to Webster, suggesting that Ballard should be considered for gentle retirement. Old Bogey, however, was the only man who knew where anything was kept backstage. Decrepit as he was, Ballard outlasted the upstart Peter Brook.'

Famous singers refused to take direction, reminding the young tyro that 'this is how we've always done it, I always enter from the left'. They complained that they could not understand his sometimes highly metaphorical stage directions, and that he had encouraged a sexy singer, Ljuba Welitsch, to vamp her role and upstage Elisabeth Schwarzkopf's Mimi in *Bohème*. Karl Rankl complained that Brook did not respect the composer's stage directions; Brook replied that they were not set in stone, and that theatre, and musical theatre, had moved on. Brook also complained about rehearsal conditions. The Opera House bowed to every whim and desire of the principal singers, who were often earning extra money recording or giving recitals, when they said their voices were too tired to rehearse. In one of his productions, Brook noted, because of last-minute changes, no fewer than four of the singers hadn't even met until twenty minutes before curtain-up. His one venture into contemporary opera, Sir Arthur Bliss' *The Olympians*, was not a powerful enough work to stir his creative juices.

It was with Brook's production in 1949 of Richard Strauss' *Salome*, to the libretto by Oscar Wilde, that his troubled term as Director of Productions at the Opera House came to a crunch. Impatient with the backstabbing, foot-dragging and hostility (not least from Karl Rankl), and stimulated by Strauss and Wilde's shocking and voluptuous work, Brook picked a provocative collaborator as designer: Salvador Dalí. In his paintings, Brook found mirrored the insidious eroticism of *Salome* – and he must have sensed a scandalous showdown with the Opera House clique. He went off to Spain to work with Dalí on what he called not so much a set, more a 'hallucinatory fantasy', with the limitless freedom of surrealist painting.

'Strauss' music,' wrote Brook before the production opened, 'is the hallucination-producing drug which induces the same emotional reaction as the highly stylised, artificial, rhetorical and elaborate visual imagery of Wilde's original . . . The task of the producer and designer is to find the same approach in "theatre style" which Wilde supplied in his dialogue.'

Brook enjoyed himself with Dalí in Spain. He noted that, despite Dalí's professional iconoclasm, he treated Brook with respect because he hoped thereby to win Covent Garden's commission for future, even wilder décors. Brook returned to London with a portfolio of Dalí's fantasies – exploding costumes and gigantic headdresses, and remembers Gala, Dalí's wife, running after him, demanding a receipt for the package of Dalí drawings that he held. The maestro of mystification was hard-headed enough to guard against plagiarism or unauthorised sales.

On his way back Brook had a dangerous encounter that might have figured in a Dalí nightmare. He and his travelling companions were held up in a forest and robbed by what the English press described as 'Spanish bandits' (though they might have been surviving Republican militia), armed with rifles, tommy-guns and grenades. They demanded the traveller's car and the contents of their suitcases. When they came to Brook, he offered them his silk pyjamas, but asked if he could keep Dalí's designs. They tied the passengers up, and threw the designs at Brook's feet.

> I was as close to death and a young life being extinguished as one could think – I know that I was terrified. But ten minutes later, I was only aware of the comic side of it, and by the time we escaped and got home all I could tell was this side. For instance, I was bound hand and foot with a man I didn't know by these partisans. When you're like that, you have to make conversation, so I said, 'What's your name?', and he had some ridiculous English name like Cuthbert Branfield-Owen. Then there was a pause, and I asked, 'What do you do?' 'Life insurance,' he said.

Brook looks back on the way he turned this episode into a comic-opera story as an example of his capacity to distance threatening reality. It's a sign, he says, of the sheer level of excitement and novelty at which he was living his life. But in reality, he recognises, the Spanish ambush could have ended badly. They eventually escaped and marched along to the next village, where they were held up by Guardia civil policemen. They had been mistaken for partisan fighters. Ironically, it was one of their number, a count who supported Franco, who negotiated their release.

Back in London, the music critics gathered to subject *Salome* to an attack more ferocious than anything Brook's 'bandits' might have unloosed on him. Sizing up 'the preposterous *Salome*' Eric Blom wrote, 'There can be no beating about the bush: the present goings-on simply will not do. I foresee that we may one day behold the heroine in a diving suit, with seven separate mechanical parts being unscrewed with a spanner during her dance.' Ernest

Newman, the elderly doyen of music critics, followed suit: 'Of the production in general, it is difficult to speak in the restrained language appropriate to a Sunday paper. One absurdity followed fast on the heels of another . . . The decapitated head looked like a large steamed pudding, though Salome's airy handling of it and the containing tray suggested that it was much lighter than this sort of pudding usually is.'

But other reviews hint that a hostile claque was at work. Headlining 'I went to deride but stayed to praise', the *Sunday Graphic*'s Hubert Griffith concluded, 'Those who booed the scenery obviously went to boo it from the outset. If they had had eyes in their heads and had used them, they would have applauded instead . . . The Strauss opera *Salome* is crude, Eastern, dramatic and barbaric. All this was expressed in the setting with imaginative beauty as well.' The theatre critic and commentator Robert Muller called the response to *Salome* 'both childish and hysterical', and echoed Brook's own critique that opera was visually and artistically retarded. With *Salome*, wrote Muller, 'the revolution has shown, as all revolutions will, its claws; there was bloodshed among memories, and we witnessed the familiar excesses of the revolutionary in power. The dust, the inefficiency, the prejudice that encrusted opera at Covent Garden for so long, have gone. Dalí is going too far, and with a bang the doghouse door shuts on Brook.' Muller called on Dr Karl Rankl to give up his petulant refusal to take a curtain call.

Brook himself, in 'an attempt to write my own notice', chose to reply to the critics with as much calm as he could muster:

> Why should we be afraid of fantasy and imagination, even in an opera house? When the curtain rises, strange vulture-like wings beat slowly under the moon: a giant peacock's tail, opening with the opening of the dance, suggests the decadent luxury of Herod's kingdom. A handful of such visual touches over the ninety-six minutes of the opera are designed to lift the audience into the strange Strauss-Wilde world. The critics all decided that Dalí and I were only out to annoy them. There, at least, I might claim that they underestimated us; if that had been our intention I think that between us we might have done much worse . . .

In June 1950, Brook's contract as Director of Productions at Covent Garden was not renewed. 'His meteoric rise to such an exalted post at the age of twenty-seven,' pronounced *Musical Opinion*, 'was an artistic mistake on the part of authorities who should have had more respect for tradition than to permit it to be the plaything of a young experimentalist.'

Brook was only to venture twice more into the traditional opera house, to do *Eugene Onegin* and *Faust* at New York's Metropolitan Opera. But this grand form of theatre continued to attract him, and thirty years later, in the intimate space of his own theatre, he staged *La Tragédie de Carmen*, in a ninety-minute, pared-down version, nothing inflated or grandiose about it, just the true voice of *dramma per la musica*.

It was at this point that Brook began a lifelong activity of writing about his work, asking basic questions about the why and wherefore of theatre. In a series of pieces for theatre magazines, he staked out the freedoms and responsibilities of a director – or producer, as directors were then called.

> It is said that the producer is the servant of his text: this cliché is as misleading as it is common. The producer is the servant of the author's intentions, which is quite another matter. The producer's task is to find new means of communicating the poetic heart of the play. The text itself can never be sacred. If the most drastic changes in the text appear essential, then they must not be shirked. A production that cuts, transposes and even re-writes a classical play, and in doing so brings the essence of that play closer to a modern audience, is performing a far more legitimate service than the production that preserves the body of the play, but misses its soul.

He was just as wary of the danger of drowning a play in directorial ingenuity and spectacle. He set out an idea of simplicity, which was to become more rigorous as he advanced: 'One must remember that there are two forms of simplicity – the one that comes from a colourless and uninventive mind, and the real simplicity, which is the hardest thing of all to attain. Real simplicity comes when the imagination has purged itself of a thousand extravagances, stripping them down to an essence that has meaning and beauty.' The rigour and ease of that purging process was to become stronger over the years.

Brook had a mentor for the kind of theatre-maker he wanted to be: Gordon Craig, the hermit visionary of the British theatre. Actor, designer, theorist, mystic and craftsman, son of the great nineteenth-century actress Ellen Terry, Craig enchanted Brook. A fragment of a Granada Television interview of the 1950s shows a mustard-keen young Brook eagerly questioning the old sage of Menton, who trots out well-used stories in reply. In 1956, Brook wrote an admiring profile of Craig in his south of France retreat. 'Craig loved Henry Irving's theatre – its painted forests, its thunder sheets, its naive melodrama – but at the same time he dreamed of another theatre where all the elements would be harmonious and whose art would be a religion.'

It was Gordon Craig's restless experimenting – wanting to rid the stage of naturalistic actors, and replace the actor with *übermarionettes* – that Brook found both an inspiration and a warning. He admired the purity of Craig's indignation:

> He retired to Italy, edited a magazine *The Masque*, firing broadsides at all that he considered shoddy and false, built himself a model and began experimenting with a system of scenery based on screens and lights. The purity of the screens, the formal beauty of the equations from which they were derived, fascinated him completely; despite many offers, he never worked in the living theatre again.

Brook tucked away as a key idea 'the formal beauty of the equations' which underpinned harmony on a stage. Craig helped him to realise that there was a deep-rooted geometry in esoteric books; this geometry of 'rightness' on the stage became a major preoccupation. Beneath the urbane play-maker who was the talk of the town was a cooler spirit, reflecting on the vocation of the director and the control of the theatre's means that it required. 'Craig preached simplicity, the beauty of harmonious form, the suggestive power of lighting. Craig advocated, aggressively and brilliantly, that the theatre must have all its elements united under the control of one man.' His aim would be to stage 'not works of literature but really works of theatre, which could not be read with any satisfaction and which only become coherent *in the full ensemble of performance*'.

4

THE PULSE BEATS FASTER
1951–53

If Brook's life and career in the 1950s were to be compared to a Rossini overture, they would now be entering that dizzying accelerando which, with a mounting intensity, gathers to it section after section of the orchestra. His energy is demonic; he does three, sometimes four shows a year. He changes tracks from Shakespeare to West End comedy, from bitter-sweet French romantic drama to opera, back to an early, savage Shakespeare play, forward to a Broadway musical set in the Caribbean. He travels from London to Paris to New York. His letters to Bob Facey are scribbled on transatlantic flights on British Overseas Airways Corporation notepaper; he has momentous meetings on cross-Channel ferries. As in Rossini, the momentum rises and rises. His intelligence, his analytical mind, his inborn ability to measure things from more than one perspective manage to contain the ferment. But emotionally, it is another matter. As well as a great beauty, there is a fierce aggression in his work, and, he feels at times, a coolness in his relationships. Sometimes he thinks he doesn't care about anyone else, that he has no emotion at all.

In 1948 he had stated in a telegraphic letter to Robert Facey: 'Self: Married – NO. Divorced – NO. Fucking – YES.' His love life and his libido are linked, sometimes productively, sometimes antagonistically, with the emotion and energy of his creative life. Talking to me in 2002, he said,

Sexual energy is the basic energy. A fanatic is misusing his sexual energy. I've been born with a highly strong sexual charge, it's self-replenishing. On the one hand, I could see absolutely no reason to suppress or to check this, so I gave it full vent, and at the same time there was more than enough going on to replenish, to drive the mind, the imagination, the activity, and although I was never *sportif*, my work in the theatre was physically on the move, I never rehearsed a play sitting down. These were all by-products of a driving sexuality.

He describes his sexuality in his twenties as self-centred and was at first astonished to find that the woman might feel differently.

The morality was to be kind and not to hurt anyone. But it took me a long time to realise that even if a woman claims to be as free in that respect as a man, it's not true. I always used to feel that if you meet someone and become friends, as men do, and have a meal or drinks with someone, going to bed together is the natural extension of it. If I was in bed for two hours in the afternoon with a girl, this would be a total meeting, a total relationship – little realising that the girl's not been looking at it the same way. In the climate of that time, the late fifties and sixties, when women were starting to be more open with men, I felt totally free. But it was a lack of understanding and imagination, to go . . . sweeping through like this.

Energised by sexual encounters, he enjoyed them with a lightness, almost a nonchalance, that, for its time, seems more French than English. Nor is it fanciful to see Brook mirroring himself as a rampant young man in Mozart's *Don Giovanni*, which he directed at the Aix-en-Provence festival in 1998. He claimed:

I defended Don Giovanni, because I believe Mozart was like his hero. The music for *Don Giovanni* shows no disapproval. He shows a man who is living the moment with total involvement. When Giovanni says to each woman, 'I love you more than anyone in the world', it's not cynical. But his lack of understanding – which I find also in myself – led him into the most terrible circumstances, and so he did great harm. Yet at the end, when I bring him on as a ghost watching the women, you can see they've all been touched by him, and not only in a bad way.

Of the many relationships with women that Brook had in his twenties, one – with Jean Boulting – stands out as a more substantial involvement. His *éducation sentimentale* begins with this woman. Brook was the young man, a modern-day Frédéric Moreau, whose eyes were opened by an older woman on to a rich, sophisticated world.

Jean was married to Roy Boulting, one of the Boulting twins, who were at that time the real off-beat element in the British cinema. I was at Pinewood, with Gaumont British, and I'd written an autobiographical script largely about school, and I went to see them. I said I'd just come down from Oxford, where I'd made a film and written this script and I wanted them to finance it. Roy looked at me a bit quizzically, and said, 'So, the new Orson Welles, eh?' They didn't take me very seriously, looked at my script and shook their heads.

But we became friendly, and I remember having lunch with – one of the twins, it must have been Roy – in a Soho restaurant, which seemed to me the height of chic, and he suddenly said, 'Oh there's my wife,' sitting having lunch with a girlfriend of hers. Chekhov would have liked the fact that he was having lunch with me and his wife was sitting on another table. As we walked past, he introduced me. She had rather heavily made-up eyelids. A big mouth. Strong blue shadow on her eyelids. She seemed to me sophisticated and glamorous.

I met her again, we went out for dinner, and one thing led to another, and I remember going to her house and her taking me upstairs, past two little children in bunk-beds. I may well have been at Covent Garden by then; but Roy was away a lot, she'd had a number of love affairs, and we rapidly became close. She told me she was going to a place in Provence where I'd never been, and I must come with her, so that became my first journey with her. We travelled a lot together. One of Jean's children caught tuberculosis and was prescribed sun and fresh air in Switzerland – and I found myself in Montana, where I hadn't been since my own childhood convalescence. Then we went off to Italy, to a tiny hotel on an island in Lake Maggiore, where we were caught.

Roy Boulting, finally deciding he'd had enough (though he was no model husband himself, and eventually married five times), summoned a Swiss lawyer who, accompanied by the British consul, in a scene worthy of an Ealing comedy, silently rowed out to the island, spied on the lovers, had the witness statement countersigned, and put the slow-moving divorce machinery into action.

> My mother was furious at the whole thing. 'You've got to break off, you'll find yourself getting married to this *old woman*! Jean was maybe 29 and I was about 23. The affair wound down over a couple of pretty ghastly years. She was intelligent and bright, and then possessive and jealous. The relationship became tortured, because we'd become really close. It was on, then it was off, then it was on again.

They went to Paris, where they had once been happy. But this time it didn't work. At a party, a woman invited them to Florence. Since nothing good was happening in Paris, they thought they might as well try Florence. They took a sad, nervous train journey, hoping to revive their relationship. But it didn't help; they separated – though by extraordinary chance, they met again the same day, in a small Florentine hotel to which each, separately, had fled. 'Neither of us,' said Brook sadly, 'accepted this coincidence as a reconciliation.'

A more turbulent view of the twenty-five-year-old Brook in the grip of his desire and emotions is provided by a letter he wrote to Facey in autumn 1950, recalling the pangs, setbacks and reversals of his pursuit of Natasha Parry. He had met her at a Covent Garden ballet matinée when she was fifteen accompanying the film director Anthony Asquith. He had been immediately struck by her beauty, and by the fact that she was called Natasha. He remembered that when he had read *War and Peace*, at the age of nine, he decided that, like Pierre in the story, he too wanted to marry Natasha.

That was the only time they met until a couple of years later. She had gone with the singer Elisabeth Welch to the Ivy restaurant. Peter was dining there. 'We stopped at his table,' Natasha recalls, 'and Lis Welch introduced me. I said, "I don't know if you remember but we did meet once when I was fifteen".'

He asked a mutual friend to invite Natasha to a party she was giving. They hardly spoke, but as she was leaving the party – 'I was almost out of the door' – he called down from the landing on the first floor and asked, 'What's your phone number, I'll call you.' To her great surprise, he did call her a couple of days later. 'Warm and friendly dinners,' says Natasha, 'a couple of long walks through London.' Then he went off to Seville for the Feria, and sent postcards. Then there was a pause: he was travelling, she was working. When he returned, he tried to contact her. Her mother told him Natasha had gone to Paris.

Finding himself obsessed with her, as he tells in *Threads of Time*, he followed her to Paris, tracked down her hotel, and walked into her in the lobby. For reasons he didn't understand, another involvement perhaps, she didn't want to see him. He retreated in confusion, and 'a year of misunderstanding' ensued. As Natasha says, 'there were also plenty of ups and downs.'

Brook's letter to Robert Facey describes the emotional tempest that followed:

Love? I've been haunted for two months by the heroine of my Paris adventure; for two months I was too proud to phone her but wandered through life looking right and left out of taxi windows, catching my breath at a passing head or the twist of a shoulder, romantic and obsessed. Then the first night of *The Little Hut* came, and with it a telegram from her. I took a deep breath and a deep risk and wrote the most beastly bitchy answer. For three days there was no word and I began to feel that my ideas on human nature had failed me.

On the fourth day I went and stood in the pouring rain in Brompton Road, watching her apartment. After an hour I gave up, drenched to the skin. I returned home and as I opened the front door I heard the phone going. I tore upstairs, fumbled with the key, dashed to the machine, but it was too late; nothing but the dialling tone. A few moments later it rang again. It was a trunk call from her, calling from Paris. We spoke for four hours. The next day I went to Stratford and again we spoke most of the night. It was arranged that she'd come over from Paris for the weekend. Complications. Cancellations. No trains. No connections. So we settled to meet in Oxford.

My fortune teller on Brighton Pier had said I'd meet her again when it was very hot. The day was grey and windy. I went to Oxford. By the time her train got in at half-past eleven at night the rain was coming down in sheets. I shivered. But she arrived. We went to the Randolph Hotel – the dining room was like an icebox, we hid from the draughts behind a screen and ate cold supper. Determined not to let my palmist down, I put a shilling in the electric fire in the bedroom. We stayed together for four days, then she had to return to a film on location, and I to London.

London is transformed, the ghost is laid: I go through the streets no longer tantalised by every passing head and shoulders. I feel full of life and ideas. And the girl? Glad to have known her. End of chapter.

But the affair was not closed. A year of keen and sometimes anguished pursuit followed. For all his growing love for Natasha, Brook was still a very driven individualist. They went to New York, the first time for her. She was twenty, a very timid girl; he had already been to New York once before. They came from the airport, deposited their luggage, kept the taxi running and on Fifth Avenue, in the middle of a gigantic St Patrick's Day parade Peter said, 'I've an appointment with a producer, so I'll have to drop you here. We'll meet at six o'clock back at the hotel, you have the address.' 'I went off,' he says, 'little thinking that for her, to be dumped in the middle of the crowds, the noise and the music would be terrifying. And when I came back I said, "Wasn't that thrilling?"' He tells these stories about his earlier self as if he's describing some coolly unkind alien.

Simon Brook, Peter's father, had clearly been struck by Natasha when he first met her, on Peter's twenty-sixth birthday. He noted in a memoir, 'Pretty figure; small; slim; soft skin; big eyes; large mouth, lips covered with plenty of colouring matter.'

At the end of a year, Natasha and Peter decided to live together, and after a further year, to marry. Peter's father tells the tale of the wedding day, 3 November 1951, in his diary: 'Yesterday, Peter rang me up and said, "Dad, are you free tomorrow, I'm getting married at Caxton Hall". That was sudden and unexpected. At ten o'clock, the clerk came to inquire who of us is getting married. But there were no traces of the bride or the groom. They both arrived, almost simultaneously, ten minutes late. Peter had no wed-ding-ring, and the official ceremony was quickly over. Peter rushed off with Natasha in his old car to have a quick breakfast, as he had to go to Brighton

to rehearse *Colombe*, she to do a radio show before her evening performance at the Aldwych. When Peter met Natasha, along with a focus and
vessel for his centrifugal, all-direction-seeking creative energy, he was
looking for a centre for his emotional and sexual life. He found it in this
beautiful, reserved and mysterious young actress, with long dark hair and
grave eyes.'

A month and a half after their marriage, Natasha fell ill with tuberculosis,
the result, said Peter, of her getting out of their car in a freezing December
fog to guide him with a torch, while being flimsily dressed after his first
night. 'It was a real pea-souper,' says Natasha, 'I walked in front of the car
from the Duke of York's Theatre all the way to South Kensington.' She
slowly recovered in their London house, treated with the still-new antibiotic
streptomycin, with a day and a night nurse and 'food treats supplied by our
kind friend Abel of the Ivy – including still-scarce pots of cream and butter',
Natasha remembers. Despite a heavy workload, Peter was always there
when she needed him.

Later, they rented a modest little house by a small beach in Spain, where
Natasha recuperated, and Peter came and went from rehearsals in London.
When she recovered, they resumed their busy lives. 'We started giving small
Saturday morning parties. Friends would come round for coffee, tea, a glass
of wine. Gradually these mornings turned into all-day gatherings, people
arriving whenever they could, after shopping, before going to the theatre. It
was relaxed, casual, informal and fun.'

Photographs of the Brooks regularly featured in the glossy magazines and
newspaper celebrity pages, Natasha as an exotic, not altogether English
beauty, Peter, in a surreal Angus McBean picture, as a puppet-master pulling
the strings of a marionette theatre.

The Brooks did not marry to 'settle down'; bouts of hard work followed by
adventurous journeys together became a *leitmotiv* of their marriage. From
their journeys to Mexico and Cuba, not to mention his frequent trips to
Paris, Brook had now begun to store up perceptions and thoughts beyond
the horizon of British experience. As he travelled, he drew political conclusions, too, seeing the economic and cultural shackles left by colonialism.

On their trip to Mexico, Brook made one precious purchase: a statuette of a laughing woman with her arms raised in delight. She stands about the height of two hands, she's made of baked clay. Her head is thrown back, her eyes closed, her mouth smiling wide. Spokes of hair poke from her head, her arms exult, palms open. Her whole body radiates the release of laughter. Below her zigzag patterned dress, her short plump legs are firmly planted on big feet. Today she stands on a shelf in Brook's Paris flat.

He presented this figure as a theatrical icon in a long article written in 1961 which ushered in his radically experimental work of the 1960s:

> I have a little figure from Vera Cruz of a goddess with her head thrown back and her hands held up – all so right in conception, in proportion and in form that the figure not only expresses a sort of inner radiance but is also a tangible object in its own right. To create it, the artist must have experienced this radiance, but he did not set out to describe radiance to us through a set of abstract symbols. He told us nothing: only he created an object that makes concrete this very quality. This to me is the essence of great acting.

Forty years later, in a documentary film his son Simon was making about him, he explained what the statuette has meant to him:

> Until I came across this statue, I thought an actor was someone who constructed, in a very complicated way, his 'character'. And then I realised this 'character' wasn't true. The actor is someone who must empty himself. So although this statue is an empty object, in its attitude one can feel fullness. It really is an expression of pure joy. So from the 1960s, I started using this object, in workshops with actors. The actor with this object understands that it's through a shedding of skills that he achieves this. It's like a direct reference to what a living actor is.

They succeeded in maintaining their nomadic life. 'I managed to retain this situation,' wrote Brook later, 'through years of marriage which, because of Natasha's oriental wisdom, never involved "settling down". Even the arrival of a first child, Irina, in 1952, was absorbed into our nomad life without too overwhelming a problem.' In a quiet passage in *Threads of Time*, where he anatomises his marriage of nearly half a century, he again

uses the word 'oriental' to describe Natasha. Given his search for the
wisdom of the East as a counterweight to Western civilisation, it's a big
compliment; for Brook it implies tradition, wisdom, journeying and hidden
realities. 'Disputes between us would never arise, even if later we both came
to understand how much tension and conflict lay painfully concealed under
the surface. Yet far below what timidity and self-restraint could hide existed
an even deeper level, more fundamental than fragility, where an almost
oriental wisdom recognised that in a relationship nothing is more precious
than the patience that brings peace.'

During 1950, Brook kept racing at Rossinian speed. Removed from the
Opera House, he tore his way through three productions back to back, two
for H. M. Tennent in the West End.

   He had already taken leave from his non-exclusive contract with Covent
Garden in 1949 to mount *Dark of the Moon*, an American play about
witchcraft which he had stumbled upon, inspired by the eerie ballad
'Barbara Allen'. He persuaded Tennent's to stage it at the Lyric Hammersmith, their house for experiments, from where it transferred to the West
End. He assembled a young cast of virtual unknowns, who could act, sing
and dance. It was, said Kenneth Tynan, a mediocre play, but 'it became a
crazily orchestrated symphony of black and amber: a jigsaw of wild super-
stitions and hot loveliness, reaching its perspiring climax in a revivalist
meeting which tore the heart out of the play and held it in its hand.'

   Later that year, Binkie Beaumont asked him to direct *Ring Round the
Moon* (*L'Invitation au château*), by Jean Anouilh, translated by Christopher
Fry. It was a fable of poignant love and lonely philanthropy, set in a filigree
conservatory designed by Oliver Messel. Brook also enjoyed the theatrical
trickery of casting Paul Scofield as twin brothers, exiting stage-left and re-
entering almost immediately stage-right as his twin. Claire Bloom played the
soulful lost girl in search of love, one of Anouilh's archetypes; Margaret
Rutherford, who had cornered the duchesses and battleaxes in the British
cinema of the time, played a *grande dame* in a wheelchair. '*Ring Round the
Moon*,' wrote the young Tynan, 'is complete wedding-cake: it has been
traced with an icing-gun on gossamer.' Brook returned to Stratford-upon-
Avon to direct his third Shakespeare play, *Measure for Measure*, certain, he

says, that his ears had been sharpened for language and speech by three years in the Opera House. As Angelo, he had one of the master-actors of language on the English stage, John Gielgud. Audiences and critics had regularly applauded Gielgud's mellifluous and witty performances; some qualified their praise by finding his mercurial mind and tongue a little self-regarding. Brook successfully stiffened him against the actor's natural desire to be liked by the audience: 'Gielgud as Angelo', wrote *The Times*, 'lets something coldly and deliberately vicious be his undoing.' In this *Measure for Measure*, which he also designed, Brook populated the play's prisons with a fantastical procession of crooks, beggars and cripples, the degenerate and wounded of a corrupt, decadent city, its stews and bordellos the mirror image of corrupt official, daylight Vienna. For the long final act of punishments and rewards, he pulled off a coup which is etched in the minds of all who saw it. Having screwed up the tension of the main action of the play, Brook asked Barbara Jefford as Isabella to hold the longest pause she could manage as she decided whether to pardon Angelo, the man who wanted to rape her. 'To these crippled final scenes,' wrote Harold Hobson in *The Sunday Times*, 'he imparts an athlete's timing that makes them genuinely dramatic. The enormous pause (during which at the first performance the audience dared scarcely breathe) that, with unbelievable bravado, he places before Isabella's plea for Angelo's pardon, is evidence by its success of the grip that Mr Brook has restored to the play.' For Tynan, these thirty-five seconds were 'a long prickly moment of doubt which had every heart in the theatre thudding'.

Returning to London, Brook now switched to something even further from the grandeur of opera or the gravity of Shakespeare: the French farce *The Little Hut* by André Roussin, in which a wife and husband and her lover are shipwrecked on a desert island. It was performed by two kings of British comedy, David Tomlinson and Robert Morley. In Morley's recollection, the two old hands told Brook how they were going to do it, and congratulated him on being very polite and considerate; he had helped Morley take off his jacket, hung it up and interfered very little. *The Little Hut* was earning him the rewards of his second and, with the Anouilh play still running, simultaneous West End success. French theatre intellectuals who came to worship at Brook's shrine when he later settled in Paris were astonished to find that he had directed hit plays by boulevard playwrights. It was as if their guru had begun his career directing Neil Simon or Ray Cooney. But this eclecticism was very important to Brook. He deplored the intellectual snobbery of the French. 'To learn theatre,' he said, 'you must explore all its forms with equal enthusiasm.'

In 1951, Brook managed to combine working for Tennent's with slipping across at weekends to the Belgian National Theatre in Brussels to supervise the premiere in that country of Arthur Miller's *Mort d'un commis voyageur* (*Death of a Salesman*), his first venture into French-speaking theatre. And he directed H. M. Tennent's two offerings for the Festival of Britain, a new play by John Whiting, and Shakespeare's *The Winter's Tale*.

Whiting's *Penny for a Song*, which opened in April 1951, was a playful comedy, in tune with the Festival of Britain, the country's cavalcade to cheer people up after the war. Whiting's play is a theatrical caprice about young lovers and their eccentric elders in a country house on the cliffs of Dorset in 1804, awaiting an invasion by Napoleon. Its tone, including its wry patriotism, is light, almost Anouilh-esque, a French *comédie brillante* in English tweeds. Brook decked out *Penny for a Song* with enchanting, Alice-in-Wonderland designs by the *Punch* cartoonist Roland Emmett, including an ornate fire engine and a decorative air-balloon. But the critics were not impressed.

He went on to direct a Tennents/Arts Council production of *The Winter's Tale* which, with its array of seasoned English classical acting talent – 'almost an ensemble, so often had they worked together,' thought Brook – was almost critic-proof. John Gielgud as Leontes, Diana Wynyard as Hermione, Flora Robson as Paulina, Virginia McKenna as Perdita, George Rose (with whom Brook had worked at Stratford-upon-Avon) as Autolycus. Ivor Brown wrote a mock-testy notice, like a twinkling uncle handing out good marks: the production, he says, 'leaves out Peter Brookishness and is admirably simple and quick'.

After its London opening, *The Winter's Tale* went up to Edinburgh, where it was also warmly appreciated. Self-congratulation seemed to be in order. But at a press conference Brook announced that while he was glad to present a Shakespeare play, he had originally proposed 'a total and perhaps a very dangerous experiment', a piece of political theatre. In Berlin a year before, he told the press conference, he had begun to think about an international political satire, whose serious political themes would have been put across 'by using the lightest of musical revue techniques'. The show would have satirised the tangle of beliefs and ideologies, past crimes and post-war reconstruction which Berlin offered, and might have wound up like a Peter Ustinov play, or a sardonic *Oh What A Lovely Peace*. But the Festival decided they couldn't take the risk.

In August 1951, Brook wrote a letter to Robert Facey to announce an exciting discovery. He wanted to enthuse about a new field: film, or at least television. 'The story is about Jonah and the whale – modern dress – in an airplane – based on my trip home from New York.' In the end, this Jonah story became an ITV television play, *Heaven and Earth*, co-written by Brook and his actor/writer friend Denis Cannan, starring Paul Scofield and directed by Brook. It was warmly reviewed by John Osborne, guesting as a TV critic for the *Evening Standard*:

> This was the most literate dialogue I have yet heard in a play written for television, and seemed to be full of such refreshingly harsh innuendoes that I was in doubt for a long time as to whether the play was simply a high-class thriller or a modern morality. The situation – that of a Holy Joe revivalist travelling on an airplane, in which the other passengers become convinced that his presence is endangering their lives – was intriguing. The standard of acting and writing was so high and Mr Brook's direction so smooth, swift and assured that I confess I was a little disappointed when it all finished.

It's intriguing to imagine what might have been if Brook and Osborne had worked together, but it was not to be; Osborne might well have dismissed Brook as an indentured servant of the genteel H. M. Tennent. But Brook's intervention on behalf of another new playwright might have encouraged Osborne. In September 1951, John Whiting's play *Saint's Day* was awarded an Arts Council prize, despite a hostile reception. In his drama of an old, angry isolated poet, with its climax of violent disintegration, Whiting conveyed a post-war nihilism, in which even the victors in the war had lost their moral compass. 'Claptrap' was one of the politer comments; *The*

Times called it 'indescribably bad'. But Brook and Tyrone Guthrie, the two most iconoclastic and unpredictable directors of the British theatre, wrote to *The Times*: '*Saint's Day* may well be strange and obscure, and entertainment is certainly a word that cannot be applied to it; but its passion and its unbroken tension are the products of a new and extraordinary theatrical mind. John Whiting is writing in his own idiom and describing his own world. For the moment this may be as strange to us as the worlds of Kafka or Virginia Woolf must have appeared before familiarity added signposts to the scene.'

These digressions over, Brook was ready to trumpet his seismic discovery, which he celebrated to Facey in a long, syntactically acrobatic sentence about philosophy, science, the fabric of life, and the universe:

The newest and overwhelming passion in life is neither play, film, female (she's a really sweet little girl, the new one, don't believe anything that other women may say!) – it is once again our old friend the UNIVERSE. Because while you were reading Toynbee I was reading the best deepest profoundest most amazing book I've ever read in my life, called *In Search of the Miraculous* by P. D. Ouspensky. Ouspensky is a Russian writer and philosopher you may have come across, who in this case merely Boswells the teaching of another Russian, Gurdjieff, who was the most astonishing superbrain containing answers to every question of life and death.

If I tell you that he proves in this book to your total satisfaction how all phenomena descend from the octave – that divine principles and cosmic energy are the same matter as atomic energy and that light, for example, is a cruder form (or a radiation or denser cluster of atoms) of the element called thought, which is a denser cluster or vibration of the one called inspiration, and so on up to God or the absolute, and down to the moon which represents the most inert form of energy and that the moon is an animal that feeds off the earth – that in the transmission of rays of energy through the entire system of Creation, organic life exists on the face of the earth as a highly sensitive ENERGY STORE for highgrade energy which is continually – in the death of the organism – attracted to the moon – and that this is the Hell and Outer Darkness that the churches have divined! Does that whet your appetite?

This shaken cocktail of magic and psychology, cosmology and science, is a sign of the way Brook was seeking to master the maelstrom of his life. Gurdjieff promised a way through his hothouse of emotions. He gave him a map of his desires. He anatomised the energy of which Brook himself was a cauldron. Gurdjieff outlined processes and laws in which human consciousness and non-human matter connected. Where life had seemed limitless to Brook, and that limitlessness sometimes lonely, the 'esoteric teacher' George Gurdjieff provided disciplines, laws and hard-edged limits.

Brook had reached Ouspensky's book by a typically circuitous route. Long before working with Salvador Dalí on *Salome* in 1948, he had begun to feel the need to seize some underlying rules or laws of stage design. He went to Cadaqués in Spain to work with Dalí, who put him up in a little fisherman's hut he kept as a guest-house. There, Brook found and read a book, *Essais sur la proportion*, by Prince Matila Ghika. Grilles of geometry were superimposed on buildings and faces. Measurements of columns and arches in classical architecture confirmed recurring patterns and intervals. 'I came across this book which says, "There are laws, there are actual, specific, physical mathematical laws. If you look and count three, that's more harmonious than three and a half or four." And that was an opening. It was hard to say why, because it demands a degree of introspection that I am sure I never had at the time.' For the first time, Brook also came across 'a spellbinding term', 'the golden section', the secret harmony of the proposition of parts.

Working with designers or making his own designs, he had seen that a certain combination of elements was 'too much', and that purely instinctive choices seemed to confirm 'a hidden order that the conscious mind was unable to define'. As a ballet critic, he had appreciated the quality of movement and groupings in choreography, the eloquent rightness of certain distances and proximities. Such experiences were immediate at a deep, preverbal level, and seemed to Brook to be at the heart of theatre. Ghika's book was not his first awareness of this; Brook had already seen how Gordon Craig had sought abstract stage elements which suggested larger emotions. Soon after his discovery of Ghika's *Essays on Proportion*, he came across another book that seemed to open out into even larger spheres: P. D. Ouspensky's *In Search of the Miraculous*.

In the living-room of some friends in Paris he picked up this book, and was amazed to discover that it had the same diagram of an octave – the ascending and descending steps of all energy – that had captivated him in Ghika's book. He quickly realised that the mysterious 'G' whose thoughts and words Ouspensky reported, as Plato had reported Socrates, was taking the octave beyond design and architecture into human behaviour and experience. 'He was referring to the musical scale and using the octave to express an amazing idea: the nature and quality of human experience are exactly determined by their place in a rising and falling scale of energies of differing intensities. This meant that even when life is in its crudest state, a process exists through which the coarser can become finer, and this process is not haphazard.'

Brook's encounter with Ouspensky's book is closely bound with his former lover Jean Boulting. After the two had found themselves by coincidence at the same hotel in Florence, Brook, in what felt like a last desperate throw of the dice to save the affair, had called Jean back in London and gone to her flat. There on her mantelpiece he discovered a newspaper cutting with a review of Ouspensky's *In Search of the Miraculous*. Jean explained that the letter G in the book stood for Gurdjieff, a Russian who transmitted ancient teaching. If Peter really wanted to learn, she said, it couldn't be done from a book, it had to be personal and direct. There was a woman she had been seeing in London, she said, who practised the Gurdjieff teachings.

That is how Brook went to an address in Hamilton Terrace, north-west London, rang the bell and met Jane Heap, who was to be his teacher until her death in 1964. She was in her sixties, a forceful woman who had given up her life as editor of the avant-garde literary magazine *The Little Review* to practise and propagate Gurdjieff's teachings. She foreshadows the other strong women to whom Brook would be drawn. He joined her 'school', and found it much more testing than Gresham's or Westminster had been. Sometimes the teaching involved physical and emotional shocks, which were not always welcome. But it was based on respect for a mentor who knew more. Perhaps Brook had found a teacher and a teaching which could pull him out of the crystal bubble of being special, of brilliance and ease and facility. 'I was being asked to work with ordinary people, with no flights of fantasy, no romance – something that forced me to face and accept, with difficulty, my own essential ordinariness.'

The teaching appealed to Brook the man and Brook the theatre-maker because it spoke of what a modern scholar of mysticism has called 'the reality of a supra-sensible world, which is neither the empirical world of the senses nor the abstract world of the intellect'. This world was bound to awaken the interest of the man who would formulate his own philosophy of theatre fifteen years later around the concept of 'The Empty Space'.

Gurdjieff himself had died just two years earlier, but left his imprint on a number of hand-picked teachers. Jane Heap was one of those who had worked directly with him; the effect she had on Brook, as an individual and in his relation with others, can be judged by his own recollection of her, written more than forty years after he started working with her, and thirty-three years after she died.

My first impressions of Jane: not tall, compact, in a navy blue artist's jacket, trousers, a shocking pink foulard, closely cropped grey hair, a clear penetrating gaze, radiating a force that was both firm and relaxed . . . She never allowed anyone to keep notes of what she said, often repeating, 'All that falls from the wagon is lost'. And constantly, she stressed, ideas by themselves are useless, speculations on cosmic questions get you nowhere – 'it's just guessing' she would say, bringing erudite interrogations about the cosmos or the afterlife down to the gritty reality of the present. Too much philosophising leads to day-dreams, she would add, while inner work is quite different, it is practical, immediate and direct – and she would show how its starting point is always what each person is, without denying any of the contradictions out of which a person is composed.

In the regular meetings which she held with her groups, she would never allow the search for meaning to remain glued to the ordinary nor exalted to the ethereal – at once she'd raise the level or prick the bubble. Within each session she would look for the link that could relate humdrum, everyday problems with fundamental, universal laws. As she spoke, each moment would take its place in a vast chain of meanings and she would open up broad perspectives far out into space and far back into history. In this way, she showed again and again that the teaching came from a great distance and was not her invention – she refused to allow anyone to make this identification – and even when she spoke with great respect of Gurdjieff it was to express that he too was not the inventor but the transmitter of a nearly forgotten tradition that preceded the great religions and had its roots in the remote past.

In Jane's approach, a teacher was not there to be obeyed blindly, a teacher was there to inspire, to stimulate, to slap, to soothe, to provide the conditions in which the pupils could face themselves, learn to question and verify and to discover how to reach with the help of others their own intensity and freedom. Of course, this was a very strong programme and the force she brought to it was inevitably too much for some – she could be ferocious and arouse great fear – while others, despite all her warnings, allowed her magnetism to draw them into adoration, hero worship and into the very dependence she abhorred.

You also ask if she influenced my own theatre work. It was quite the contrary. From the start, she instilled in me a repulsion towards exploiting a sacred teaching to further one's own worldly occupations. In the East, she would repeat, true knowledge is carefully hidden away, like a precious jewel. To use ideas or experiences gleaned from the groups for one's own personal profit would make one – and she'd punch out the words with vehemence – 'a thief!'

At the same time, all her efforts were devoted to opening her pupils to an awareness of the reality of finer energies and to be present to them, to become gradually aware that at every moment we have a responsibility – a responsibility for the quality of energy that enters into the activities of daily life.

FROM THE BEGGAR'S OPERA TO THE BOLSHOI 1953–58

In 1953, taking on a new role, Brook directed a feature film. As with *A Sentimental Journey*, its subject was a much-loved work of eighteenth-century English literature. *The Beggar's Opera*, based on John Gay's satirical ballad-opera of 1728, might have been made to express Brook's ambivalent feelings for English landscape and London wit. It was a film soaked in ironic satire and cheerful eroticism, the simplicity of Gay's traditional airs and ballads married to a virtuosic cinematic style. Brook's producer was Herbert Wilcox, then the middle-brow master of the British cinema. He had Britain's greatest actor, Laurence Olivier, to play the raffish rascal, Macheath. Olivier, alerted by his experiences in *Wuthering Heights* (1939) and *Rebecca* (1940) and having acted, directed and produced his 1948 *Hamlet*, insisted that he be made co-producer as well as the star.

This did not bode well for Brook. While Olivier saw Macheath as an opportunity to shine in a sardonically comic role and to charm the audience with his swashbuckling and singing, Brook had something edgier in mind, a cinematic equivalent of what John Russell Taylor calls his 'theatricalist' stage productions – *Dark of the Moon, Ring Round the Moon, Penny for a Song, Colombe*. He wanted the then unknown Richard Burton as the lead, but Olivier and Herbert Wilcox had turned him down, Wilcox sending a terse telegram claiming, 'This man will never make it, even as an extra.'

Brook asked Denis Cannan to write a screenplay from Gay's play and Christopher Fry wrote additional dialogue and lyrics. Georges Wakhevitch created eighteenth-century London interiors and exteriors. The songs, sweetly arranged by the Master of the Queen's Musick Sir Arthur Bliss, were dubbed by leading opera singers of the day – except for Macheath; Olivier, with beetle-browed determination, set himself to strengthen his naturally light baritone voice.

Brook contrasts the exhilarating expanses of Bagshot Heath, with the highwayman Macheath galloping like a spirit set free, against the labyrinthine interiors of the jail, with its acrobatic fights and grizzled prisoners' faces behind bars. He would have preferred to shoot in Hogarthian black-and-white, but Wilcox insisted on colour; he wanted a sumptuous, charming film for the royal premiere on 3 June 1953, part of Queen Elizabeth's coronation festivities. The Queen's guests were received by a court official who Brook and everyone working seriously in the British theatre was soon to cross swords with: Brigadier Sir Norman Gwatkin, K.C.V.O., D.S.O., Assistant Comptroller of the Lord Chamberlain's Office, which was the headquarters of theatre censorship in Britain.

Most critics damned the film with faint, respectful praise. But the *Observer* praised the direction's 'astonishing range of speed. Perhaps the most brilliant passages in the film are those that show us contrasted studies of the doxies, the Ladies of the Town; caught in the vivid whirligig of the dance, or taken listless, still, and off their guard. The composition of these latter groups in particular is remarkably fine and full of character.' It noted that the film, with all its audience-pleasing qualities, 'is oddly unlike any other film that we have ever experienced'. This fate, of making films estranged from the cinematic mainstream, was to apply to many of Brook's subsequent films.

The film did not do good business; in fact, Wilcox and Olivier had to face the fact that they had produced a prestigious flop and Brook did not get any film offers in Britain for years; his next film, *Moderato cantabile*, was to be made in France. As he pointed out when that film opened in 1960, 'when you flop to the tune of a quarter of a million pounds, you have to do penance until the people concerned forget you or die off'. But in 1961, eight years after *The Beggar's Opera* first came out, the doyenne of American film critics, Pauline Kael, gave it a belated accolade. It may have suffered, she thought, from the word 'opera' in the title; film-goers had endured too many reverential screen versions of grand opera. Her enthusiastic account makes the film sound like a precursor of *The Marat/Sade*:

> The brilliant, unabashed theatricality, the choreographed chases and betrayals and captures, the elegant march to the gallows, the dazzling, macabre ballet under the titles at the end as the prisoners and jailers whirl amidst their stocks and irons, may have been too much of a jolt for movie audiences. . . . Here, artifice is used with the carefree delight and audacity of early Douglas Fairbanks films – delight in the film medium. Not even in Pirandello productions is there a more exquisite stylization of the derangements of art and life than in the hanging scene. We wait for the rescue, we know something must save Macheath, and something theatrically perfect does: Macheath as the actor playing Macheath simply refuses to be hanged.

Kael shrewdly speculates that some of the film's lack of success in Britain may also be due, paradoxically, to Olivier's stature as 'the champion of the English-speaking theatre, the actor who so rarely has an opportunity to demonstrate that he is, in addition to everything else, a great comedian. Olivier's stature may, ironically, have contributed to the film's failure: the critics were so happy to pounce on any possible weakness in an actor of such heroic dimensions – and Olivier's pleasant baritone, though adequate to the demands of the score, is not a *great* voice.' The critics were so happy to pounce: if Kael's guess was true, Brook might well have notched it up as another symptom of the 'Lilliputian mentality', the wish to 'take down a peg or two', so strange in 'can-do' America, so frequent at the blasé end of English culture.

Throughout the 1950s, Denis Cannan, actor, playwright and screenwriter, was one of Brook's closest collaborators and a friend with whom he relaxed in green rooms, bars and on tour. Cannan played Samuel Breeze in Brook's 1951 production of John Whiting's *Penny for a Song*; he and Brook had written the television film, *Heaven and Earth*, together, and Cannan adapted Anouilh's *Colombe* later that year. He wrote the screenplay for Brook's *Beggar's Opera*, appearing in a cameo role, and adapted Graham Greene's *The Power and the Glory* in 1956. A tall, shy, romantically handsome man with a saturnine sense of humour, he captures in a set of sharp vignettes he wrote for this book the insatiable curiosity of Brook in his twenties, his gleeful sense of the incongruous and his tendency to super- stition.

A director has to anticipate the reactions of spectators. Peter himself was an ideal audience. On tour with *Colombe* I went with him and Binkie to see *The Great Caruso*. At one especially nauseating moment Mario Lanza sang a lullaby to a sleeping baby. I looked round to see the reactions of my cynical and worldly companions. Both had cheeks wet with tears.

Peter's choices of events we had to go to were always unexpected. I remember visits to The Crazy Gang, to midnight masses at Downside Abbey and an orthodox church in Paris and to Billy Graham's first mass rally in England. At Earl's Court – to a full house, Peter noted – there were long preliminaries with acolytes banked on the platform and music by massed choirs. Peter was restless. Was something bothering him? 'I can't make out where Billy's going to make his entrance from.'

Dr Graham was announced. Suddenly he stood up. He'd been there all the time, unnoticed until now. I'm sure Peter made use of this effect in some future production. After Dr Graham's exhortation and more singing, we were asked in conclusion if all those willing on this night to give themselves to God would come forward. To my alarm, Peter rose and, with an expression of ecstatic reverence, went forward to the platform. With other postulants he was led out of the auditorium. After a long wait I went in search of him. I found him coming out of a marquee.

'I had to see him in close-up,' he explained.

'What happened in that tent?'

'Oh, they just took our names and addresses.'

'Now you're in trouble. They'll come to your door and pester you to death'

'Oh no they won't.'

'How can you be so sure?'

'Because I gave your name and address.'

I was always wary of his interest in the occult and his mystical leanings. He thought me an old-fashioned Fabian rationalist, impervious to the wisdom of the East. He had what I thought an unhealthy interest in that old fraud Aleister

Crowley whom he once interviewed. There was a famous palmist on Brighton Pier called Madame Binney. When one of his shows opened in Brighton, Binkie always consulted her about its prospects. Peter sometimes went with him. I am not sure which of them told me that during one consultation, Madame Binney said, 'Excuse me, dears', lifted her skirts and hauled up a flapping mackerel, caught on a line that passed through a hole in the floor.

For all his irreverence, there was a side of Peter I found naively superstitious. He would never direct *Macbeth*, he said; its reputation for bringing bad luck was well founded, because – and he really believed this – one of the witches' spells was a genuine invocation of evil.

Books on Peter, including his own, give the impression of a remote and solemn guru – a description he has said he detests. Of our times together, what I remember most is laughter.

In 1950, Brook had opened the Stratford season with *Measure for Measure*, starring John Gielgud. Of the two English actors who inspired Brook, Gielgud resembled Ariel – light and mercurial – where Scofield was more like Caliban – dark, secret, the instrument of a mysterious music. Gielgud, the most graceful voice of his theatrical generation and one of its most active, fizzing minds, moved towards the manic end of the spectrum; Scofield, darkly handsome, with a voice that was creased and gut-wrenched, seemed to rise from some broken melancholy. Scofield looked older than his years; Gielgud seemed to have eternal youth. 'In John,' wrote Brook, 'tongue and mind work so closely together that it is sufficient for him to think of something for it to be said; his tongue is the sensitive instrument that captures the most delicate shades of feeling in his acting and just as readily produces gaffes, indiscretions and outrageous puns.'

Brook had first met Gielgud when, as a bumptious young man, he thrust his way into the Haymarket Theatre to borrow costumes for *The Sentimental Journey*. Now, a decade later, he cast Gielgud as the lustful and anguished Angelo in another play that continued to tease and concern him, *Measure for Measure*. In 1953, Brook also brought Scofield and Gielgud together in Thomas Otway's 1681 tragedy *Venice Preserv'd*, Scofield playing the fiery young revolutionary Pierre, Gielgud his Brutus-like friend Jaffier. 'A prodigy has been brought to birth,' announced Kenneth Tynan.

'By which I mean a pure, plain, clear, classical production of the last great verse play in the English language . . . Otway allows Jaffier far too much self-pity, a mood of which John Gielgud, as an actor, is far too fond. The temptation sometimes proves too much for him: inhaling passionately through his nose, he administers to every line a tremendous parsonical quiver.'

Brook spent the rest of 1953 in New York, and did three productions – an opera, a televised Shakespeare and a Broadway musical – which, though received with varying degrees of warmth, began to imprint his name in Manhattan. He took Rolf Gerard with him into the Metropolitan Opera to design Gounod's *Faust*, stripping it of its medieval frippery to make something more immediate to a contemporary eye. The conductor was the veteran French maestro, Pierre Monteux, who exercised a calm authority over the orchestra and who Brook, who has always been fascinated by the longevity of conductors, admired. He also warmed to the Met's general manager, the Viennese-born Rudolf Bing. 'He was the best administrator I'd met. Just when you were going to explode about some shortcoming in the opera house, Bing would bustle in, waving his hands, and saying, "Oh I know just what you mean, it's intolerable, nobody should be obliged to work in these conditions, I'm working on it already, the next time you come it will be fixed." ' Brook was also impressed by the stream of pretty women beating a path to and from Bing's office. 'Whenever I went up for meeting, one would slip out as I went in. His secretary and I would exchange a look.' Gerard and Brook decided that it would be a mistake to be authentically early-medieval for Gounod's *Faust*, whose music was written in a resolutely nineteenth-century idiom, complete with waltzes. So they dressed the characters accordingly, putting Mephistopheles into an opera cloak and a top hat.

America was beginning to open up for Brook. *The Beggar's Opera* had been received much more warmly there. *The Little Hut* transferred to the Coronet Theater on Broadway, with the French-born Anne Vernon taking over the lead role of wife and mistress. It, however, was not well received, and closed after only twenty-nine performances. Meanwhile, the eminently visible Brook had been approached by CBS, producers of a prestigious cultural slot on American television, *Omnibus*, to do a classic drama production for them. Brook had proposed *King Lear*. It would be shot live, as all television drama was at that time, and the transmission slot meant that the play had to be condensed into ninety minutes – seventy-five actually, allowing for the commercials which, in deference to the grandeur of Shakespeare, were crammed together at the end. For Lear, Brook wanted Orson Welles.

Brook was still working at Covent Garden when he first met Welles one moody, foggy night on a ferry to Ostend, in an atmosphere like the vision of Vienna in *The Third Man*. Welles had loomed up on deck with the lights behind him, an ominous, Reed-ish apparition. Brook had introduced himself, asked Welles if he'd be interested in directing an opera. Nothing came of that, but when CBS approached him, he remembered Welles, offered him Lear, and Welles accepted.

Preparations and casting took up a number of lavish dinners at Peter and Natasha's house in Gordon Place. Welles had been travelling, and in Dublin had met the cream of Irish actors. He introduced Brook to Micheál Mac Liammóir, the sophisticated Irishman (actually an Englishman passing for Irish) at whose Gate Theatre in Dublin Welles had learned his first lessons in Shakespeare. Mac Liammóir played Poor Tom, a separate character, not Edgar in disguise; Brook thought this would clarify the plot. The cast was split sharply between towering talents like Welles and Mac Liammóir and run-of-the-mill secondary players. Brook and Welles with their quicksilver theatrical instinct would bewilder the rest of the cast and the crew by suddenly changing the moves; and dishearten some of the unknown actors with barely disguised exasperation at their delivery. The music, including every sound effect, was composed by the avant-garde American Virgil Thompson.

The reviews were respectful but, when Brook did not ask Orson to repeat the role on stage, a chill seemed to develop between the two men; Brook didn't think Welles had the staying power for it. 'Orson could only work in close-up,' Brook told me. 'Line for line, there were wonderful moments, you could imagine them in performance as very telling. But for the rhythm of a whole performance, he lacked the stamina.'

Brook came back to London, and staged for Tennent Christopher Fry's verse play *The Dark is Light Enough*, an elegiac tale about an *ancien régime* countess, played by Edith Evans. This was genteel drama. More robust was Arthur Macrae's comedy *Both Ends Meet*, a comedy about cheating the taxman which Brook directed in the summer of 1954 at the Apollo Theatre. Some years before staging the play, Brook had a meeting with Alfred Hitchcock.

Hitchcock rang up the Opera House one day, and asked me if I would direct a stage scene in one of his films. I looked at my diary and said, 'Very sorry, I'm not free'. Hitchcock replied, 'Will you come and have a drink with me at the Savoy?' 'What an elegant way of reacting when a young person refuses you something,' I thought. 'I must remember this.'

I go; we spend two hours in a magnificent suite overlooking the river, having a conversation about everything under the sun. It gradually got dark, but he never turned on the lights. We finished one bottle of scotch and he opened another and poured me a glass. 'So what date can you start?' he said. 'I can't,' I said. He took back the bottle and the glass and, firmly replacing the stopper, said, 'Then why are you wasting my time?'

I had my revenge two or three years later. I did *Both Ends Meet* by Arthur Macrae. Arthur was a gay, droll friend of Tennents; he collected fine china. He said, 'I'm writing a play; you must direct it.' It was a little West End comedy, about a tax inspector, and Arthur played a writer who has been fiddling his tax. In the first scene, the bell rings, and a man comes in. The writer takes him for a journalist and is very friendly. After a lot of chat and several drinks, Arthur becomes impatient. 'Are you here about the interview?' Arthur asks. 'No, I'm from the Inland Revenue,' says the man. At which point, I remembered Hitchcock and we did the gag with the bottle, only Arthur improved it: glass in one hand, bottle in the other, he slowly poured the drink back again and got the biggest laugh in the play.

He had scored a modest West End comedy success (284 performances); a Hitchcockian television play he had written about a man, Robert Helpmann, wheeling and dealing against the clock in a telephone booth, had been well noticed. Now Brook was off again to New York, to direct his first Broadway musical, *House of Flowers*, based on a novella by Truman Capote, with music by Harold Arlen. It dealt with the rivalry between two brothels on an island in the Caribbean. One was the eponymous House of Flowers, the other the *maison close* of Madame Tango, played by Pearl Bailey. Rehearsals turned out to be volatile, to say the least. 'On the first day of rehearsal,' Brook says, 'Harold Arlen, a blue cornflower in his button-hole, turned up with champagne and presents for everybody. Truman Capote whispered to Brook, "It's love today; the lawyers will be in tomorrow." And, within a few weeks, they were; Pearl Bailey, the lead, objected to Brook's constant rewriting of the second act and, with the play still touring, served a $50,000 writ on Brook. Later, in New York, he had to do most of the direction at long distance, from his hotel room by way of the choreographer.

Capote had met Brook in 1952, been impressed and had insisted to producer Arnold Saint-Subber that Brook must direct the show. It was a ninety per cent black cast, Afro-American and Caribbean. It contained black actors and performers who would go on to star in American theatre and dance, including Arthur Mitchell and Alvin Ailey, both of whom would lead formative Afro-American companies. Brook did little to win them round with his opening speech assuring them that he was 'not prejudiced'. And, according to cast member Geoffrey Holder, he proceeded to put his foot still further in it, addressing the cast as 'you people'.

The producer had hired the Russian ballet maestro George Balanchine to do the choreography. Coming from an alien ballet tradition, he spent two days breaking a mambo down into dance units, unaware that he could have had a rough but lively version at once, 'because we did it every night at the Palladium', says Holder. Balanchine resigned during the show's Philadelphia try-out, and was replaced by Herbert Ross – who also took over direction of the show from Brook. Brook had not been getting on well with Pearl Bailey. 'When Brook told her, "We have to create a new Pearl Bailey," she replied, "Honey, I'm not through with the old one yet." '

Brook was becoming aware of new voices in American theatre and American art which were less socially hidebound, freer in their form, and more truthful in their voice than the typical English play of the times. Tennessee Williams' searing plays, from *The Glass Menagerie* to *A Streetcar Named Desire*, with their exposure of vulnerability and the complexities of sexual desire, had enlarged American theatre's emotional space. McCarthyism and the Cold War shadowed the plays of Arthur Miller with the elegiac *Death of a Salesman* (1949) and the polemical *The Crucible* (1953). The elemental new dance of Martha Graham and the neo-classicism of George Balanchine were at their peak. The Abstract Expressionist painters of the New York School – Pollock, De Kooning and Rothko – gave licence to the instinctive gesture, to dream and imagination. All these currents stimulated Brook to push beyond the limitations of the culture in which he had grown up, to further stretch his artistic muscles.

Brook's drive to crack open the decorum of his own culture came to a head in 1955 with his fourth Shakespeare production at Stratford-upon-Avon, *Titus Andronicus*. It was the least well known and most spurned of the Shakespeare plays he had staged, customarily written off as a young man's attempt, perhaps in collaboration, to write a Senecan play of horrors, a *grand guignol* of violence and blood, crime and vicious retaliation, its horrors wreathed in sonorous rhetoric. T. S. Eliot called it 'one of the stupidest and most uninspiring plays ever written, a play in which it is incredible that Shakespeare had any hand at all'.

Brook liked it for its unfamiliarity, it being unlikely to trigger stock responses. He wanted to do it because it was theatre of the streets and the sawdust, a shocker to please the popular audience, and because he believed he could find a human reality in the suffering, absurdity and carnage. And as Titus he had Laurence Olivier, the British actor who embodied danger and risk-taking vitality, who was capable of fearless assault on tragic peaks, but also of languorous world-weariness.

Brook decided to design, direct and compose the electronic music. It was a stylised production, transposing the worst horrors into emblems, drawing on what Brook had seen in dance and learned about oriental theatre. Lavinia, raped, her tongue cut out and her hands cut off, trailed red ribbons for streams of blood and traced the letters of her rapists' names in the sand with a stick held between her arms. Brook cut risibly melodramatic lines like 'baked in that pie', and composed instead what he called 'a powerful and extremely barbaric ritual' in which violence, hatred, cruelty and fear, presented with an almost antiseptic coolness, became a credible world. He yoked atrocity to a cats-cradle of theatrical signs, which were almost

Japanese in their obliquity. The production had a power new to the British theatre because it yoked such extremes in Brook himself, between his forceful understanding of Shakespeare's violent story and his cool, filmic mastery of the devices of theatrical poetry.

The play hit the critics with a force like dynamite. 'This is tragedy naked, godless, and unredeemed,' wrote Tynan, 'a carnival of carnage in which pity is the first man down. We have since learned how to sweeten tragedy, to make it ennobling, but we would do well to remember that *Titus* is the raw material, "the thing itself", the piling of agony on to a human head until it splits.' Tynan exults in Olivier's battered sorrow: 'A hundred campaigns have tanned his heart to leather, and from the cracking of that heart there issues a terrible music, not untinged by madness.' He is, however, acerbic about Vivien Leigh who was both the wife of Titus on stage, and Olivier's wife in reality. 'As Lavinia, Vivien Leigh receives the news that she is about to be ravished on her husband's corpse with little more than the mild annoyance of one who would have preferred foam rubber.' Others were not affected by such unevenness. Peter Shaffer, seeing the production eight years before he was to work with Brook, still retains an indelible impression of being 'inducted into its force-infused ritual'.

The Polish critic Jan Kott, who saw the production in Warsaw on its Eastern European tour, regarded this as Brook's initiation in Shakespearean tragedy, even if *Titus* was an apprentice play.

> *Titus Andronicus* is already Shakespearian theatre; but a truly Shakespearian text is yet to come. Brook and Olivier have both declared that they had been encouraged to produce *Titus* on realizing that this play already contained – though still in a rough shape – the seed of all the great Shakespearian tragedies. No doubt Titus' sufferings foretell the hell through which Lear will walk . . . Mr Brook did not discover *Titus*. He discovered Shakespeare in *Titus*. Or rather, in this play he discovered the Shakespearian theatre, the theatre that had moved and thrilled audiences, had terrified and dazzled them. He has created sequences of great dramatic images. He has found again in Shakespeare the long-lost thrilling spectacle . . . I count this performance among the five greatest theatrical experiences of my life.

In the autumn of 1955, as one of three plays with Paul Scofield at the Phoenix Theatre, Brook staged *Hamlet*, his first mature Shakespeare tragedy. Before it came to the Phoenix, the production was invited to the Moscow Art Theatre, a tour funded by the British Council and Brook's first visit to the country of his ancestors. The newspapers beat the drum for this first appearance by a British company since the Revolution. 'Bang! Hamlet hits Moscow' headlined the *Daily Express*, reporting that scenery and props had been stranded in Berlin and that the doors of the Soviet plane sent to bring them were too narrow. Brook, who spoke more than passable Russian, was reported as cajoling authorities and patiently explaining to the Russian stage staff what he wanted them to do.

For him, Moscow was full of puzzles, contradictions and elusive emotion:

> This was the moment I had waited for so long, the return to the land of my fathers, and my first emotion was amazement, amazement that there was no other emotion; that no electricity called soul-of-Russia tingled up to the tear-ducts through the first leg that met the soil. Not a trace of it. Not like going into a Tzigane restaurant in Paris where, passing through doors, hearing the balalaikas play, seeing the waitresses in peasant costume, the tragic-princely maître d'hôtel bowing, the lit-up view of the Ukraine on the walls, even bogus Russians burst into tears. I had expected this emotion and was cheated.

Instead, Brook found a country and a people that felt themselves besieged. Khrushchev's reforms, leading to the Thaw, had just begun. People who had spent their lives following Soviet orders and threats were bewildered by new revelations about Stalin, and were tentatively allowing themselves to remember the reflexes of freedom. The arrival of the British theatre company was greeted with excitement, but an excitement shadowed by apprehension. Brook went on:

> The Russian sees himself continually in a state of siege. His revolution was recent, it was precariously won. For us, governments have changed, times have passed; but for the Russian the ridicule, the hostility and the armed intervention of the rest of the world after the Revolution is as vivid as the Troubles are to the Irishman pointing out the Dublin Post Office to the foreigner . . . They

take a joy in self-criticism, they will grant you a thousand bizarre hang-overs of the past, a mass of inconsistencies not yet cleared up. However, this is their state of siege. They see themselves surrounded by enemies and are very aware of the enemy within themselves.

Brook's empathy for the grandiose myths that propelled this society – wanting the new and yet not wanting to throw away the old – gave him insights into the monumentality of the Soviet performing arts:

> One would expect the Russian theatre to be vigorous, with its genius harnessed to furthering the developing of the new society. In practice, this is not so. The Russian has fallen into a subtle trap. He wanted both to win his war and yet preserve all that he treasured. The Russian revolutionary (to his undying credit, it must be said), having recognised the value of his opera and ballet and his dramatic theatre, preserved these institutions complete with their traditional way of work. This was cultivated and leisurely, contemplative, civilised and gracious.

Nineteenth-century operas and ballets, to which Brook was taken, were solid and reassuring, could be safely served up to visiting dignitaries. They sometimes transcended kitsch by virtue of their commitment to scale and grandeur, but their conservatism, in a society once dedicated to revolutionary change, was paradoxical.

> The old works were performed in the only style Russia considers worthy of them – in what we can call the Bolshoi Theatre style – where splendour is coupled with reverence, lavishness with mastery of execution. This style is an expression of the deepest Russian identification of the noble with the opulent. Bit by bit it came about that the theatre of an actively militant nation became deeply traditional: slow in method, mature in result, romantic in quality, escapist in effect.

He went to Baku, and saw *Hamlet* directed by Okhlopkov, the director who had invited Brook's *Hamlet* to Moscow. Here was another variation on the decorative and pictorial theatre: 'Despite many cuts in the text, the *Hamlet* lasted some four hours and a half. Much of this time is taken up with the decorations that amplify the text, the pauses, the great moment of declamation, the interludes, the effects, the *grands tableaux*. Although the execution is always masterly, much of this would seem to us superfluous.'

The showman in Brook, who had rehearsed his own economically budgeted production for H. M. Tennent in just four weeks, could only admire Okhlopkov's *coup de théâtre* for Hamlet's play scene. 'The panels in the great gates suddenly opened, revealing an opera house sliced in half, three tiers of boxes crammed with excited, screaming, hysterical courtiers looking down onto Hamlet's *Mousetrap* played below. This was electrifying and I would have given anything to have had it in our production.'

In Moscow the box-office was mobbed, all tickets were sold in hours. The first-night audience included Olga Knipper, Chekhov's widow, the leading ballerina Maya Plisetskaya, diplomats and politicians, even, rumour had it, Stalin's daughter Svetlana. Paul Scofield and Mary Ure, who played Ophelia, were fêted like pop stars. In Moscow, at a time of lifting away layers of a cruel past, this *Hamlet* spoke to audiences reawakening to hope. To this culture of what he called '*Hamlet* Fat', he brought a *Hamlet* which would strike the Russians as '*Hamlet* Lean'. Brook understood that Russian tradition had gradually turned Hamlet into one of their own national stereotypes, 'the superfluous man', the weak, neurasthenic outsider who finds it difficult to take up arms against 'a sea of troubles'. But he also sensed that Russian politics was reaching a point where an active, un-neurotic hero, ready to purge the kingdom, could begin to be imagined, in real life as well as on stage. And the Russian critics warily greeted Scofield's Hamlet as 'a truthful, clean, honest, very lively youth, deeply indignant at the evil that is going on around him. His lofty daydreaming, his moral purity and humanitarian views are in sharpest conflict with . . . the ocean of evil with which he suddenly finds himself surrounded.' Brook was alert to the audience response:

They were fascinated to find that a naked staging made the drama not duller but more tense, that without underlining, without flourishes, the emotions were still expressive and harrowing . . . Above all, they kept commenting on what they termed our simplicity, austerity and economy. Suddenly they realised that they were using the very words with which Khrushchev had launched his new line in architecture. Suddenly it became clear that this visiting *Hamlet* was strangely opportune; they realised they could relate it to the great struggle between the Bolshoi approach to art, for which they have so overwhelming a natural taste, and the urgent need for art that is practical and direct.

After many evenings in Moscow theatres seeing slow-moving, overloaded productions, Brook was desperate to see something that was carrying on the vitality and iconoclasm of the Russian experimental theatre before and for a while after the Revolution; the theatre of Meyerhold and Mayakovsky, of Vaghtangov and Tairov. His hosts had mentioned that the talk of unofficial Moscow was a new production by Valentin Plouchek of Mayakovsky's *Klop* (*The Bedbug*).

The original production in Mayakovsky's lifetime in 1929 had been stopped by the censors; for this play to be revived in 1955 was seen as a retrieval of an emblematic work. On the first night, people had been afraid to show their reactions. Then positive reviews prompted a rush for tickets. As Brook watched the performance, he had the strange sensation of thinking, 'Now, that's exactly how I would have done that scene.' Spellbound by Plouchek's production, Brook discovered a powerful and witty piece of theatre. More surprisingly, he also discovered a long-lost relative.

His father had told him about his favourite sister, Faynia, who had stayed in Moscow during the Revolution when her two sisters had left. Having married a Russian, Faynia hadn't wanted to go. Brook's father, realising that letters from him in London would have put her in danger, had stopped writing to her in the 1930s. Brook recalls the reunion with his cousin in Moscow in 1955:

Valya – Valentin Plouchek – came in to my hotel room, and said, 'I'm Faynia's son.' He was ten years older than I am. He'd been running the Moscow Satirical Theatre through thick and thin, good times and mostly bad. He started with Meyerhold, first as an actor and then as Meyerhold's assistant. I never managed to find out how he survived during the worst Stalinist period, as a Jewish theatre director of a satirical theatre. Everyone says he was clean and honest, there was no word of his being a collaborator. He must have had great guile and subtlety to survive.

Brook kept up the connection with this Russian relative, a good director, whose life, though in entirely different circumstances, mirrored his own. For Brook, it was as if Plouchek was a kind of notional double: 'If my father had never left Russia and I'd been born there, Plouchek's life could have been mine.' He saw Plouchek's production of Nikolai Erdman's savage play *The Suicide*. Plouchek travelled to Milan to see Brook's *Carmen*. Brook planned to film an interview with Plouchek about Meyerhold, but Plouchek died in 1991.

In Moscow, Brook's *Hamlet* was an arresting arrival from an unknown country. When it came to London's Phoenix Theatre in January 1956, it got a cooler reception. John Gielgud, writing to the American critic Stark Young from London, laid about it with typical insouciance: 'The Scofield–Brook *Hamlet* is really disgracefully bad – not even a correct text spoken, and not *one* decent performance. Such a pity it should have been seen in Moscow. They must have thought us sillier than ever.' The *Observer* berated an uppity pupil – 'Give Peter Brook the impossible and he will solve your problem. But it would be unwise, I fancy, to trust him with safe jobs' – before writing it off as 'a melancholic and soporific presentation'. Brook was the first to admit that he failed to realise the ghost scenes – 'I fell headfirst into the trap of making the Ghost into a human figure . . . it was against the whole concept of ghost-ness and the scene just seemed drab and under-played.'

Brook completed his Scofield season at the Phoenix with Cannan's adaptation of Graham Greene's novel *The Power And The Glory* and *The Family Reunion*, T. S. Eliot's modern-day verse response to *The Oresteia*. 'Occasionally, things go terribly wrong,' says Peter Hall, looking back on Brook's season with Scofield. 'The *Hamlet* – it was perfectly boring, routine, there was no interpretation. *The Family Reunion* – it was arid, in an ascetic way. *The Power and the Glory* – a great performance by Scofield in a poor play, the only vital experience in their whole season. What was wrong

with him? He was doing it out of "observance", to show he was being a
good director.'

But Brook now changed tack, turning to one of the new American plays
that had attracted him in New York with its vernacular eloquence and
moral force: Arthur Miller's *A View from the Bridge*. Miller's tragedy
starred Anthony Quayle as Eddie Carbone, a Brooklyn longshoreman
whose obsession with his pretty orphaned niece spirals out of control. It is
set in a close migrant community bound by Italian codes of summary
justice and the strict laws of US immigration. Eddie knows the rules, but
he cannot restrain himself when he and his wife take two illegal immi-
grants into their home. When Eddie publicly kisses one of them, insulting
him as homosexual, he breaks the code of honour and triggers his own
death.

In 1956, it was impossible to perform Miller's play, with this strong
homosexual undercurrent, in a public theatre in London. But Binkie
Beaumont negotiated this problem by transforming the Comedy Theatre
into a private members' club, and topping up the ticket price for a club
membership. So smart was Binkie that even the play's American co-producer
never thought until it was too late to demand his cut of this added price.
'And when he did,' Arthur Miller recalled fondly in his autobiography,
'Binkie produced one of his smiles – what I called "English impish," of which
he had a stock in hand – wearing down with it not only Bob but also my
agent in his demands for my percentage. When I complimented him on his
beautiful Rolls, in which we were all driven to my play's opening, he had a
one-word response, "Rented" (no doubt to sidetrack any further discussion
of percentages).'

At the auditions, held in a theatre in the Covent Garden fruit and
vegetable market, Miller saw another side of the English culture Brook
was engaged with: class. He watched genteel young actors painfully pick
their way through the speeches he'd written for Italo-Americans on the
Brooklyn waterfront. Seeing Covent Garden market outside, he asked Brook
why he didn't audition some of the Cockney hawkers for the parts.
' "Doesn't a grocer's son ever think of becoming an actor?" I asked. "These
are all grocers' sons," Peter replied, indicating the group of young gentlemen
awaiting their turns at one side of the orchestra, "but they have trained

themselves into this class language. Almost all the plays are written in that language and are about those kinds of people."'

Miller was happy with the way Brook realised the mythic dimension of his play, and after mercenary Broadway, he appreciated the humanity of London theatre. On the Sunday before opening, Brook invited the families of the stage crew in to see how the elaborate set, with its revolves, and mobile trucks, was put in and operated. 'The families oohed and aahed,' wrote Miller. 'In New York I had never had interest of this kind on the part of the backstage people, and the realization was saddening. With us it was all pure bucks.'

In 1957 Brook returned to Stratford-upon-Avon to work with John Gielgud again, casting him as Prospero in *The Tempest*. Once more, Brook designed the sets and the production's eerie electronic music, creating a landscape of mists and shifting perspectives. The *New Statesman* praised a reformed Brook, no longer the confrontational *enfant terrible*. 'Peter Brook has not forgotten those tricks which he sometimes used too exuberantly, as the young are inclined to; but he has acquired a reverence too. His *Tempest* at Stratford is a most imaginative conception, beautifully carried out. Long wide vistas open and close between the towering rocks: at one moment it is luxuriant with growth, at the next bare sea-swept caves.' The same reviewer also noted the modernity of Gielgud's performance: 'His Prospero is under threat of being engulfed by his sense of being wronged. He has to fight against the temptation to give way to it. His very magic is a part of that temptation, leading him into fearful territory. He is perhaps as frightened of his powers as he is proud of them.'

In December 1957, when the production came to the Theatre Royal Drury Lane, where the state-of-the-art stage enabled Brook to increase his scenic magic, the *Spectator*'s reviewer started a tradition of seeing Brook as a wickedly clever but unemotional young man: 'Mr Brook is very intelligent; he has a genius for outlines and essentials; he likes big sights and hard, strange sounds; he throws a clear, sombre light on things. In other words, he is not the man for *The Tempest* any more than he would be the man for *A Midsummer Night's Dream*. Gielgud's voice nearly effaces the cacophonies of Mr Brook's harsh island.'

That autumn Brook returned to the Metropolitan Opera, New York, where, with his designer Rolf Gerard, he staged Tchaikovsky's *Eugene Onegin*. Brook wrote in the *New York Times* about his affinity with the realism of Russian romantic art:

> The romantic quality, whether of *Anna Karenina*, of *The Cherry Orchard* or of *Eugene Onegin*, is not distortion of events by authors who see life in dreamy, rose-coloured terms; on the contrary, it is photography – exquisite photography – of real people, whose true relations to circumstances lead them to what we now consider romantic behaviour.

After reviving *Titus Andronicus* for a tour throughout Europe, in 1958 Brook returned to Paris to direct a new production of a play he had staged in London. He had already made his Paris debut in 1956 with a production of Tennessee Williams' *Cat on a Hot Tin Roof* (*Chatte sur un toit brûlant*), starring Jeanne Moreau; the critics had variously dismissed it as a symptom of American sexual hysteria, or slavered over Moreau's lasciviousness. Brook was at first unwilling to accept theatre owner Simone Berriau's proposal to do *Vu du pont* in Paris less than two years after he'd done *A View from the Bridge* in London. But Arthur Miller's agent Micheline Rozan confronted him and, with a bluntness he would come to know and respect, told him that his production of *Chatte* hadn't been a great success, that his Parisian career hadn't begun very well, that Miller's play was a sure-fire hit, and that if he wanted to get on in Paris he would be well advised to do it.

Brook agreed and thus joined the small but select clientele of Micheline's talent agency, which included Jeanne Moreau and Jean-Paul Belmondo, who she had picked out of the Conservatoire National d'Art Dramatique, both of whom would star in Brook's first French film, *Moderato cantabile*. Another of her clients, the young playwright and screenwriter Jean-Claude Carrière, would later become Brook's invaluable collaborator.

In 1958 Brook opened *Vu du pont*. Parisian critics appreciated Miller's social awareness, Brook's dynamic décor of fire escapes and wharves, and the sensitive performance of Italian film-actor Raf Vallone, playing Eddie Carbone. As the newspaper *Combat* pronounced, 'You expected to find an actor. You found instead a man.'

While in Paris, Brook saw a production of Friedrich Dürrenmatt's *The Visit* (*Der Besuch der alten Dame*), a 'macabre parable', as its English translator put it, of revenge, greed and moral collapse which the Swiss writer had created out of his own sarcastic humour and in the footsteps of Brecht. It is a play of pitiless revenge, by an unforgiving millionairess, who many years ago, as a young pregnant woman, was jilted by the man who is now the mayor of a small town. She buys up the town's businesses and industry and squeezes them dry but promises to save the town if they will kill her seducer, their mayor. Which they do. It is easy to see why the sceptical, cutting side of Brook would have been attracted to this parable, the more so since it offered two great parts for senior leading actors. He announced his casting brainwave to Binkie Beaumont: they had to get the two greatest stars of the American theatre – the Lunts, Alfred Lunt and Lynn Fontanne. A longmarried couple, commanding the stage, regularly performing together, theirs was a fabled Broadway double act, comparable to Sybil Thorndike and Lewis Casson or Laurence Olivier and Vivien Leigh. They had even appeared on a US postage stamp as icons and aristocrats of American culture.

Brook's production of *The Visit* had a curious history. It played in Blackpool, Stratford-upon-Avon, Dublin and Edinburgh. It opened in Brighton on Christmas Eve, to 'an audience of uncles and aunts, already full of port, nuts and good cheer', wrote Brook. 'They had made up their minds that this would inevitably be a sweet tale of candles and champagne, carrying a nostalgic reassurance that the aristocratic virtues of elegance and taste still rule the world. Instead, they got a bitter and important play about the evasions and dishonesty of provincial minds. When the curtain fell on Alfred Lunt's corpse being carried away under twinkling Christmas lights, it was a blow in the teeth for the audience, and they filed out of the theatre in angry silence.' It's interesting, that phrase 'a blow in the teeth', serving as a reminder of the aggression, the sadistic incisiveness that, from *Titus Andronicus* to *The Visit*, was at work in Peter Brook's theatre-making at this time.

But the 'pre-London tour' never made it to London. Binkie Beaumont said that his theatres were all busy, other London theatre managers closed door after door on the play. There was nowhere for it to go in England, so Brook went back to Paris to prepare his very different next show, a cheeky musical about a whore with a heart of gold, *Irma la douce*.

Then a fortuitous meeting on a train with a New York tycoon who was looking for a play with which to open a theatre he had just built gave *The Visit* a new life in New York. And so, halfway through the first night of his *Vu du pont* in Paris he rushed out of the theatre to catch a plane to New York to open the *The Visit* there:

> From Orly Airport I phoned the theatre and heard the applause that indicated all had gone well with *Vu du pont*. A few weeks later that same heart-warming sound meant that New York had accepted this harsh, violent play in the new theatre to which the Lunts have now given their name.
>
> The next day I was back in London at work on *Irma la douce*. It is here that the wheel comes full circle. If I hadn't worked in London I would never have come upon *A View from the Bridge* to take to Paris; if I hadn't worked in Paris I might never have found *Irma la douce* to bring to London.

This is the pitch and tempo of his professional and emotional life in his thirties: relish in the whirring of showbusiness wheels, jubilation in luck, coincidence and last-minute reversals, success snatched out of the jaws of disaster. He was living on surges of adrenalin. The electrical charge he emanated, his dynamism and energy, imprinted itself on actors, singers, designers, writers and producers in London, Paris and New York. 'Like a Svengali', as one of his actresses said about him. He believed that nothing was an accident, that everything was preordained, and that he had to seize the unforeseeable:

> Now my experience was swinging like a great pendulum, pulling me between countries and people, between travel and theatre, between various ways of life. I have always been suspicious of any creed, of any conviction, of any programme that ignores contradictions. The meaning of chaos, the need for order; the wish for action, the power of inaction; the silence that alone gives sense to sound; the necessity to intervene, and the virtue of letting go; the balance between inner and outer life; the dilemma of what to give and what to withhold, of what to take and what to decline – then, as now, I was driven by

these shifting themes. The changing of styles, places and rhythms created a wilful, joyful way of life, but the sense of being a swinging ball also carried a deep need for the ball to be attached to a thread, a thread that should be there at all costs to save the ball from spinning irretrievably into outer space.

The Visit opened at the refurbished and re-baptised Lunt-Fontanne Theater on 5 May 1958, and was greeted with an accolade from Walter Kerr who, along with Brooks Atkinson on the *New York Times*, had the power to make or break a show in New York. 'The new Lunt-Fontanne Theater, with its powder-blue walls, floating gilt feathers and tapering candles reflected on crystal, is as soft as a theatre can be. The play, with its fanged heroine, its symbolic black panther loping through small-town streets and its bitter stare into the corrupt hearts of a whole community, is as hard as the nails in the coffin that waits patiently in the wings for a victim all night.'

He describes the kinetic power of Brook's groupings and configurations of bodies on a largely bare stage, praising 'Peter Brook's manipulation of abandoned figures in constantly constricting space. The idle, silky, subtly threatening movement of presumably innocent townsfolk as they halt their man's escape by night, the terror of a line of stubborn backs blocking his every turn, the infinitely slow and quiet encircling that ends in a most discreet murder – all are images of insinuating power.'

In June 1960, buoyed by its Broadway success, *The Visit* opened in London, at another new theatre, the Royalty. Brook, along with many theatre-artists in Europe, had been impressed by Brecht's Berliner Ensemble, who had paid their first visit to Paris in 1954 and to London two years after. As he later wrote, 'The Brecht theatre is a rich compound of images appealing for our belief. When Brecht spoke contemptuously of illusion, this was not what he was attacking. He meant the single sustained picture, the statement that continued after its purpose had been served – like the painted tree.' *The Visit* spanned the full spectrum of theatre imagery, from emptiness – Clara Zachanassian and her one-time lover meeting again after years on a black void stage – to fullness – the baroque entrance of Clara, red-haired, in a sedan chair with a butler, husband number seven, two hired killers, a retinue of blind eunuchs and a panther on a lead.

Bernard Levin, writing in the *Daily Express*, vividly conjured up the impact of the production:

> Expecting, no doubt, another of the confections with which Mr Lunt and Miss Lynn Fontanne have for so long delighted their fans and infuriated their admirers, they got instead a story of horror within horror, a pitiless exposure of human weakness, an unrelenting assault on those philosophers who tell us that man is good. The whole thing is as fine as a steel blade, as clean as a bone, as free of fat as a greyhound, as effective as a hammer, and as merciless as hell . . . The result is to focus the attention as the sun's rays are focused through a burning-glass.

Binkie Beaumont must have been pleased to read such notices, and happy that this tough-minded play about society caving in to the lure of money was likely to make money for him. But the London theatre was changing, and an alternative to the hegemony of his company H. M. Tennent Ltd was arising. Its figurehead was John Osborne, whose *Look Back in Anger* at the Royal Court Theatre in 1956 had spearheaded the new British drama. In a vitriolic piece for the left-wing weekly *Tribune*, Osborne settled scores with the theatrical management for whom Brook had done so much work. It was the voice of new England contesting the rule of the traditional masters:

> When I first entered the profession, the London theatre was dominated by H. M. Tennent and its subsidiaries. It was the General Motors of British show business, presided over by Mr Hugh 'Binkie' Beaumont. Binkie, a tough, shrewd professional – in a field where the amateurism of showmanship was almost matched by the amateurism of its business – possesses the charm of an antique dagger and the manners of a diplomat overawed by his own archetype.
>
> For a brilliant decade or so, Binkie exercised a virtual monopoly of taste, backed by his superior acumen, his control over theatres, and his history of first-class personal relations with the starriest talents in the profession, and aided considerably by the mediocrity of his competitors.

By now, Brook was no longer, if he had ever been, a creature of H. M. Tennent. But he was just as unlikely to sign up to the club of the opposition, the new-wave playwrights of the Royal Court. Brook didn't plan on joining any of the clubs which made up British theatre culture. He had given Tennent's a range of quality work, and built relationships with some of England's foremost actors. He had seized on five of Shakespeare's plays and lifted the scales of familiarity off them. He had made a feature film. He had spread his wings with opera and a musical in New York, and begun to open a path for himself in Paris. He had sounded his Russian ancestry. He was too swift and mercurial to be pinned down into purely English structures. Playing one genre against another, asking himself where he felt most 'at home', what he hated about home and whether 'elsewhere' promised something better, he was beginning to become the man without borders.

PART TWO

BREAKING THROUGH BOUNDARIES

EMBRACING FRANCE
1958–60

Searching for a hub to his many-spoked wheel, over the next two years, Brook continued to pursue things French: a feather-weight French musical in London, a bitter comedy by Anouilh in New York, the stormy premiere of a Jean Genet play about sex and power in Paris and *Moderato cantabile*, a passionate, contemplative French film. The flair and seductiveness of French culture, the sensuousness of Paris, continued to stimulate him.

He had discovered the pocket-sized French musical, *Irma la douce*, playing in a fringe theatre far from the bright lights of the *grands boulevards*. A cocktail of the myths of raffish Montmartre, it told the story of a whore, Irma, the charming pimp she's in love with, the comic gendarmes, the philosophical barmen of the all-night bars, the street people making a living out of sex. It was a comic inversion of romantic love, the world of Brassaï's *Paris by nuit* conjoined with the irreverence of a Feydeau farce. With a cheerful score by Marguerite Monnot, and book and lyrics by Alexandre Breffort, an all-night taxi driver familiar with his subject, *Irma la douce* appealed to Brook the Francophile showman, and he took it at once to Binkie Beaumont. He wanted to expand it into a dancing as well as a singing show, he said; he needed a big West End stage, not the tiny cabaret space in which it was born.

A new British musical about a talent agent, *Expresso Bongo*, starring Paul Scofield, had just had a West End success. Its authors – Wolf Mankowitz, Monty Norman, David Heneker and Julian More – had wanted Brook to direct it, not least because of his closeness to Scofield, but he had not been free. Now he invited the team of writer, lyricist and composer over. Julian More takes up the story:

> He said, 'Boys' – we were always known as the boys, and there were four of us, with Wolf – 'I've got a wonderful musical for you. What I'd like you to do, Wolf, is to draft something freely around this story.' He didn't like what Wolf did; there was too much Cockney slang so Wolf left the team. Brook said, 'There's only one way of doing this show, which is to find a language like Damon Runyon did for *Guys and Dolls*.' I was the only French speaker; they put me together with a strange old lady, Moura Budberg, who had been the mistress of Gorky, H. G. Wells and Alexander Korda. She knew the most bawdy phrases in French slang, and became my adviser. In the end, we decided to keep most of the French slang in the original French; Peter was very thrilled by this.

Brook began hunting for a singer-dancer who could play Irma. Another hit of that year's London season was the musical *The Pajama Game*, with its show-stopping number 'Steam Heat', sung with guts by a gamine young woman, Elizabeth Seal. Brook went after her. 'She turned out to be exactly right,' says Julian More. 'Very English, almost English suburban, but Peter saw something, and thought, yes, I can do something with this girl. The magic of Peter is that he can get together a group of people with very little in common – there was Monty from the East End, David Heneker who had been a brigadier in the army, me between the two, public school but sort of veering to the Left, Liz Seal who was suburban, Clive Revill, a wonderful comic from New Zealand, and Keith Michell, an Australian – but Peter managed to pull everyone together.'

Irma la douce is a simple story. Irma, a prostitute in Paris, meets a law-student, Nestor le Fripé. He falls in love with her, and soon becomes jealous of the clients who line up for her services. In a virtuoso *commedia dell'arte* routine, quick-changing and dodging either side of a large circular pillar, Nestor invents an alter ego, Monsieur Oscar. This rich old gentleman gives Irma 10,000 francs each time, in return for her exclusive attentions. She hands them back to Nestor – who next day, in the character of Monsieur

Oscar, gives them again to Irma. All goes well, until Irma falls in love with Monsieur Oscar. Nestor finds himself obliged to bump off the imaginary 'suitor'. He is caught, sentenced to Devil's Island for life – like Captain Alfred Dreyfus – but escapes and is reunited with the now pregnant Irma for a Christmas finale.

Julian More tells how *Irma* opened in a very unlikely out-of-town theatre:

We opened in Bournemouth in the middle of the summer, the most unlikely time and place to do it. After the dress-rehearsal, Binkie Beaumont said, 'Brooklet, I give this show two weeks, if that.' Binkie liked to call Peter 'Brooklet'. They were very fond of each other, but I thought Binkie was almost in awe of Peter.

The ladies of Bournemouth didn't know where they were when it started; but after our first love-song, 'Our Language of Love', it became clear that although it was about a pimp and a prostitute, it was a love story and they could relate to it, and we got a standing ovation. We all thought, 'Ah, this is going to work, we've got it made.' We then went to Brighton, and it was a disaster, with waspish gays saying, 'Oh this is just too silly, what has Peter been up to?' That woke us up to the bad things in the show, so we spent the two weeks writing, rewriting, polishing, and came out thinking, 'This is still going to be all right.'

The first night was all right, but at the party after, I remember Hal Prince saying to me, 'Oh God, Peter should never have blown this thing up, it was quite charming in Paris.' He was the ghost at the feast. Next day the notices were half good, half bad, and we were really worried. Until Harold Hobson on Sunday gave it a *whoop*. He loved the French theatre, and I have to say, he went over the top.

Irma la douce gave Harold Hobson, drama critic of *The Sunday Times*, one of his finest hours. From the late fifties, there was a weekly contest between the two leading theatre critics: Kenneth Tynan, a recent convert to Brecht, who wrote like Oscar Wilde; and Harold Hobson, who also wrote pithily, and had an encyclopaedic passion for French theatre. Naturally, Hobson had been across to Paris to see the sweet and unassuming original and he contrasted Parisian innocence in matters of love with London's unliberated cynicism:

It is a play that is wholly, from the first minute to the last, about *sex*, but into which no thought of sex, in any sexy way, is ever allowed to enter. It deals with the commercial excitation of the senses: and its unique merit is that the senses are never excited. It is about a prostitute and a *souteneur*, carrying on their trade in a disreputable Montmartre bar among other prostitutes and thieves who live off street women's earnings, and its effect, which is held steadily throughout the performance in Paris, is one of tranquil purity.

Hobson specialised in the spiritual paradox beloved of his favourite Catholic French writers like Claudel, that something can be dirty but also near-divine; his celebratory prose is studded with last-minute redemptions, finding a wondrous innocence in the heart of sexual degradation:

It is almost impossible to resist the temptation to produce the piece as if it were daring and saucy and naughty. One congratulates Peter Brook on having avoided this so enticing trap. *Irma la douce* is completely without offence. That acrobatic dance which Elizabeth Seal does in a dream of Nestor's, which is one of the hits of the show, is not in the least erotic. Miss Seal's professional walk, her grins, her flashing eyes, are bright and gay but they have nothing to do with impropriety.

Elizabeth Seal remembers a working relationship with Brook which involved attraction, backstage excitements and a good deal of power play. The only time she really argued with him was when it became clear that the show had been such a hit in London it was going to Broadway, and the producers, Beaumont and Donald Albery, decided they were not going to take her to America to play the lead; they wanted an inter-nationally known performer or an American star. She recalls how the news was broken to her:

Peter came in just after the half-hour and said, 'We're not going to take you to America, because we're not sure your performance will carry in the large American houses.' Peter then left, I was crying, the curtain went up late. Then later Donald Albery, who had a share in the show with Binkie, came in and said, 'Well, of course, if you did go to America, we couldn't pay you the full

Broadway salary.' The next thing was that all these people came to watch me –
Juliette Greco, Brigitte Bardot, Leslie Caron.

It's a part where you need to be able to sing in very low keys, too low for my
natural voice, to give an illusion of the French thing. Sometimes I would get
croaks and growls in my throat – which was quite helpful – but then Peter
would want a purer tone. One day I was fed up with him, and I said, 'Peter, if
you think that there's such a woman, who can dance like Margot Fonteyn, act
like Anna Magnani and sing like Maria Callas, you jolly well go and find her!'
He went completely motionless. And I rushed off, not letting him see I had
tears in my eyes. And then it was reported to me that he'd gone back to Binkie
and said, 'That girl, you know, she's got a lot of passion and woof.'

Elizabeth Seal got the part for the Broadway opening. When she started
working with Peter in New York, she discovered he had found a new
enthusiasm: Method acting and its memory recall exercises.

I went on ahead, to get into training and work with the American dancers.
Peter arrived, and went straight to the Stella Adler studios; he was really
obsessed with the Method. He comes into rehearsal and asks me to tell him the
story of Irma's childhood. 'You must be joking,' I said, 'don't be ridiculous, it's
not going to help.' And when he's difficult, he's steely, the twinkle goes out of
those blue eyes. So I realised, I've got to do it, and I made up this whole thing. I
went on and on, but I managed it. He then wanted me to write it down. This
was completely foreign to me – I was used to the dance classroom and the bar.
So after many a private tear I did it – because one thing you mustn't do in front
of Peter is to cry. You're a girl, don't do it; be a fella. He's quite manipulative
and domineering, or he was at that stage.

Brook had tickled London palates with his teasing fairy tale about sex and
love, and went on to repeat his success with it in New York, even though it
didn't have a big American star in the lead. But for his next production in
New York he did have a star – Rex Harrison, who had scored a career-lifting
triumph as Henry Higgins in *My Fair Lady* (1956) and he had Natasha
Parry, Brook's wife, playing opposite him. The play was another sour-sweet
Anouilh play, with the accent on the sour: *L'Hurluberlu, ou le reactionnaire*

amoureux which, in Lucienne Hill's version, became *The Fighting Cock*. Brook had now staged three plays by Anouilh, who could be said to have been his presiding playwright through the 1950s. In *The Fighting Cock*, Anouilh creates a misanthropic old general in bitter retirement, who plots with his *anciens combattants* to rid France of the 'maggots' of opportunism and self-interest which have infected it, and is defeated and disgraced. He is not without some resemblance to a real life aloof general with a national mission, Charles de Gaulle, who had returned to power in 1958. Despite Rex Harrison's touching performance, New York critics dismissed the play as 'a tedious Gallic fable'.

Brook's capacity to override setbacks, his appetite and curiosity about what lies round the corner, was demonstrated when he turned his back on New York and in 1960 headed for Paris, to prepare one of the most sulphurous plays in modern French theatre.

He had been given a copy of Jean Genet's *Le Balcon* (*The Balcony*) during the visit of *Titus Andronicus* to the Théâtre des Nations festival in 1957, which Genet attended and liked. Genet was already a famous, not to say notorious, author. The illegitimate son of a Parisian prostitute, abandoned by his parents, he grew up in a series of institutions for delinquents. He had rambled his life across pre-war Europe, living as a thief and a male prostitute, and making a morality out of rejection and rebellion. By the age of twenty-three, he was sleeping with a one-armed pimp, lice-ridden and begging on Spanish streets, experiences which spawned the dry gallows humour of *The Balcony*. It was Genet's fastidious stance of total insubordination that fascinated Brook.

The Balcony, written in 1958, was the play which most dazzlingly displayed Genet's conviction that life is not merely a dream, but a conspiracy of illusions, a carnival of servitude. Brook was stirred by its brutal yet refined theatrical language and its classical tirades. 'I was astonished by the purity of theatrical thought that it revealed. Conditioned by the tolerance of English liberal thinking, far from the intense partisan climate of French politics that coloured that country's intellectual life, I could not understand why no theatre had taken up this bold and subversive work by an already famous author.'

Brook and his producer were running into French police repression that made the Lord Chamberlain's censorship antics look mild. In a club theatre in London, *The Balcony* had received its British premiere, in a production by Peter Zadek which Genet disowned. But it had at least been done.

Why was *The Balcony* considered so repugnant and subversive in France? Set in a brothel, it showed emblematic figures – the Bishop, the Judge, the General – stripped down to their basic lusts in sexual, often sado-masochistic tableaux. If you were the real Prefect of Police you would not be best pleased by Genet's Police Chief. But perhaps the threat of *The Balcony* lay even more in Genet's scathing rhetoric that undermined society and what was commonly accepted as reality itself. Sartre, embarking on his mammoth study, *Saint Genet, comédien et martyr*, remarked, 'It is the element of fake, of sham, of artificiality, that attracts Genet in the theatre.'

Between November 1957 and 1960, when it opened, *Le Balcon* passed through the hands of the owners and producers of the Paris equivalent of 'off-Broadway'. Passed through their hands and passed on: no one had the courage to agree to do it. The satirical paper *Le Canard enchaîné* explained that the police were threatening to intervene because they had information that performing the play would lead to a breach of the peace. 'A conspiracy of right-thinking people, emanating, as one might well expect, from the hushed cabinet of the Prefect of Police himself, has virtually banned the play on the flimsy excuse that on its first night two hundred bawlers (affronted right-wing nationalists) would be present.'

The mists cleared when Marie Bell, a pre-eminent classical actress who had played the great tragic heroines of Racine at La Comédie-Française, said she would like to play Madame Irma, the keeper of the brothel. Bell, who, said Brook, 'wore large hats, strong make-up, had the panache and style that belonged to her role, and in her extravagant diva way was a free woman,' could clearly match Genet's huge character. She brought with her the Théâtre du Gymnase, a large, nineteenth-century boulevard theatre which she directed, where the plays of Scribe, Alexandre Dumas *fils* and Sacha Guitry had been performed. Rehearsals began. Unable in his limited re-hearsal time to forge the ensemble that Genet required for his hieratic style, and his assistants scoured the bars of Paris for striking faces and bodies to add to his core cast of professionals. He used improvisation for the first time, enacting scenes from brothel life, the more exotic the better. They were not much help in delivering Genet's highly worked text, but were useful in creating a climate, and doubtless good, though not so clean fun. 'The work in improvisation,' wrote Brook 'was liberating through the sheer delight of playing for the sake of playing, and as we laughed and entertained one another, a large degree of coherence appeared in this very eccentric band of performers, creating a sort of ensemble.'

Brook designed the sets himself, creating 'a labyrinth of picture frames' to embody Genet's house of distorting mirrors. He and Genet had been accomplices during the long struggle to get the play staged, and so it was something of a surprise to Brook that once rehearsals started, Genet disappeared to Athens and cut off all contact, perhaps acting out his belief that friendship demands betrayal. One day Marie Bell got hold of him by telephone. 'Would you like to speak to Peter?' she asked. 'On no account. You know he's someone I never could bear,' was the reply. It was like two worlds colliding – Brook, tough but never really rough, coming up against this creature of the doss-house and the streets, and being reminded how sheltered his own life had been. 'I was very far from the furious climate of rebellion and political violence that his whole way of life had pushed to an absolute extreme.' Is this Brook admitting that he was a tiny bit intimidated by Genet?

The Balcony did not trigger right-wing nationalist riots, as the Prefect of Police had anticipated, but it did call forth some inflated critical writing. Harold Hobson came up with his usual dialectic of religious inversion: 'What Mr Brook has given us is all the splendour of vestments, an evil glory of speech, a strangely compulsive parody on the "Marche Funèbre", a church service as a church would be if a church service were obscene.'

The *Observateur Littéraire* compared *Le Balcon* to Sartre's *Huis clos*, the first play about a *maison close* that Brook had directed. 'With its red velvet drapes which are soon reduced to rags, and its mirrors emptied of their intolerable reflections, the house of Madame Irma resembles the room of *Huis clos*. But here, hell is not "other people", it's in each person, in this bottomless abyss which these impostors try hopelessly to fill with their games . . . A great baroque hymn to death . . . theatrical material of incontestable richness'

Le Balcon opened up new ground for Brook. The adventure and the antagonisms inside Parisian theatre and French culture spurred him to cross boundaries, test limits. For the first time he was directing the premiere of a new French play in France; not Arthur Miller or Tennessee Williams imported, but a challenging French text for French audiences, the polar opposite of Anouilh's well-crafted plays. He was certainly inspired by Genet's descent into disorder, bringing back severe truths about *la vie sexuelle*, domination, rebellion and mortality, transgression and sadistic pleasure. All these elements, and the pleasure of working in Paris, where 'the sharp scent of Gauloises was strangely exciting, and everything from the Metro to the cafés had a special sexual glow,' conspired to rouse Brook, opening paths to a greater plenitude, to a fuller *jouissance*, the French term for complete fulfilment – or orgasm.

While still rehearsing *Le Balcon*, Brook began work on his first French film, indeed his first in seven years since *The Beggar's Opera* in 1953. It was Micheline Rozan who opened the door. A friend of Marguerite Duras, and agent and manager of Jeanne Moreau, Rozan introduced him to a minimalist novel by Duras, *Moderato cantabile*.

Duras had become famous for her screenplay and dialogues for Alain Resnais' incantatory film *Hiroshima mon amour*, which embedded a love affair in the nuclear holocaust of Hiroshima. On the strength of her fame, and the growing reputation of Jeanne Moreau, the search for a producer began, with Brook coming from *Le Balcon* rehearsals to pitch his film to French businessmen and financial institutions. After almost a year, they found their man: Raoul Lévy, who had made millions producing Brigitte Bardot films. 'He went to his group of financiers,' Brook remembers, 'and said, "Look, you turned down *Les 400 coups* because you couldn't understand the script; you turned down *Hiroshima mon amour*. Well, I can't make head nor tail of this script and what's more I'm not even going to show it to you – but I want 30 million francs".' Raoul Lévy's chutzpah paid off; he got the money, and he agreed that he would have no say in the cast or the cut. This was a classier kind of film than his Bardot movies.

Moderato cantabile tells of a love affair that is never physically consummated but which sears both its protagonists: Anne (Jeanne Moreau) the neglected wife of a local industrialist and Chauvin (Jean-Paul Belmondo) a drifting, rather dazed employee of her husband. The location, a small town by a river in the Gironde, shapes the emotional lives of the protagonists. 'You can't say the characters behave as they do because they live by a river in a dull town,' said Brook, 'but you can't ignore the way these things relate to them either.'

The two meet at the scene of a *crime passionel*: Anne takes her son for his piano lesson, which is brutally interrupted by the scream of a woman in agony. In the café below her piano teacher's flat, a woman lies dead on the floor, the consequence, Anne assumes, of a tragic love affair. She exchanges words with Chauvin in the crowd around the corpse, then has to leave with her son.

We see them in the café again, by the river and in a tumbledown house. Their words are stumbling. The boy is there, watching, playing, and so everything between them remains suppressed and suggested. Back at her home, Anne's husband throws a black-tie dinner party for their stuffy friends, she gets drunk, she runs in her little black dress back to the café where she first met Chauvin. The film comes full circle with her howl, her scream of agony as she lies on the café floor, poleaxed by an impossible love.

In his work up to this point, Brook had often see-sawed between fullness and emptiness: between the romantic happy ending of the reunited lovers in *Love's Labour's Lost* and the sudden intrusion into their happiness of Mercadé the messenger of death; between the violence of *Titus Andronicus* and its refined, formal expression; between the Brechtian sparseness of *The Visit* and the baroque profusion of *Le Balcon*. Now he makes a film which is as stripped down, as minimal as anything by the Japanese master Ozu.

Brook described his process of elimination: 'There is this completely lost little town where there is no distinctive feature whatsoever. We then take out anything that dramatises the story. We take away the element of narrative; we avoid scenes, big scenes in the dramatic sense; and we avoid emphasis, avoid underlining and pointing a thing. Avoid anything in the camera work, in the movement of the camera, the lighting, the music and the cutting, to dramatise it; so that eventually one has done a process of total elimination. This is real film direction.'

Moderato cantabile recalls *Brief Encounter*, but it's as if the lovers have been slowed down, subtracted from conventional cinematic conventions and exposed to a diagnostic examination. This cinematic self-denial left

Brook free to make further discoveries about acting, especially with Jeanne Moreau. 'Jeanne Moreau works like a medium, through her instincts. She gets a hunch about the character and then some part of her watches the improvisation of that and lets it happen, occasionally intervening, a bit like a good technician, when, for instance, she wants to be facing the camera, to be at the right angle . . . The result is that her performance gives you an endless series of tiny surprises. On each take she knows exactly what is going to happen.'

This description of Moreau at work recalls Brook's description of Paul Scofield's 'mysterious alchemy of the imagination'. Like Scofield, Jeanne Moreau was seeking not just a conceptual or mental truth, but a physical one. Like Scofield, Jeanne Moreau has an ageless beauty.

The reception of *Moderato cantabile* was rather chilly. From its premiere at Cannes, *Le Monde*'s critic wrote, 'I have sympathy for *Moderato cantabile*, a work that never leaves you indifferent, that is neither banal or vulgar, I feel a kind of friendship for it, in which esteem has a place. That said, I find it an irritating film. Irritating because one constantly has the impression that very little would be needed to make it a success, that one awaits from scene to scene this "something", which never arrives.'

The British critic John Russell Taylor expressed the same frustration:

> We were prepared in advance to find that the film reflected his current interest in drama without exposition, development, story, characterisation, construction, and above all with no tempo but 'the tempo of life itself'. This might to some extent explain the sections of the film in which Brook actually departed from the 'classical' form he seemed to have prescribed for himself: mainly long, long close-ups of Jeanne Moreau just thinking or, more vaguely, just being. Admittedly there are few people on the screen that one would rather examine in this way, but what comes over is big star magic, and reality has little to do with it.

Stung by these, and other criticisms, Brook retaliated in his *Guardian* interview with two leading (and Francophile) film critics.

> Shakespeare would have provided powerful words and metaphors to convey what we in film were trying to communicate with that weight of silence. And it

wasn't actually silence that one was photographing, or a Japanese composition of an empty white screen, but a look on her face and a tiny movement of
her cheek, which to me were valid because she was actually *and at that
moment* experiencing something which therefore became interesting to look at
as an object. The particular documentary aspect of filming, the catching of
something as it happens, relates in this way to acting: the aim is always to
capture that look in someone's eye.

Then Brook praises the flexibility and low costs of French film-making,
compared to the British film industry. *Moderato cantabile* had cost a mere
£80,000 and been shot in seven weeks.

> The fact must be faced – it is owing to the French being so highly organized,
> adaptable, resourceful, economical, imaginative and above all flexible in
> interpreting their union privileges and rules, that one is able to get the same
> result infinitely quicker and cheaper than in England or in America. And this
> matter of a relatively low cost is all-important, as it is the price of freedom.
> Quite simply, there is a price which makes producers nervous and a price at
> which they are prepared to take a risk . . . What is important to me is that
> having passionately wanted to make this film in a particular way, it could be
> done. And once made, that it was received, dissected, accepted or rejected with
> equal passion. In England, the greatest danger that awaits such enterprises is
> indifference.

This tense, restless, searching Englishman was learning that France, because
it did not share its language with America, could make original works for the
cinema for less money and with hand-crafted, artisanal care.

In 1961, Peter Hall invited Peter Brook to join him, the French director Michel
St Denis and Peggy Ashcroft as an Associate Artist, to form a new directorate
of the Royal Shakespeare Company. For all his pugnacity as the formative
politician of post-war British theatre, Peter Hall had a sense of his own
solitude at the head of what would become Britain's largest theatre organisa-
tion. He wanted to work in what he called a 'collegiate' way, with colleagues,
notably with older colleagues (St Denis was sixty-four, Ashcroft fifty-four,

while Brook was thirty-six, and Hall himself thirty-one), who would prod and stretch him. 'I always chose associates who were in some respect better than I was,' he frequently said. Brook would be one such colleague and provoker, encouraged by Hall to make him question everything. Brook told Sally Beauman, who was writing a history of the RSC, of his dissatisfaction with the company's ideal in the early 1960s, which was, he said, 'to do good things very well, the traditional target of liberal England'. He agreed to feed the company's two main stages by doing Shakespeare at Stratford-upon-Avon and modern drama at the Aldwych, but as a condition of joining, he wanted to run a completely experimental activity, a piece of research with a group of actors that might fail, or deliver results that were never shown to the public. He got his wish, and joined the RSC.

But the newborn RSC was having growing pains. Harold Hobson bemoaned in *The Sunday Times* the company's lack of shared style. 'The unfortunate players are blown about in gales of contrary doctrine. Sometimes they have a curtain, sometimes not; sometimes they imitate the previous performances of greater players than themselves, sometimes they are built on novelty. Often they match ducal costumes to dustbin voices . . . As a preparation for a National Theatre this is no good at all. We need a style, and Stratford ought to be able to find it for us.'

But creating an ensemble, what Sally Beauman calls 'a confederacy of individuals, tastes and beliefs', with a coherent way of speaking Shakespeare's verse and directors and designers creating visual, metaphorical worlds was precisely what Hall, with his collaborators, aimed to do. He was also driven by a wish to expand the RSC, for both aesthetic and political reasons. Brook was never sure about the wisdom of Hall's drive to expand. He could see that the actors, signing up for two-year contracts, could become the nucleus of a creative ensemble. He could see too that they were drawing on their Shakespearean skills to play Pinter and their Pinteresque skills for Shakespeare. There was no doubt that this theatre in London and the Midlands, its actors and executives burning up motorway miles, brought forward a group of remarkable talents: in 1962 the company could boast Vanessa Redgrave, Ian Bannen, Max Adrian, Diana Rigg, Keith Michell, Irene Worth, Hugh Griffith, Ian Holm, Tony Church, Ian Richardson, Alec McCowen and Judi Dench.

Brook's doubts about Peter Hall's expansionism, even if it aimed to entrench the RSC as a national institution and not leave the National Theatre to make all the running, arose from a concern that it might result in a lowering of standards. Brook had, after all, participated in Sir Barry Jackson's revitalising of the Shakespeare Memorial Theatre in 1946. He had learned to deal with a very uneven group of actors, coming from very different Shakespeare traditions or from none, within a short rehearsal period. 'In every production of that period, the director *had* to find a way of injecting animation into actors. One had to play a sort of game: you'd take a small part actor who had been bored all season, and say, "Why don't you play this part as a hunchback with one eye?" – that sort of thing, you *had* to make a stage picture, and bring as much vitality out of the actors as you could. To bring out ensemble strength was impossible.'

By making it a condition of his joining that he could run an experimental season, Brook marked himself out from his colleagues. He shared with them experience in the West End theatre and in the craft of playing Shakespeare. But he steered from other points on his compass: to Shakespeare's text he brought different perspectives: from the French theatre and from the value of straddling French and English; from his exploration of minimalism in his recent feature film; and from the radicalism of the American experimental theatre. And, more than any of these, he came from an affinity with Shakespeare, with the world view of a writer who could put kings and murderers in the same frame as ghosts and witches; an affinity that respected the words of Shakespeare's plays, for the way that they had surfaced out of an inner journey through levels and detours to arrive at conscious expression. He had said that Jeanne Moreau worked 'like a medium'; he had a hunch that Shakespeare did too.

When *Encore* magazine asked him in November 1960 to write about the Living Theater's production of Jack Gelber's *The Connection*, Brook seized the opportunity to tear into the most basic assumptions of what theatre is for, what is real in theatre and how far British theatre was from being free. Gelber's play, which hadn't even reached London at the time, had radiated shock waves from New York – not only because of its subject, a room full of junkies waiting for a fix that was in some sense simply an update of what Maxim Gorky had written in *The Lower Depths* – but because of its hyper-naturalism, its dismissal of the shortcuts we take for granted in conventional dramaturgy. Brook greeted that total lack of artifice:

> The actors who are portraying these characters have sunk themselves into a total, beyond Method, degree of saturated naturalism, so that they aren't *acting*, they are *being*. And then one realises that the two criteria – boredom or interest – are not in this case possible criticisms of the play but criticisms of ourselves. Are we capable of looking at people we don't know, with a way of life different from our own, with interest? The stage is paying us the supreme compliment of treating us all as artists, as independent creative witnesses . . . *The Connection*, though 'anti' in terms of stage convention, is supremely positive – it is assuming that man is passionately interested in man.

Leaving *The Connection* behind, Brook shot from the hip, refusing to take the prevalent theatrical realism for granted, embracing abstract art, which theatre, alone of all twentieth-century arts, had virtually ignored, and finally rising to a rattle of questions about what our experience now is like.

> I'm interested in why the theatre today in its search for popular forms ignores the fact that in painting the most popular form in the world today has become abstract. Why did the Picasso show fill the Tate with all manner of people who would not go to the Royal Academy? Why do his abstractions seem *real*, why do people sense he is dealing with *concrete* vital things? We know that the theatre lags behind the other arts because its continual need for immediate success chains it to the slowest members of its audience. But is there nothing in the revolution that took place in painting fifty years ago that applies to our own crisis today? Do we know where we stand in relation to the real and the unreal, the face of life and its hidden streams, the abstract and the concrete, the story and the ritual? What are 'facts' today? Are they *concrete*, like prices and hours of work – or *abstract* like violence and loneliness? And are we sure that in relation to twentieth-century living, the great abstractions – speed, strain, space, frenzy, energy, brutality – aren't more concrete, more immediately likely to affect our lives than the so-called concrete issues? Mustn't we relate this to the actor and the ritual of acting to find the pattern of the theatre that we need?

This text is crucial for Brook's development. It is shaped by a French map, that sees the birth of 'the modern' in the French and European avant-garde at the start of the twentieth century. These movements had shaped the thinking of Europe's contemporary artists, except in aesthetically conservative societies like England. True, Virginia Woolf in London had testified that 'in or about December 1910 human character changed'. But Elgar and Thomas Hardy were the exemplars of modern English artistic expression; Walter Sickert and Stanley Spencer, not Picasso, Lutyens, not Gaudí, its pathfinders in painting and architecture. The French embrace of modernity had the edge – not least because so many key modern art events happened in Paris. And Brook the artist, who had French intelligence and instincts, had that modernity in his bones.

That same sense that the arts, and theatre especially, had to be changed to measure up to the new world of what Brook in *Encore* called 'speed, strain, space, frenzy, energy, brutality' – that same sense he found in Antonin Artaud, the French poet, actor, theatre-maker and sublime manifesto-writer. Artaud was to be the sovereign spirit for Brook's RSC experimental event; just as Brook's dissatisfaction and determination to go beyond theatre's 'continual need for immediate success' raised a flag for the rest of his long march.

JOURNEYS INTO DARKNESS
1960–63

For two years, Brook did nothing in the theatre. He was, he told his son Simon, 'fed up with theatre'. Instead he devoted his energies and powers of persuasion to trying to set up a film of William Golding's novel *Lord of the Flies*. 'You should make a film of this,' Kenneth Tynan had said when he gave Brook the novel. Its title is a translation of 'Beelzebub', its plot a hellish story of marooned English schoolboys descending into anarchy. Golding's dystopian fable electrified Brook. He set about trying to acquire the rights, only to find that Ealing Studios had bought them, indeed had already commissioned a screenplay. Brook, crestfallen, was assured by friends in the film industry that Ealing would never make it; and this indeed is what happened. Ealing put the rights up for sale. 'When I heard this,' wrote Brook, 'I rushed to Sam Spiegel.'

Spiegel, one of Hollywood's most outrageous and enigmatic figures, had gained his reputation as a discerning independent producer with two films – *The African Queen* (1951) with Humphrey Bogart and Katharine Hepburn and *On The Waterfront* (1954) starring Marlon Brando. When Brook approached him, he was preparing David Lean's *Lawrence of Arabia*, which would win him a Best Picture Oscar for the third time in 1962. Spiegel was in the line of central European émigrés who had stamped their image on Hollywood movies. Born in 1903 in the Czech part of Austro-Hungary, 'Spiegel's first fifty years read like a racy picaresque novel co-written by Harold Robbins and Saul Bellow,' wrote Philip French. A convinced Zionist, he took off for Palestine in the 1920s, launched a number of shady businesses, married the daughter of a well-to-do Jewish family, sired a child, and decamped without his family in 1927.

Using forged documents and leaving a trail of unpaid bills, he made a series of unremarkable films in Austria, Britain, France and Germany. Jailed for fraud in Britain and America, he bounced back and with his friend Otto Preminger fled Nazi Germany for the USA, where he changed his name to S. P. Eagle. David Lean called him 'a dictator with no respect for human dignity and individuality'; Gore Vidal worked for him a second time 'because I couldn't believe it the first time'. Billy Wilder called him a modern Robin Hood, who steals from the rich and steals from the poor. For Brook and *Lord of the Flies*, things seemed to go well at first. 'All I wanted was a small sum of money,' wrote Brook, 'no script, just kids, a camera and a beach. All the producer wanted was a detailed screenplay which would guarantee him that the film had "world values" before any big money was spent.' The British playwright Peter Shaffer was hired to write the screenplay, and he and Brook set to work. They did not know at that time that Spiegel had simultaneously hired the British novelist Richard Hughes to write another screenplay of the novel.

As they worked at the screenplay, Brook and Shaffer kept getting ideas from Spiegel, phoned in from his yacht: couldn't there be girls on the island as well? 'We followed that up for quite a while,' says Shaffer. 'It was quite interesting. One of the girls developed a strong character and became a sort of priestess. But we gave it up eventually; we were getting too far away from Golding.' Couldn't all the kids be Americans? Is there one big part for a star? They found rationalisations, as every Hollywood writer learns to, and continued. 'Shaffer wrote a remarkable six-hour epic. There was a giant trek up a mountain and an extraordinary sequence, lasting nearly an hour, in a cave. I remember three complex rituals playing at once, each of which would have served a whole season of the Theatre of Cruelty.'

Shaffer became a good friend of Peter and Natasha, going round daily to their tiny house in Gordon Place, and staying for dinner at weekends. He remembers arriving in the morning to find Brook still in his bath.

I recall him slowly rising through a thick blanket of soapsuds, drying and then anointing his torso with an exquisitely scented French toilet water mysteriously named *Vent Vert* – and all the while he was delivering a perfectly seamless, enthralling and ever-widening discourse on Golding's aggressive children. I can still see him standing naked in the now empty bath, his delicate fingers curling incessantly as if seeking to give some physical shape to an endlessly arriving stream of insights. His voice throughout remained always light in tone, carefully phrasing his words with a kind of professorial precision. But above all, I remember his eyes – those pale turquoise eyes – benignly lit with expectation.

Shaffer also remembers 'the beauty of Natasha – displaying with perfect definition an unforgettably Russian radiance.' When Natasha gave birth to Irina in 1962, Peter was by her bedside. He came back and told Shaffer that Natasha had gone white with dismay when he said he wanted Jean Genet to be godfather to their daughter. 'Then he asked me to be her godfather too, to correct the imbalance, I suppose. I accepted.'

For Shaffer it was intimate, engrossing and revealing work, each day a new insight into Brook's mercurial mind. He remembers

the most remarkable and certainly the funniest incident to illustrate how deeply Peter could immerse himself in the racing tide of his incoming thoughts, to the total exclusion of the outside world. It occurred one morning in London when he suddenly proposed that he drive us both to Oxford to watch his wife Natasha acting in the matinee of a play. I recall he climbed into his car, I sat beside him, and he drove off. However he also chose that exact moment to begin speaking one of those characteristically original, highly cerebral monologues, becoming entirely absorbed in it. To my utter amazement I observed him drive for a full ten minutes in a complete circle, talking all the way from Gordon Place along Kensington High Street, up Church street and back down over Campden Hill – arriving in the end at exact spot from which we had just departed, across the road from his own house. Here he halted and continued to speak with the same riveting intensity for at least another five minutes. Finally he fell silent, calmly turned on the ignition again as if for the first time, and headed serenely for Oxford without referring to the incident in any way. To this day I wonder if he ever became remotely conscious of this astounding performance.

But Brook was beginning to see the film he wanted slipping through their fingers, and experienced the brew of emotions – determination, guile, cussedness, rage – that made them lose their way with a canny adversary like Spiegel. 'Our eighth script was a scarred and pitted battlefield, but we were so identified with it that I think we would have gone ahead.'

At which point, Spiegel abandoned the project. A year had passed, and they were back where they had started. Meanwhile in New York there was a young producer, Lewis Allen, who had staged several off-Broadway successes, such as Jack Gelber's *The Connection*, and had produced Shirley Clarke's low-budget feature film of it. Now he came to Brook with a new idea. As he had done with *The Connection* movie, he said, he would approach a large number of small investors, sending them Shaffer's now-voluminous screenplay and asking them for a maximum of a couple of thousand dollars each. By this means, a production budget of £80,000 was raised. Spiegel agreed to sell back the rights for £50,000 plus one third of the producer's profits. 'We had spent over half our capital on the rights,' wrote Brook, 'which must be some sort of a record.'

Brook and his small team set out to find thirty-five English schoolboys living in America (they had located an island for the shoot just off Puerto Rico, and air-fares would be saved if the cast lived in America). Expatriate British businessmen were canvassed, Brook's assistant stood at New York's port and airport and scrutinised arriving British families, Old Etonian and Old Harrovian Clubs were discovered in the New York telephone directory, an entire Scottish village moved by a distillery to New Jersey was vetted. Three thousand adolescents were interviewed. The children were offered pocket money and a share of profits, one day, maybe, perhaps.

Brook abandoned Shaffer's script with regret, tempered by an excitement at taking the risk of improvising with the children on the basis of Golding's story, rather than have them act a written script. He knew that their attempts to act a writer's words would be less real than their own improvised dialogue. 'I believed that the reason for translating Golding's very complete masterpiece into another form in the first place,' he said, 'was that although the cinema lessens the magic, it introduces evidence.'

The island, with curving bays, palm trees and rocks, was owned by

Woolworth's who lent it free, in exchange for a credit. As soon as the unit was installed, they collided with history: they found the other side of the island swarming with US marines, soldiers and helicopters. America had chosen it as a base from which to launch its invasion of Cuba in 1961; a puppet dictator was on hand, waiting to make his historic entrance as the Cuban people's liberator. In the end the shooting of Brook's film lasted longer than the failed American invasion.

They spent most of their money on taking care of the children, for this was going to be a demanding and at times even a frightening ordeal. That and unlimited amounts of film-stock. 'It had always obsessed me,' wrote Brook, 'that the accountants of the most expensive productions will happily condone all sorts of ludicrous expenses but are strangely horrified by the least waste of the raw material, film-stock; it is like a writer who is afraid to cross out in case it uses up paper.'

Brook's principal cameraman, a stills photographer, Tom Hollyman, was working on his first feature-film. Equally important and a man who would become a good friend, was the second director and all-purpose assistant and accomplice, a documentary film-maker called Gerry Feil, who had been introduced by Lewis Allen. Feil, an energetic young man, had led a varied career in theatre, documentary, television and film. He knew the skills of film-making from every angle, and brought a freewheeling gaze and tech nical savvy to Brook's risky way of filming Golding's book. 'Peter gave me complete freedom to do what I wanted,' Feil told me. 'When we later looked at his rushes and at mine, we frequently saw that they could be cut together.'

They had no daily rushes to view, they just kept on shooting, accumulating sixty hours of footage and miles of sound tape, recorded day and night, 'on-set' and off. After the shoot, because teachers would not release their pupils to do any more work on the film, Brook and Feil trudged from public school to public school re-recording scraps of dialogue on an ingenious system which Feil invented that enabled speech to be synchronised without projecting the film. In a suburban Paris cutting room which gave them credit, a year's editing followed, involving collaging together fragments, sometimes syllables, of unscripted speech recorded days and weeks apart. As they laboriously put it together, the two of them gradually realised that they had made a dark, ominous picture which packed a fierce kick

The film opened at the Cannes film festival on 21 May 1963, in New York in August and in Britain a year later. It was given an 'X' certificate, which meant a limited release and prevented the boys in the film from seeing it. Brook arranged a private screening and took them all to lunch afterwards.

In a gleeful *New Yorker* review Jonathan Miller especially welcomed Hugh Edward's performance as Piggy.

> Stumbling along the strand in his long baggy shorts, this extraordinary young man has mastered the style of Golding's fat, cowardly pragmatist . . . Piggy has all the dreary realism of someone whose physical handicaps have driven him to resignation. Disqualified by his bulk from the sporty heroism of his colleagues, he has a plodding common sense that provides a perfect counterpoint to their cruel Jungian fantasies. He is just too fat and breathless to be swept away by their athletic volatility of spirit. . . . The whole thing has been cut with sabre-toothed abruptness. The sound track is conspicuous for a fine, harsh sibilance – the crackle of branches and the hot whine of insects.

Miller's key point bears out Brook's belief that what film can bring to a novel is *evidence*. The film, says Miller, is 'specific, not straining after universality; it is a brilliant local satire . . . an undressed version of familiar public school vice.' Although Brook doesn't wallow in the unpleasantness of his school days, it's hard to imagine that this film doesn't carry some traces of his emotions at Gresham's School.

Penelope Gilliatt wrote an equally penetrating review, attacking those who would prefer a softer, more sentimental view of human nature:

> It is an implacably pessimistic fable, and its effect is to make practically every other morality story look like a paternalistic con-trick to encourage the useful virtues at the expense of the truth . . . The film is a sour social history of England run backwards from post-Imperialism to woad. It is true that the speech of the children is not at all like the improvised ideal of grown up acting but then it isn't in real life either; the way a child speaks often has a weirdly staged quality, as though he were repeating messages, because speech is not yet natural enough not to have to be rehearsed first in his head.

There is one outstanding ancestor in the history of the cinema for a story of a group of adolescents and their instincts – Jean Vigo's *Zéro de conduite*. Since *Lord of the Flies* there have been a number of powerful pubescent tales – Kubrick's *A Clockwork Orange*, Ken Loach's *Kes*, Louis Malle's *Lacombe Lucien*, Stephen Daldry's *Billy Elliott*. But none of them has the uncomfortable immediacy of a social statement that is also a personal metaphor. It feels as if Brook is wrestling with some of the accepted English ghosts and demons that had surrounded and haunted him. *Lord of the Flies* was part of his reckoning with England before he moved on.

In 1962 Brook embarked on his first production for the Royal Shakespeare Company, *King Lear*. It proved to be a moment of accumulation, a new synthesis. In the life of every true artist, works erupt in which previous achievements and intuitions are gathered up into a new, often surprising whole: think of Stravinsky's *Rite of Spring*, Eliot's *The Waste Land*, Picasso's *Demoiselles d'Avignon*. The *Lear* which the thirty-seven-year-old Brook now directed was to be, like Shakespeare's tragedy itself, a mouldbreaker. It was to banish for ever the archetype of the poor old white-haired patriarch, born of nineteenth-century bathos.

Brook showed every sign of treating this encounter with *Lear* as a championship bout; either he would rise to meet the challenge of this earthquake of a tragedy, or he would slope away from it, a humbled contender. *Lear* stretched theatre to its severe extremes; it broke to the surface in verse which cracked all the rules yet remained craggy, volcanic. Brook told Sheila More that James Booth, playing Edmund, had suggested in rehearsal that it might be amusing to skip during a scene with his father. 'Alas, you can't do that with a masterpiece,' he said. 'It has to be done only one way: the right way. And because of that it's very difficult to find.'

To compare this Peter Brook with the twenty-eight-year-old director who only nine years earlier had flung himself at *King Lear* in a New York television studio with Orson Welles as the king, is to measure the distance Brook had travelled, as a director and as a man. Above all, he was learning how to divest himself of things – not unlike King Lear himself, believing that he is divesting himself of the kingdom and its cares – only to find out painfully in the rest of the play what divestiture at every level really means.

'I came to *King Lear* early on,' Brook said, 'I was young, here was this angry old man, and then the play's process of going through all these painful experiences, from being the unquestioned dictator, until he reaches the point where there is nothing left and he's a completely open human being. It's the process of being within one's own citadel and painfully coming out of it. I could identify with the whole story.' For years, Brook had been inhabited by this play, with its unflinching portrayal of someone trapped in the armour of his own 'character', status and familiar actions – not unfamiliar to Brook in his own life. Lear also seems an archetypal tragic protagonist, compelled to abandon the prisons of illusory ideas about his self, going through disintegration to a tragic acceptance of the instability and unpredictability of human life.

Brook had a cast of fine actors – Scofield as Lear, Alec McCowen as the Fool, Irene Worth as Goneril, Brian Murray as Edgar, Alan Webb as Gloucester, Tom Fleming as Kent. He had invited a spindly young American writer and director, Charles Marowitz, to be his assistant on this production, and it was he who wrote a '*Lear* Log' of rehearsals.

Marowitz's chronicle is full of accounts of the Royal Shakespeare Company grappling with a newfangled thing called improvisation. 'Another, older RSC actor entered during one improvisation. When it was over he questioned the use of improvisation, saying everything was in the text. Brook and Marowitz replied that this simply wasn't true with a number of the characters and relationships in the play. Brook explained afterwards that for certain actors – he cited Scofield – it was not only unnecessary but wasteful. "Paul is already struggling with what is essential in Lear. For him, improvisation would only be a diversion of energy."'

There was a baleful power in many of the rehearsals. It exploded in the scene in which Lear, flanked by a big retinue of his knights, returns from the hunt to his daughter Goneril's home, demanding to be fed and housed. She slights him, and he hits the roof – only at this rehearsal, it was a rather tame explosion. Brook gave the knights a pep talk, asking them to go for broke. 'On Lear's cue, which is "Darkness and Devils", one could almost see a dozen acting missiles rev up for the blast off,' wrote Marowitz. 'As Lear overturned the table, the stage exploded and sent shrapnel flying in a dozen different directions. Tankards whizzed through the air hitting actors and ricocheting into the laps of stage-managers below; set pieces were smashed over up-ended bits of furniture and a chandelier above the rehearsal stage was splintered into a thousand pieces.'

In the storm scene, Brook brought the sheets themselves on stage: three steel sheets, discoloured with rust and time, were slowly flown in, like guillotine blades. Seeing the production at Stratford in 1962 and watching these sheets inexorably descend they also brought to mind the rough tongues of giant monsters. Then they began to vibrate, gently at first, making a distant growl, then more violently as the electric motors powering them accelerated, until they were shaking and buckling alarmingly above the solitary Gloucester; everyone else having rushed indoors for shelter. Then, as an electronic score amplified the thunder-sheets, Kent and the Gentleman were hurled on and, like Japanese actors, began to mime the effects of a storm, a shift to abstraction building to Lear's entrance. The young Tom Stoppard, writing for an arts weekly, was viscerally grabbed by these wraith-like figures: 'never more effective than in the storm scene, when with three thunder sheets drumming overhead, the first entrant is flung into view by the gale, a black wheeling shape that might have been an empty cloak or a broken umbrella'.

An umbrella perhaps carried by a Beckettian tramp. Kenneth Tynan, in the first of his two rhapsodic reviews of *Lear*, had made much of this resemblance: 'Lear is by now a rustic vagabond: cf. the classless derelicts of Samuel Beckett.'

Shakespeare and Beckett present essentially the same double act: King and Fool, master and servant, like Pozzo and Lucky in *Waiting For Godot*, Hamm and Clov in *Endgame*. The Fool in *Lear* has licence to puncture his master's illusions, which he does with anxious care, and to divert him from his madness, which he does with zany riddles; and it is with a Beckettian resignation, a shared, old-couple exhaustion, that Lear and Fool mutter quietly, seated at the edge of an empty stage. Lear caps it by breathing, 'Let me not be mad.'

The encounter of mad Lear and blinded Gloucester was an even more pitiful example of Beckettian pathos. Two kinds of blindness meet in this scene: Lear's moral blindness to those who care for him most, and Gloucester's literal blindness, his eyes gouged out by his son-in-law. Beckettian wraiths to be sure, but also Biblical: two old clowns playing the Book of Job, like Max Beckmann's crumpled and exiled kings, journeying they know not where on a Ship of Fools. Later, in his book *The Empty Space*, Brook noted that while all Beckett was already there in Shakespeare, the 'Beckett-ness' of *Lear* waiting to be seized, the reverse wasn't true until the fragmented 1960s. Only then could the age begin to see the Shakespeare in Beckett.

Eyebrows were raised at Brook's cutting the lines of the good servant, who rushes to stop his master blinding Gloucester and is killed. Even this little crumb of comfort was refused; he didn't see the play in a soft-edged light, he was bringing the story and the characters to life in a pitiless society. 'This production brings me closer to Lear than I have ever been,' said Tynan. 'From now on, I not only know him but can place him in his harsh and unforgiving world.' Stoppard responded fully to Brook's placing of the unqualified blinding scene as the culmination of Part One. 'Gloucester is left alone with the servants. As they start to clear the furniture, he is buffeted and jostled by them until he gropes his way upstage, with the house lights going on, a broken figure long in view of a mesmerised audience sitting in full light.'

Irving Wardle picked up the oriental signs in Brook's work, praising the 'stylized and detached posture of a Buddhist monk' held by the eyeless Gloucester sitting alone on a totally empty stage furnished only with the off-stage clash of distant battle.

It was perhaps a sign of a shift in British culture that as Brook's *King Lear* was shaking its audiences, a group of poets – Ted Hughes in Britain, Robert Lowell in America, Zbigniew Herbert in Poland – were taking a new stance which A. L. Alvarez, the *Observer*'s poetry critic, labelled as 'against the gentility principle'. In the aftermath of Auschwitz and Hiroshima, of the Gulag and the Cold War, poetry, he said, in his introduction to his anthology, *The New Poetry*, had to let in the extremes of life now. It had to write about zero-degree survival in concentration camps, about the sedatives and mental hospitals, about the brutality of family life, about the wellsprings of cruelty as well as kindness.

In such a climate, Brook's *Lear* thrust Shakespeare's most splintered tragedy into the wind-tunnel of the twentieth century. After the brutal depiction of lost innocence in *Lord of the Flies*, it was further evidence of his own well of night and darkness. And it is the production which, with *A Midsummer Nights Dream* (1970), probably more than any other changed the way directors came to grips with Shakespeare.

Brook drew upon the continuity within the troupe for his first RSC production at the Aldwych, for which he returned to Friedrich Dürrenmatt. Irene Worth, Brook's Goneril, Alan Webb, his Gloucester and Diana Rigg, his Cordelia, starred in Dürrenmatt's cutting comedy of madness and nuclear weapons, *The Physicists*. The play takes place in a lunatic asylum presided over by a hunchbacked chief doctor. There are three apparently crazy inmates. One believes himself to be Isaac Newton, the second Albert Einstein, and the third that he can communicate with King Solomon.

It turns out that, far from being mad, the first two inmates are simply rival agents of superpowers each trying to kidnap the third, who has invented a weapon of universal destruction. But he is a kind of secular saint, who chooses self-imprisonment rather than let humanity suffer from the application of his scientific discoveries. 'Only in the madhouse can we be free,' he tells his colleagues. If Dürrenmatt's play has something of the moral gravity of Shakespeare's *King Lear*, its ending, as critics who could recall Brook's *Huis clos* noted, is like the doomed double-bind of Sartre's 'Hell is other people'.

Tynan admired Brook's 'icily flawless' production, praised the play but had reservations: 'The outline is fixed and inflexible; you feel that Dürrenmatt never allows his characters to take him by surprise, since that might spoil the pattern; but beneath the Arctic cap of the argument there simmers a passionate concern for human survival, and this wedding of logic and charity is what prompts me to hail the piece as Dürrenmatt's finest work.'

Dürrenmatt's play acquired extra resonance from the ever-present threat of the Cold War. The spread of nuclear weapons fed people's minds with visions of devastation, and the Cuban missile crisis which so nearly triggered a nuclear confrontation was fresh in memory. It is to such shared nightmares that Tynan is referring when he praises the play's 'wedding of logic and charity'.

What did Brook feel about these collective nightmares of annihilation? Did they mirror his own dark imaginings? Scars of recent history seem to haunt many productions of Brook's first twenty years; not just the top-down view of Hiroshima and Nagasaki victims fleeing and crumbling, but also the cruelty of torture and the brutal treatment of the insane, the industrialised death-camps of Hitler and Stalin. The graphic torture in his production of Sartre's French Resistance play *Men without Shadows* (1947), the trans-posed but nonetheless extreme violence of *Titus Andronicus* (1955), the sado-masochism of *Le Balcon* (1960) the cannibalism and total abandon-ment of constraints in *Lord of the Flies* (1961) – all these point to a deeply rooted aggression and anguish in Brook's psyche. It's as if Brook had his own nightmares of a *tabula rasa*: earth, cities and human bodies scorched into a raw void; as if he adopted Shakespeare's grim picture of the human species cannibalising itself:

> It will come.
> Humanity perforce must prey upon itself,
> Like monsters of the deep

Irving Wardle who, as *The Times* drama critic, reviewed Brook's major productions from the sixties onwards, had a similar insight: 'These are expressions of anthropological despair, re-examining the nature of man in the light of Auschwitz and Vietnam by a process of immersion in the "destructive element" . . . It is worth noting that the blackest of these works were produced while he was still a prisoner of the "glamour circuit": before he kicked the careerist ladder aside and went his own way.'

The Royal Shakespeare Company, entering its third year, was beginning to feel severe political and financial pressures. Peter Hall was at the vortex of these pressures. Hall's chairman had agreed that the company's reserves could be used to finance the expansion plan into London, but they would soon be exhausted. There were still too many productions with a directorial concept, but a patchy delivery of the text. What was needed was a landmark production that would weld the nascent talents with the senior actors, like Peggy Ashcroft. Hall sensed that this could come through a 'revisionist' production of Shakespeare's English history plays, yoking classical form to a contemporary view of power play and political expediency. He wanted to do the little-performed three plays of *Henry VI*, continue their story into the more familiar *Richard III*, and call the result *The Wars of The Roses*. At the end of 1962 he asked John Barton to reduce the *Henry VI* trilogy to two plays. Cutting Shakespeare's text and writing iambic connective tissue against the clock, Barton managed to meet the deadline, with morning and evening sessions with Hall, who was rehearsing *A Midsummer Night's Dream*. Brook advised that in spite of the pressures on him as chief executive, Hall should direct them himself. Hall began, and two weeks in, collapsed in the rehearsal room.

He withdrew to a darkened room. One of the diagnoses of his multiple symptoms was shingles. 'Hall suffered a variety of physical symptoms – in his stomach, head and sinuses – and mental turmoil,' wrote Stephen Fay. 'He fell into one of his periodic fits of weeping, and, he says, thought about suicide. To occupy his mind he built a battleship out of matchsticks. William Sargant, a fashionable Harley Street psychiatrist who advocated shock therapy in severe cases of depression, thought Hall a suitable case for treatment.'

Today, Peter Hall remembers a very different kind of shock therapy administered by Brook:

In 1963, the Royal Shakespeare Company was three years old. We had no grant, and we were fast using up the reserves. My first marriage, to Leslie Caron, was breaking up. I was trying to run the Aldwych and Stratford-upon-Avon at the same time. I offered Peter the *Henry VI* plays to do. 'They're not for me,' he said, 'You do them.' And I did. I was doing the biggest and most frightening production of my life. I was dead tired, miserable, and I knew that if this production didn't come off, the Royal Shakespeare Company was finished. I rehearsed for two weeks and then collapsed. In my memory, it seems to me that I woke up, and standing round the bed were Peter, Peggy Ashcroft and Leslie. After much discussion, Peter said to me, 'Get up and go back to work.' 'I can't,' I said, 'the doctors won't let me.' He said, 'Fuck the doctors; if you don't work now, you'll never work again.' I got up and went back to work. I hated the work, and it was probably the greatest success of my career, and the start of the RSC as an international force. Peter was delighted; he radiated 'told-you-so'. Had I just been breaking up with Leslie and said, can we talk, he'd probably have said, sorry, I'm busy.

He doesn't waste time on the beta plus. It's the same in friendship; I learned early on that to ask him for help on a relatively minor matter was a total waste of time. But if it was a major one, he not only had the instinct to suss out that it was major, but he was there.

Meanwhile, in *Encore* magazine Brook continued analysing and reflecting on theatre and film, the abstract and the concrete. The magazine had asked him to review Samuel Beckett's *Happy Days*, directed by Alan Schneider in New York, and rejected by audience and critics. He began by recalling the little clay statuette from Mexico which in an earlier *Encore* he had used as a touchstone for a new kind of acting. Now he applied it to Beckett's ability to make an irreducible stage image:

> Beckett at his finest seems to have the power of casting a stage picture, a stage relationship, a stage machine from his most intense experiences that in a flash, inspired, *exists*, stands there complete in itself, not *telling* not *dictating*, symbolic without symbolism.
>
> Before Oedipus and Hamlet were born in their authors' minds all the qualities these characters reflect must have been in existence as nebuloid formless currents of experience. Then came a powerful generative act – and characters appeared giving shape and substance to these abstractions. Hamlet is there: we can refer to him. Suddenly Jimmy Porter is there – we can't throw him off. And Beckett's Vladimir and Estragon, or his bosomy, cheery Winnie in *Happy Days* – once imagined and embodied, they can't be thrown off, they become part of our 'field of reference'.

Little is wasted with Brook. Thirty years after writing about *Happy Days*, he went on to direct it himself. In 1962 he formulated his first insight into this play which is, he says, of all Beckett's work perhaps the most corrosive and Shakespearean:

> Certainly this is a play about man throwing his life away: it is a play about possibilities lost: comically, tragically it shows us man atrophied, paralysed, three-quarters useless, three-quarters dead – but grotesquely it shows he is only aware of how lucky he is to be alive. This is a picture of us ourselves

endlessly grinning – not as Pagliacci once grinned, to conceal a broken heart –
but grinning because no one has told us our heart stopped beating long ago.
. . . In showing man bereft of most of his organs it is implying that the
possibilities were there, are there still, buried, ignored. Unlike the other Beckett
plays this is not only a vision of our fallen condition, it is an assault on our
blindness.

And then, reminding us that New York rejected this play, Brook extends
Beckett's image to assault American culture and to flay the political class:
'Here is the audience (and the critics) at any play (or film) which after two
hours finds the answers, which glibly asserts that life is good, that there is
always hope and that all will be well. Here is Walter Kerr, and the audience
of *The Miracle Worker* and Ike and most of our politicians grinning from ear
to ear and buried up to their necks.'

Brook now scurried into a trio of productions, the first of which was his one
incontrovertible flop. *The Perils of Scobie Prilt* was a musical by the team that
had made such a success of *Irma*, Julian More, Monty Norman and David
Heneker. More remembers how the idea came up. 'We were sitting on the
terrace of the Café Flore – where else does one have ideas that will lead to total
disaster? – and one of us said, Wouldn't it be fun to do a James Bond movie on
the stage, with a cast the size of *Beyond The Fringe*? And Peter said, yes and at
the end I'll have this paper rocket and it will just rise in the air and burst into
flames.' Excited, Brook took the idea to Binkie Beaumont and Donald Albery,
Binkie's West End co-producer. From then on, as More says, 'It was like an
amoeba that grew into a colossus, that could not control itself.'

The story was about a scientist, Scobie, who produces a highly intelligent
robot from the genes of a serial killer. Worried that the West will use it for
destructive purposes; he absconds with it. He's captured by Them, the other
side, in the shape of a glamorous spy. He falls in love with the spy, the West
is trying to ambush and capture him, and it becomes a James Bond pastiche.
Jullan More recalls how it went so wrong:

The trouble was that by now the original cast of four had grown into twenty-
four, the paper rocket was replaced by a real rocket, and we practically blew

up the New Theatre, Oxford. On the opening night, all that could have gone wrong technically did so. And Peter also went wrong. He didn't realise that you couldn't do a small-scale experiment in the conditions of a commercial production, with only four weeks' rehearsal. I remember especially Nigel Davenport, a very conventional actor, who played the James Bond character, crawling around under the grand piano, with Charles Marowitz, who was the assistant director, standing over him. I said, 'What are you doing under that grand piano?' 'I'm in a fucking Viennese sewer,' said Nigel, 'I don't know what they're doing, we open in two weeks and why can't Peter get on and direct this show?'

Their out-of-town premiere, at the New Theatre, Oxford, had to be cancelled. It opened on the Wednesday, and closed on the Saturday.

The four men behind *Scobie*, Julian More admits, had succumbed to showbiz delirium, carrying each other away, calling for more experiment, more daring; 'but we lost sight of the original idea of the show, which was a love story. Monty had written some wonderful, strong music, but when we hired a very gifted jazz composer, Bill Russo, he orchestrated a pit show for cellos and trombones, big banks of them. You couldn't hear anything. That was the end of it, in England at least. Peter seemed to have come to the show tired, after *King Lear*. I think his spirit was moving in another direction. But we did look on him as the magician who would pull us through.'

Brook now took a break.

After a holiday in Tunisia, he and Natasha and the now eleven-year-old Irina moved house to Holland Street, in Kensington. Looking back, in 1989, on the birth of his first child, Brook had a clear memory of the miraculous convulsion with which she came into the world: 'A little shoulder and an arm were the first signs of Irina, and then suddenly, there she was, complete. Something to do with the way her body linked itself together and the manner in which she looked around gave her the appearance of being very definite, a solid character, a real Aries. In that moment I had the impression of seeing not her babyhood, but her essential nature.'

Irina, who herself has become a gifted director, remembered her father making up endless stories. One of the stock characters was Mr Ubu, 'a fat villainous man who spent the whole day doing villainous things and who, at the end of the day, would always proclaim: "I'm never going out again!" ' Growing up 'watching actors in faded jeans rehearsing in old warehouses', Irina wanted to follow suit and go to stage school. 'Being his daughter I was a good talker and in the Brook way I would carefully explain the pros and cons of such a plan. It never cut any ice. He'd say, "If you want to be an actress, you wait until you've finished school, and that's that." It was good advice; acting is a narrow enough field without entering it too early.' Brook added, 'I never encouraged Irina to be an actor; in my view, if anyone can be saved from this misfortune, they should be.' But when she did become an actor and was recommended to change her name so she could be seen as separate from her famous parents, Brook was against it: 'Your name is part of your skin.'

About her upbringing, Irina says, 'He gave me the freedom to do exactly as I wanted but always with quiet authority. It may appear indulgent that he imposed so few restrictions but it was never without thought: it was all part of his conscious training to allow you to discover things for yourself. He directs his family as he directs his actors, subtly: you have the freedom to express yourself while he retains the vision of the whole.'

Brook's son, Simon, born in 1966, also remembers his father's gentleness and pleasure in play. Stepping out from the shadow of his father's fame, he has become a documentary film-maker. His film about his father, *Brook by Brook* (2001) is elegant, searching, poised and tender.

In London Brook had not connected with the playwrights of the English Stage Company at the Royal Court Theatre. But now, in Paris in 1963, he staged one of the Court's outstanding – and most contentious – new plays, *Serjeant Musgrave's Dance* by John Arden. Arden's play tackled the uncomfortable issue of colonial violence (it was prompted by a retaliatory raid after a British soldier's wife in Cyprus had been killed by guerrillas), the rigidity of moral principles in war, their ambiguity in peace-time, the necessity and difficulty of pacifism. In form, it drew its strength from the vivid world of traditional ballads, the irony and vernacular poetry of Yorkshire speech and the Puritan Bible. Directed by Lindsay Anderson, it opened at the Royal Court in October 1959, and was greeted, as John Whiting's *Saint's Day* had been a decade earlier, with a sharply divided critical response. Now Michael Billington wrote of the Paris production, 'This is spell-binding, mind-challenging drama that touches greatness: and what is more, it is written in that wonderful Arden language that seems to be hewn out of granite.' *The Sunday Times*, however, greeted the play wearily as 'another dreadful ordeal'.

Set in the mid-nineteenth century, the play focuses on four British army deserters returning from a war in some far corner of the Empire to bring the body of a dead soldier back to a mining community. Their leader, Serjeant Musgrave, plans to hold the town at gunpoint and confront its people with the realities of warfare. The stage becomes the town-hall square and we the audience are the town-folk at the meeting, with Gatling guns pointing down our throats. Musgrave's righteousness turns to zeal, his zeal to near-madness. The soldiers' rebellion collapses in chaos and confusion. But a seed of resistance has been sown.

Brook saw the play less as a political parable that could apply to Suez, Cyprus, Algeria and Africa, more as a microcosm of how 'true theatre' is born, out of an excess of passion, a bonfire of existing forms. Writing three years later, he related the play to Antonin Artaud's image of the transfigured actor or artist, 'burnt at the stake, signalling through the flames'.

> The demonstration that [Musgrave] improvises is like a genuine piece of popular theatre; his props are machine guns, flags and a uniformed skeleton that he hauls aloft. When this does not succeed in transmitting his complete message to the crowd, his desperate energy drives him to find still further means of expression, and, in a flash of inspiration, he begins a rhythmic stamping, out of which develops a savage dance and chant. *Serjeant Musgrave's Dance* is a demonstration of how a violent need to project a meaning can suddenly call into existence a wild unpredictable form.

'A violent need to project a meaning.' It's a phrase that could be applied to Brook himself, and it drove him to mould Arden's play to meet his concerns and French perceptions. Arden had firmly outlined the heightened quality of the world he sought to portray, with its primary colours of ballad- and broad-sheets. 'Black is for death and for the coal mines. Red is for murder and for the soldier's coat the collier puts on to escape his black.' But Brook wanted a very different, Parisian, abstract aesthetic: a modernist sculpture of elemental grey-green slabs, which split open to make interiors and smaller spaces, and looked as if it were made for a modern ballet.

In their study of Brook, Albert Hunt and Geoffrey Reeves, both of whom later worked with him, accuse Brook's production of leaching out the social texture of Arden's world in favour of generalised dance-like gestures. The result, both authors conclude, is to 'put *Musgrave* firmly back into the slough of post-war pessimism in which Brook himself felt most at home'. This is perhaps to read too much ideological meaning into the work of a mercurial director. It remained for Harold Hobson to come to the Athénée and make his symbolic act of recantation. In *The Sunday Times* he noted that 'M. Jean-Jacques Gautier asserts that the one kind of theatre no one will make him endure is the theatre of boredom, of which he claims that *Serjeant Musgrave's Dance* is a prime example. These words are to me the more resonant in that I used them myself when I first saw the play in 1959.' Now, however, rejoices Hobson, 'Mr Brook has put the ball right into the net. Mr Arden's play is as full of checks and balances as the American constitution itself, but Mr Brook has found a way of making them all harmoniously contribute to one total, dark and overwhelming effect.'

It was not half as dark or contentious, though, as Brook's final production in Paris that year. The director of the Théatre de L'Athénée, Françoise Spira, another of those fearless women in the French theatre towards whom Brook was drawn, had acquired the rights to Rolf Hochhuth's *The Representative*, a play which attacked the Pope's conduct in the Second World War, and was stirring and offending audiences all over Europe. Hochhuth had unearthed documentary evidence that the Pope had done nothing to protest or prevent the extermination of the Jews, had, in fact, turned a blind eye to them. Out of his discoveries, he wove an impassioned documentary play which, performed at full length, would have lasted seven hours.

The 'representative' of the title is a young Jesuit, Fontana, based on a real priest, who to his horror is drawn to face the irrefutable knowledge of the extermination camps, and pleads with Pope Pius XII to raise his voice against them. When he fails, he puts on a yellow star in solidarity with the Jews, and follows them into the gas chamber.

Brook co-directed *The Representative* with Francis Darbon, who had appeared in his *Musgrave*; Jorge Semprun, the Spanish Communist writer who had been in Buchenwald, translated and trimmed the text. Praising Semprun's 'sense of stark testimony and sharp dialogue', Bertrand Poirot Delpech in *Le Monde* compared the Paris approach with the productions in Berlin and London: 'It acts on the mind rather than the nerve-ends. Avoiding on the one hand the trap of caricaturing men of the Church – as Piscator did in Berlin, or of tugging the audience's heart-strings once more with documentary film of the camps, as was done in London – they have given the whole production the uniform tone of a neutral, icy, Cartesian demonstration.' The result was to restore to an audience the freedom and responsibility of a jury.

There was no curtain-call. It would have been outrageous to solicit applause. But the restraint on stage did little to calm infuriated right-wing Catholics in the auditorium. Demonstrators, organised by an ad hoc 'Pius XII Committee', shouted 'It's a scandal!' 'A gross caricature!' 'All fiction!'; leaflets fluttered down from the balcony, whistles were blown, tambourines beaten, tributes to Pius XII from the chief rabbis of Rome and Bucharest and from Golda Meir quoted. But the play ran for six months, and it gave further impetus to a new theatrical genre of the 1960s, the 'Theatre of Fact'. Peter Weiss' *The Investigation* (1965) was one of the plays that followed Hochhuth's, and Brook would co-direct it at the Aldwych Theatre. But he was never keen on the 'Theatre of Fact' label: he told me, 'You can never get to the facts. I'd rather call it the theatre of myth.'

With the pitiless cruelty of *King Lear* and *Lord of the Flies*, the bitter lucidity of Dürrenmatt's *Physicists*, the protesting soldiers of *Serjeant Musgrave's Dance* and the dissident priest of *The Representative*, Brook at the beginning of the sixties was far from retreating into a resigned 'postwar pessimism'.

FROM ARTAUD TO THE ASYLUM
1963–65

'When I was a young director,' Brook told Michael Billington in a Theatre Museum interview in May 2002, 'I was looking for energy, vitality, dynamics. It was a response to middle-class ennui, the boredom of what I saw: the West End theatre, the first Shakespeares I saw, the dreariness of Stratford-upon-Avon, the ugliness and also the lethargy, the lifelessness, the "traditionalness", in the worst sense of the word, of everything I saw in theatre. So I searched for life, new life, surprise.'

He did so with conscious mischief. In 1963, at a notorious Drama Conference organised by Kenneth Tynan and the publisher John Calder at the Edinburgh Festival (which made the tabloid front pages because a nude model was wheeled across the stage), Brook had asserted that the theatre had to face 'the death of the word'. The idea quickly became currency in discussions of poetry, cinema and theatre; verbal expression, it was said, seemed to be buckling in the force-field of contemporary life and modern history. Allied to this scrutiny of language 'under pressure' (the title of an influential book by the critic A. L. Alvarez) was a belief that the artist might have to skirt and even succumb to insanity in order to bring back telling insights. R. D. Laing, the anti-psychiatrist and writer, was advancing a new theory and practice which claimed to lay bare 'the politics of madness', and proposed a more existential kind of journey through what society defined as insanity than that offered by psychotherapy and medication.

All these ideas interested Brook, and many of them could be traced back to the jagged life and work of the French actor, artist director, poet, playwright and seer Antonin Artaud (1896–1948). The young Brook would have heard about Artaud in his trips to Paris in the 1950s, when in avant-garde circles Artaud had cast himself as a revolutionary martyr in the cause of modern art – Artaud Agonistes, surfacing from months of electro-shock therapy to write his late, hectoring texts and to have his final radio play, *An End to the Judgement of God*, banned by French state radio. Artaud conducted a critique of language in well-written theatre: 'To break through language in order to touch life is to create or re-create the theatre.' He joined the Surrealists and then split from them when they threw in their lot with the French Communist Party. He wrote electrifying manifestos calling for the subversion of theatre as it was. These were collected in a sulphurous book, *Le Théâtre et son double*, published in 1938 and reissued six years later, the year of his release from the sanatorium at Rodez. Two of its manifestos called *Le Théâtre de la Cruauté* gave Brook the name of his experimental laboratory, which marked the beginning of his break from the mainstream.

Brook does not recall when he first read Artaud's texts but in the late fifties and early sixties, Artaud came to influence people more by osmosis than close study; William Burroughs, free jazz, the earliest American alternative theatre with Julian Beck and Judith Malina's Living Theater, all succumbed.

In New York, Brook had seen the work of Joseph Chaikin, an ex-Living Theater actor who had started his own company, inspired by Artaudian ideas. As Peter Feldman, one of Chaikin's fellow actors, put it: 'Our object was to make visible on stage those levels of reality which are usually not expressed in situations: the elusive, irrational, fragile, mysterious or mon-strous lives within our lives; to break down the actor's reliance on mundane social realism and watered-down Freud.' Brook absorbed Artaud's influence through a variety of channels and cities. Now, thanks to Peter Hall's undertaking to give him an opportunity to experiment at the Royal Shakespeare Company, Brook was about to take on Artaud, refracted by early-sixties London, its new waves, its rock and roll, its flirtations with madness, its nonchalant utopianism.

Beginning in a small church hall near the Royal Court Theatre in Sloane

Square, Brook launched an arc of work that carried him and a nucleus of actors through 1960s London and swept him away in search of currents and meanings beyond Britain. The early sixties was also the time when Brook wrote incisive pieces for *Encore* magazine; in tone, they have much in common with the convulsive, fractured language of Artaud's writing: 'Either we restore all the arts to a central attitude and necessity, finding an analogy between a gesture made in painting or the theatre, and a gesture made by lava in a volcanic explosion, or we must stop painting, babbling, writing, or doing whatever it is we do.'

In his *Encore* texts calling for far-reaching theatrical reform, Brook wrote with the same passionate, angry edge. But could his adoption of Artaud's suggestive, unfinished legacy, 'work that cancels itself' in Susan Sontag's words, go farther than that? Could it start a new direction for Brook's own theatre?

Glenda Jackson, who began work with Brook in this experiment, describes how she came into the group:

One had to do an audition, which Peter and his assistant director Charles Marowitz ran. You were told to go with a prepared piece and so I went and was told to do my prepared piece but within the context of a woman who opens her front door and is immediately bundled into a straitjacket and taken off to a lunatic asylum. So that was the first thing. Then, if memory serves, I was called back for a second. Then I heard absolutely nothing and then I was told that I was one of twelve who would start on what became known as the Theatre of Cruelty. And we started work I think in a room over a pub in the King's Road or a church hall.

No one had ever asked me to do that kind of work in my life before, and I have to say it was an oasis in the desert. First of all, Brook was somebody who paid us the great compliment of believing that we were what we said we were, namely actors, and therefore we could do absolutely anything that was demanded of us. In many ways, he took things right back to very basic essentials – I can remember a great deal of time with us all sitting around in a circle on the floor beating out the stresses in a line of Shakespeare. Essentially he was looking for something that was not rooted – as I think British theatre was at that time – in a literary exposition of emotion.

Sally Jacobs joined Brook for *Theatre of Cruelty* and went on to design his key shows of the 1960s.

> I was already doing some work with the Royal Shakespeare and then I read a small piece in the newspaper that he was about to put together a group – no big names – everyone was going to earn the same money in order to do what we used to call in those days 'experiment' and make a laboratory. I had no specific role, so I didn't have a conventional relationship with the director. I didn't take part in improvisations but I absorbed and witnessed and I often did drawings of what they were doing and kept myself steeped in it. I managed to provide not only what a designer could but something more that triggered further work. And then they'd work with it and I'd work directly with some of the actors. I began to participate in the making of work in a way that I hadn't had the chance to do before.

They had twelve weeks in all for training and for a five-week showing of work in progress at the LAMDA (London Academy of Music and Dramatic Art) theatre in Kensington. They explored sounds, banging and scraping objects, seeing how much variety they could make; they worked with rhythms, both the rhythms of their percussive objects, and then their voices and bodies; they began to use a sound and a movement to respond to a new situation. Soon they ran into the limitations of purely formal experiments. 'Very quickly, frighteningly quickly, actors became as glib with non-naturalistic sounds and movements as they were with stock dramatic clichés,' wrote Marowitz.

But Brook had faith in the occasional signs of uncanny contact between actors, things invisible made manifest. A few years later, in *The Empty Space* he wrote about these instants of invisible but tangible communication.

> An actor sits at one end of the room, facing the wall. At the other end is another actor, looking at the first one's back, not allowed to move. The second actor must make the first one obey him. As the first one has his back turned, the second has no way of communicating his wishes except through sounds, for he is allowed no words. This seems impossible, but it can be done. It is like

crossing an abyss on a tightrope: necessity suddenly produces strange powers . . .

The actor then found that to communicate his invisible meanings he needed concentration, he needed will; he needed to summon all his emotional reserves; he needed courage; he needed clear thought. But the most important result was that he was led inexorably to the conclusion that he needed form.

The actor/*auteur*, Brook came to see through this work, needed 'to mint a new form which would be a container and a reflector for his impulses. That is what is truly called an action . . . This is what some theatres call magic, others science, but it's the same thing. An invisible idea was rightly shown.'

From January 1964, the *Theatre of Cruelty* work went public for five weeks. The running order, periodically shuffled, included nonsense sketches by an absurdist writer, Paul Ableman; a short Artaud play, *The Spurt of Blood* about a knight and big-bosomed wet-nurse, in a medieval setting, performed first in sounds, then as written; scenes from Genet's *The Screens*; a playlet by John Arden, *Ars Longa, Vita Brevis* and Marowitz's cut-up *Hamlet*. Sometimes Brook and Marowitz went on stage to discuss why they were doing the whole thing, or Brook rehearsed a Shakespeare scene – one night a scene from *Richard III*. But there was one piece devised by Brook which stood out.

It was called *The Public Bath*. Brook had turned the theatre around; the performance took place on the raked, stepped slope on which the audience normally sat; the audience sat in the well of the theatre, and looked up. Glenda Jackson appeared at the top of the slope, dressed in a tight black dress, black stockings and high heels, the uniform of the high-class hooker. Coldly, almost haughtily, high above the audience and as far away as she could be, she did an antiseptic strip-tease. There was no come-on in the way she displayed her naked body.

She was led down to floor-level and put into a tin bath and washed, then dressed in the rough, shapeless clothes of a prisoner. She knelt next to the bath. From the top of the slope, elderly judges and lawyers – the sort of people who could have been the clients of a whore – intoned a text that Brook had stitched together from press-cuttings of one scandal and one tragedy that had dominated British headlines that year: Christine Keeler, the call-girl who brought down the Tory Minister of Defence, John Profumo, and unleashed a flood of hypocrisy, and Jacqueline Kennedy, the widow of the assassinated President of the USA. Keeler, the pampered luxury call-girl, had to submit to the humiliation of being scrubbed and disinfected in a tin bath. The same bath, upturned, was then sublimated into the coffin of the martyred widow of President Kennedy at the state funeral.

The audience was left with the sight of a grieving woman, the Madonna and the Whore, exposed to 'the public bath' – the bath of voyeurism, sexual fantasy, vicarious emotion – a curdle of emotions repeated nearly half a century later, when Princess Diana died. It was more than a tough little revue-sketch. Martin Esslin, an early advocate of the Theatre of the Absurd, compared *The Public Bath*, a touch fulsomely perhaps, with 'the total involvement of the participants in some primeval magical rite or Aztec sacrifice'.

Years after *Theatre of Cruelty*, Glenda Jackson painted her own picture of Brook at work, as tough-minded and down-to-earth as she was:

> He was given an award by a university in Dallas, Texas, and I was asked if I would go along for the award ceremony. Before the ceremony Peter held a workshop. We sat on the stage with all these students and theatre people sitting in the auditorium and he was introduced and he just sat there. Now I knew what he was doing: it was about the power of silence and how you get people to concentrate. He does it very well. He goes through that whole process of people watching, then getting anxious because they're not used to silence and then becoming a bit embarrassed – has something gone wrong? – and he still sits and he still sits – and then at precisely the right moment he'll say, 'This is what I am doing.' And he can be very precise in his exposition – on that occasion I think he was talking about how irrelevant theatre is. But the way he took control of the event was a way of showing how relevant it could be.
>
> What he says is always very fluent, very lucid, very clear, it's rooted in a philosophy which informs what he's talking about. When he speaks to actors as a group he's useless. He can't speak to actors in a group unless – well he can if he's angry. But he's always nervous, because he knows how dangerous words are and how very easy it is to push actors in the wrong direction. Where

he's absolutely brilliant, I think, is that he cuts you off if you're going down the wrong way. He just stops it dead. Someone once asked me what was the word that was most synonymous in my mind with working with Peter Brook, and the word is 'No'. That's the word you hear and he doesn't need to embellish that, he'll just say 'No'.

Then he might take you off into a corner and have a little talk with you. When he's actually engaged in a production, he has a willingness always to be as vulnerable as all the actors. When he doesn't know, he doesn't know. He knows what he doesn't want, like all great directors, they all know that, but they are absolutely vulnerable, like babies; you have to show them what they want, they don't know what that is. And that's where his great genius is, I think, in choosing from what you feel confident enough to offer.

Meanwhile *King Lear*, after its brief London season, was on an international tour in Eastern Europe, from Berlin to Leningrad, via Budapest, Belgrade, Prague, Bucharest, Warsaw, Helsinki and Moscow. After Russia, *King Lear* went to America, and wound up its tour at the new Lincoln Center for the Performing Arts in New York. No one had paid any attention to the acoustics for spoken drama at this theatre, and they were appalling. They had been designed to work for music and dance, but not theatre. Brook had to get his actors to speak louder and stand more frontally, with considerable damage to his work. After the painful first performance, Brook insisted that the entire board of trustees of the Lincoln Center be summoned for a meeting. Clifford Williams, whose production of *A Comedy of Errors* would be next to open there, remembers Brook lambasting the cowering chairman and the trembling trustees for their impoliteness in offering an acoustically unsuitable theatre. He demanded a public apology in the press the next day. It duly appeared, and every critic blamed the Lincoln Center rather than Brook's actors. None of this seemed to harm the reception, however, and it was this visit which cemented Brook's American and international reputation. Jack Kroll, *Newsweek*'s seasoned drama critic, talked of its 'stripped, merciless action' and called it 'a hard, implacable, revolutionary production that can change the face of Shakespeare for our time'.

Charles Marowitz, now working as a theatre critic, railed against this adulation: 'I couldn't disguise a sense of disgust over what had become not only "a hit" and a *succès d'estime* but a historical event in English theatre ... The show had become not an imaginative, brilliantly executed, somewhat flawed and erratic Shakespearean production, but a "milestone".' Marowitz's deflation is a reminder of the myth-making clouds of praise that were beginning to surround the celebrity director.

Back in London, Brook moved the company which had performed in *Theatre of Cruelty* onwards, into Jean Genet's *The Screens*. It seemed a perfect follow-on to the LAMDA season; its language was harsh but lyrical, it played with flat painted images and three-dimensional objects, it was even more scathing about the European power elite than *Le Balcon* had been. Brook staged the first twelve scenes of the play in London, in 1964, two years before the French got round to staging it. For *The Screens*, Brook expanded his LAMDA core company, and added actors such as John Steiner and Morgan Shepard, who were to go on to play in *The Marat/Sade* and, in some cases *US* and *A Midsummer Night's Dream*, his chain of productions through the 1960s. Within the Royal Shakespeare Company, he was building his own group, with a common training and a shared line of work. The actors took to Genet's repertoire of theatre languages in *The Screens* with relish: the switches from the verbal to the graphic, the continual reshaping of the space in the spartan Donmar studio by wheeling around Sally Jacobs' steel-framed screens – all this was grist to their mill. The design relationship between Brook and Jacobs deepened, as she responded to Genet's luxurious imagination with a fairground peep-show display of 'an Academician, a Soldier, a Vamp, a News Photographer, a Widow, a Judge, a Banker, a Little Girl wearing a communion dress and a General' – the colonial elite on show 'like coconuts on a shy'. She also set up a naked articulated tailor's dummy that, festooned with glitzy medals, became an imperial totem.

Tom Milne, who had not been bowled over by *Theatre of Cruelty*, wrote in *Encore* of *The Screen*'s 'series of shattering images: as two Colonialists chat cosily about the aesthetics and economics of their plantations, Arab terrorists creep stealthily in to draw tiny flames on the screens behind them;

Peter Brook, aged
twelve, curious
about film.

Brook aged twenty-one in 1946,
when he staged *Love's Labour's Lost*.

Brook at twenty-one
celebrated by *Vogue* as a
rising star, 1946.

Brook directing *A Sentimental Journey,* Oxford, 1944.

Peter Brook and Natasha Parry around the time of their marriage, 1950s.

Brook with John Gielgud (*left*) and Anthony Quayle (*right*) in the stalls of the Stratford Shakespeare Memorial Theatre, 1950.

Alec Guinness
distraught in Sartre's
Vicious Circle, Arts
Theatre, London, 1946.

Captivating post-war elegance in Jean Anouilh's sweet-sour characters, including
Paul Scofield (*right*) playing twins, in Oliver Messel's filigree conservatory, *Ring
Round the Moon*, 1950.

Peter Brook and
Natasha Parry
with Fidel Castro,
Cuba, 1953.

Paul Scofield as a mould-breaking
King Lear, Stratford, 1962.

Paul Scofield as Lear
in the film of *King Lear*, 1969.

Descent into savagery, *Lord of the Flies*, 1963.

The inmates of Charenton asylum in the pit, *The Marat/Sade*, 1964.

At work on the Vietnam War material for *US*, 1966, with Peter Brook (*centre*);
Michael Kustow, Patrick O'Donnell, Hugh Sullivan, Clifford Rose (*to the right*);
Mike Pratt, Barrie Stanton (*to the left*); and stage management (*upstage*).

Model of Sally Jacobs' design for *A Midsummer Night's Dream*, 1970.

Snug the Joiner (Hugh Keays Byrne) transformed into Lion frightening
the 'mechanicals' as Puck (John Kane) looks on, *A Midsummer Night's Dream*,
Stratford, 1970.

The trapeze-borne Oberon (Alan Howard) and Puck (John Kane) in the fairy realm
above Bottom (David Waller) in the arms of Titania (Sara Kestelman),
A Midsummer Night's Dream, Stratford, 1970.

Brook and Ted Hughes, poet and *Orghast* playwright, Persia, 1971.

Orghast at Persepolis in rehearsal, 1971.

The birds set out on their voyage of discovery, *The Conference of the Birds*,
Bouffes du Nord, 1979.

Scenes from *The Mahabharata*, 1989. Arjuna (Vittorio Mezzogiorno), the hero.

Lord Ganesha, the scribe of the *Mahabharata*.

The battle begins.

The aftermath of battle.

Drona (Yoshi Oida)
drowned in his own
blood.

Peter Brook demonstrating at a theatre day in the Bouffes du Nord, 1982.

The Man Who, Bouffes du Nord, 1993. Yoshi Oida as mental patient.

Matilda (Marianne Jean-Baptiste) and her 'lover', *The Suit*, Bouffes du Nord, 1999.

Hamlet (Adrian Lester, *back left*) watches the player king re-enact the murder of his father. *The Tragedy of Hamlet*, Bouffes du Nord, 2000.

Sotigui Kouyate as Tierno Bokar, Bouffes du Nord, 2004.

then more Arabs, more flames, until the action seems to dissolve in a sheet of fire . . . The result is electrifying: naked hatred is present on the stage. In both cases we are presented with an image apparently derived out of fantasy but which, like Picasso's *Guernica*, is a poetic distillation which contains a truth more bright than reality.'

Two members of the Lord Chamberlain's staff, Mr Heriot and Mr Hill, attended a Donmar showing to judge whether the play might be authorised for public performance. 'The author seems preoccupied with anal eroticism,' Heriot wrote wonderingly, before banning the play's roll-call of profana: 'fucking, pissing, farting, screwing, shit, b'Jesus, unbutton my fly, bugger off, bullshit.' 'Forbid all farting,' he then instructed, as well as 'up my arse . . . a spot of sperm . . . it was my pair of balls. Otherwise recommended for licence.' The Lord Chamberlain did not license the play, and it was given two performances only to invited audiences.

Then came a piece of theatrical manna from heaven: Martin Esslin, the dramaturg of BBC Radio, rang Brook from his office and enthused about a play which had just been sent to him from Germany. Brook read it overnight, and it was translated in twenty-four hours. The Royal Shakespeare Company immediately bought an option on it, beating the National Theatre, which had sent Kenneth Tynan to see it in Berlin. It was by the Swedish playwright Peter Weiss and was known as *The Marat/Sade*. Or to give it its full erudite, cod-eighteenth-century title, *The Persecution and Assassination of Marat as Performed by the Inmates of the Asylum of Charenton under the Direction of the Marquis de Sade.*

It's not hard to see where some of the theatrical seeds of Brook's stunning production of *The Marat/Sade* sprang from. The effigies of the powerful, improvised out of broomsticks and vegetables, as in *The Screens*. The buckets of paint and brushes, the discontinuous playing, and sub-textual shifts, as in *Theatre of Cruelty*. The cool Brechtian semiology of the stage-space, as Brook had practised it in Dürrenmatt's *The Visit*. The parade of the world's follies and crimes, as in Lear's accusations in his make-believe courtroom in *King Lear*.

But none of these encompasses the 'something more' that people who saw his production of *The Marat/Sade* still recall, and that Bernard Levin, this time convincing in his enthusiasm, tried to capture: 'Its breadth, its totality, its breathtakingly rapid and varied use of every imaginable technique, dramatic device, stage-picture, form of movement, speech and song make it as close as this imperfect world is ever likely to get to the *Gesamtkunst-werk* of which Richard Wagner dreamed, in which every element, every force that the theatre could provide would fuse in one overwhelming experience.'

Brook was energised by the shifting planes and abrupt gear-changes of Weiss' play:

> Starting with its title, everything about this play is designed to crack the spectator on the jaw, then douse him with ice-cold water, then force him to assess intelligently what has happened to him, then give him a kick in the balls, then bring him back to his senses again. It's not exactly Brecht and it's not Shakespeare either but it's very Elizabethan and very much of our time. Weiss' force is not only in the quantity of instruments he uses; it is above all in the jangle produced by the clash of styles. Everything is put in its place by its neighbour – the serious by the comic, the noble by the popular, the literary by the crude, the intellectual by the physical: the abstraction is vivified by the stage image, the violence illuminated by the cool flow of thought. The strands of meaning of the play pass to and fro through its structure and the result is a very complex form: like in Genet it is a hall of mirrors or a corridor of echoes – and one must keep looking front and back all the time to reach the author's sense.

Brook stage mastery took this dynamism to its utmost, filling and emptying his designer Sally Jacobs' tiled, slatted bath-house with abrupt transformations. When the bath-house was empty, it was hard not to be chilled by its reminder of an Auschwitz shower-room awaiting its victims.

Critics who complained that the play lacked a plot missed the point. It had a plot – Charlotte Corday's murder of Marat. That operated in one time frame, the early fervour of the French Revolution, which is refracted through quarrelling viewpoints: Marat's self-sacrificing service to the Revolution, de Sade's tormented individualism, the sarcasm of the fairground quartet, cynical entertainers of the street, and the urgency of the radical Socialist, Jacques Roux.

But the action of *The Marat/Sade* simultaneously operated in another time frame: the here-and-now of the performance in the asylum, as Coulmier, Charenton's director, displayed the progressive treatment of his patients to an audience of Parisian *bien-pensants*. Fifteen years after the Revolution, the rationality of the scientist was constantly punctured by insurgent inmates, who were clubbed to the floor when they got out of hand. And finally, there was the here-and-now of today. The horde of madmen advanced on us, the audience in the auditorium, here and now, crying 'We want our revolution *now*!' – a cry that resonated most strongly when they performed in America, where the civil rights movement was at its height.

Brook had asked the Royal Shakespeare Company to suggest a poet to make a new version from Geoffrey Skelton's literal translation, since the text required a spectrum of verse styles. Jeremy Brooks, the RSC's literary manager, knew Adrian Mitchell, a radical poet, and recommended him. Mitchell received the Skelton translation sixteen days before rehearsals were due to start, and meeting Brook for the first time, had an arresting image of the man. 'I thought, this man looks like a rhinoceros. I think I can say that because very soon when I began to get to know him, he looked to me beautiful. But at first, the shape of his head and his proboscis reminded me of rhinos. I got to love that face; it's a very wise face, and of course there are those astonishing eyes, the power of those blue eyes. He explained very carefully what he wanted: would I do a couple of pages. So I went and did them as a test piece overnight and delivered them next day. He said yeah, I want you to do it. It was about ten days before rehearsals started.'

But Brook didn't need a script for the first days of rehearsal. He set the actors to 'find the madmen in themselves' through a mixture of research – nineteenth-century medical textbooks, the paintings of Hogarth and Goya, meetings with psychoanalysts and visits to mental hospitals. Mitchell watched this prolonged process of immersion in madness:

I was watching these actors starting to pretend to be mad, from their experiences of mad people. The ones that worked best were based on actual people they knew who were nutty. But of course, as Peter explained, nuttiness is different now, because we have drugs and people are drugged up to the hilt if they're thought to be violent.

It was an incredible company to watch rehearsing. There was Patrick Magee who was like a volcano, a volcano thirsting for Guinness; he was lovely but intimidating. He didn't need to intimidate me – I was pretty scared of him anyway. It was my first real job in the theatre and apparently I was going around looking as if I was going to be hit.

Mitchell was pushing himself to the limit to keep pace with rehearsals, punching out couplets, free verse and song lyrics while holding down a job on the *Sun* newspaper.

I was very tired a lot of the time. Rehearsals all day and writing all night – I was also a TV critic at the time. I don't think Peter understood the situation. There was a speech I gave him which he read and laughed. I said 'What's funny about it?' 'It's this bit where Marat says "I sank into the swamps of over-work,"' he said. 'What's so funny about that?' I said. 'I'm sinking into the swamps of overwork, Peter. I'm not complaining but I know I'm working more than my brain can take.' He said, 'There's no such thing – the brain's very flexible.' That surprised me, but I didn't resent it. I would have worked to death for Peter and for that show and for that company.

Brook went on, day after day, asking the actors to improvise madness, and not to repeat themselves. Mitchell kept bringing in hastily typed new sections of the play. Brook didn't give much in the way of direction, just spoke to individual actors quietly, in a corner of the Donmar rehearsal room, as the new sections came in. Insecurity was coming to a head among the company, as Mitchell saw.

They had to be on stage through the whole play, often with only a few lines. People were going on working and working on madness, and Peter wasn't telling them what to do, he was saying, 'You can't do anything wrong, just do it, its okay, don't worry.' He must have known exactly when the tipping point came.

One day, when we went back after lunch, Peter called the actors together and said 'Now come round, I want to remind you of some things.' To one actor he would say something like, 'Freddie, remember what you were doing last Wednesday when you were imitating that friend of yours who lives in Brazil – that's perfect, but if you could give us a bit of the fear which you were working on yesterday and fuse that with it, that would be fantastic.' And he went through everyone, told them what he wanted from what they'd created.

When the play opened in London, it became the prize exhibit in the so-called 'dirty plays row'. Emile Littler, a governor of the Royal Shakespeare Company, accused Peter Hall of turning over the Aldwych Theatre to 'dirty plays'. He deplored David Rudkin's *Afore Night Come*, in which an old man is murdered and decapitated; Roger Vitrac's scabrous, Surrealist play about childhood, *Victor*; Samuel Beckett's *Endgame*; and first and foremost, *The Marat/Sade*. Littler, backed by Keith Prowse, owner of London's largest ticket agency, and Peter Cadbury, a right-wing moralist, traded blows with Peter Hall, who replied by calling for Littler's resignation as an RSC governor.

The most surprising voice of reason came from the conservative play-wright Terence Rattigan. 'I do think,' he wrote to *The Times*, 'that Mr Cadbury's and Mr Littler's mildly fatuous but no doubt well-meaning vapourings on the nature of entertainment, silly-seasoned by the press into a mildly fatuous news item, have been allowed, with resignations of responsible people from responsible posts, and television nightly treating the subject as a crisis of national importance, to get entirely out of hand. I would like to see it silly-seasoned back to its original, miniscule dimensions.' But before it did so, it had inflamed the critical atmosphere. Some reviewers, attuned to mainstream theatre conventions, could not see the production's radicalness or the play's intense debate about revolution because of its 'general turbulence' (John Gross); 'Brook's direction never allows a moment to dry off' (Alan Brien). Others recognised a play of embodied thought. 'What Peter Weiss has produced is an image which . . . revolves and unfurls itself, throwing off glints of possible meaning from different aspects, without reaching any fixed premise or conclusion. The image is superbly powerful, a living Géricault: a dungeon of bleached, fantastic ghosts mopping and mowing round the waxy tableau of death in cold water . . . De Sade's great cry in the play, "This is a world of bodies", gives Brook the license to indulge his strongest gift, the building of stage-pictures out of massed, writhing limbs.'

In *Burnt Bridges*, his memoir of the 1960s, Charles Marowitz rather acidly noted how Brook was defining his own unique field of work:

> One way to transcend criticism is to create an artifact so unique that conventional criteria cannot be applied to it. A play must answer a play's critics, but a performance piece, a happening, a surrealist vaudeville, an eight-hour evocation of ancient rites and unfamiliar mythology eludes the critical tentacles of those who would clutch, squeeze and ultimately label what artists do. By creating outside the established convention, you rob convention of its power to circumscribe you.

In January 1966, *The Marat/Sade* opened in New York at the Martin Beck Theater, one of Broadway's prime sites. It was presented by David Merrick, one of its most buccaneering impresarios. Although initial audiences were disconcerted, the response picked up rapidly, prompted by some discreet marketing of its sex and violence, and by every New Yorker's deep-seated conviction that everyone is a dangerous lunatic out to get you. The play also took on the colouring of America's great racial fracture, the *sans-culottes* of revolutionary Paris echoing the civil rights marchers and rioters. In such ways does a molten theatrical image draw to itself society's splinters.

Stanley Kauffman in the *New York Times* caught the kinetic energy of Brook's production: '[It] surges, opens and narrows like the iris of a camera, using its members in mad, stuttering, but carefully composed movement.' The *Herald Tribune's* critic Walter Kerr evoked a heap of humanity out of Breugel or Bosch: 'The untormented faces beneath matted hair, with mismatched eyes or with skulls cracked open like reddened eggs mesmerise us. Together they are a chorus of universally condemned mankind, the mankind that continues to perpetuate its follies today, and when their voices mass they make a singing sound of doom, due tomorrow, not the day after.'

In a follow-up piece, though, Kerr questioned the value of Weiss' text, claiming that Brook had been obliged to supply the author's deficiencies. This started a running debate about the play, with Robert Brustein, drama critic for the *New Republic*, and Susan Sontag, modernism's most eloquent advocate, defending its vertiginous gear-shifts, while Harold Clurman, founder of the famous 1930s Group Theatre, agreed with Kerr that, once the shock of the spectacular shell of the production had worn off, 'all the lovely tools of total theatre will in the end produce little more than the equivalent of sober-sided revue sketches.'

Brook maintained a complete loyalty to Peter Weiss and his kaleidoscopic play: 'The author had an extraordinarily complex and daring vision, and one that was very hard for him to put down on paper. The nearest he could get was a title which reflects a complex stage machine we had to recapture. And I think that what we do on stage, for better or worse, is exactly what the author was seeing on the stage of his mind, seeing in his vision.'

With his film of *The Marat/Sade*, shot in seventeen days in May 1966, Brook managed to combine the thrust of live theatre with the precision of film. David Picker, the head of United Artists, offered Brook's producer Michael Birkett $250,000 – a low budget for a feature film – on the basis that Brook could make the film any way he wanted, without any interference, provided it came in on time and on budget. This meant, said Brook, 'keeping as close as possible to the stage version, which was rehearsed and ready. At the same time, I wanted to see if a purely cinematic language could be found that would take us away from the deadliness of the filmed play and capture a purely cinematic excitement.'

The film drove forward on the rhythm and pulse of the playing, ripened by eighteen months' performances. 'With three, sometimes four cameras working non-stop and burning up yards of celluloid,' wrote Brook, 'we covered the production like a boxing match. The cameras advanced and retreated, twisted and whirled, trying to behave like what goes on in a spectator's head and simulate his experience, attempting to follow the contradictory flashes of thought and stomach blows with which Peter Weiss had filled his madhouse.' Brook's indispensable ally in this *corrida* was his cinematographer David Watkin. Together, they worked out an overall lighting plot which covered the entire set, within which there were special spots where close-ups and groups could be shot. Opaque white windows were added to Sally Jacobs' set; lit from behind, they diffused an overall wash of white light. Setting a group of madmen in silhouette against this white glare and turning the lens out of focus produced abstract, prismatic outlines reminiscent of the calcinated figures of Giacometti. Time and place vanished with such images: one was looking at the burnt ruins of humanity.

Brook keeps the metaphorical force of make-believe images from the stage. A bucket of paint becomes the guillotine's blood. Charlotte Corday knocks on Marat's non-existent door; the rat-tat-tat is provided by the herald's staff on the stage. The play of hands – Corday's, de Sade's – around the real knife with which she will murder Marat gives the action its multiple meanings – political, erotic and histrionic – for everything we see is make-believe, a charade played out by the insane.

At the same time, what Brook called the 'merciless literalism' of photography delivers the matter of madness, its straitjackets, blank stares, blinding rage, deep inertia, with the matter-of-factness of a Diane Arbus photograph. On one level, the film of *The Marat/Sade* is a distressing illustrated record of the behaviour of people called mad in an age before tranquillisers and anti-depressants. Then we are removed and distanced from being in the den with the inmates as the camera pulls back and we view the whole stage as if we were part of the Parisian audience of the day, peering through real bars. And in a final threatening free-for-all, in which Brook himself took charge of one of the hand-held cameras, the inmates literally rip the place apart, destroying the studio set – actually setting it on fire – a scene which could never have happened on stage.

'The difference between theatre and cinema', Brook said when the film was released, 'is that in cinema the power of the image is so great that it engulfs one . . . When the image is there in all its power, at the precise moment when it is being received, one can neither think, nor feel, nor imagine anything else.' In theatre, on the other hand, the conditions exist for that fluctuating, magnetic quality called 'presence'. 'The true theatrical relationship,' Brook continued, 'is like most human relationships between people: the degree of involvement is always varying. This is why theatre permits one to experience something in an incredibly powerful way and at the same time to retain a certain freedom.'

In 1964, nearly midway through a decade in which his gifts as a director were becoming more varied, more violent, more potent, Brook accepted an invitation to give a series of lectures which became the basis of a vastly influential book on theatre. It came from Granada Television, with which, through his friendship with its founder Sidney Bernstein, he already had connections; indeed it was for Granada that he had made his long, and long-lost, interview with Gordon Craig as a young man. He accepted their invitation because it prompted him to set down comprehensively what he'd been doing in the theatre since he started – and because his fee would pay for a long-planned trip to Afghanistan. He turned the lecture series into *The Empty Space*, which, translated into sixteen languages, has become something of a bible for theatre-makers. Its two opening sentences are arguably the most inspiring theatre writing since Aristotle. 'I can take any empty space and call it a bare stage. A man walks across this empty space whilst someone else is watching him, and this is all that is needed for an act of theatre to begin.'

Granada had endowed a lecture series to be delivered at universities in the north of England – Manchester, Keele, Hull and Sheffield. Brook carefully prepared his lectures through the latter part of 1964, and delivered the first one, 'The Deadly Theatre', on 1 February 1965 at Manchester University, in Granada's heartland. In his four lectures, Brook mapped out his now-famous four-part taxonomy of theatre – the Deadly, the Holy, the Rough and the Immediate. *The Empty Space* is a book compiled, like many of Brook's key texts, from a process of immediate delivery followed by distillation: into a speech delivered for a particular audience on a specific occasion, he splices additional material.

In *The Empty Space* you don't feel the joins; it moves smoothly between magisterial abstractions, a skill he had certainly sharpened in all his years speaking and thinking in French, and easygoing vernacular anecdote. He stumbles upon a performance among the rubble of 1945 Hamburg. He sees in close-up the backstage absurdity of the opera house ('a nightmare of vast feuds over tiny details; of surrealist anecdotes that all turn round the same assertion: nothing needs to change'). He discovers the paradoxical limits to freedom in totally unconstrained experiment. With its touchstone of Shakespeare and 'the Elizabethan', *The Empty Space* is very English but in its dialectic and search for universals it is very French. The book's final chapter, 'The Immediate Theatre', is its most intimate. He insists there is no secret, no mystique to directing. He puts language on its tiptoes to convey the theatre's special gift of animating the present moment, making it more immediate, more packed.

Attacking the translation of Stanislavski's book as *Building a Character*, as if a character could be constructed like a wall, he offers an alternative analogy for the actor's creative process: the idea that a part is not built but born. Here a French comparison helps him sharpen the argument.

> The actor must destroy and abandon his results even if what he picks up is almost the same. This is easier for French actors than for English ones, because temperamentally they are more open to the idea that nothing is any good. And this is the only way that a part, instead of being built, can be born. The role that has been *built* is the same every night – except that it slowly erodes. For the part that is born to be the same it must always be reborn, which makes it always different. Of course, particularly in a long run, the effort of daily re-creation becomes unbearable, and this is where the experienced creative artist is compelled to fall back on a second level called technique to carry him through.

This is not the voice in which he wrote his call-to-arms pieces in *Encore*, it no longer stands in the slipstream of Gordon Craig's rhetoric, the rallying cries of Artaud, the impassive theoretical analyses of Brecht. Voices like these can be found in *The Empty Space*; but the final chapter is quieter, more ruminative.

'When a performance is over, what remains?' he asks. 'Fun can be forgotten, but powerful emotion also disappears and good arguments lose their thread. When emotion and argument are harnessed to a wish from the audience to see more clearly into itself – then something in the mind burns. The event scorches on to the memory an outline, a taste, a trace, a smell – a picture. It is the play's central image that remains, its silhouette, and if the elements are rightly blended this silhouette will be its meaning, this shape will be the essence of what it has to say.'

He turns to three words in the French language to clinch his description of what is needed to bring this theatre event about: *répétition, représentation, assistance*. Like many an expatriate, Brook is struck by the slight disjunction of meaning that the same set of letters takes in another language. *Répétition*, the French word for rehearsal, confronts the fact that things have to be repeated in rehearsal until one day a spark may flash and an insight take root. 'Anyone who refuses the challenge of repetition knows that certain regions of expression are automatically barred to him.' But at the same time, repetition leads to 'all that is meaningless in tradition: the soul-destroying long run, the understudy rehearsals, all that sensitive actors dread'.

What lifts theatre out of the rut of repetition is what is evoked by the French word for performance – *représentation*. A performance in this sense is not just another delivery of what has been rehearsed and repeated. It is 'a making present'; 'something that once was, now is'; 'it takes yesterday's action and makes it live again in every one of its aspects – including its immediacy.'

And finally, Brook comes to the audience. French has many words for theatregoers – *le public, les spectateurs, l'assistance* – but Brook seized on the one that strikes the Anglo-Saxon ear most strangely: *assistance*. 'I watch a play – *j'assiste à une piece*.' The actor, says Brook, may have gone through the whole creative process of turning rehearsal into re-creation and yet, faced with a dull, predictable or detached audience, his work may crash to the ground.

> This is where the meaning of 'assistance' in the French term is needed. Occasionally, on what he calls a 'good night', the actor encounters an audience that by chance brings an active interest and life to its watching role – this audience assists. With this assistance, the assistance of eyes and focus and desires and enjoyment and concentration, repetition turns into represen-tation. Then the word representation no longer separates actor and audience, show and public: it envelops them: what is present for one is present for the other.

Brook reminds us that the essence of the theatre event still eludes static definition, because truth and meaning in the theatre are always on the move, and one can always begin again. In a glimpse of personal insight into why theatre matters for him, why making theatre gives him a metaphor for renewal, Brook affirms that 'unlike a book, the theatre always has one special characteristic. It is always possible to start again. In life this is a myth; we ourselves can never go back on anything. New leaves never turn, clocks never go back, we can never have a second chance. In the theatre the slate is wiped clean all the time.'

By the mid sixties, the Vietnam War had begun to eat into public con-sciousness and the body politic. The theatre responded to America's military and political mobilisation with a movement, soon labelled 'theatre of fact', which set out in documentary style to explore the drama of political life. Even if the first examples of this were not directly linked to the Vietnam War, they bore witness to a widespread new awareness of – and scepticism about – the actions of politicians and public figures. The rhetoric of history was thrust at us by television and newspapers; perhaps the theatre could distil an essence of truth from the flood of reporting, or de-mystify media rhetoric by holding up language for inspection.

In the spring of 1965, Brook received a copy of Peter Weiss' 'oratorio-stage-documentary', *The Investigation*, based on the concentration-camp trials that had recently concluded their two-year hearing in Frankfurt. Weiss had taken the mass of material – testimonies, interrogations, evidence – and structured it in the style of Dante's *Inferno*, breaking it down into cantos, with titles such as 'Zyklon B' and 'The Fire Ovens'. He had carved the words into a very modest verse form whose line-endings lifted the frequently appalling words of the prosecution, the witnesses and the accused to a level beyond the merely evidential. Thirteen theatres in East and West Germany had decided to present Weiss' spoken oratorio on the same night, 19 October 1965. This European co-production came about not only as an act of civic expres-sion but in Germany as a specific protest against the Bundestag's intention to end the statute of limitations on war crimes, and thus allow war criminals to go free.

When Brook learned of this theatrical solidarity, he wanted to associate the Royal Shakespeare Company with it. A late-night performance was arranged, with Brook and David Jones co-directing the entire Royal Shakespeare Aldwych company, on the same night as the European presentations. Brook wrote an acidic programme note, which not only introduced *The Investigation* but pointed ahead to his further questions about theatre: how could aesthetics and beauty co-exist with the barbarous worlds of Auschwitz and napalm? He began with a stream-of-consciousness sentence.

> It's the German's business not ours teutonic guilt complex it's all over it's buried a thing of the past what good will it do let's forget bygones be bygones no muck raking we know it by heart sick of it.
>
> What label can we put on Peter Weiss' script to make it respectable as theatre?
>
> How can we defend it against the predictable attacks?
>
> I don't know.
>
> I only know that hearing that 13 German theatres and also the Berliner Ensemble were making a collective manifestation with this play we felt this to be right and we wished to stand with them. We share their belief that the ingredients of the camps have not vanished from this world and that the topic of man's indifference is not yet out of date.
>
> I suppose I've never got over hearing Alain Resnais' film about the concentration camps described as 'beautiful'.
>
> With more time we could have prepared a more polished performance, built a set, made music. What for?
>
> We feel our job is to transmit this text at once – to whom it may concern.

There's a belligerence, an impatience, in this text which indicates the strength of Brook's anger and his burning dissatisfaction, not only about the concentration camps, but about the insufficiencies of an entire culture. There was one performance only of *The Investigation* – a reading from scripts, rehearsed over a weekend. It began at eleven p.m. and finished at two a.m. One by one, every actor of the Royal Shakespeare Company stepped into a semi-circle of red leather chairs, delivered a statement, was cross-examined, recovered memories, had memory lapses, told lies, all with the utmost transparency; acting at a minimal threshold, the actor not as character, but as chronicler. It had the sober authority of fact, transmitted by actors who were not impersonating but were as savagely impersonal as they could constrain themselves to be.

9

TELL ME LIES ABOUT VIETNAM
1966

Brook was now looking for every kind of Archimedes lever to prise open the box in which theatre had, as Arthur Miller said, 'hermetically sealed itself'. He could not fail to be aware of the conflicts which were shaking the rich part of the world to which the theatres of London, Paris and New York belonged. The war in Vietnam was increasingly becoming the focal point for disaffection and disquiet. Out of this turmoil, and out of Brook's own self-communion and self-questioning, came his most directly political and reflective theatre-piece, *US*.

Seeking a way to bring theatre up to the tempo and ferocity of the age, to hold a mirror, in Hamlet's words, to 'its form and pressure', Brook was writing with increased violence, as if the temper of the times licensed him to show even greater asperity. 'There are times when I am nauseated by the theatre, when its artificiality appals me, although at the very same moment I recognize that its formality is its strength. The birth of *US* was allied to the reaction of a group of us who quite suddenly felt that Vietnam was more powerful, more acute, more insistent a situation than any drama that already existed between covers.'

He knew it was time to test theatre against the convulsions of the Vietnam War, using as a title two letters, a U and an S, to articulate 'US': the United States of America, our friendly superpower, and 'us', our bewilderment, our rage and our torn certainties. As if by chance, Brook found an echo of the emotions swilling in and around him in the Hindu poem of the *Bhagavad-*

Gita, which a young Indian writer had brought into a workshop Brook was running. It's an exchange between the god Krishna and Arjuna the warrior, who comes to a halt on the battlefield, and learns that he is gripped between the difficulty of taking a right action and the impossibility of taking no action at all.

But Brook wanted to go beyond holy texts, indeed beyond all pieties. He drew on the counter-culture, of which he had not noticeably been a part, though in its own way the path he had been following in the sixties was nothing if not counter-cultural. Adrian Mitchell opened the way. In London in June 1965, Allen Ginsberg, the magus of American poetry, had joined British and European poets at the Albert Hall in *Wholly Communion*, an event which was a landmark in poetry, counter-cultural energy and political protest. Adrian Mitchell stood up before 7,000 people and, with clipped, syncopated rage, read his poem 'To Whom It May Concern', which, as well as being taken up by the anti-war movement, became a key song in *US*:

> You put your bombers in, you put your conscience out,
> You take the human being and you twist it all about
> So scrub my skin with women
> Chain my tongue with whisky
> Stuff my nose with garlic
> Coat my eyes with butter
> Fill my ears with silver
> Stick my legs in plaster
> Tell me lies about Vietnam.

Brook put to Peter Hall a challenging proposal: a play about Vietnam and us and the USA in the main London theatre of the publicly funded RSC. To make things even riskier, the experiment would start out with no script. Instead, on day one of rehearsal, there would be a mass of research documents – books, testimonies, films, videos – a long, fourteen-week rehearsal period, and a group of creators – playwright Charles Wood, assistant director Geoffrey Reeves, who had done bold work at the Royal Court and the National, and Albert Hunt, who wrote acute theatre criticism for *New Society* and had developed political pageants at the theatre department of Bradford College of Art. Mike Stott and I, working with Brook for the first time, were responsible for documentary material, Adrian Mitchell and the jazz-influenced composer Richard Peaslee for the songs. Designer Sally Jacobs soon created a gigantic horror-comic effigy of a soldier which was to hang from the proscenium arch at the Aldwych, bleeding the war into the auditorium.

Work on *US* began in December 1965 with an immersion by the team in every kind of material, not only about the war in Vietnam, but about the pop culture that sometimes opposed the war, and sometimes gave it a mythology, especially in America. History books and *Marvel* comic books; the US Senate hearings on Vietnam and China and the writings of John Cage; the history of Vietnam and monographs on Happenings; TV documentaries and reports; Lyndon Johnson's speeches and Mao's *Little Red Book*; rock and roll and the *Bhagavad Gita*. People came in to see us – button-down types from the US Embassy, Buddhist monks in saffron robes, war reporters, news correspondents.

Brook talked about an American Quaker, Norman Morrison, who had burned himself to death, following the example of the Buddhists of Hué, whose self-immolation had toppled a local warlord.

Brook was fascinated by the New York avant-garde, and asked the actors to improvise on Happenings, especially on John Cage's 'Composition 1960 number five', in which a butterfly is turned loose in the concert hall, and the piece is the sound of its wings fluttering. 'Mike Williams suddenly demonstrated the kind of theatre language we were looking for,' wrote Albert Hunt, 'by bringing together the world of the Buddhists and Quakers with the world of John Cage. He put a chair on a table, crumpled some paper and took a match. Then, speaking very simply the words of the letter about the butterfly piece, he climbed onto the chair, and pretended to drench himself in petrol. As he reached the words "Isn't it wonderful to listen to something you normally look at?", he struck the match.' Joseph Chaikin, the director of the off-off-Broadway troupe The Open Theater, which Brook had seen in New York, arrived and wrote back uneasily to his playwright friend Jean-Claude van Itallie about the rehearsal work:

July 6, 1966: Peter was interested in NY happenings. But his interest was to show the decadence, the emptiness of the happenings and the people making them. He's very interested, as the whole company is, in American values. That is, they are interested in looking into the fact that nothing is valued over anything else except money, of course, because 10 is greater than 9. The company is very fired up about the similarities of the American myth figures – James Stewart, Johnson, John Cage, Andy Warhol, etc. Even though the attitude is a sensitive and understanding one, these British are really filled with alarm about what's going to happen, because America has lost its rocker.

A Vietnamese monk from the Vihara on Haverstock Hill came to talk to the cast about war and non-violence; a tiny man, on the brink of tears. Albert Hunt noted that when someone put Brook's original question to him: Would he fight? the monk answered that he himself would not fight, but the soldiers would fight – that was their job.

While improvisations and interviews continued in London, Peter had slipped over to Paris, met the Polish theatre director Jerzy Grotowski, and invited him to come and work with the group in London. He was looking for a way to get beyond the well-worn social and political arguments, and touch the furies that perpetuated the war, and the energies that might end it, visible in the actors' bodies. He believed that letting Grotowski into the process would shake up certainties and dynamite prepared positions.

When Grotowski walked into the rehearsal room, I had not seen him for five years, since I made what felt like a pilgrimage to his tiny 'theatre-laboratory' in the small Silesian town of Opole. A friend at the Lodz film school had made his graduation film about Grotowski, and invited me to come to Poland in 1961, to see the work and meet the man. I had shown the film to Brook, who was immediately gripped, met him, and struck up one of the most formative relationships in his work and his life. Grotowski was exacting and uncompromising, a director in the line of Meyerhold and Vaghtangov, a teacher in the tradition of the seer and the shaman. Picking his way through the thorns of Communist Poland, he had run a theatrical research institute and a tiny theatre in a dull industrial town that had once been part of Germany. He travelled widely in the East, learning and passing on the traditions of India, China and central Asia. He mounted classic plays or montages of texts, because the censors weren't equipped to see the transgressive force of his *mise-en-scène*, and the script on the page looked harmless enough. After the declaration of martial law in Poland in 1981, Grotowski's work was finally closed down, and he left for the West the following year, with Ryszard Cieslak, his astounding leading actor, who came with him to the *US* workshops. Grotowski in 1966 was no different from the way he had struck me first in a bare little café in Opole, smoking incessantly, thin, excitable, dressed in black, with dark glasses, very white skin and small, plump hands. Once more I felt in the presence of a zeal that might as properly have been found in a Catholic crusader or a Communist militant. Grotowski may have seemed unworldly, but when it came to money or politics he was sharp as a pin; Brook was urbane, but Grotowski reinforced Brook's other impulse – towards severity, discipline and a continual work of spiritual refinement.

With Ryszard Cieslak, Grotowski took our actors through two taxing weeks of 'psycho-physical' work. Writing about Grotowski in 1968, Brook emphasised the confidentiality of the work, and its impact. Refusing to describe what the work with Grotowski was, Brook nonetheless went on to say what it did. Borrowing a term from Gurdjieff, who prescribed the giving of 'shocks' to awaken 'sleeping humanity', he described with existential sharpness Grotowski's effect on the actors:

> The shock of confronting himself in the face of simple irrefutable challenges.
> The shock of catching sight of his own evasions, tricks and clichés.
> The shock of sensing something of his own vast and untapped resources.
> The shock of being forced to question why he is an actor at all.
> The shock of being forced to recognize that such questions do exist and – despite a long English tradition of avoiding seriousness in theatrical art – the time comes when they must be faced. And of finding that he wants to face them.

In Grotowski, Brook had spotted a fellow theatre-worker with even more single-mindedness than himself, and with a battery of techniques. Of course, the societies and the theatres in which they worked were very different. Grotowski was the incarnation of Brook's Holy Theatre:

He runs a laboratory. He needs an audience occasionally. In small numbers. His tradition is Catholic – or anti-Catholic; in this case the two extremes meet. He is creating a form of service. We work in another country, another language, another tradition. Our aim is not a new Mass, but a new Elizabethan relationship – linking the private and the public, the intimate and the crowded, the secret and the open, the vulgar and the magical.

Rehearsal was now at the mid-point of its fourteen-week life, and Brook had gone to a far point of the actors' inner processes. He had seized on the brash energy of pop art, comic books and American heroes, explored the flat speech of soldiers on the battlefield and politicians in the US Senate, opened doors into Buddhist clarity, recalled the Hindu insights of Arjuna, listened to the butterfly wings of John Cage. But a rift was about to open which would test Brook's ability to hold the team together. One of his greatest gifts as a director is his ability to provoke a kind of psychological depth-charge. He chooses people from very different positions and backgrounds, and allows their situation and their differences to stretch to their utmost. Sometimes, as in *US*, almost to breaking point.

Some of the group, while appreciating the vocal and physical dexterity Grotowski had been able to draw from the actors in his two-week residency, found the reverent atmosphere that surrounded him – Brook impassively translating even his most demanding directions, becoming a mouthpiece of the Master – distasteful. Adrian Mitchell, who had been attending every rehearsal, went off to write song lyrics. Albert Hunt, repelled by an improvisation in which Glenda Jackson as Juliet had been forced to put up with Romeo's prolonged sexual advances, had split off with a group of supporting actors to carry out improvisations which he knew would never feature in the show. The extremity, the toughness on the self, which was part of Grotowski's appeal to Brook, was hard for many to take.

After Grotowski left, the team met to plan the next phase of the work. Mitchell and Hunt argued for a Dionysiac, song-studded, grotesque pantomime, extending the style of the comic-book scenes and the people's pageant history of Vietnam, intercutting them with hyper-realistic scenes of American soldiers and politicians. Brook said that after Grotowski's visit more thought had to be given to the question of form, and announced that he had invited Denis Cannan to join the team. Cannan and Brook had known each other since the fifties.

The group had been working without a playwright since Charles Wood had left to work on a movie. One interpretation of Cannan's arrival, said Hunt, was that 'we non-established playwrights had failed to come up with what Brook saw as a workable script, and that in his desperation he went to someone who had at least had plays on the London stage. An alternative explanation could be that he'd given the left-wing radicals their head and created something for a different kind of writer to bounce off, and that this is what he'd intended all along. I don't think Brook had intended anything all along; I think he thought he was genuinely open to ideas, if the ideas were good enough.'

In any event, the team agreed that the main focus of the action of part two would be the self-immolation by fire in protest against the war. The suicides had started with the Buddhists in Hué and had spread to America with the death on 2 November 1965 of the Quaker Norman Morrison, about whom Mitchell had written a poem. This story had horrified and haunted Brook, who saw it both as a desperate self-sacrifice and as a metaphor for religious fervour. Mitchell now says that Norman Morrison did what he did, 'to show the people of Vietnam that someone in the West – and an American too – cared enough, but now it's done, for ever, and there's no need to do it again. Much harder to go on living and struggling against the war. So I thought that too much concentration on that burning was not helpful. It ignores what it's about: people dropping a lot of fire, people burning thousands of people. The act of martyrdom becoming the focus of attention, instead of the mass slaughter.'

Nevertheless the second act of US became the story of a young Englishman, played by Mark Jones, determined to burn himself on the steps of the American Embassy, and of a young Englishwoman, played by Glenda Jackson, who probes his motives and tries to dissuade him. Its crucial speech, delivered by Glenda as if out of her own worst nightmare, brings the war right back home to the lawns of England:

So you end the war in Vietnam. Where's the next one? Thailand, Chile, Alabama? The things that will be needed are all ready in some carefully camouflaged quartermaster's store. The wire, the rope, the gas, the cardboard boxes they use for coffins in emergencies.

I WANT IT TO GET WORSE! I want it to come HERE!

In Peter Whitehead's documentary of the making of the play, *Benefit of the Doubt*, filmed during one Sunday on the Aldwych stage, Glenda is shot in tight close-up doing this speech. As she raises her voice here, her eyes glint with tears.

I want to see it in an English house, among the floral chintzes and the school blazers and the dog leads hanging in the hall. I would like us to be tested. I would like a fugitive to run to our doors and say hide me – and know if we hid him we might get shot and if we turned him away we would have to remember that forever. I would like to know which of my nice well-meaning acquaintances would collaborate, which would betray, which would talk first under torture – and which would become a torturer.

Whenever I heard this it always struck me as a kind of inherited nightmare, the tribal trauma of the son of an émigré, still wary, after so many years of success and recognition, that he would be 'outed' as an alien, treated with sadistic disdain by well-mannered Englishmen, as his Magdalen College professors had treated Peter and his father. Did Brook ever feel this? Or did Denis Cannan just intuit it and use it for his own self-accusation as an 'untested' Englishman?

But as Adrian Mitchell says, 'I didn't want it to come here. I wanted it to stop in Vietnam.' And so, after another late-night meeting, an alternative ending was offered. Hunt said, 'after Glenda had made her speech, one of us should walk onto the stage carrying a bunch of flowers and say, "That was marvellous, darling. Would you do it again?" When we suggested it to Brook, he assumed the hurt look he used to make you feel you were offending his deepest sensibilities, and that was the end of the argument.'

There were many such disagreements about this ending as the first night approached. But Peter stuck to the dramatic line which culminated in Glenda's speech, strengthening the songs and documentary scenes that alienated and punctured it. We were struggling with the limits of group authorship. But a further disagreement – about a butterfly – was still to come.

Taking a cue from the group's early work on American Happenings, that Zen-like piece by John Cage scored for the sound of a butterfly's wings, Brook asked Robert Lloyd, a trim figure in a white suit with black gloves, to pick his way through the stage full of motionless actors, carrying a small black box. Stopping behind the frozen figure of Mark Jones, he opened the box, inserted his hand, and released a butterfly. It fluttered and flew up into the roof of the Aldwych Theatre, drawn by the warmth of the spotlights. Then Lloyd released a second butterfly. Then, reaching into his pocket for a cigarette-lighter, he extracted a third, and set fire to it. Then everyone stood still, until the audience decided to leave.

This was the final litmus test of the evening, the last attempt to wrap around Cannan's self-mutilating rhetoric a skein of competing, distancing elements. One night, a brave, middle-aged woman climbed up on stage and tore the lighter out of the actor's hand, was confused to discover that the butterfly was paper, but turned to the audience in astonishment, and cried, 'You see, we can do something!' Brook was delighted by the gesture but warned that if anyone disclosed the trick again they would be forced to burn a real butterfly.

None of this could quite compete with Glenda's snarling dissatisfaction, and her final speech is what most audiences remember from the show. But just as powerful were the songs – Mitchell's lyrics and Peaslee's deft, infectious jazz score. 'Tell Me Lies', a child's counting song of moral anguish; 'Make and Break', in which three Americans tout rifles and surgical scalpels, as they alternately 'maim by night and heal by day'; and the joyful talkin' blues 'Moon Over Minnesota', celebrating the 'sewer-realist' protest of Barry Bondhus of Big Lake, Minnesota, father of ten, who goes to the local draft board office and 'lumps in, dumps in . . . two full buckets of human excrement' rather than send his ten sons to Vietnam.

In *US*, self-accusation and moral paralysis struggled with exuberance and the spirit of jazz. It was Brook's first tussle with not one living playwright, but a whole group of author-collaborators, dealing with a subject that was in every sense a burning issue, a war that was being waged as they performed. What drove Brook and infuriated many who criticised the show from an anti-war position, was the quest to go beyond protest, beyond having 'a position', 'a point of view'. Just when any spectator might feel that his convictions or prejudices were confirmed, the piece, like a slippery fish, wriggled and turned and upset fixed positions. It was a pyrotechnic, Meyerholdian montage, a kaleidoscope of furies and guilts, more dazzling than most musicals, made by a man fiercely in search of a human centre in an inhuman war. It is not only surprising that the piece came to fruition on the Royal Shakespeare's main stage, despite the Lord Chamberlain's attempts to emasculate it, and even to withdraw the RSC's grant. It is a miracle, given the strength of the disparate viewpoints, that Brook managed to hold together a fissiparous group and make a piece that deployed arguments, developed a dramatic line and was unmistakably theatre. Looking back now, from a time in which much 'political theatre' frequently sacrifices theatrical resources to documentary or 'verbatim' presentations, *US* still stands as a template of what theatre about immediate conflicts can be.

The most notorious reaction to the show came from Kenneth Tynan. As he sat in the Aldwych Theatre stalls after Bob Lloyd had 'burned the butterfly' and watched the entire cast stand motionless, reflective and, in his view, ineffably superior, he could not restrain himself from calling out, 'Are you waiting for us or are we waiting for you?' In a letter to Robert David Macdonald, the translator of Rolf Hochhuth's political play about Churchill, *The Soldiers*, which he was trying to get the National Theatre to stage, Tynan elaborated: '*The Soldiers* is all that Peter Brook's *US* isn't – it is precise and specific instead of vague and general, it's informed and impassioned instead of ignorant and tepid and it has a blessedly fearless point of view.' But Hochhuth's play, which, it is worth pointing out, never made it to the National, was dealing with events half a century in the past, not with a war that was daily breaking news.

It was this matter of 'having a point of view' that engaged Brook the most. He took his reservations about agit-prop theatre to a Dadaist extreme, when we held a post-show discussion with the public, in a small – and packed – Catholic church hall off Leicester Square. Brook and the rest of the team sat behind a long table, facing the audience. Hanging from its front were hand-painted signs, saying OPINIONS COST MONEY. IT'S FREE IF YOU

SPEAK. YOU MUST PAY IF WE ANSWER. IF WE SPEAK FIRST, WE MUST PAY.

We sat there and sat there. The audience waited, and began to get impatient. What the hell was this all about? We've come to get some answers! In the annoyed silence, a sound could be heard, the sound of coins chinking in buckets, which were being carried around by stage managers. 'For God's sake, what do you think you're doing,' asked one angry punter. 'Have you paid?' replied Brook. 'If you pay, we'll give you our opinion.'

No one wanted to put money into the buckets. Who would crack first? After a while the penny, as it were, dropped, and people began to discuss the play, its politics and morality, its relevance to Britain now, between themselves. 'It's up to us to talk,' said someone. 'There are no experts.' The panel became the audience to a lively debate. Brook looked satisfied, though his interventions in the debate showed a kind of clipped fury, as if the tensions of making a collective show and his dissatisfaction at English milk-and-water attitudes were still at boiling-point.

The US experience became a watershed for Brook's beliefs about the powers and limits of political theatre. 'If democracy means respect for the individual,' he wrote, 'true political theatre means trusting each individual in the audience to reach his or her own conclusions, once the act of theatre has performed its legitimate function of bringing the hidden complexities of a situation into light . . . A great dramatist can without judgement launch opposing characters against one another, so an audience can be at one and the same time inside and outside them; both successively for, against and neutral.'

This was echoed in one of the most striking press responses to US. Writing in the Listener, the Bishop of Woolwich saw US as a liturgy, because it 'involves its participants in the saving acts of their redemption'. Though his account slightly cleans up the show's rudeness and raucousness, the Bishop hits the nail on the head in his conclusion: 'The reiterated theme is of a reality too painful to be evaded and too profound to admit of any verbal or rational solution. It can be resolved only in action which is itself suffering, and in suffering which is itself action. It is not specifically Christian: far from it. It spoke of confession but not of absolution, of fraction but not of communion. It judged, but it did not pretend to save.'

Though Brook is not a Christian, nor what the French would call *un militant*, the most common question he had to answer about *US* was, 'Do you imagine your play will stop the war?' It was a disguised put-down for which Brook had a reply:

> If no act of theatre can stop a war, if it can neither influence a nation nor a government nor a city, this does not mean that it is impossible for a theatre to be both objective and political. An auditorium is like a small restaurant whose responsibility is to nourish its customer. In a theatre perhaps a hundred and rarely more than a thousand people come to a performance: the field is circumscribed by the walls of the place and duration of the event – this is precisely where our responsibility to provide good food begins and ends. A performance has the possibility to turn words about a better life into direct experience, and in this way it can be a powerful antidote to despair. There is only one test: do the spectators leave the playhouse with slightly more courage, more strength, than when they came in? If the answer is yes, then the food is healthy.

When the stage show of *US* ended its well-attended run, Brook took fragments of it – songs, speeches, documentary material – and, together with improvised and *verité* scenes of London in 1967, made a feature film, *Tell Me Lies – A Film About London*. The protagonist of this cinematic collage, as in the stage play, is the actor, Mark Jones. His indignation drives him into a picaresque journey through London from a protest march to an Angry Arts festival, from fundraising tea-parties in Hampstead to direct action in Grosvenor Square. In a scene which says much about Brook's opinion of England's political and intellectual culture, Mark confronts a bunch of silver-tongued politicians and pundits at a party, including the sarcastic novelist, Kingsley Amis, the brittle editor of the *Sunday Telegraph*, Peregrine Worsthorne, and two gentlemanly Labour MPs, Tom Driberg and Ivor Richards. They run rings around his arguments, but Brook's extended sequence of their mannered and highly comic debating-chamber fluency seems to pass a damning judgement on a section of society he had been groomed and educated to join. Then Mark meets Stokely Carmichael, the American Black Power activist, who tells him with quiet vehemence that there's no hope for the white race, and three left-wing scientists who lecture him about the bad deeds of the Americans and a Buddhist priest who seems above the fray. Brook combines a hand-held, rough style, inspired by the *cinéma-vérité* movement of the time, punctuated with dramatically lit, tightly edited song-sequences, filmed as if for a musical but subverted by horrifying newsreel footage. The stylistic span of *Tell Me Lies* is as exhilarating as its pessimism about the likelihood of change is bleak.

10

A MYTH, A DREAM, A DEPARTURE
1968–70

By the late 1960s, Laurence Olivier's National Theatre at the Old Vic was riding high. Blessed with a company which included John Gielgud, Irene Worth, Robert Stephens, Maggie Smith; a quartet of dynamic directors – Bill Gaskill, Michael Blakemore, John Dexter, Jonathan Miller; prodded by an inventive literary manager, Kenneth Tynan, and led by a titanic actor-manager, Olivier himself, it had produced a stream of successful productions. Now Olivier, prompted by Tynan, wanted to direct Gielgud in a relative curiosity, the Roman dramatist Seneca's *Oedipus*. Then Olivier fell ill, the first signs of what was to become a prolonged and debilitating decline. Brook, who was completing the *Marat/Sade* film, was approached and agreed to direct, stipulating a ten-week rehearsal period for a piece less than ninety minutes long. He needed this time, he said, for his new rehearsal methods, to stretch and extend the actors of the National's ensemble, with whom he had not worked before.

A translation made for BBC Radio by David Turner already existed, but Brook wanted the text to be handled by a greater talent, and approached the poet Ted Hughes. Hughes had an affinity for myths – he studied anthropology at Cambridge – and he had a poet's ability to bring the old stories fiercely into the present, to find the mythical dimension of contemporary experience. His verse had a brutal, hard-wrought immediacy that spoke to Brook's own impatience and iconoclasm. (David Turner was generous enough to say that Hughes' version was on another plane altogether.)

Hughes was still writing the script until halfway through rehearsal, so there was ample time for Brook to explore with his actors. The Northern Irish actor Colin Blakeley, who played Creon, explained in a characteristically robust interview how the actors found their way, for Brook imposed very little:

> He would only tell us what not to do. So we just rummaged about within ourselves and in ten weeks came up with something to suit our requirements, and, ultimately, his too . . . For instance, we connected the speeches to a deliberate type of breathing, not normal – the kind one uses in voice exercises. This idea grew out of our listening to recordings from various primitive tribes . . . But we didn't want to copy a native ritual, so we made up our own rituals. Breathing was our beginning.

The exercises involved communicating without language; at times the actors banished voice altogether and just aimed to communicate through breathing in and out. Blakeley described an exercise which used Hieronymus Bosch's painting of hell: 'We had to describe this painting, without words, to a blindfolded actress – as if we were dumb and she were blind.' As a member of the company which Olivier had trained to speak with clarity and force, Blakeley also embraced Brook's non-verbal rehearsal process: 'You always, I think, start from the premise that you should be able to do a play without the words. If you can do a play without the words, and get some emotional meaning, then you know you have really understood the play.'

Everyone, Gielgud included, did the rehearsal exercises. Brook describes Gielgud, the past master of beautiful and thoughtful textual delivery in the British theatre, getting to grips with these new methods, surrounded by a much younger company, many of whom rejected the well-groomed theatre which, in their eyes, Gielgud stood for:

> John knew that after the confident young actors he could only appear ridiculous. But, as always, his reaction was immediate. He plunged in. He tried, he tried humbly, clumsily, with all he could bring. He was no longer the star, the superior being. He was quite simply there, struggling with his body, as the others would be later with their words, with an intensity and a sincerity

that were his own. In a matter of seconds his relation with the group was transformed.

Meanwhile, Ted Hughes was chiselling his version of Seneca's play. He used an unpunctuated line of syncopated phrases, which he had found in translating the bony Eastern European poetry of Zbigniew Herbert, Vasko Popa and Miroslav Holub. He was already hacking out the hellish ironies of his book *Crow* in the same poetic form. Its parallelisms jangle, its abrupt cuts and line-endings gouge the mind:

> he was raging as he spoke   his face throbbed darkred   his eyeballs seemed to be jumping in their sockets   forced out from the skull   his face was no longer the face of Oedipus   contorted   like a rabid dog   he had begun to scream   a bellowing animal   anger   agony tearing his throat his fingers had stabbed deep into his eyesockets

The headlong, torrential force of this verse, its seeming refusal to take a breath, dictated a single tragic act, with no interval. Brook's challenge was to sustain audience involvement over such a span of unmitigated transgression, violence, sexuality and pain. The long rehearsal period had produced material for a palette of sound, which Brook orchestrated with the virtuosity of a Stockhausen or a Berio; but could he supply enough dramatic impetus to carry the evening?

The audience entering the Old Vic was wrapped in a tapestry of noise that swept the entire space; members of the chorus were planted throughout the auditorium, live caryatids were bound to the pillars and balconies. Into this soundscape, Brook presented an abstract space of geometrical shapes, a giant silver box revolving centre-stage, smaller cubes and plinths around the stage. Nothing was suggestive of the classical world; the actors wore dark trousers and pullovers, Oedipus had a robe and Jocasta a long dark dress. After Ronald Pickup's account of Oedipus' self-blinding, blind Tiresias handed a pair of dark glasses to Gielgud as Oedipus, who had sat impassively listening to the horrifying speech. The elemental became tangible: Jocasta, stage-directed by Seneca to stab herself to death in the womb, lowered herself painfully slowly around one of the pointed stage obelisks, her bent knees bearing her weight, her face frozen in a rictus of death.

The performance was not for the squeamish; some people fainted, some walked out. But the biggest onslaught on the audience happened in the final minutes of the piece. In classical tragedy, a satyr-play concluded a trilogy of tragedies, performed by half-human half-animal creatures, the actors donning horns and hairy goat-legs. The satyr-play took some aspect of the serious drama of the preceding tragedies, and turned its seriousness topsy-turvy. Dionysus replaced Zeus and Apollo, the tragic action was displaced by humour, licentiousness and wine. Brook rounded off his Senecan drama with a Bacchanalian finale.

A carriage entered veiled in glittering fabrics, drawn by revellers who lifted off the coverings to reveal a fifteen-foot-tall phallus (the actress Coral Browne, in the stalls, was heard to remark, 'No one we know, dear'). A jazz band shuffled on behind, playing a Dixieland version of 'Yes We Have No Bananas'. The procession spilled over into the auditorium, the actors inviting the audience to dance. There were giggles, blushes ('Women in the front rows bowed their heads,' wrote Charles Marowitz, 'whether out of respect or embarrassment one couldn't say'). After ninety dense minutes of Ted Hughes' word-tapestry, here was the Crazy Gang, here was riot and disorder, capping what Ted Hughes had called Oedipus' 'sacred, ritual progress under the marriage of love and death'. Colin Blakeley bluntly summed up the applause at the end and the meaning of the phallus: 'It got quite a reception, from guffaws to tuts, from boos to feet-stamping applause, and it was very funny and outrageous, a stunning *coup de théâtre*. What was it about, though? What it said to me was: One: you've just seen a load of cock. Two: in olden days the Romans used to do this after the play. Three: you see what can happen when you fuck about? Four: don't go to bed with your mother. Five: don't take it too seriously, now you've been through hell, forget it, you can deal with it. Number five is valid. The rest is ultimately belittling.'

Inevitably, there was a huge outcry from the British press, echoing London's recent 'dirty plays' row. Interviewed on BBC Radio, Brook gave a straightfaced justification for his ending:

Birth, bed, womb, blood – every word Seneca wrote seemed to prepare for the confrontation with this object. The phallus is a religious object throughout the world. We offered not a closed interpretation, but a colourful opening-up of real speculation upon the mystery and real meaning of the active and masculine force of life. The religious rites of Seneca's time related not only to the phallus, but to how in a religious society one could pass from tragic emotion to obscenity and blasphemy, as intrinsic portions of one religious ceremony. We're confronting great mysteries in which our divisions of tragedy for one night and comedy for another have become very debased.

Charles Marowitz, however, was sceptical: 'What in Grotowski or the Living Theater appears to be an inevitable expression of personally-arrived-at discoveries, looks, in Brook, like elaborately camouflaged second-hand goods. However effective theatre may be, some part of ourselves demands to know we are being overwhelmed for some reason greater than a director's desire to overwhelm us.'

Marowitz was touching on a truth. Brook had enfranchised himself of the conventions and rituals of theatre, at the price of summoning some of his harshest energies. There was a strain, a tension, a violence, as he sought to break the bonds. More things needed to shift before he could tap into his finer energies.

During the 1960s, Brook kept chasing the elusive film he dreamed of making. While rehearsing *Oedipus*, his producer Michael Birkett was setting up Brook's film of *King Lear*, which he finally shot in 1969. It is a grave, muted film, black and white, without music, pared down, scrubbed. Although influenced by Brook's stage production, it has its own independent vision; when Michael Birkett took the screenplay to Paul Scofield, the actor said, 'I've erased all the tapes in my head of what I did on stage, you know.'

It was shot in the treeless, hostile, snow-covered plains of Jutland; all the sound effects have been honed to a sharp edge. Horses drive across the snow-scape, the bellowing of their riders and clashing reins and hooves providing a percussive reminder of the bitter struggle with nature. The sixty-four-year-old Russian designer Wakhevitch provided sparse, elemental interiors, a log fire, rough-hewn tables, cloth partitions, animal-skins for clothes. At key points of the story, this realistic environment melts away to a non-place, made of curtains of light and abstracted shapes, streams of rain and depths of darkness. In a play in which the word 'nothing' tolls, this cinematic void resounds to it.

In Brook's film career, *King Lear* is a milestone of shooting, editing and fragmented telling. Scofield as Lear, striding about the court in a massive black fur coat that looks like a bear slung across his shoulders, emerges out of pools of darkness into light, like a depressive coming to the surface. Faces are sliced in half by the screen-edge, profiles face up to each other from either end of the screen with a void between them, features are dislodged from the whole physiognomy. 'Look,' Brook's device seems to say, 'in this world of apartness and isolation, only these fragments exist, these cropped faces, these clips and scraps.' For seconds at a time, the screen goes black while the words of a speech or the sounds of the wind continue, as if a void had taken over. As Lear builds up to his outburst on the final brink of madness, control seems to abandon the camera's gaze too. 'O reason not the need,' he pleads to Goneril, and in a long take Scofield's face veers out of frame and back again, into focus and out. From a screen of refracted, unfocused shapes comes 'O Fool, I shall go mad', and on 'Blow, winds, and crack your cheeks', we see Lear's face nestled in thorns and briars, stung by pouring rain, illuminated by a sudden lightning flare, indistinguishable from microscopic close-ups of the worms and rodents among whom he has fallen. The cuts are so rapid that sometimes there is no time to recognise whether what you're looking at is animal, vegetable or human. It is the most radical vision of Shakespearean disintegration ever brought to the screen.

The closest analogy is perhaps with Brook's near-contemporary, Francis Bacon. Bacon's paintings have the same retinal violence, the same visceral bite at the world, the same ectoplasmic after-images as this film at its peaks. David Sylvester, Bacon's greatest interpreter, defined the painter's strategy in a 1954 review: 'It is one of his main preoccupations as a painter to see how far it is possible to twist appearances out of shape without depriving them of conviction, and by this act of taking reality to the brink of unreality, to heighten our awareness of it.' The vision of both artists has roots in the films of Eisenstein, Bacon gripped by the violence of the screaming bespectacled face in the Odessa Steps sequence of *Battleship Potemkin*, Brook by the almost silent-cinema vividness given to close-ups of hands, eyes, the back of a head. 'The dissolution produced by the paint,' says Sylvester, '*acts directly upon our nerves*, suffices without further explanation to convey a sense of tragedy' (my italics). That is how Brook's film-language works in *King Lear*. It is a spasm tearing a path to the central nervous system. Brook and Bacon both convey a pitiless world ruled by power and lust and greed. But Brook's Lear works his way back to a devastated humanity in the scene on Dover beach with the blinded Gloucester, played with suffering courtesy by Alan Webb. His tragicomic attempt at suicide by throwing himself off a non-existent cliff is shot from above; a crane shot looks down on this old man's body from above, lying like a sack flung away on the beach. And then Lear materialises, and we watch two old men, groping for each other, one without sight, the other out of his wits. As paroxysmic as the storm and madness scenes have been, this oasis before the end is filmed with simplicity and humanity.

After which, the film hurtles to an end. Cornwall, who blinded Glouce-ster, dies, stabbed by a servant. Goneril beats her brains out against a rock. Edgar swiftly despatches Edmund with a fearful blow from an axe. And with a cut like the hammer-blow in Mahler's *Sixth Symphony*, Cordelia's body is seen hanging from a noose. And then Brook cuts to Lear, holding her, howling to an empty horizon. Recalling Eisenstein's *Ivan The Terrible*, Lear falls out of the frame like a slow-motion collapsing palace. What Sylvester said of Bacon is true too of this *Lear*: '(its) disturbing effect resides far less in its premonitions of disaster than in the sheer weight of its sense of reality.'

This was Brook's seventh film, if you count his undergraduate *A Sentimental Journey* as his first. What is his relationship to film? Where do his films stand compared with his theatre productions? How good a film-maker is Brook, who from early adolescence to apprenticeship in a film studio, wanted more than anything to make films? He said drily that he chose theatre because he found one could get a play on quicker than one could make a film.

In his most successful film, *Lord of the Flies*, he exploited cinema's unique quality: its ability to provide what he called 'evidence', the documentary *vérité* of a face, a place, a time of day, a quality of light. It was this merciless literalism of the camera which was the bedrock of cinematic truth for Brook;

he knew equally well that film was merciless in turning the most luxurious décor and design into laths, paint and canvas. He constantly called on the evidential realism he had learned from cinema to give edge and reality to his theatre work: Isabella's painfully prolonged here-and-now pause for decision in the last act of his *Measure for Measure*; the gritty waterfront tenements of *A View from the Bridge*; the sparseness of *The Visit*, throwing into close-up relief the confrontation of the rich vengeful woman and her former lover.

But another side of Brook sought something less certain and self-evident than photographic realism, and that side was inspired in the *King Lear* film to use cinema in a Shakespearean way. What he loved in Shakespeare's plays, he told the émigré Czech film critic Antonin Liehm, was their mercurial, shape-and-genre-shifting quality. Since *King Lear* was not a documentary picture of primitive England, it should not look like a museum exhibit, a historical reconstruction. Fire and fur, defences against hostile nature, said Brook, became the structural mainstay of the reality on screen. The verisimilitude and detail of interiors and landscape was just enough for spectators to take it in their stride without posing unnecessary questions about its historical veracity, while shooting in black and white gave a further cohesiveness to the screen. '*Lear* is so complex that if you add the slightest bit of complexity to it, you are completely smothered,' Brook told Liehm. 'So the process of preparing *Lear* was elimination all the way – of scenic detail, costume detail, colour detail, music detail.' This restraint, economy and elimination enabled Brook to move from the outside world to minimal interiors to the inside of Lear's mind to the cosmos.

It's this prepared fluency that Brook sought, and continues to seek, in his film-making. In some of his films to date, he believed he had found a personal cinematic voice. The mosaic of harsh nature and children's improvisation in *Lord of the Flies* enabled him to create with arresting strangeness a visceral image of society shattered. In the *Marat/Sade* film, he successfully converted theatrical rhythms and space into filmic language. Both of these films were made under pressure of time and finances; but perhaps the resultant cliff-edge adrenalin is what compels Brook.

Lord of the Flies was a commerical success; Brook's other films have become arthouse treasures, but have hardly thrust him into the cinematic mainstream, something of which he is well aware. As he wrote to Robert Facey,

> I haven't yet made a film I like. In the theatre, certainly, I'm not attached to what I do, but there are about six or eight productions which I know were complete – they could not be developed further within their own terms of reference. I haven't found this yet in film. It's hard to analyse – I think making a film is excruciatingly difficult – and the very empirical nature of theatre is in a way a bad preparation because it makes me flexible towards detail and in a sense accommodating when one works, while proper shooting of a film requires every stroke to be right there and then. It is far, far more concentrated. I think that as I entered the cinema at a time when technique was considered so important I've always spent a lot of energy on a sort of technical virtuosity, not so much because it interested me as because I wanted to demonstrate how easy and unimportant it was! But this unimportance assumed a too large role. The film this year, *Tell Me Lies*, was very different, very free, very improvised. But I'm still searching for the form and the language.

This comes from a long letter written in 1968. Brook is forty-three and at a turning point of his life. He has been thinking about Dylan Thomas' line in 'Poem in October', which he misremembers as, 'It was my fortieth year to heaven', and what it means to him. He is alone in Dolgellau, North Wales, on New Year's Eve, rehearsals for *Oedipus* suspended for the Christmas break, recovering from mumps which he caught from one of his children. As he writes to Facey, he finds himself conducting a stock-take of his life and sizing up the idea of leaving England.

For months he has known it is time to leave, time to start again. He knows that he must conduct a great shift in himself, abandoning an overabundance of choices and stimuli. He knows himself enough to recognise that some things cannot change.

> I am deeply conditioned, over Pavlovian light years, to be everywhere and nowhere, en route between too many equally attractive alternatives. This can't be changed with one wrench and perhaps will never change. But the bias can change even if the ball keeps on rolling. I've never wanted the tie and

responsibility of a theatre of my own – now, and only gradually at that, I'm beginning to prepare for the need of having a group for which I can be totally responsible on all levels for a substantial period of time. It now seems that this is the only possible evolution after so many years of attempts and experiments.

It's as if a parade of triumphs – and occasional disasters – of forays into Shakespeare, the West End, musicals, philosophical drama, opera, movies, French theatre, political drama is being rounded up by this prodigal son, who wants to turn himself into a prodigal adult, the parent of a theatre and a troupe, with a parent's responsibility. And step by step he relates his professional life and its freedom to the demands and rewards of a real-life family. His second child Simon is just eighteen months old.

Of course, it's inseparable from the problem of having a family. Having been the Favoured Son for so long and so accepting without any resentment all the advantages of a benign paternity observed by others (film producers, impresarios, theatre owners and managers), I even managed to retain this situation through years of marriage which, because of Natasha's oriental wisdom, never involved 'settling down'. Even the arrival of a first child, Irina, was absorbed into our nomad life without too overwhelming a problem. However, as others predicted, it's two that changes all, that makes a family.

With the first night of the new production, with an aggressive assertive penis there, to boot, I saw that one whole world was over and another one would have to take its place. This transition is only in its infancy and I can assure you it is very difficult. You don't get childhood illnesses like mumps for nothing!

[Here is added a drawing of four arrows pointing out from a centre.]

In the theatre there's been a big change of direction for me. For years all went outwards as I tried to touch and explore as many forms, genres, media, countries as possible. Now, passing that crucial landmark of 40, the direction changes and I want to try to concentrate, exploring in depth rather than breadth. Of course, all such theorising is dangerous and misleading (most of all to myself if I take it too literally).

He looks back at his charmed life in commercial theatre, opera, film and subsidised theatre. He is thinking of Barry Jackson, who took him to

Stratford-upon-Avon; Binkie Beaumont, his guardian angel in the West End theatre; Peter Hall, who invited him to join the Royal Shakespeare Company; David Merrick and Alexander Cohen, the producers who paved the way for his reputation in New York; David Picker, who found money from an American studio for the low-budget *Marat/Sade* film; Peter Sykes and Gerry Feil, who followed his instincts in the *Tell Me Lies* film; Simone Berriau and Françoise Spira who produced his work in Paris, and Micheline Rozan, who has wisely guided his Parisian career, and will soon play a decisive role in his new life – all his backers, protectors and benefactors. With them, he has been able to play the indulged child, almost at times the spoilt son.

The 'aggressive assertive penis' which Peter Brook put on stage as the climax of his *Oedipus* was also the masculine life force with which he had conquered the theatre on many fronts, over the previous twenty-three years of his professional life. It was the energy with which he had pushed himself to the limits, journeyed to far corners of the world, plumbed ideas and plundered forms, like Marlowe's restless Faust in Brook's first production at the age of eighteen. With Faust, he might have boasted of the 'world of profit and delight / Of power, of honour, of omnipotence' he has conquered. He had long since ceased being a 'directorial' director. Beginning with *Theatre of Cruelty*, *The Marat/Sade* and especially in his long preparation of *Oedipus*, his hours and days of seemingly rudderless searching in the rehearsal room, renouncing the masculine role of director as commander – these began to point towards a new integration ahead. 'The conjunctions are complicated,' he continues in his letter to Facey, 'by the fact that Natasha, after some years now of maternity and domesticity, is suddenly desperate, in a most legitimate way, to express herself in her own field as an actress. Which also isn't easy, because acting for a woman is either unemployment and frustration or – for a film actress – unexpected departures for God knows where. When I'm rehearsing *Oedipus* she and the family will be in Paris and I'll commute every weekend. So the peaceful integration is a long way off!'

And then there is the further complication of money. There have been acrimonious exchanges with the National Theatre about the low fee he was being offered to direct *Oedipus*. 'By not exploiting my position and going after art for art's sake and experiment,' he continues, 'I'm finding myself in more and more complicated finances. Again, for years this could be ridden – now, as father of the family, suddenly another element of humdrum reality that has to be grappled with!' And to conclude, Brook closes this letter of reckoning with a stream of restless thoughts to himself about 'the true issue – what is this unfolding texture in constant movement and change? Why? What for? What is its place? What can be influenced and by whom? What can evolve, and in what direction?' It is a Hamlet-like self-questioning.

Brook's next step was towards internationalism. Jean-Louis Barrault, the actor and director who had enlarged French theatre with the expansive plays of Paul Claudel and lit up French cinema as the pantomime artist Baptiste Debureau in *Les Enfants du paradis* (1945), was running the Théâtre de l'Odéon and an annual international festival, the Théâtre des Nations. In 1967 Barrault invited Brook to stage a Shakespeare play in Paris. Brook, with the research process of *Theatre of Cruelty* and *Oedipus* still resonating, said he would rather hold an international workshop about Shakespeare with actors from many countries and cultures. The play he would like to explore, he said, was *The Tempest*, which he'd already staged twice and which still tantalised him. Barrault agreed, and Brook set about gathering a most diverse group to travel further down the paths he had opened in London. 'These bodies had all been British,' he wrote, 'and now like an Elizabethan explorer I wished to discover continents remote from my native land.'

Brook brought to Paris eight British actors from *US*, including Glenda Jackson, Robert Lloyd and Henry Woolf; two experimental directors, Joe Chaikin and Victor García from Argentina; a French writer, Claude Roy, and a group of French actors, including Delphine Seyrig and Michael Lonsdale; Brook's wife Natasha Parry; and Geoffrey Reeves once more as his assistant director. Barrault, whose own work as an actor had been refined by Japanese theatre and its philosopher Zeami, was keen to have a classically trained Japanese actor join the group. He found Yoshi Oida, an actor trained in the disciplines of Noh theatre and its comic counterpart Kyogen. Yoshi spoke no English, greeted Brook in Barrault's office with bows and smiles, joined the group and remains until today a cornerstone of Brook's international company.

They began work in Les Gobelins in the south of Paris, in a vast stone storehouse, the Mobilier National, where the French state stored the furniture and trappings of its official apartments. In his book, *An Actor Adrift*, Yoshi gives glimpses of how his different point-of-departure from Western and European actors enriched the mixture of the work. Early on, Brook had asked the actors to improvise on an elemental scenario in which they were to begin as water, become a typhoon, then its victim, then become wind, then fire, then soil. Yoshi watched the other actors, who all seemed enormous compared to him, throw themselves about the space, wriggle and writhe, bellow and roar. He didn't think he could do the same; a diminutive Japanese among these massive actors, he thought, would have looked like a mosquito buzzing round the room.

Instead, Yoshi had recourse to the 'hara', a Noh theatre name for a point just below the navel which is 'considered to be the centre of a person's energy and sense of being'. Taking this inner focus, Yoshi 'sat on the floor, like Buddha, concentrating himself with all his energy, so that he might transform into fire or water. It must have looked quite odd; a small Japanese man in a cotton kimono, sitting in the middle of this wild activity.'

Beyond the stone walls of the Mobilier, the paving-stones of Paris were being torn up and its buildings festooned with revolutionary posters by the *enragés* of May '68. What began as a carnival against repression became a movement, spreading from students to workers, that threatened the French state. Brook's response, as a man of forty-three engaged in his own rigorous artistic reassessment, was less elated than those who prematurely rejoiced at French society being brought to a halt by its Dionysiac confrontations with the police: 'I was less impressed than they were by the sudden discovery that everything needed to be questioned. This was after all what had brought us all together in the first place and I felt more than ever that we needed to carry on with what we had begun in our own field. Outside, it was often hard to discover what was concrete and what was dream.'

In *Threads of Time*, Brook tells two stories of May '68. He tells how he was summoned by a 'lieutenant' of one of the leaders of those who were now occupying Barrault's Théâtre de l'Odéon. He met the leader in the dressing-room, was not impressed, and found out later that like a character in Genet's *Le Balcon*, he was a police spy. Then there's the veteran Vietnamese

Communist who begins by being overjoyed by the euphoria of '68, going night after night to the occupied Sorbonne to drink deep at the hopes which had once inspired his own youth. Then one night, he has an insight. 'The old man was not deceived,' writes Brook. 'His sensitivity took him beyond his wishes; he saw the invisible worm, he sensed the canker as it invaded the bloom. He stood quietly in a corner, watching and listening. Then he went home and took his life.'

These brief sketches of the delusive aspects of insurgency and the suicide of an exiled old militant reveal an unromantic, dialectical view of human life. Paris in 1968 reminds Brook of being in Cuba just after the revolution: 'I had experienced the intoxicating marvel of a sudden liberation and had naively believed that this could continue, without understanding the complex processes that develop after every new beginning.' It is also likely that his outlook was affected by what he had learned – from Yoshi among others – about the three-part rhythm shared by all Asian theatre, called Jo-Ha-Kyu: 'slow, or introductory; middle, or unfolding; fast, or ending and conclusion.' In his book, Yoshi analyses the action of *Hamlet* and *Macbeth* in terms of Jo-Ha-Kyu, the slow beginning of the ghost and the witches, the rapid action and development in the middle of the plays, their finales in battles and duels. 'But it is important to realise,' warns Yoshi, 'that the "Kyu" section of a play does not always involve high-speed action, although this is fairly common. What makes it "Kyu" is the fact that the interior energy of the scene remains very strong and active. "Kyu" is energy, not merely speed.'

One can see Brook initially annoyed by the intrusion of the passions of the street into his work, then buoyed up by the festivity of the streets, the eroticism of release – and immediately checked by the anti-romantic Brook, sensing that something was missing in the 'Jo' of 1968. Its energy was too rash, too Romeo-like; from such a beginning could only flow what he later saw inside the Théâtre de l'Odéon: 'a non-stop marathon of speech making, which had begun on the first evening, had now become repetitive and self-indulgent. The hedonistic sex in the corridors was sinking into an apathy of drugs and squalor; dealers, thugs and operators were taking over the theatre, and boredom was overcoming the last handful of listeners still scribbling notes in the stalls.'

Outer circumstances and opportunities dictated the outcome. The French

Equity actors' union went on strike, the French government panicked and shut down all public buildings, including the Mobilier National. An appeal to friends and supporters in London enabled Brook and the group, minus some of its French members who had stayed behind to see the uprising through, to come to the Roundhouse, a former locomotive turntable in Chalk Farm, which playwright Arnold Wesker was trying to turn into an arts centre for working people. The French airports and railway stations were closed, the roads blocked; the group took off from a military airport and landed at an RAF airbase in outer London. In June they opened their workshop presentation of *The Tempest*. Inside, the Roundhouse is an epic, circular building, rising to a conical roof. The predominant materials are wood, for the floors and the roof, and iron, for its handsome Victorian pillars. Being circular, it's not hard to disorient an audience, and with a white tent canopy overhead, and a set of scaffolding towers for seating, with railings when the contraption shuddered and began to move, Brook created his labyrinth. Elements of *The Tempest*, currents which Brook and the group imagined swirling in Shakespeare's mind and surfacing as *The Tempest*, were set in motion. Margaret Croyden picked up on the deconstructive texture of the event: 'not a literal interpretation of Shakespeare's play but abstractions, essences, possible contradictions embedded in the text. The plot is shattered, condensed, de-verbalised; time is discontinuous, shifting. Action merges into collages, though some moments are framed, then, as in a film, dissolve and fade out.'

This was, in every sense, work in progress; progressing, as Brook had begun to realise, towards the goal of an ongoing international group. The interaction between styles and traditions was everywhere apparent, as when Yoshi, playing Ariel, yoked himself back to back to Bob Lloyd playing Ferdinand, and doubled up Lloyd's lines in the Japanese language of Noh drama. The 'mirror' exercise, in which one partner takes the lead, the other follows and the lead role passes back and forth with tiny transformations, was a *leitmotiv*, as were the mutual dependencies of Prospero and Caliban, 'civilised' and 'barbarian', human and spirit. It was, in one sense, a defini-tion-postponing frolic with the impulses that gave birth to Shakespeare's text. One image may have linked with *mai soixante-huit* in Paris. Miranda marvels at the 'brave new world' she sees and Prospero replies, 'Tis new to thee', in the manner of the former militant who had killed himself in Paris, knowing what the future held.

There were stabs of pure throat-catching magic, in which the other-wordliness of Ariel (played by Yoshi in Japanese), the presence of things of darkness, were shown and swept away in the scenic whirlpool. The urgency, the order sought through fragmentation of Brook's workshop, were images of the atoms of change whirring inside his head.

At the same time, during 1968 and 1969, in trips to Paris and America, he was beginning to draft proposals, sound out possible backers and plan strategies to make his departure from London a reality, and his work in and out of Paris with a group for which he took responsibility something tangible.

In 1970, Brook began rehearsing what was to be his last production on an English stage before leaving England. 'There are plays that are perfect in their form,' he said. 'I think that *A Midsummer Night's Dream* is a perfect, Mozartian construction, where you can't cut a note out of the score without harming it.' He chose to do one of Shakespeare's plays held in most affection by British audiences. In the collective British psyche, *A Midsummer Night's Dream* had become a fairy tale, symbolised by Arthur Rackham's charming but childish Edwardian illustrations. Brook wanted to reclaim it as an adult's play of celebration, but also of fright and darkness, desire and dream, and magical powers which really were powerful. He knew that everything he had learned over the past eight years would be needed to release what Ted Hughes, talking to Brook, called the play's 'single battery of energy':

If your job is to bring these plays off the page into living form, you must always prevent yourself, as far as possible, from imposing anything that is going to cut down those areas to your own chosen ones . . . To approach Shakespeare and produce either 'style' or clarity of certain ideas is only a reduction of the play. It's not possible for any of us to reveal the complete play . . . But the direction we can take at each point can try to capture in our net the richest amount of the contradictory, clashing, opposed, discordant elements that criss-cross these plays . . . It's a concord-discord. There is vulgar sex, there is metaphysical love, and the two exist side by side. In all our work, we try to replace *either/or* with *both*.

To the rehearsal room Brook brought the panoply of exercises, improvisations and games he had built up in the past decade's experiments. He was dealing with a Royal Shakespeare Company nucleus of actors – including Alan Howard, Sara Kestelman, Ben Kingsley, David Waller and Frances de la Tour. Brook wanted to profit from their skills; but he also wanted to disrupt them, with an almost mediumistic approach to the play. John Kane, playing Puck and Philostrate in this play of doubled roles, felt the difference between the RSC approach, in which 'we do something with the play', and Brook's: 'He wanted the play to do things with us.'

Bamboo sticks, plates, drums and percussion, plastic tubes, hoops, paper, string, cushions, mats, instruments, funny noses and hats and soon a scaffolding version of the set with its two levels and its trapezes turned the rehearsal room into an adventure playground. The six sturdy actors playing the very un-sylph-like Fairies were given full licence. They soon became not just mischievous but subversive, seizing actors in mid-scene and plonking them down at the other end of the space, mocking the Mechanicals, blowing raspberries, sending-up, invading. These 'Audio-Visuals', as they were nicknamed, became a troubling, not merely decorative presence in the play, dislodging preconceptions, opening doors into dark forces. 'The forest and its inhabitants exuded a primitive savagery that infected everyone who came in contact with them,' wrote John Kane, who played Puck. 'As the group feeling grew, a wild gaiety seized the company.'

It culminated in a memorable rehearsal of the wedding of Titania and Bottom. Kane later recalled:

> The thing took off and went at incredible speed. We tore everything up, newspapers, we threw cushions about. At the end, when everything quietened down and the last newspaper flicked to the floor, we stood and looked around at the incredible chaos – the debris – we had created during the course of rehearsal. We had wrecked the entire studio. Hardly a chair was left with a leg on it. It was the first glimmer we had had of how a play . . . can drive you. We had got a hint of that 'secret play' that Peter still talks about: the play that will never be found by us, but we keep working at it.

Frances de la Tour, playing Helena, and Sally Jacobs, the designer working with Brook on *A Midsummer Night's Dream,* offered vivid insights into the creative shorthand he establishes with his collaborators.

> *Frances de la Tour*: I had heard that Brook had asked for people who had been at the Royal Shakespeare Company. I was called for a collective audition with him and then I heard I was going to play Helena; I was up in the air.
>
> I soon realised Peter was an incredibly serious man of the theatre. He started by just working on the text with us, but working so delicately. You could be running around, or spending the whole day on just three lines of text. I asked him once if he would always direct like this and he said, 'No, not at all. This is because we're doing Shakespeare and this particular play in this particular time.'

Sally Jacobs, who had been working for Brook for a decade, since the *Theatre of Cruelty* season, talked about how the production's iconic 'white box' came into being.

> *Sally Jacobs*: We kept meeting in New York – I was living in LA, he was in Paris – so we'd meet at the Chelsea Hotel in New York. We'd correspond – there was no email in those days. What we'd got was our white box with its gallery above; we'd got the wires to make the forest; we'd got the bower so Titania could stay in sight but be lifted up. But we had all these young lovers asleep on the stage getting in everyone's way. It started to look all wrong, we could never get any clarity. I'm looking at this model I'm building in Los Angeles and thinking what am I going to do with all these sleeping people? Where are Puck and Oberon going to overlook this lovers' madness?
>
> Then I realised, I've got to use the vertical space. I'm already flying the feather, so – fly them too, make two trapeze bars as their special place, where they can hover above the action! And that connected with circus which we were interested in.

> *Frances de la Tour*: Peter had to go away in the middle of rehearsals for a week or two and left us to rehearse by ourselves. It was a very strange time. We never knew when he was going to walk in. So we spun plates, ran a few scenes.

Alan Howard sort of took the lead. Peter said to us before he left, 'I want you to tell me what the secret of the play is.' We talked about it for a bit before he left and we said, 'Love? Er . . . hate? Power? Dreams? What?' and he said, 'Now I'm going away.' And when Peter came back, I said, 'I know what the secret of the play is. The secret of the play is me, meaning Helena, because this is my story.'

And then one day, rehearsing with Ben Kingsley, my text was essentially saying, 'Don't leave me, don't leave me, I love you.' And Ben started to go, to leave the stage. So Ben would go off and I said, 'If he goes off, how can I say the speech?' I just flounced. I was very upset, I started to cry, and Peter said, 'Now why are you crying?' We had these steel coils for the trees of the forest, and I said, 'These steel things are banging on my head, it's not my idea of a forest, I don't know where I am and Ben won't stay for the speech and' – you've got to remember we're in the 1970s – I said, 'I don't feel there's a lot of love here.' And Peter said in that hushed voice of his, 'That is absolutely right, Frankie. Now go and do the scene.' So Ben came on and I rugby-tackled him. I pinned him down and shouted, 'The more you beat me I will fawn on you!'

And Peter went 'Good'. And then he said, 'That was right. Do you know why it was right?' and I said 'No'. And I thought, 'It's like the secret of the play. Will I be able to learn why it was right?'

Sally Jacobs: We put down the anchors, but it had to be the kind of design that remained open for the discoveries that were going to be made in rehearsal. But you mustn't let this openness neutralise the idea, otherwise you just finish up with an empty stage all the time and these plays demand an invented world.

Frances de la Tour: Another time I said to him, 'I don't know how to make it real, because it's Shakespeare and it's not just Shakespeare, it's rhyming couplets. And it's a soliloquy. How do I make this real, Peter?' And he said, 'You're in close-up, your face is probably forty feet high. So if you even just move an eye – anything that goes on, they're going to see.' And far from it being daunting, it was great. I felt that the audience knew exactly what I was thinking, what I was feeling. It gave me the most enormous confidence.

Sally Jacobs: Everyone took part in making all the toys work, they weren't just presented with things. Alan Howard worked directly with the prop department to make his stick bounce – it had a tiny spring at the top so that when he received the spinning plate thrown down by Puck from the gallery, he could catch it more easily because it had a tiny bit of give in it.

Frances de la Tour: Like a great painter or like Pablo Casals, Peter had more knowledge of the instrument that he was dealing with – in his case, the text – than anybody else. But it wasn't just academic, he was a real artist, with demands that went beyond what is commonly known as acting, that nobody else had. I didn't necessarily think that then. Then I felt he had a mischievous quality that went beyond the text, as if he felt, 'I'm having fun with this, I'm exploring my own nature with this, I'm discovering who I love in this, what I really think about life in this.'

Sally Jacobs: It's a continuous development – there's no end, no answer. It's a continuous exploration of the questions – it throws up questions and explorations that can only be met through creating a piece of work. He has so many aspects to him – and this must be one of the good things about Gurdjieff – the acceptance that we're all made up of many, many different parts and we only use a fraction of them and we have to work hard to make sure we try to use them all. That's been Peter's blessing – that he's always found an outlet for whatever complexity is in him.

Frances de la Tour: One day he took me for a walk down by the Avon, and said, 'I think you might have to make a decision, Frankie. Either you're going to be a very serious actress, and I think you will be and can be because you remind me of Glenda (which is a nice thing to say) – in fact you remind me of Paul Scofield sometimes in the way you look at a piece of text – or you're going to be a personality. You can come on and razzle-dazzle or you can just do the work and get just as much as you can out of it.'

In the terrible mid-eighties, when I hadn't worked for two years, I wrote to Peter Hall, Trevor Nunn and Peter Brook and said, 'I'm after work, will one of you work with me?' Trevor wrote back a couple of weeks later – his secretary obviously typed it – 'Dear Frankie, I'm thinking about your past, present and future, Love, Trevor'. Peter Hall said 'Nothing for you at the moment' – very straightforward and by return. I got a handwritten letter from Peter Brook. I was so desperate, I said, 'I'll do anything, can I come to Paris?' I think he was about to do Glenda's Cleopatra at Stratford-upon-Avon, so I said, 'Could I play Iris?' and he said, 'No, you've got to play Cleopatra one of these days. You can't do Iris – you're not going to be happy doing Iris. Take care, etc'. It was all handwritten. Just a lovely, lovely letter.

Sally Jacobs: He has to satisfy himself that he has explored every nook and cranny, over the hill, round the corner, taking every part as seriously as the next part. He will not allow himself to fix anything until he's gone around and around and turned over everything thoroughly. Then the brilliance comes in; he edits and fine-tunes it and chooses how to put together what's been discovered. But the discovery takes him into areas where he has the courage to go, because he's not worried about the outcome. These explorations that he makes always come up with something that is finally the only way to do it.

He's a super technician. When he's done all the exploration and you get on the stage and you have a commitment to get the thing on, he is a most wonderful commander of this enormous crew. He knows exactly what to tell everyone – 'come in there, go out there, I want a bit more light here, stop here, move there, I want this to be three seconds longer'. He's like a magician who's got everything at his fingertips and he pulls it together impeccably.

Frances de la Tour: Working with him on *A Midsummer Night's Dream* was about exploration – of everything you did: the sexual exploration of love, what makes two human beings want to go off together and then maybe want to go off with somebody else, what that's all about. It's just a continual searching – I suppose it's what he means by the secret of the play, its dark side, perhaps. We want the loveliness, the union and the roses and everyone getting married at the end – but you have to get through such a dark passage to get there. And that has to come out; how can you be creative if there's just a perfect house with roses round the door?

I think there's something devilish in him, like Picasso. You can't put sanctions on Peter, you can't put full stops, and I imagine it must make it very difficult to live with him. And another thing. Peter is maybe one of the greatest comics of all time. I think he's a clown, and a real clown can break your heart.

The *Dream* left those who saw it with many etched images, the acid test, in Brook's terms, of a good piece of theatre. One such image was the ease with which Oberon, balancing on a trapeze, slid a spinning plate from a thin wand across on to Puck's wand. The plate became Shakespeare's magic flower to enchant Titania. 'And with the juice of this I'll streak her eyes / And make her full of hateful fantasies': the words were reignited by the physical acrobatics and equilibrium of the two actors.

There was the Feydeau-farcical mirth, laughter building on laughter, that greeted the quarrels and bewitched infatuations of the lovers. Or the even bigger laugh, a laugh of complicity with the audience, when Oberon berates Puck for screwing up the magic with the lovers: a slow descent of the trapezes from which they've been watching his botched work, a raised eyebrow from Alan Howard, a slow burn worthy of Jack Benny, and the words, 'This is thy negligence.'

That sudden shiver of fear, like an icy gust, as Puck made a line stand out with a chill: 'Night and silence. Who is here?' Richard Peaslee's nightmarish horn-blasts, sounded from elephant-trunk-long instruments, that aurally poked you awake from 'the fierce vexation of a dream' into the daylight world of Theseus' hunting party. Or the weight of meaning the word *imagination* bore as Theseus spoke 'The lunatic, the lover and the poet / Are of imagination all compact.' Brook had plugged the fantastic workings of the imagination, its dream-logic, gear-shifts and transpositions into a charged playing space which the actors ceaselessly transformed.

An almost universal chorus of approval greeted this production. *The Times'* Irving Wardle noted the production's sense of a culmination: 'It is not only the apex towards which the RSC has been moving for the past two years, it brings Brook himself to a new point of rest. You could not have predicted what he would do with the play; but after seeing the production you feel you ought to have known, and it is a simple and inevitable crystallization of what has gone before.' In the *New York Post*, Clive Barnes, reviewing it when it transferred to Broadway, simply asserted that this *Midsummer Night's Dream* was not only a distillation of the past, but a beacon for Brook's future, for theatre's future: 'Once in a while, once in a very rare while, a theatrical production arrives that is going to be talked about as long as there is a theatre, a production which, for good or ill, is going to exert a major influence on the contemporary stage . . . If Peter Brook had done nothing else but this *Dream*, he would have deserved a place in theatre history.'

PART THREE

CUTTING LOOSE

11

TO PARIS AND BEYOND
1970–73

When Brook cut loose from the English theatre in 1970, at the peak of his success, he had been increasingly aware that England was not fertile ground for a radical innovator. English society had remained largely static since the war; it kept art and artists within bounds or dismissed troubling talent like John Whiting, or tried to clasp rebellious writers like John Osborne into its soft embrace. In the sixties, with the arrival of Peter Hall's Royal Shakespeare Company, windows began to open, but the RSC as an institution still seemed to be pushing against a fog of Bardolatry and undemanding pleasure seeking. England used 'quality' as an alibi against innovation.

'Beware of quality', Brook had already announced in 1962, the year of his searing *King Lear*. As yet another campaign to create a British National Theatre took off he gave a warning to those who thought it could be made by the mere accumulation of recognised talent:

In the hall of the National Theatre I would put up a great gold sign reading 'Beware of Quality'. There is a large slice of the English audience that is bedazzled by Quality . . . The easy danger and death trap for the National Theatre could lie in persuading the audience that it represents the best we have to offer by the seemingly irrefutable evidence of marshalling, even in the smallest parts, the greatest performers of the land. The Elizabethans strove for expression so hard that the edges were rough: in the Elizabethan tradition

quality served a purpose. The aim was meaning. In artistic matters quality in
itself cuts no ice.

Brook also felt constrained by a kind of decent reticence, exemplified in
the modest ambitions of the 'movement' poets – Kingsley Amis, John Wain,
Philip Larkin. English philosophy was also modest: essentially empirical,
anti-metaphysical, tied to fact and evidence. The clipped lawn which Denis
Cannan had summoned up as an image of safe England for the culminating
speech in *US* remained velvet-smooth.

Brook, by the late sixties a thinker as well as a practitioner of theatre,
pushed further, led by a strong metaphysical drive to see beyond the
surface of things. Although the Royal Court 'revolution' had brought a
new social realism and sense of debate into the British theatre, for Brook it
still operated on too narrow a waveband. The Elizabethan theatre, wrote
Brook, 'was far ahead of our present theatre, which can only be acutely
partisan or weakly liberal. Furthermore, the Elizabethan theatre passed
from the world of action to the world of thought, from down-to-earth
reality to the extreme of metaphysical inquiry without effort and without
self-consciousness. Here again, it is far ahead of our own theatre which
has the vitality to deal with life but not the courage to deal with life-and-
death.'

In 1970, he faced the fact that he'd had enough of his love-hate relationship with the English-speaking theatre. Taking further the diverse group of
actors in the Roundhouse *Tempest* company, which had been his first
experience of working with a group not defined by its nationality, he began
to lay plans for an international group.

To begin with, he wanted to work free from box-office pressures; he
needed funds to subsidise the freedom to perform to audiences only as and
when the work needed it. He wanted to see whether theatrical meaning
could be made, using the simplest means available, by a group of performers
who did not share a language – the pioneering group of 1970 with which he
began his journey of exploration came from Japan, Britain, France, Mali and
America. What were the common stories, the recognisable shorthands, the
instant abstractions, the shared outlines of story and character with which
an international group could work? What was a group, anyway? How could

it become more than a collection of individuals? What would be its myths, its basic impulses, its comedy beyond words?

Brook had been raising the questions which were to lead to his departure for Paris for more than two years before he finally left London in the autumn of 1970. During his seven months editing the *King Lear* film in Paris in 1969, he wrote a manifesto to spearhead funding applications for a '*Centre International de Recherches Théâtrales*, the International Centre for Theatre Research' (CIRT is the French acronym, which has stuck) and to run it for three years without any need for box-office income:

> The world's theatre has rarely been in so grave a crisis. With few exceptions, it can be divided into two unsatisfactory categories: those theatres that remain faithful to traditions in which they have lost confidence, and those that wish to create a new and revolutionary theatre, but have not the skills that this requires. And yet theatre in the deepest sense of the word is no anachronism in the 20th century: it has never been needed so urgently.
>
> The special virtue of the theatre as an art form is that it is inseparable from the community. This could mean that the only way to make possible a healthy theatre is by first of all changing the society around it. It can also mean the opposite. It can mean that although the world cannot be reformed in a day, in the theatre it is always possible to wipe the slate clean and start again from zero. Total reform can be put into immediate application.

There are many ingredients here that sprung from Brook's work and his encounters over the previous decade: the idea of calling the organism a research centre, as Grotowski, seeking to evade the censorship of the Communist authorities, had done. A research centre, with its aura of science, is also something which sober foundations would find easier to fund than a theatre, which to some still carries associations of profligacy. In Brook's text there is also a submerged political thread, a dialogue with the *révoltés* of 1968 who had insisted that the world must change before true art can be made. Brook turns the argument on its head: just as the slate can be wiped clean in the theatre, by the same token everything within the theatrical experience can be utterly transformed – if only for the 'two hours' traffic' of a play. It is the Shakespearean magic of his *Midsummer Night's Dream* applied to his own field of work.

The actors must become as skilled with their bodies as with words, 'actors of many nationalities and very different backgrounds, with all skills and no prejudices, actors belonging to no school, who learn to master the arts of all schools, actors who can move like dancers and acrobats, but who are capable of just the same dexterity with words'. And free expression, American style, is not enough: 'Only a disciplined actor is free.'

He ends his appeal document with a call to enlarge and develop the audience around a shared search for theatre's necessity and, echoing all the modern theatre's reformers, from Ibsen to Stanislavski and from Copeau to Grotowski, a commitment to renewal.

> The problem today is not one of restricting the theatre to any single group of spectators. On the contrary, it is a matter of making theatregoing a necessary experience and consequently a social activity that is essential to a community as a whole. This cannot be achieved by popularising the theatre in a naive way. This cannot be achieved by adapting the theatre to the tastes of its audiences. It cannot be achieved either by limiting the theatre to the expectations and criteria of an elite.
>
> Such a theatre can only be created on the basis of a new audience with the intention of serving all those members of a community who see theatre as a possibility of renewal for themselves.

These were the questions behind the flow of position papers which Brook and Micheline Rozan sent out to foundations, festivals and governments to raise the $300,000 per annum needed for the first three years' work of his international group.

It is commonly felt that Brook left London for Paris because French culture, with its monarchical and centralist traditions, was more generous to outstanding individual artists, and more cosmopolitan in giving foreign artists a home. Culture, even in a republican state, meant *gloire*, and Paris thrived on it. In fact, for the first three years of the group's work, the French state did little more than provide a rent-free space in a vast warehouse in Les Gobelins, on the Left Bank of Paris. The funding came from a variety of international sources, and could have been applied to Brook's 'work in progress laboratory', if he had chosen to base it in London or New York. Indeed, Peter Hall had pleaded with him to delay his departure so that funds might be raised and a space found for Brook to conduct his explorations in England.

For Brook, that wasn't the point. He knew English culture and English theatre through and through, from the Royal Shakespeare Company to Binkie Beaumont's West End, from the fiefdoms of the Royal Opera House to the cosiness of British cinema. He needed to cast it off, he needed to unleash himself into a new climate, different sounds, sights, tastes and appetites.

He was hardly a stranger to French culture. But, even in the cosmopolitan French capital, he stood apart. Clearly well versed in French theatre, an early admirer of the exquisite designer Christian Bérard, the presenter to the English of the plays of Anouilh, Sartre, and Cocteau, at ease with the outrages of Surrealism and in sympathy with French cinema's *nouvelle vague*, he also trailed an exotic aura that came from the regular visits of his English language productions (*Titus Andronicus, King Lear*) to the Théâtre des Nations, with legendary British actors – Laurence Olivier, Vivien Leigh, Paul Scofield. It was as if he were at once an accomplished Parisian director, and an envoy from another culture. He spoke French fluently and thoughtfully, though with no attempt to make his accent any better than he needed to. But when he took off for Paris he had a longer journey in mind.

There had always been an otherworldly side to Brook, noticed by many, from the young Tynan to the actors who enjoyed imitating him. It was something about his tempo, his long ruminative pauses, the way he sought for an idea or a word with his fingers, the steadiness of his eyes. More and more, in the decade leading up to his departure, he could have been saying, like Coriolanus, 'There is a world elsewhere.' That world was also a spiritual world.

In fact, his deepest reason for going to Paris was neither its cosmopolitanism nor that 'England destroys its artists', as he had written in *Encore*, nor that it supplied a place to work and, in Micheline Rozan, an effective producer who he respected. No, he said, the real reason was Jeanne de Salzmann. Since the death of his Gurdjieff teacher Jane Heap in 1964, Brook had increasingly looked to Jeanne de Salzmann, who had formally inherited the mantle from Gurdjieff himself after his death. She was now living in Paris as the successor to Gurdjieff, his inheritor and 'transmitter', a striking woman of eighty, still an example for Brook. He wrote about her with a dedication due to someone who had attained a higher level of living: 'Through her own unremitting struggle, she had gained the capacity to transmit to others a unique quality of experience, and I now made a vow to myself always to be available whenever the opportunity arose to be near her.' Living and working in Paris would make this much more possible.

Then there was the other remarkable Parisian woman in his life: his agent, producer and manager Micheline Rozan, who he had met twelve years before, when she'd persuaded him to do Arthur Miller's *A View from the Bridge* in Paris, and had guided his Paris career ever since. In Brook she encountered not only a talent she admired, but a bold thinker whose ambitious schemes stimulated her own strategies as a producer. Together they turned Brook's vision into a theatre, production budgets, a troupe, tours, and, as time passed, the reputation and the clout to raise development money for Peter's next experiment. They attained a shorthand which meant they hardly had to exchange a word to know what the other thought: a glance would be enough, or merely a raised eyebrow in a meeting with others. Their partnership, their creative complicity over thirty years, can be compared with modern theatre's great double acts: Stanislavski and Nemirovich-Danchenko, Giorgio Strehler and Paolo Grassi, Joan Littlewood and Gerry Raffles.

She was combative, relishing hard negotiation. She worked long hours in an office attached to her flat in the rue du Cirque, telephoning between the world's time-zones, pushing herself and her tiny staff. She had a brain and a tongue like quicksilver.

It was she who found for Brook the ruined theatre he turned into a theatrical emblem of enduring transience; she scrutinised every nail and wire in it. She barred the door to time-wasters and took care of the theatre's budget and Brook's finances. She drove a hard bargain, knowing Brook's worth to the world's international promoters and presenters. Recognising that Rozan was an exceptional force of nature, Brook heeded her warnings, for she had an awareness of dangers ahead, and a refusal to look on any illusory bright side. Brook made himself available for key meetings, delivered speeches, drafted appeals. She believed in him, even when she questioned some of his shows, and he supported her during the good times and the inevitable bad ones. Perhaps he had never had such unconditional support since his father.

Brook's eloquence and Micheline's energetic networking bore fruit. One wealthy American triggered all the other foundations. Brook and Rozan's International Centre for Theatre Research ended up receiving substantial grants from the Ford and Gulbenkian foundations, from UNESCO in Paris and from a Persian commission to make a new work for the Shiraz/Persepolis festival. In New York the swashbuckling impresario David Merrick, who had presented *A Midsummer Night's Dream* on Broadway, made a donation from his fund.

Brook called up all his international contacts to find actors for the group. Ellen Stewart, founder director of the La Mama Experimental Theater in Greenwich Village, suggested a great range of high-spirited American actors; Grotowski proposed actors who had come to his workshops; Jean-Louis Barrault remembered actors who he had met through his Théâtre des Nations; Brook himself canvassed the more adventurous talents of the Royal Shakespeare Company, and kept an eye on the bolder spirits playing in the nooks and corners of London theatre. The group assembled in Paris in October 1970, in a dingy hall in the Cité Universitaire, since their future home, the Mobilier National, was not ready. 'What, in the theatre, is "a company"? What is "a troupe"? What is "an ensemble"?' asked Brook. The group of actors that was to go with Brook to Paris in 1970, Persia in 1971, Africa in 1972 and America in 1973 was a company of no fixed abode. It had a base in Paris, but it emanated outwards, it was, in Brook's own terms, 'a shifting point'. Its cohesion rested on what Brook, in an interview with David Williams, scientifically defined as 'the pre-expressive substrata that underlie cultural stereotypes and imitations'.

They wanted to reach the greatest diversity of audiences. Audiences of strangers, coming from distant worlds of belief and values. Audiences who had never been inside a theatre, who did not even have a concept of theatre. Audiences separated from the actors by language, religion, ethnicity.

Brook's group in 1970 was neither an expatriate English company nor an expatriate French theatre troupe; it was, like the astronauts, extra-terrestrial. It was the beginning of something unprecedented: a planetary theatre.

As Brook and his group stood at the threshold of their three-year odyssey of research, one can see clearly the variety and flavour of the actors with whom he launched his international group for the testing journeys of its first three years

Yoshi Oida had perhaps made the longest journey and the greatest displacement. An outstanding Japanese actor, trained in the disciplines of classical Noh, Kyogen and Bunraku theatre, and an adept in Zen prayer and meditation, Yoshi had stamina, taut concentration, power mixed with humour.

Bruce Myers, the Englishman in the group, met Brook at Stratford-upon-Avon, where he'd been a dissatisfied Royal Shakespeare Company actor, and had left – unable, he said, to understand a word the other actors were saying, though the sound was beautiful.

Andreas Katsulas, an expansive Greek-American and Michele Collison, a big, beautiful actress and singer, both came from the New York off-off-Broadway scene, as did the extravagant Lou Zeldis and the wiry composer Elizabeth Swados. They came from many places and situations: Malick Bowens from Mali, who had stayed in Paris to work with Grotowski; Miriam Goldschmidt, daughter of a Malian father and a German mother, sharp featured, full of edgy energy; Helen Mirren, breaking away from her successful career as a young theatre and film star, and proving herself to be a gifted comic improviser. She joined late, in 1972, and had to deal with resistance in the group to working with the woman the tabloids called 'The Sex Queen of the Royal Shakespeare Company'. She was seductive, could be brusque and relished playing hags, against her innate glamour. Natasha Parry, Brook's wife, bringing a quiet beauty and an inner tension. Sylvain Corthay came from Parisian experimental theatre, and had played Shakespearean leads with Jean Vilar and Jean-Louis Barrault. François Marthouret, handsome and reflective, had started his own experimental theatre in Marseilles, and was now well known as a film and television actor. A member of a Trotskyite *groupuscule*, he was to have reservations about the group going to the Shah's Persia.

On their first day in the Cité Universitaire hall, Brook told the group that what is done on the first day of anything shapes everything that follows. 'Our job is to animate,' he said, 'to put life into the lifeless. So go ahead and transform this sad little hall into a place of excitement, of food and enjoyment. You have three hours to bring it to life.' With wide ribbons of coloured paper they constructed a big tent with slits in its walls. From *traiteurs* and *charcuteries* and *épiceries* across Paris came good things to eat, and soon the room was full of the scent of spices. They ate, they sang, they danced, all beginning to get to know each other.

A girl from the street came in, attracted by the sounds and smells. 'They sat her down, fed her and sang to her,' wrote A.C.H. Smith, chronicler of the group's beginnings and first journey. 'The excitement of making the transformation gave life to everything that was done within it. Then it was all cleared away, not a trace left. It had been, said Brook, "the essential blueprint of what we are learning about popular entertainment, the ability to assess a whole situation".' And the first of many lessons in transience, the empty space and how to inhabit and transform it, how to say goodbye to it.

It was some time before they recaptured that bold innocence of what Brook called 'the beginner's mind', that explosion of joy and colour of the first 'consecration of the house' – even if the Cité Universitaire hall was not their house. The question, said Brook, was not about the quality of the material they were performing, 'but of the completeness of the circle we make'. And that circle, as the next three nomadic years were to show, did not need a house to contain it; it could be spun anywhere.

They worked with sticks. Long thin bamboo wands, a heap of them in the corner of the Salle Peret of the Mobilier National to which they had now moved. They threw them to each other in a circle, they hoisted them aloft, together, gently, into a cone, a spire, then slowly lowered them, careful to preserve a circular shape. Then they worked with boxes. Cardboard boxes, sturdy and floppy boxes, they did everything they could do with boxes – wore them like frocks or hats, crawled into them like houses, made a train out of boxes and travelled. They worked with shoes. Scuffed and battered shoes which they treated like delicious fillet steaks, or tottered about in, squeezed big male feet into dainty female slippers, or turned into jewellery or telephones.

They made long keening sounds, choppy syncopated noises. They tried to give sequences of noises the shape and meaning of simple sentences, and hoped to be understood. Then they spoke the sounds and meanings of languages long dead or from a long way off. The ancient Greek of Aeschylus. The Latin of Seneca. From Persia, the ancient Zoroastrian language, Avesta. Arabic, Armenian, Japanese, Spanish. Then they invented their own language, from the syllables they used most. *Bash. Ta. Hon. Do. Bashtahondo.* They went hunting for the flesh and body of a language, the meaning inseparable from the sounds. They became language mystics. Brook participated in the exercises, a little clumsily according to some of his actors, but with determination and a strong will to break through the shackles of his own constraints.

Stories saved them from losing themselves down the paths of language. Language was the abstraction, stories were specific, though they could become universal. Some of the languages came embedded with stories and myths. The Prometheus story told by Aeschylus in Greek: stealing fire from the gods and being punished for it. Calderón's *Life's A Dream* (*La vida es sueño*): the hero imprisoned away from the world at birth and released into it as a young man. A similar story of a human like a blank slate, told in Peter Handke's German-language play *Kaspar.* They took *Kaspar* apart and put it together in countless different ways, and played it in schools and community centres in the *quartier*. But their work kept rotating around the Promethean story, man's first mastery, fire stolen from Olympus.

Ted Hughes, who had worked with Brook at the Old Vic, joined their sessions, in preparation for the piece they would create in Persia. The anthropology he'd studied at Cambridge fed Hughes' poems; Brook wanted him to devise a comprehensive myth, weaving in and out of the Prometheus story, to be performed at the Shiraz/Persepolis festival in Persia, which had given the group its first commission. What language would he write it in? An invented language, of course: Hughes called it Orghast, and this also became the name of the piece.

The poet and the director engaged intuitively and deeply. Brook was seeking to renew the powers of theatre in ancient traditions and sources.

Hughes was seeking to plant his personal experience and his country's psyche and language in myth and legend. This search underpinned not only Hughes' poetry, but a vast study of 'the tragic equation' in Shakespeare's last fourteen plays, considered as if they were one immense drama. He was bringing this to completion while he was working with Brook; it was published as *Shakespeare and the Goddess of Complete Being*. Hughes' powerful speculations wonderfully complement Brook's ventures into Shakespeare's impersonality and multiplicity. Hughes had a technical/mystical vocabulary for his obsessions; Brook was opening up the physical, psychic and vocal force of truthful performance, which in turn stimulated Hughes to map the sites of language in the body. *Orghast*, the group's first public performance at an international event, would contain the forces that drove both men.

In an interview with Tom Stoppard during the making of *Orghast*, Hughes explained it further:

> What you hear in a person's voice is what is going on at the centre of gravity in his consciousness at that moment. Imagination and concentration are decisive. The action of the mind at that moment is decisive. When the attention is scrambled the voice loses its anchor, or its roothold rather, in what is really going on in the man. This is the voice most of us are producing most of the time. Our real message is getting jammed. We are speaking a sort of gabbled gibberish of static interference. But when the mind is clear and the experience of the moment is actual and true, then a simple syllable can transmit volumes. A survivor only needs to sigh and it hits you like a hammer.

Stoppard's response was a mixture of awe at the immensity of the enterprise, and concern at its renunciation of storytelling: '*Orghast* aims to be a leveller of audiences by appealing not to semantic athleticism but to the instinctive recognition of a "mental state" within a sound. One can hardly imagine a bolder challenge to the limits of narrative.'

Brook was now heading his theatre into realms of radical experiment, of abstraction and non-naturalism. What music, fine art, surrealism and anthropology – perhaps *the* archetypal modernist field of study – had opened up, this theatrical saga in Persia, a country between East and West, a land of live popular traditions and evocative ruins, could now explore. Stoppard was right: there was only a minimally comprehensible narrative in *Orghast*, though Hughes had written out an immense scroll of interconnected back stories, an epic cycle of which the dramatised events of the play *Orghast* were a suggestive and tantalising slice. But there were tonal resonances of *Prometheus*, of Manichean creation myths and of the historical defeat of the Persians by the ancient Greeks at the formative battle of Salamis; and Brook and Hughes in the choruses of *Orghast* sought to connect the psyche of the actors to the psyche of the audience, at a level deeper than its cultural formations, its specific roots and local codes.

In the summer of 1971, they took their group and their *Orghast* to Persia, to the festival of Shiraz/Persepolis, at the invitation of its patron, the wife of the Shah. They worked on the piece for three months, in preparation for a single performance in the ancient ruins. There's a photograph of Brook at rehearsal in the hall of the Baghe Ferdous, a slightly battered old mansion on the outskirts of Teheran, where the group worked for its first seven weeks in Persia. A lofty space with arabesque cornices and windows opening on to a walled garden, where people went off to work in smaller groups, the room is strewn with mattresses. On one of these, Brook lies back, barefoot, leaning on one elbow, laughing like a contented child as he watches an improvisation, at ease like a pasha on a divan. Next to him is Natasha, long haired, equally relaxed; to his left, Arbi Ovanessian, his Persian assistant director; behind him Mahin Tadjadod, the academic whose researches offered the group clues and diagrams of the pronunciation of the extinct ceremonial language of Avesta. Behind Brook, hunched intently on a heap of mattresses is the language master of *Orghast*, Ted Hughes. Next to Brook a script, and a cymbal suspended in an iron frame. In his hand he holds a stick, to beat the cymbal when he wants to halt the work. The tiled floor gleams in the reflected sunlight.

At times, the three months spent working in Persia was as idyllic as this photograph conveys. There were big ideas swirling through their work, a majestic ruined site which awaited them, villages where they would try out their popular theatre work. Brook the spokesman was carefully keeping his options open about the result, at the risk of sounding abstract: 'We are not making a dramatic esperanto. The result we are working towards is not a form, not an image, but a set of conditions in which a certain quality of performance can arise. This sort of work takes a long time, and unfortunately it is in contradiction to the budgets and building schedules of festivals.' Sometimes the work, the physical conditions, the light, were magical. Other times, the group, far from home and searching for a path whose direction was often hidden and obscure, went a little crazy. They were staying in a far-from-idyllic motel in the Teheran suburbs. They thought they were being scrutinised by SAVAK, the Shah's secret police. They had borne the brunt of criticisms before they left, people telling them they shouldn't be performing in a police state. Eric Bentley, the translator and advocate of Brecht in America, wrote that Brook had missed a trick by agreeing to go; refusal, he wrote in the spring 1971 issue of *Partisan Review*, would have been a small act of 'political warfare'. There was dissension within the group, too, about who they were performing to. The normal audience at an international festival in a country which has been cut off from world developments is local artists, the intellectual and social elite from the host country and abroad and young people, eager to taste the best and most radical work. Once Brook's group arrived, they learned that they would have to give one special performance exclusively for the Shabanou and her rich, famous and official guests. A bitter discussion took place. Those who were most unhappy pointed out that Persia was not only under authoritarian rule, but that the Shah was also pocketing oil revenues which could have been used to help the poor. They reiterated that other American and European companies had refused to take the Shiraz/Persepolis estival's 'dirty money'. While that may be so, replied those who were for performing in Persia, you had to look at who *has* performed at the Shiraz/Persepolis festival – Jerzy Grotowski, Joe Chaikin and Victor García, all of who had been valued collaborators in Brook's work.

For Brook, the fact that Persia was lodged between East and West and that the sites where they played were drenched in ancient history and religion mattered every bit as much as the political behaviour of the Shah's regime. 'It would be complete humbug,' he said, 'for us to work in France as though we naively believed that there was no repression or police brutality there, and suddenly discover it in Iran.' He had a ninety-minute audience with the Shabanou, which he called 'a direct confrontation' and said he was able to air a number of criticisms which in his view managed to 'balance the account'.

After the event, Brook concluded, 'Iran is not a country that I've broken relations with. It's a very complex country, with good and bad elements. You might say there are two Irans: an Iran that one dreads and an Iran of great quality. One positive quality is that we were able to do this piece, *Orghast*, within a particular tradition, which was a necessary base for this stage of our work . . . If I can set foot in the United States, then I can set foot in Iran.'

Prickly relationships with the nine Persian actors in the group came to a head when it was time to distribute parts for the forthcoming performance of *Orghast*. The Persian actors felt that these 'Western' theatre people had passed them over for the main roles and relegated them to the chorus.

But as Brook's assistant director Geoffrey Reeves bluntly put it, 'Despite their talents and vocal abilities, most of the Persian actors were unable to achieve any flexibility of pitch or rhythm, or to find outlets for their emotions within the strict discipline of the work. After six weeks, only two could handle *Orghast*; the rest were chorus material.' Brook called the Persian actors to a crisis meeting. Some resented being tutored by a woman. Some hated the fact that a group of foreigners were taking over their own archaic language, Avesta. Brook listened, remembering that when they did exercises in producing pure sound, the Persian actors had gravitated towards a melancholic, plaintive note. Believing that 'a man's musical pattern is as revealing of his essential nature as a Rorschach test', Brook saw this as the result of centuries of social stagnation, of European hostility, an unresolved ancestral attitude of inner defeat.

A. C. H. Smith, in his book about the play's process and production, pictures Brook getting tougher as the final weeks of preparation wound down:

> He told them: 'Maybe you didn't know what you were joining. The Paris group understand the condition of our work together: to work for the sake of the work, even if you've got only one word to do in a day.' If anyone was not prepared to be in the chorus, to do the complex work of the chorus really well, this was the moment to leave. Three of the thirteen did leave. One of them had been given, to work on, the Messenger speech in *The Persians*, 'perhaps the

greatest speech in world theatre,' but felt humiliated because he had been given
no Orghast.

The Persian actors who left had to report their departure to the Ministry
of Culture. They laid complaints against Brook and his troupe: an actor and
an actress had, scandalously, been thrust together in one of the large
cardboard boxes for an improvisation; Brook's actors had lifted ideas from
performances of the indigenous folk-theatre, *ruhozi*; and, by choosing part
of Aeschylus' *The Persians*, Brook was rubbing the country's nose in its
greatest defeat. No one at the Ministry took these complaints seriously.

The following day, Brook talked to the group of actors who had started
with him in Paris. It's his clearest statement to date of the dynamics of a
theatre group:

> Inside the group one should recognise that all everyday emotions have to be
> kept out, and – this is the prime discipline – one should rigorously prevent
> them from ever creeping into the work. For this ideal working state one needs
> a great sense of realism, and one must take care not to be seduced by certain
> dreams. For instance, exercises like those we have been doing – the sticks, Tai
> Chi, etc. – can make a group play rapidly and intuitively together. It's a lovely
> reassuring feeling: nobody at any moment stands out. Then the exercises come
> to an end. Now suddenly one will have a lot to do, another a little. The
> beautiful circle is broken. The strength of mind of each of us comes into
> question.
>
> Last night I called together the Persian group and spoke at length about
> these things, the condition of our work being that everyone accepts and tackles
> totally whatever possibilities are offered. The Persian actors had come into the
> work not knowing about us. Perhaps they had many misunderstandings,
> thinking it would be something to show to their friends or to improve their
> status. So I said that things were still in evolution and reminded them that no
> promises had ever been made to anyone.

For many of the group, perhaps the purest expression of their work in
Persia was not the grand *Orghast* drama at the ruins of Persepolis and the
tombs of Naqsh-e-Rustam, which went round the world as a series of vivid

press pictures and awe-struck accounts. No, the most satisfying work, the work most performers would have liked to continue with was the performance at a little village, Uzbakhi. It was one of the earliest of what they came to call 'carpet plays': a carpet is laid down to make a playing area, villagers are invited without being imposed on, and the players try to reach them without falling back on the circus tricks and roll-up routines with which countless street-theatre players have made a quickly forgotten mark.

The group had been working on a Ted Hughes scenario, *Difficulties of a Bridegroom*, about a tongue-tied lover and his adventures with his in-laws and with a rival suitor who is accidentally killed and, in a time-honoured routine, becomes a corpse that will not lie still. This was a bare basis for improvisation. The props were a beautiful set of boxes and the ever-useful bamboo sticks. The language was Bashtahondo. With the help of a Persian *ruhozi* actor, they found Uzbakhi, a village eighty kilometres from Teheran and one afternoon, while the villagers were finishing their work in the fields, arrived to set up. At the heart of Uzbakhi was a large clay compound, a courtyard with rooms scooped out of the enclosing mud wall. A little low-key negotiation – also part of the process – led to the unrolling of the carpet in the centre of the courtyard. By five o'clock, some two hundred people had gathered to watch, of which more than a hundred were children. The response was quick, attentive and lively. The women of the village, faces shrouded, laughed less openly than the men. (Out of deference to a society which does not accept woman acting in public, Brook had decided that the actresses in the group should not take part, but watch. Later the women villagers asked the actresses why they had sat at the side and not performed.)

The villagers, though not completely untouched by city life – some had worked there – had never seen live theatre. But they quickly picked up plot points and comedy routines; the actors managed to play in a calmer, more relaxed, less excitable way. The experience was simple, but it was complete. The festival audience, however, was very different. The Shabanou and her entourage – international festival cognoscenti and drama critics from around the world – needed a different mode of approach. Brook wrote a donnish programme note for the performance: 'What is the relation between verbal and non-verbal theatre? What happens when gesture and sound turn into word? What is the exact place of the word in theatrical expression? As vibration? Concept? Music? Is any evidence buried in the sound structure of certain ancient languages?'

The first part of the show unfolded at Persepolis, at the tomb of Artaterxes, up a steep mountain track. Around a huge open cube cut into the mountain, the actors were disposed, most prominently Prometheus, chained to the rock. A molten globe of fire snaked its way down from the heights, the original theft of power to make or destroy which humanity received. Krogon, Hughes' Zeus-figure, steals the fire back, to defend himself against his sons who, it has been foretold, will kill their father. In a desperate struggle, he kills and eats his offspring. And all the time the sonorous sounds and teasing patterns of Hughes' Orghast-language echoed round the rock-chamber and entered the audience's ears:

BULLORGA OMBOLOM FROR
darkness opened its womb
SHARSAYA NULBULDA BRARG
I hear chaos roar
IN OMBOLOM BULLORGA
in the womb of darkness

Orghast Part II, planned to start at four-thirty a.m. and end at dawn at another historic site, Naqsh-e-Rustam, nearly didn't happen, because of a skirmish with the Shabanou's security apparatus. They prevented Brook, his actors and his advance technical team from getting into the site. Brook was furious, in his contained, cutting way; indeed he claims he was shoved by an officer and responded in kind. He took the entire company off to a coffee house and refused to respond to increasingly frantic royal messengers, come to tell him he couldn't keep the Queen waiting. Eventually, the technicians were allowed in and, more than an hour late, the performance began, conjuring up the ghosts and memories of another epic event, the defeat of the Persians by the Greeks, as dramatised by Aeschylus.

From the beginning, with a great bowl of fire descending on the saga's massive figures against the pitted, bas-reliefed walls, to the distant, solitary shepherd in the dawn at the end of Part II walking his cow on a leash along a ridge that led to the plain, the audience was spellbound. 'The focus changes,' wrote Irving Wardle, 'from swirling mass effects to luridly illuminated single figures, from impassioned utterance in Greek to the stonily remote rhythms of Avesta, from human spectacle to an unearthly stirring into life of the mountain itself.' Richard Findlater was overwhelmed, but shared the bewilderment of much of the audience: 'What we saw and above all, what we heard was riveting, beautiful and disturbing; but what it meant, precisely, was elusive.'

Findlater was also aware of an 'Emperor's Clothes' theorising and veneration around *Orghast*, 'a noticeable element of wool in the verbal cloth of gold that shrouds what Brook *says* he is doing; but in what he does there shines out, repeatedly, the unmistakable *mana* of the arch-magician, a self-renewing Prospero with enough of Puck in him to change his staff in time, before it is snapped by theory.'

Andrew Porter, opera critic of the *Financial Times*, who had played a key part in getting Brook invited to the Shiraz/Persepolis festival, noted the parallels between Brook's sound-world and the structure and ethos of contemporary composers such as Berio or Stockhausen. *Orghast Part II* reduced him to a state of near-worship: 'When from the darkness of Darius's tomb-mouth the solemn shape stepped forth, the effect was overwhelming, and the impulse to fling oneself on one's knees along with the actors became hard to master. What could have been just melodramatic became thrilling and awe-ful. The playgoer who has entered deeply into *Orghast* has passed through fire, and can never be the same again.' Porter's sense of transformation echoes Brook own half-voiced beliefs about the fleetingly redemptive powers of theatre.

Brook's loosening of old ties and his building of a new way of working had three phases. The first, starting in November 1970, had been the intensive work in the laboratory of the Mobilier National, turned towards the actors, and in *Orghast* what they could discover across demarcations of race and culture. The second, more outward-turned phase, their two-month trip to Africa, which they began in December 1972, was a rough, often desolate, and now and then exalting trip. Within the group, traditions continued to mingle: Brook's own eclectic but ultimately rigorous explorations met the instinctual, freewheeling, jazzy energy of new American theatre; Africans bedded down side by side with Europeans and Americans in the sleeping bags that sheltered them from the cold Sahara night. And Brook urged them to destroy the boundaries between art and life, to see even the chores of group camping – the washing-up rota, latrines, setting up lights to eat by – as part of 'the whole exercise, the mega-exercise'. When things went wrong, as they inevitably did, John Heilpern writes in his picaresque New Journalistic account of the safari, 'Brook would call another of the countless group meetings, say that he refused to be put into the position of a teacher ticking off pupils who were not pulling their weight in washing-up duties, and utter his mantra, "These things should be *sensed*".'

He must have had second-sight reminders of the authoritarianism of his own school experiences, and of the group anarchy he had let loose in *Lord of the Flies*. But any fears of repeating the past were countered by excitement at his real goal: a functioning, creative group that meshed at all levels, a life/art ensemble which he could lead and join.

Heilpern captures the fervour of his commitment:

'See the camp as an *extension* of the work,' Brook kept telling us. 'See it as an improvisation. Either it lives or it doesn't.' And on another occasion, when fatigue and depression took over the group, he called the actors together. He was shaking with anger. He confronted them in silence on the carpet. 'I am prepared to stop this trip at any time,' he began. The force of it stunned us. 'I will stop it this minute if necessary! If I'm to be put in the position of a schoolmaster it would be intolerable. But if we cannot work together at every level there is just no *point* in us being here. This isn't a sightseeing tour. If there is anyone who thinks it is, then say so now and go home. It isn't just a challenge. It's something far more than this. It's in the nature of a super-challenge. It is for us the whole point of being here. Are we aware of this? It is the word that summarizes this whole discussion – *awareness*.'

In Salah. Agadès. The Tuareg people, the Peulh people. These are some of the places and the people where the group succeeded in bridging the cultural abyss, and through loosely prepared scenarios, on-the-spot improvisations or soaring musical riffs, reached their audiences. The group would arrive, ask the village chief or the regional authority if they could perform – they didn't call it theatre, for there is no place in the mind of Africans for the word 'theatre', they called it 'story', 'music'. They obtained permission and agreed a space where they could lay out their magic carpet, in the shade of a big tree if possible. They had done exercise after exercise, standing in a circle looking straight ahead, but becoming aware that a movement had been made by their neighbour and it was their job to pass it round the circle, looking neither at the one who had passed on the movement nor the one to whom it would be transmitted.

In Paris they had prepared small, wordless plays. Heilpern had done one, *The Shoe Show*. Ted Hughes had done another, *The Ogre Show*. The actors invented their own, *The Bread Show*, and a hundred varieties of box shows. With the right conditions, the whole thing could ignite, as it did early on, in In Salah in the Sahara, when Sylvain Corthay soloed wildly above a pulsing bass from the group, and immediately the audience responded with laughter and enthusiasm to a quality of sound. Or in the second performance in Agadès in Niger when, in Heilpern's words, 'at times it was as if they were playing in a frenzy, switching direction time and again, risking more and more in an effort to catch all the moods and lightning responses of the people.'

Often an extraordinary sound or gesture came from the Africans themselves, and the actors simply gazed in wonder and tried to offer a response, witnessing the sky-storming visions of Antonin Artaud sung and danced out before them with a composure, a relaxation, a humour, even a high-camp glee, that exploded the solemnity of many of Artaud's manifestos. The laughing villagers of Wuseli performed an infectious celebration ceremony made up of hoots and shuffles, with an ambling insouciance and ease that went on for hours. The village of the loonies, Heilpern called it. And the Peulhs, a gorgeously tricked out group, face-painted and bejewelled, who disdained all the musical offerings from Brook's actors until they finally decided to join them in a long sustained 'ah' sound: 'It was as if the Peulh were pulling the sound from them. They pointed to the sky . . . Somehow the sound makes itself.' The next day, the group set up under a tree in the fields to give a farewell show for the people of Agadès. They waited and they waited, until sunset, singing. Then they realised that nobody would come. The village was virtually deserted. The people had left in search of better land. They knew famine was on its way.

As the group went on, they introduced a new element into their shows –
birdsong, the voices of hoopoe and nightingale, dove and swallow and a
multitude of other exotic birds which they had explored in Paris. This had
come from a sequence of bird-poems which Brook had asked Ted Hughes to
write, as a preamble to their work on Brook's next project: a Persian Sufi
poem by Farid Uddin Attar, *The Conference of the Birds*, which used the
journey of a flock of birds as a metaphor for human life. In Africa they took
the first steps into this material, trying out birdsong, bird journeys and bird
fights.

Of course, there were misunderstandings and misapprehensions. The poet
and playwright Tony Harrison, who speaks some of Nigeria's many
languages, was amused to see a subsequent documentary in which Brook
arrived by boat in a village in backwoods Nigeria where they were going to
perform. An old man on the bank muttered *Kwabo, kwabo* as they
approached. Brook, picking the phrase up quickly, stepped out of the boat,
advanced beaming on the old man, threw his arms open and said, '*Kwabo,
Kwabo*', with long English vowels and diphthongs, evidently unaware that
the word meant 'Give us a penny'.

But out of the testing journey, out of the encounters good and bad, Brook
had reason to feel that his hunch about a common theatrical language and
the rich resources of a diverse group was working out.

While Brook had been in Paris, Persia and Africa, the *Dream* had been on
the road. In January 1971, it opened in New York, at the Billy Rose Theater,
produced by David Merrick. At the end of its Broadway run, a young
producer called Harvey Lichtenstein came to see Merrick with a proposition. 'When your run is finished, could we have the show in Brooklyn for a
final two weeks? We'd like to present it to a new audience at less than
Broadway prices.' Merrick was scornful at first. But finally, seeing that it
could be perceived as a noble act of philanthropy, he agreed.

A Midsummer Night's Dream played in the Brooklyn Academy of Music
(known in New York parlance as BAM), which Harvey Lichtenstein was
running as an avant-garde centre for opera, dance and what their brochures
called 'next wave' performance, from Philip Glass to Laurie Anderson. Most
of the seats for the *Dream* cost less than Broadway and two hundred young

people sat on cushions in the front stalls at five dollars a head. Lichtenstein's enthusiastic embrace and advocacy of Brook's work was to give him a regular base in Brooklyn, and an even higher profile in the press and media.

A Midsummer Night's Dream took to the road in north America, followed by a season at the Aldwych Theatre in London, and then a year's world tour through Europe, Japan and Australia. Its high-wire magic, its nightmares in full daylight and its shifts from the lofty and poetic to the simplicity of Shakespeare's own 'carpet play', spoke across language barriers, as Brook and his actors were concurrently trying to do in their travels.

In July 1973, as the *Dream* was concluding its antipodean tour, Brook and his CIRT group arrived in California to complete the third part of their research journey, bringing with them the immense Persian carpet, the *Ur*-carpet of their roll-it-out-and-start-right-here performances; their richly coloured and patterned Nigerian blankets, made out of sewn-together panels of dyed and woven cloth, and of course their bamboo sticks and cardboard boxes.

They arrived in San Juan Bautista, a former Spanish mission town two hours' drive from San Francisco. It was the home of *El Teatro Campesino* (The Farm-workers' Theatre), a Spanish-speaking theatre run by a playwright and director, Luis Valdez. It had grown out of the struggles of the grape-pickers against exploitation, racism and the monopoly of the corrupt Teamsters Union in the vineyards of Southern California. The *campesinos* were migrant workers from Mexico – they called themselves *chicanos*. Their strikes, boycotts and demonstrations had been organised under the charismatic leadership of Cesar Chavez, an outstanding labour activist, a public speaker with the rousing appeal of his contemporary, Martin Luther King. In 1968, inspired by the example of Gandhi, he had gone on hunger strike for twenty-five days.

Early on in their Californian journey, Brook and the group went to meet Chavez. The *chicanos'* ultimately victorious recent strike against the grape-growers of the Delano district had lasted for five years. It became known by its Spanish name, *La Huelga*, and acquired an aura of meanings beyond the specifically political. *Huelga* stood for strength, morality, the life force itself. *Huelga* became a deep motivating force, connected with the spirit of the serpent – 'living, pulsating, flowing like a snake', said Luis Valdez.

Valdez had learned his craft with one of the leading American radical theatre groups, the San Francisco Mime Troupe, who made a theatre of instant outline and chutzpah in the city's parks and plazas and street corners. In 1965 Luis Valdez left the Troupe and joined Chavez in the fields, creating urgent, immediate political skits – *actos* – performed by a handful of actors with a guitar. *Campesino's actos* framed demands and triggered action, in a swift style drawing on the *fiesta* of street theatre. Brook had met Valdez and seen their affirmative, joyful work at the Nancy International Theatre Festival in 1972. He realised he was watching theatre from a situation of oppression where agit-prop, and the song and poetry of an old tradition, were an earned right, not a metropolitan nostalgia.

But there were other currents in the work of *El Teatro Campesino*. These performers had a culture which few white North-American groups could match. Starting with Chavez himself, they were largely observant Catholics, but they had a darker legacy. Through acts of 'miscegenation' between Spanish colonial conquerors and local Indian women, the *chicanos* were also inhabited by the dreams, mythologies and magic of the non-Christian world of American Indians. *Chicanismo*, as it came to be known, was a rich brew of beliefs. Beyond the social satire and the jauntiness, there was a sombre meditation on the mystery of life and death. Luis Valdez wanted to add to the political immediacy of the *actos*, the timeless side of his people's experience, its *mitos*, its myths. This wish to find forms to express the invisible and permanent aspects of humanity was the common ground of a discussion between Brook and Valdez when they had met in France. For Brook, *El Teatro Campesino* was rough theatre incarnate; it pulled him down from his more abstract research, and put the stress on the audience as much as the actor. In California a year later, the two groups began work together, showing each other performances, swapping exercises, jumping in on each other's improvisations like jazzmen. *The Conference of the Birds* became the pole around which their theatrical encounter crystallised. It tells how all the birds in the world gather together to seek a king for themselves. The hoopoe, an enlightened bird, tells them they already have a king, the Simorgh, but that he is far away, and that to find him will mean a long and arduous journey. One by one the birds' initial enthusiasm for the quest falters; their excuses all point to their reluctance to change their lives. Tiny allegorical stories are grafted into the action to draw lessons from each bird's reluctance to change. Nonetheless, they do set out behind the hoopoe, travelling through seven valleys of enlightenment to arrive at the Simorgh's court. When they are finally admitted, they find that the Simorgh is not an outside ruler, but a faculty, a possibility, a source within them. The journey will never end.

In California, Brook's actors and the *Campesinos* developed their *Birds* improvisations, as well as returning to another text of their early work at the Mobilier, Peter Handke's *Kaspar*. They gave performances of *Los Pajaros* (*The Conference of the Birds* in its Spanish-language version, performed by both groups) in high school playgrounds, at Union meetings, in a Catholic seminary. The *Campesino* actors brought their very different energy and experience to the piece. Sometimes the results were thrilling, sometimes confusing. Midway through the work, Brook took the measure of the two groups' different paths and set out his own reason for doing *The Conference of the Birds*.

Brook was seeing *The Conference of the Birds* as a kind of meta-journey for the actual journeys he and the group undertook during these three years. Each member of the group was tested, just as the birds had been tested by the quest to find the Simorgh. Each of them – through fatigue, the irritations of group living, prejudices, habits, attachments – was tempted to drop out, to find excuses and rationalisations to stop. Each and all would be summoned to try to surmount their limitations.

At short notice they took a version of the piece to Four Acres Farm in Delano, where the United Farm Workers' strike was still holding out. (Eventually, in 1977, their union won the exclusive right to organise grape- and lettuce-pickers.) Rapidly, they put together a new version to perform at the strike headquarters. Michael Wilson reports it:

> The Simorgh became the thunderbird of the Union flag; the journey became the struggle of La Causa. Unity became union. The audience was remarkably cosmopolitan: Portuguese, Chicanos, Arabs, even two Sikhs. The opening routine, an argument in which everyone speaks a different language, came off brilliantly and was immediately grasped by the crowd. The journey and the Simorgh were described with reference to the Huelga and the Union. Felix was a Ridiculous Farmworker, Andreas a Grower. A new element had been added:

a chorus, made up of all the players not directly involved in the plot, led by Helen Mirren. Peter thought it had been the best performance ever, a real beginning.

The encounter with the *Campesinos* had turned out to be everything that Brook might have hoped for. In their eight weeks together, there had been real exchange: through improvisation, argument, sacrifice, myth, language, music, politics, celebration, food, and love affairs. *The Conference of the Birds* had been wrenched by turns towards the spirit, towards popular comedy, towards political struggle, songfest, wisdom tale; in whatever form they re-modelled it, it continued to fly.

Brook and his actors moved on to a variety of different audiences and spaces: an Institute for Humanistic Studies in the chic ski-resort of Aspen, Colorado; the Chippewa Indian reservation in Minnesota, where they worked with the Native American Theater Ensemble and members of the Nez Percé Indian tribe. They swapped hand- and sign-language, learned dances and songs. One night they witnessed a crowd of Chippewas dancing 'in a slow cosmic circle' at the lake's edge, to the sound of songs and drums. The dancers were unhappy about being watched, and Brook and his group were abruptly asked to leave; a small aftertaste of America's harsh treatment of 'native Americans'.

Nearing the end of the three-year CIRT research trip, the shape and meaning of Brook's journey, which he had embarked upon not knowing where it would lead, was now clearer. He was making a peripatetic theatre that had no home, only a rehearsal space; no common language; for three years, no need to perform in order to survive. It was that radical. In these first three years of the 1970s, Brook pushed to the outer limits the successive self-questionings, the *contestations* he had conducted during the past decade. He had questioned language in theatre; he had stripped Shakespeare of his sanctity and dug into unfamiliar myths; he had improvised in every way conceivable, and opened himself to powerful innovators, such as Grotowski and Joe Chaikin; he had measured film language in the light of stage expression, and vice versa; he had thrust theatre into the heart of urgent political conflicts and mass murder; he had redefined the expression of madness and magic, spirit and dream on the stage.

*   *   *

They arrived in Brooklyn to round off their quest with a six-week residency at Harvey Lichtenstein's Brooklyn Academy of Music. Brook set the group an arduous schedule. He invented the format of a 'Theatre Day'; demonstrations by the actors in exercises and games in the morning; participation by performers from the audience in the afternoon; and a performance of *The Conference of the Birds* at night. No less important, Brook and the group regularly went out into Brooklyn and played on street corners, in church gymnasia, museum forecourts and housing estates, doing improvised carpet shows for audiences, often made up of unruly black teenagers or tough young Italian men. In the daytime, the company was showing the tools of its trade and conducting 'master classes' for professionals; in the evening, they rolled out the great Persian carpet, lit lamps, put on their loose white costumes, took up their masks and props and stepped into the light of the cavernous ballroom to deliver the most exquisite performance of *The Conference of the Birds* they could muster.

Talking to the actors at the outset, Brook had laid out a clear idea of the two poles of what they were doing:

We have a-situation-which-is-not-prepared-at-all, and one which is highly prepared. In the latter case, it is as if a glass box surrounds the performance for the audience to admire, or to forget themselves completely and become one with what happens: a total experience, an astonishing level of experience.

In the first case, however, one is going out where life is happening anyway. One can't cheat: almost always what is prepared ahead of time in such cases ends by negating the actual living conditions and creating that glass box. By not preparing at all, one can be open to seize the current, ride the wind, deal with the forces that are there at that time and only at that time. There are unexpected surprises, involvement in the life-flow itself. But the chances of higher quality become even rarer in this situation than usual. There may be a current of feeling running between audience and actors, but not usually a 'great' performance. So neither pole is complete, neither is truer or realer than the other.

The group was now drawing on all the theatrical parameters they had used in countless environments. The *Orghast* experiments, planted in specific holy sites, and their first attempts at popular theatre in Persian villages. Their freewheeling African sorties into villages, picking what Brook calls the 'conducive' spot, making comedies, ceremonies, contests, probing audiences to participate. The encounter with the political struggle and intensity of the *chicanos*. Now in Brooklyn, as the research approached its end, they were, Brook reminded them, like trained warriors: 'The training of an actor is like that of a samurai: it may last for years and lead up to one sudden confrontation. The only rule is that one is *never* prepared for the situation one really meets.'

The one sudden confrontation would be their final night in Brooklyn. For the last week, they spent the time recapitulating the fruits of their expeditions. They picked up the text of *The Conference of the Birds* and from a hundred attempts to improvise around it, tried to return to the thing itself. Each night, they gave a different version of it, led by two different actors. Each performance attempted completeness, but it was not simply a 'glass box' performance; it trailed some of their busking, comedic improvisation. One night it might be low-life and vulgar, another night musical and solemn, another night arcane, a meditation on their work as a group of actors.

On the final night, they prepared three versions, one at eight p.m., one at midnight, one starting at five a.m. and ending at daybreak. Brook found the first 'rough theatre, vulgar, comic and full of life'. The second, he thought, was 'a quest for the sacred', intimate, whispered, played in candlelight. The third, in which he participated, was 'a kind of chorale, made out of improvised music'.

As the last notes died away and dawn came up, a cover was removed from a low table which Brook had prepared. On it were a row of carved wooden birds, the birds they had been bringing to life in so many ways for so long. Sitting in a circle with his actors, Brook poignantly rounded off all the experiences they had shared, recognising that the group had reached a peak just as the door marked 'Enter' is closing.

> If we had touched the quality of this night's performances one month ago, two months ago, three months ago, it would have been a springboard for something even more. But things are only exactly what they are; what's important is that we've finally touched it. This clarity could never have arisen through

theory, which is at best a basis, a link, a help. The quality which informed the night's performances could only have arisen through real experience.

The work becomes meaningful only when all our talents and skills are to serve something other than the actor's ego, or even the group, or good work. Imagination and humour, excitement, energy and passion must be devoted to something more: this thing which is called, on paper, *Conference of the Birds*. This is when theatre takes on the promise of something real, when it becomes more than just a poor thing to get involved in.

Three unremitting years of experiments, exercises and trials, of thinking and doing, doing as thinking, of encounters with other cultures, had brought Brook and his actors to a tangible apprehension of the 'something more' that made sense of their work. As they packed up for their return to Europe, where would they house their skills, how would they channel their experience?

12

THE WAY OF THEATRE
1974–78

Micheline Rozan had found the answer, or at least the beginning of an answer. When Brook returned to Paris, she took him up behind the Gare du Nord, into the *quartier* of small shops, immigrant communities – Arabs, Indians – bazaars and street markets. They stopped at a boarded-up building on the corner of the Boulevard de la Chapelle and the Boulevard Rochechouart, with its elevated Metro. 'Bouffes du Nord' said a sign above the boards. They prised open some planks, crawled along a tunnel, found themselves among debris and shattered plaster. Then Brook saw for the first time the theatre which would become the site of three decades' work. A door opened and there was the Bouffes – a majestic space with light streaming down through the dome and the dusty air on to what looked, at ground level, like a bomb site. There was a heap of rubble in the middle of the space with wires hanging everywhere, evidence of destruction in progress. Brook described his first impressions of the place:

> I was immediately certain that this was the right place for us. Even in its suffering condition there was an elegance to the proportions, a dignity to the atmosphere. It was clearly a theatre, but it looked nothing like it must have done previously: the 'cultural' skin of architectural finish had been cauterized away. All the stalls seats were missing, except a few that had been smashed up and thrown to one side. It seemed obvious that all we had to do was sweep away the rubble and find a means to sit people at the ground level. The

balcony seats were fine – they could be used as they were. And the walls could also stay as they were – covered in pockmarks, flayed raw by time, weather and human destruction.

The Théâtre des Bouffes du Nord had opened in 1876 and had led an erratic life, going from popular music-hall and *café-concert* entertainment, to the high-art drama of Lugné-Poë's Théâtre de l'Oeuvre, with its premieres of Ibsen's plays, to closure during both world wars and, after a stuttering post-war season or two, final closure in 1952 when its owners could not afford to meet security regulations. Although it had been built as a proscenium theatre, its very ruined state immediately suggested to Brook an Elizabethan plan with an open thrust stage circled by ramped seating and three balconies.

Brook, invited to direct a Shakespeare play for the Festival d'Automne, had chosen *Timon of Athens*, and now passionately wanted to do it at the Bouffes du Nord, 'otherwise,' said Brook, 'we'd be in the situation of using someone else's space, and our group would have nowhere to go after the production'. Other directors and companies had looked at the Bouffes, but their refurbishment plans, making the whole building good, were prohibitively expensive. Brook made a radical proposal: to keep the chipped and discoloured walls, the marks of work and history which embodied the soul of the building and finish the seats, exits and entrances just sufficiently to carry an audience and meet safety requirements. This 'ecological' approach, plus Micheline Rozan's hotline to Michel Guy, who after directing the Festival d'Automne had just been appointed Minister of Culture, ensured that funds and permits were found.

Time was still desperately short, though, as Brook was well aware: 'The designer Georges Wakhevitch put a team of his assistants to work at phenomenal speed, building seats out of wooden planks with straw cushions, making adjustments for fire safety, levelling the floor surface to make it into our new stage. The deadline was so soon upon us that some spectators on the first night were literally glued to their seats because the varnish hadn't had time to dry – we ended up paying them compensation for the bits of skirt and trouser they left behind.' Brook and Rozan also decided to have a single, low-cost price of admission and to reach out to the *quartier* with special performances and visits to schools and hospitals. They changed the name of the CIRT (International Centre for Theatre Research) to the CICT (International Centre for Theatre Creation), signifying to donors and public that they were in the business of creating productions, not merely researching theatre in test conditions. Opening the Bouffes du Nord in 1974 with a Shakespeare, and, with *Timon*, a very raw, angry one at that, Brook continued with a trio of productions in his first three years at the Bouffes that drew together his themes, his sources and his theatrical signatures, in an environment that, for the first time in his career, he could control and really get to know.

Three hallmarks characterised Brook's new venture, as he spelled them out: 'continuity, internationalism and research'. The next thirty years would show what a range of meanings he could give each of these terms. In all of the opening productions at the Bouffes du Nord, Brook relished the new space, learning to make finer and finer adjustments to its colour, texture and volume. At the same time there were after-echoes and continuities with his earlier work. With *Timon d'Athènes* (1974) he recalled his confrontational *Titus Andronicus* of 1955, but in another language and an environment very unlike Stratford-upon-Avon. The desolation of *The Ik* (1975) recalled the harsh worlds of *King Lear* and *Lord of the Flies*. With *Ubu aux Bouffes* (1977), a conflation of Alfred Jarry's King Ubu plays, he harked back to the anarchic comedy of madness and the absurd which had lit up *The Marat/ Sade*. With *The Conference of the Birds* (1979), he distilled the lessons and the style of the Persian poem he and the group had explored so persistently, in so many places.

If *Timon* can be seen as a Shakespearean prologue, Brook soon came to see inner resonances in the subsequent trio of productions. By 1980, he was talking about the *Ik*, *Ubu* and *Conference* as a thematic trilogy. 'We want to do these three pieces as a cycle,' he told New York journalist Margaret Croyden.

> It's a real progression of meaning. First, you go through the low, the world of
> the stomach, which is really the world of *Ubu*. Living with the stomach and yet
> living with another world the whole time is *The Ik*. Which is a picture of our
> world, a picture of London when we play it in London, a picture of Paris when

we play it in Paris, and a picture of New York now we're here. The picture is of a tragic modern world that is betraying its possibilities. And then *The Conference of the Birds* is a conference because the birds are living in a world of chaos and the question is implied: Is it true that there's something else? There it is – complete. A three-part play.

Timon d'Athènes is virtually unknown in France and often dismissed in England as a misanthropic rant. Shakespeare's tale of a compulsive philan-thropist, flattered as long as he opens his wallet, reviled when his funds run out, interested Brook because it was discordant and extreme. Timon, like Lear, responds with fury to the ingratitude of former friends, fulminating against fickle mankind, digging into the earth to denounce gold as the root cause of human betrayal and prostitution. No wonder that Marx used the play to reveal the corrosive effects of capitalism in tearing apart the bonds that make us human. And in 1974, as the oil crisis made the world realise how much it relied on one source of energy like a greedy addict, the play acquired yet another edge.

But its action is inward, too. In the fawning upon Timon ascendant, there is mismeasure; in Timon's manic tearing down of human ties, his reduction of life to perfidy, there's an imbalance even more extreme. Jean-Claude Carrière's lucid, immediate French version excited Brook. The fury of Timon's English ignited Carrière's French, giving his syntax heft and thrust. He dug his way into the play by uncovering its most frequent 'radiant words', *des mots rayonnants*, as he called Shakespeare's keywords. Brook approached it as if it were a new play.

Jean-Claude Carrière was to become Brook's creative mainstay for his first fifteen years in France. A well-known playwright and screenwriter, he had written some of Buñuel's greatest films, including *That Obscure Object of Desire* (1976). He was quick, craftsmanlike, dapper, flexible and a hard worker; Brook couldn't have wished for a better counterpart, and Carrière enjoyed the lightness he found in Brook. Carrière catches the pleasure the two men took in each other:

A journalist asked Peter, 'What are the supreme qualities needed to be a director – or to express things in general?' And he answered, 'To be an experienced child – *un enfant experimenté.*'

Peter has a very strong presence, but what most strikes me is his lightness. He's the opposite of heaviness in every way. When he travels, he just has a little bag on his shoulder, an Afghan bag made of knitted wool.

When I met him and discovered what he was doing, I said to myself, this is the most famous theatre director in the world going back to the sources, to the most basic things. So I asked if I could go along. And that was our first professional contact, at the Mobilier in 1970. I asked Peter if I could watch, and he said, no, you can't watch, but you can participate. So I went, once a week, once a fortnight. And finally, he asked me to do the French version of *Timon of Athens*.

Carrière also perceptively reveals the secret of the strength of Brook and Rozan's partnership:

Peter's relationship with Micheline Rozan isn't like the standard one between manager/producer and client. She has a character as abrupt as Peter's is sweet; he always seems suave, calm, a *brahman*. This contrast has helped them to stay together. He could never have done what he has without her. She didn't always like Peter's shows, but she's been miraculously well placed to help him, and together they made a moment of theatre history.

In recruiting actors for *Timon d'Athènes*, Brook was able to call on a young woman, Marie-Hélène Estienne who had joined the company as a press attaché after writing about art and theatre for French weekly magazines. Her husband, an art critic, had died suddenly, and Rozan invited her to join the theatre, to deal with the press. Estienne had seen *Moderato cantabile* and *Lord of the Flies*, but not his theatre work. She told him she wanted to learn about theatre from within, not just as a critic. Estienne's work was to evolve, from observer at rehearsals, to production assistant, casting director, dramaturg, assistant director, translator and writer. A restless, questioning woman – 'she changes her mind even more often than I do', says Brook – she was to become his artistic collaborator.

Doing *Timon* in French, Brook satisfied his instinct to purge a classic play of cultural accretions. With Estienne's help, he gathered a hybrid cast. Brook had seen John Schlesinger's production at Stratford-upon-Avon, with Scofield playing a youthful Timon, and it had given him a new vision of a play he'd regarded as tiresome. What came across at the Bouffes du Nord was entirely contemporary: the charming young boss of a corporation, free with his favours, bounteous to his friends, who turn their backs on him when the shares of his company start to tumble. It was not a deliberately topical production or a political allegory, but, thanks to Carrière's direct translation, and the barely salvaged, battered Bouffes du Nord, a classic text became immediate theatre.

Actors entered from all directions on a catwalk across the back wall, from a cavernous pit upstage, through holes punched in the proscenium arch, from the curved, shallow balconies. If there was a spatial freedom within the volumes of the Bouffes, there was a *bricolage*-liberty in the fragmentary costumes, often worn over everyday contemporary clothes. Alcibiades, the general who Timon invites to destroy his city, looked like a Latin American general. The Athenians flocking to Timon's banquets and parties wore cheap, glistening cloaks and huge, flapping capes which, as David Williams notes, made them look like crows. The pleasure Brook had taken in skilfully staging the opera chorus as far back as *Boris Godunov* had not deserted him. Writing in the *New York Review of Books*, Elizabeth Hardwick, a sophisticated writer once married to Robert Lowell, brought a disabused Manhattanite's familiarity with conspicuous wealth to bear on *Timon*:

> *Timon* itself, Shakespeare's play, is in a state of reduction, at the least unrevised, thin in parts, late. It is perfectly served by the thrift of the staging, the challenging scantiness. Nothing could be worse than gold and silver, cloth from the ancient world, gilded sandals. The banquet scene with its Cupid, lutes and Amazons is given by suggestion almost, without *luxe*. Instead a moody hashish-blurred atmosphere, high shrill sounds from the Arab quarters and, mercifully no orgy or spot of nakedness standing out from the surface like a pimple upon which we are to gaze without pardon. The riches, the waste, are all in the mind.

This patching together of places and cultures was theatrical suggestiveness at its most potent, and was to become a hallmark of Brook's work at the

Bouffes. Brook's theatrical language, as David Williams remarks of the stage itself, was 'never locked within a single frame of reference'.

At the hub of these shifting frames of reference, François Marthouret played Timon with self-absorbed grace. He wore a white silk suit with a Mao collar over a gold lamé shirt; when his money vanished, the suit was torn to pieces. Elizabeth Hardwick's beady New York gaze saw the end of this Timon foreshadowed in his beginning.

> Timon is a romantic, a spendthrift, full of longings for something perfect, if only the perfect gift, the dazzling charity, as if he were too young for lust. Or perhaps something warns him even at the first that the acute, burning misanthropy lies waiting for the exhausted innocent and the weary aesthete. Brook helped Marthouret to play the upheaval and reversal of this cool, un-self-knowing character with a virtuosic clarity and force. And once more he offered the audience the dramatic frisson that comes from the dizzying sense of the ground giving way beneath our feet.

With *The Ik*, Brook's next show at the Bouffes in 1975, he plunged again into that chasm of uncomprehended, perhaps incomprehensible, suffering which he had sounded in the previous fifteen years – in *King Lear*, in *Lord of the Flies*, in *The Investigation*. *The Ik* was based on a book by ethnologist Colin Turnbull, *The Mountain People*, which told the tale of Turnbull's nine-month stay with the Ik, a Ugandan tribe that at first fascinated, then puzzled, then horrified him, finally challenging all his professional and human assumptions and leaving him in impotent rage. The Ugandan government in its wisdom had resettled the Ik, mountain people who survived by hunting and gathering, moving them far away from their homeland and telling them to become farmers. Under the shock of this radical change, their entire social and family structures, their beliefs and human bonds had collapsed. Turnbull witnessed a people who had no scruples in stealing food from a corpse's mouth or from their closest family, laughing at the misfortune of their fellows, casting out the old and mad to die in the bush, relieved at having one less mouth to feed.

The actors playing the Ik (Malick Bowens, Michelle Collison, Miriam Goldschmidt, Bruce Myers, Yoshi Oida, Maurice Benichou, Andreas Katsulas and Jean-Claude Perrin, who had joined the company for *Timon*) had come from or travelled with Brook to Africa. They rehearsed by building an Ik hut in a corner of the Bouffes du Nord and painstakingly going through the reduced actions of Ik everyday life. At the start of the performance they re-created the environment, pouring brown earth from sacks on to the Bouffes' stone floor, plaiting twigs together to make a roof over their heads. They spoke in a made-up language that sounded like manic birds, occasionally dipping into French to subtitle their words for the audience, an offhand distancing effect. The reality on stage was full of such gaps and holes, asking the audience to enter them with its imagination. Brook was finding his way towards the essence of his late style, a wise naiveté, which he compared to telling a child a bedtime story: 'I'm going toward the essential elements. Not the essential experience, but the essential elements. That's really like in writing when you go back and cut out all unnecessary adjectives. You're not really against the adjectives themselves but you look at what you're trying to say and you see that the adjectives are fogging the meaning . . . You are trying to find the most appropriate form for reflecting something.'

Gestures in *The Ik* are performed with riveting concentration. A boy digs in the earth to pull out pebbles and swallow them. The same boy is taught a hard lesson by his mother, who calls him to join her by a fire and take food from her hand; when he reaches out, she withdraws it, and he is burnt. She laughs, but she has given him a survivor's lesson in mistrust. An amiable antic fellow who befriends Turnbull continues taking food rations for his wife long after she has died. He has buried her in secret, to avoid giving a burial feast to the villagers. Turnbull emerges from a sleeping bag, sets up his folding stool, lights his primus stove, warms the teapot and is about to throw away the water when he becomes aware of four pairs of Ik eyes watching him, their hungry gaze estranging every object and action. Framed in Brook's stark stage space, these acts have a Brechtian fastidiousness.

But some critics were uneasy about the aestheticising effect of playing out these agonised lives in such a refined way. Irving Wardle, The *Times'* critic, called it 'an event trembling on the brink of obscenity', when he saw it in the Roundhouse in London. More acerbic was Albert Hunt. 'Listening to the applause the other night that burst out in the crowded Bouffes du Nord after the last *Ik* had vomited up in front of the audience his last sack of relief grain, and then dragged his twisted limbs into a hole at the back of the stage, I couldn't help thinking that Brook, the miracle worker, had pulled it off again. He'd made the Iks enjoyable.'

This ironic judgement concludes an attack by Hunt on Brook's underlying nihilism and pessimism, which he traces back to *The Marat/Sade* and *US*, and Brook's *Encore* articles which mock 'facile optimism' against the gritty, bracing truth of Beckett. He contrasts the overall impression of *The Ik* on stage with Turnbull's final affirmation in the book that something must and can be done. 'In *The Mountain People*,' says Hunt, 'Turnbull's faith in his own values was questioned by the evidence offered by the Iks. Brook's faith in futility is not in any way questioned by Turnbull's intelligence. This seems to me to represent the other side of the coin from the "facile optimism" Brook wants to challenge. In place of such optimism he offers an equally facile despair.'

But to gaze deeply does not mean to fall under the spell of what is gazed at. And the despondency of Turnbull as Brook portrayed him on stage is not Brook's own position – indeed, when Turnbull finally saw the stage version, he recovered a sympathy for the Ik that he had lost. Brook saw the play as a picture of 'a tragic modern world that is betraying its possibilities'.

'Brook believes,' writes David Williams, 'that the Ik story offers a rare challenge to the limitations of a strictly Marxist analysis. Fundamentally, the pre-"fall" unity of the Ik did not have an economic basis; collapse has resulted from the removal of cohesive spiritual traditions.' Williams sees Brook's production as 'a form of myth about the loss of tradition', about the tragic destruction, through necessity for survival, of everything that had made their lives meaningful. Yet even in this descent there are moments when one is made acutely aware of 'the potentiality, the virtuality that is being missed'.

One such was the ascent by the Ik to a mountain top which they believed was inhabited by a god. They climbed up the pitons of the Bouffes' back wall, like insects on a rockface. As they climbed they sang a radiant anthem, and one wondered how long a people so degraded by privation and hunger could hold on to this scrap of shared beauty. And then Turnbull appeared, and suddenly they stopped. In the silence we were made aware of what Brook called 'the force of tradition through the sense of its disappearance'.

Brook followed the sparse *Ik* with a jamboree of rough theatre, *Ubu aux Bouffes*, a raucous, improvisational, post-Shakespearean *grand guignol* based on the scathing plays of French theatre's *enfant terrible*, Alfred Jarry (1873–1907).

Brook treated Jarry's *Ubu*, which he had considered mounting for his *Theatre of Cruelty* season in London, with radical disrespect. Originally premiered in 1896 (when a shocked W. B. Yeats had exclaimed, 'What more is possible? After us the Savage God'), the plays had been turned by the French into lovable modern classics, held in the same affection as the jokes of the venerable satirical weekly *Le Canard enchainé*. But Brook wanted to restore Jarry's comic violence and vulgarity, drawing out its roots in Aristophanes. Perhaps he also saw it as a comic inversion, in another, ruder key, of the Ik's heartless survival tactics.

Ubu and his consort Mother Ubu decide that they can become king and queen of an imaginary Poland ('The action takes place in Poland', says Jarry's notorious opening stage direction, 'that is to say: nowhere'). They hack, cheat and bully their way to the top, seeding Europe with corpses. Their power play, without any hinterland of belief or value, strikes a chord in today's audience, all too familiar with the tyrants of contemporary history.

Brook restored the play's force by employing the street theatre and roadside riffs in which his company had become so expert. To the anarchic joy of these off-the-cuff performances Brook now added *Ubu*'s unruly rage and derision. They constructed a new iconography for *Ubu* out of urban bric-a-brac: bricks, sticks, rubber balls and two man-sized drums on which electric cable had been wound, spotted by Brook in roadworks around his theatre. The bricks became money or food or a peasant's hovel. A mangy old rug became Ubu's monarchical robe. The giant spools became tables, chairs, thrones, and, at the peak of Ubu's martial triumphs, a fearful war-machine rolling down towards the audience. Andreas Katsulas' Ubu skipping to keep his balance on top of this juggernaut, a bulldozer demolishing houses and people, seems to foreshadow images of the West Bank today.

Brook's Ubu was not inflated or distorted, but a down-to-earth member of the French lumpenproletariat, a plumber or a removal man, sporting sturdy braces over his long-sleeved vest. The playing space swelled and shrank as the actors tumbled into the auditorium, scaled ladders to the balcony, buttonholed spectators and tugged them into their disputes and tirades. It was like *The Goon Show* and *Hellzapoppin*, transforming a handful of props in countless ways, and summoning the spectator's imagination to 'fill the gaps'. Brook was to carry this alchemy of objects, this gift of making the part summon up the whole, into longer perspectives and deeper questions. But here, after the sombre worlds of *Timon* and *The Ik*, Brook used his stagecraft and skill to release the company's huge ability to cavort and to laugh.

After *Ubu*, Brook made the journey back to England, to direct an English-language Shakespeare, *Antony and Cleopatra*. Returning to the Royal Shakespeare Company at Stratford-upon-Avon was like returning to the scene of an old love affair: the partner has changed, and the lover wonders how he could ever have had such fervent feelings. Brook had crowned the English phase of his life in 1970 with his 'white box' *A Midsummer Night's Dream* rehearsed and premiered at Stratford-upon-Avon during a sensuous, creative summer. Now, in 1978, he returned to do a play he had loved for a long time, but had sworn not to attempt until he had found the right actress for the lead. And then, in the sixties, he found her. After working with Glenda Jackson throughout the sixties, he realised she was ideal: explosive sexual, dangerous. Opposite her as Antony he cast Alan Howard, the RSC's leading actor, who had played a memorable Oberon/Theseus in Brook's *Dream*. To design the production, Brook again called in Sally Jacobs.

It was a reunion of some of his closest artistic associates in a place where he felt happy; he says now that if he had to choose one landscape in the world in which to end his days, it would be the uneventful Warwickshire landscape, 'midmost England' as Henry James called it. But somehow the plant failed to take root. This *Antony and Cleopatra* was a fleetingly brilliant but fitful account of Shakespeare's tragedy of love and loss, a play about a passionate woman and a man who throws away his whole world for her, a play which ends in the double death of the lovers whose desire has seemed to bestride the world. Maybe there was too little sexual chemistry between Alan Howard, broody and touching, but rarely expansive and conquering, and Glenda Jackson, prowling like a panther, combustive, fiercely possessive. Howard gave it everything he had – his command of the tidal lift and syncopation of Shakespeare's verse was matchless – but he rarely seemed equal to Glenda's flame-like temperament. This Cleopatra might well have eaten this Antony for breakfast; it was harder to imagine her melting in his flame.

Which is not to say that there weren't wonderful things in the production. There was a dizzying moment when Sally Jacobs' vast carpet, on which the world's commanders caroused together, was suddenly hoisted from the floor of a ship to become a vertical wall, a tottering world, sending drunken men rolling and tumbling as Antony hung on to the fabric, teetering but not drowning in drink and appetite.

Perhaps also it was the Royal Shakespeare Company that had changed. Nina Soufy, Brook's assistant, noted that 'between scenes supporting actors would run down to the green room to finish a hand of poker, or watch telly. I couldn't believe it.' Many of the Stratford actors did not appreciate the warm-up exercises which Brook, for whom they were now a regular part of rehearsal, asked them to do. After his international group and its encounters and creative shocks around the world, this must have seemed to Brook a very routine way of making theatre.

Glenda Jackson recalls the experience:

We'd done the film of *Marat/Sade* and we were doing *Tell Me Lies* and he said to me, I want to do *Antony and Cleopatra*, so don't do it until I'm ready. One day in 1978 the phone call came. At that stage Antony was going to be Stacy Keach [an American movie actor]. Then he had trouble with the Customs and he pulled out. So Alan Howard did it, and he was not best pleased that he wasn't first choice. So we arrive at Stratford. It's the last play of the season, and it's a company where everyone knew everyone, and there are two new people coming in: me and Brook. In the first staging, at Stratford-upon-Avon, Alan was more passionate about Enobarbus than he was about Cleopatra. But it got better when we got to the Aldwych. By then the company had all stopped thinking, 'Oh she's just come swanning in here, big film star'; they never said it out loud but it certainly informed everything they did.

What was interesting about the work was that Peter immediately started in on the text. It was the first time I'd worked with him where you were immediately on the book. Of course there were lots of other exercises and we were inundated with pictures of Tutankhamen and Egypt and we did physical exercises. But when we moved into the rehearsal rooms at the Memorial Theatre at Stratford, it was absolutely text-based.

He was horrified at the state the company was in. I've only seen him lose his temper twice and one of those was during that production. He said, 'When I call rehearsals at ten o'clock I expect you to be ready to work at ten o'clock, I don't expect you to be reading newspapers.' It was the last production that year, and it hadn't been a very good season for them and they'd just got into that rut that happens in that benighted place if you're there for a whole season.

But then the magic began to work, but not as potently as it had with other groups I had been in with him. He would never ever say, 'Oh if only I'd had Olivier', about an actor who wasn't doing whatever it was he wanted, even though he didn't know what he wanted. He always worked with the people he'd got. There was never any backsliding or whingeing about that: this was the company he was working with, these were the people he'd got and these were the people who had to make this production.

It got better when we got to the Aldwych, partly because the company was getting better and it's also a much, much better house for that play, which should be done in a very small space, not that ghastly theatre at Stratford. But I don't think he was happy with the experience. It had to do with the amount of work that he suddenly found necessary to get a company together, which he had not been used to doing. He'd had his own company in Paris and that came as a bit of a shock to him. It certainly came as a shock to me. I was absolutely bemused that all those bloody actors could think they were better than he was. Amazing.

Brook came back from Stratford to the Bouffes to mount *Mesure pour mesure* (*Measure for Measure*), a play which had fascinated him since he'd staged it at Stratford in 1950, with Gielgud as Angelo. Brook loved this riddling play, its mixture of disparate elements – high-mindedness in public and lewdness in private; the unmasking of hypocrisy; the tug-of-war between justice and mercy; the energy of the belly and the genitals under-cutting the high principles of the law and morality.

But this too failed to kindle, despite a troublingly comic performance by Bruce Myers as Angelo, his first leading part in French, and a fine Duke in a monk's habit played by François Marthouret, keenly watching the behaviour of his deputy and his citizens once they believed his back was turned. The *Observer*'s critic Robert Cushman came over to see it, but was largely disappointed. 'The whole company is, as ever, commandingly unfussed . . . but in this neat *Mesure*, Brook's ideal *Measure* has gone by default. On this occasion he has stretched the mind, not blown it.' *Mesure* did not fill houses, and its run was truncated. There was now a hole in the schedule.

Having one's own theatre was a responsibility as well as a pleasure. Brook was no longer supplying productions to someone else's commercial operation, as he had done for Binkie Beaumont. Nor was he contributing as a member of a subsidised ensemble, as he had done for Peter Hall's RSC. He was well aware of the big shift in his working life and responsibilities. With Rozan, he was taking on the risks of theatrical self-management. If a production was not a success, they would have a gap in their schedules, and something would have to be found in its place. They had a small subsidy, but not enough to feel safe if one production went down. The price of freedom was insecurity. 'In France,' Jean-Claude Carrière told me, 'there are two ways to subsidise a theatre. You can fund a theatre, which is then obliged to do three or four new shows a year, to employ a certain number of people, to become, in effect, an institution. Or you can give a director less money, for which he has more freedom and fewer obligations. Peter chose the second solution. He got half the money that other companies got, much less than Patrice Chéreau or Jean-Pierre Vincent. But he had more freedom.'

Timon had been a success, selling out all its scheduled performances. *Mesure* was not. Rozan fired typically forthright questions at Brook: 'You have a mobile company – they mime and make wonderful sounds. Why make them play Viennese senators in *Mesure*? Why not revive *The Conference of the Birds*? Round off all the work you've done on it. And let's take it to the Avignon Festival next summer. It's time for us to make a splash at Avignon.'

When Brook came to round out the work on *The Conference of the Birds* in 1979, it had to be a summation. In Les Gobelins in Paris, in Persepolis, Africa and America, the group had taken episodes of the Sufi poem and worked them every which way. Brook had told the company that he could foresee a time when everything they had been doing on the *Birds* fragments would have bedded in, and they could try to seize *The Conference of the Birds* in something like its totality.

He did not begin the attempt in the Bouffes du Nord, but in a stone courtyard in the South of France, one of the sites of the Avignon Festival. Founded in 1947 by the great French actor, director and theatre-maker Jean Vilar – 'a republican monarch' as French critic Bernard Dort calls him – the Avignon Festival became a symbol of France's regeneration after the war and the Nazi occupation. The open-air performances, in the grand courtyard of the Pope's Palace before a 3,000-strong audience, assembled a galaxy of future stars, the young Gérard Philippe and Jeanne Moreau among them, renewed the classics of French and European theatre – Corneille, Marivaux, Shakespeare, Büchner, Brecht – and began searching for new theatre sources and forms. The energy and sensuality of the town in high summer and the responsiveness of its audiences made it a vital centre. Brook found the ideal space in the cloisters of a former monastery, the Cloître des Carmes. For the premiere, designer Sally Jacobs made a small addition to the walled cloister gardens: a mound of earth topped with a tree was set in one corner. 'The tree presented certain technical difficulties,' write Todd and Lecat, 'it had be lifted into the cloister with a crane lent by the army. It was bedded in sand from Roussillon, which had been specially chosen for its delicately varied colours. In the heat of a Provençal July its leaves promptly tuned brown and fell off. They had to be glued back on one by one and restored to their original green colour by careful painting.'

When the production went up to the Bouffes for its Parisian opening, Brook and his new designer Chloe Obolensky created a new environment with three large and intricately patterned Persian carpets, two on the floor and one hung floating a little in front of the walls. Not only did these carpets make a bridge between the here and now and the Persian ancestry of *The Conference of the Birds*, their worn surfaces and faded colours also melded with the nature of the Bouffes, and, as Lecat and Todd note, became 'an ordinary-extraordinary artefact *par excellence* – a launchpad for the imagination which has its foundations in our world.' A vital contributor to the production's imaginative richness was Tapa Sudana, a Balinese actor, and an expert in Balinese masks, who joined the company for *The Conference of the Birds* and stayed for further productions – *The Tempest*, *The Mahabharata* and *Carmen*.

What truth did this production of the long-stalked *The Conference of the Birds* present?

'A near-Eastern *Pilgrim's Progress*', as many commentators have noticed, Farid Uddin Attar's twelfth-century poem uses birds, as Aristophanes had done in *The Birds* and Chaucer in *The Parliament of Fowls*, to illustrate human characters, to chart the growth of a soul and its initiation into the divine. Its story belongs to the Islamic tradition in which a bird frees itself from the burdens and traps of this world to return to its true King. Brook asked his collaborator Jean-Claude Carrière to extract a script from the poem's four thousand lines. With a screenwriter's skill, he produced a text which provided what no group exploration or improvisation had managed: a shapely overall storyline, in which every element could find its proportionate place.

The journey of the birds was expanded by set-piece allegorical stories. When the Sparrow tells the Hoopoe that he feels too weak to undertake the journey to the Simorgh, a man enters, walking extremely slowly. In Brook's telling translation:

'Do you remember this man?' asks the Hoopoe. 'He was a saint, more perfect than can be imagined: Hallaj. He was at home in both science and wisdom. He was an unmatched example to humanity, a flag raised in this world. When he was about to be executed, all he said was, "I am the truth". They cut off his hands and his feet, to punish him. Blood flowed abundantly from his body; he grew pale, so he decided to rub his bloody wrists against his face, saying "Since blood colours man's complexion, I want to use it today to make my face look ruddy. I don't want anyone to see me pale, they will think I was afraid. When the executioner comes to me he'll see a brave man. The world is just the corpse of nothingness. Why should I be afraid?'

The man slowly exits. The birds are silent. 'So?' says the Hoopoe, 'you've nothing more to say? Are you so afraid of this death?' The Hoopoe goes from one to the next, and the birds hang their heads as he speaks to them one by one:

'This bird only loves his cage. That one doesn't want to leave his lake, or his mountain. That one thinks he's a worm, this one a king. Thousands of creatures have applied themselves to the pursuit of the corpse of this world. And they all say, 'Why should we abandon quiet happiness?''

Brook found in *The Conference of the Birds* a tough-mindedness, a contempt for the ego's quibbling and a devotion and dedication to the task which are almost ruthless. He was working with a fundamental text of Sufism, whose conviction of the illusory nature of the world connected with Brook's own sense of the ephemeral, mask-like quality of all forms of theatre. What Brook sought from his actors had nothing to do with the subjectivity and 'emotional memory' of Stanislavski's American disciples. He wanted to find a 'transparency' freed from the 'personality' under whose spell Sufis and other mystics believed we wasted too much of our lives. The other facet of Sufism which spoke to Brook was love as a way of discovery. *The Conference of the Birds* is eloquent about the path of love. This is very Shakespearean: it recalls the power of love to break through the immature affectations of the lovers of *Love's Labour's Lost*, and the crazed young lovers in *A Midsummer Night's Dream*, lost in a labyrinth of unassuaged desire.

Brook knew that the poem's levels and layers made a straightforward anthropomorphic version of cuddly creatures in bird-heads and bird-skins impossible. As he told Margaret Croyden, if he wanted to transcend pantomime, he needed 'a double image':

> The double image is the one thing that arises through play. All children's play is based on this idea. Children don't forget that they're running about in a playground, and yet they have the double image that they're pirates on a ship, or gangsters on a street corner. It's evoked with a stick. It's evoked with a twig. It's evoked by a way of standing or of shouting. And this double image is the force, the power, and the meaning of everything to do with the theatre.

The piece could only be released if the bird-reality and the human-reality could be shuffled like cards, now one more present, now the other.

For the actor to become a bird and then a dervish or a princess, it became necessary to find an instrument, something which is like an extension or an exaltation of the basic impulse. To dress the actor as a bird with a mask over his head would be too heavy; we needed instead to give a swift suggestion which would not encumber the imagination. At certain moments, one needs to feel the figurative side of the bird more fully, at others, less so. In this way, without thinking about it and often without knowing, we used a disparate range of expressive elements, coming from sources which corresponded with the collective experience of the group.

So no actor in *The Conference of the Birds* encased his head in a bird-mask. Instead the most delicate forms of expression were used. Sometimes an actor carried an effigy of a bird; sometimes two crooked fingers signifying a beak, and emerging from a gorgeous wrap slung over the arm sufficed. You saw and heard a nightingale, a sparrow, a bat, a heron, a dove, and then you didn't see them, only their player and puppeteer, their human double. The reality on the stage was eclectic, fluctuating, morphing between modes.

A certain kind of English empiricist temperament finds the 'mysticism' in Brook's work since he left London hard to swallow, or sees his journeys into the hidden, the esoteric and the 'invisible' as a surrender to subjective fantasy and narcissism. To which Brook replies with a judgement on his own work in *The Conference of the Birds*: 'Our point of departure was necessarily ourselves. But to avoid going round in dangerously narcissistic circles, it is vital that we rest on something bigger and stronger coming from outside; something which challenges our understanding and makes us see beyond this personal universe that we set before ourselves and confuse with reality.'

The stage language which Brook fashioned with such fleeting beauty and immediacy in *The Conference of the Birds* was inseparable from the interplay of impulses and identities he had now forged in his group. The counterpoint of their different performance traditions, their ability to take rhythm and tone from each other and top them with a new voice or transform them, were the theatrical equivalent of free life within a form, as in jazz and traditional African music. The pleasure audiences across the world took in the delicate strength of their performances, seemingly afloat between cultures and national identities, speaking with the freedom of 'the in-between', was a sign that Brook was now reaping the harvest he had planted nine years before. Perhaps this internationalism, this 'inter-cultur-alism' in performance had achieved such free play that other paths could at last be opened. Brook now felt confident enough that he had sufficiently embodied the truths of his study of Gurdjieff to relax the barrier he had set against letting the personal work appear in public. His vehicle was to be, not a theatre piece, but a searching film.

MEETINGS
1978–84

Brook had acknowledged that his move to Paris was motivated in large part by his respect for Jeanne de Salzmann, Gurdjieff's successor. Since he arrived, he had been nursing a project which would involve her and be inspired by her: she had suggested he make a film based on Gurdjieff's book telling the story of his youth and awakening, *Meetings with Remarkable Men*. Throughout the 1970s, parallel to his work in the theatre, he wrote and rewrote a screenplay with her, and busied himself raising funds for the film. In May 1977, dovetailing with a tour of *The Ik* and rehearsals of *Ubu*, he began shooting the film.

It was his first work overtly to acknowledge the sources of Gurdjieff's teachings. In the deliberately naive and simple style of an oriental tale, it tells the story of the young Gurdjieff, born in Kars on the borders of Russia and Armenia (Afghanistan was the film's location), known for its traditions of bardic poetry and oral storytelling. Gurdjieff's book *Meetings With Remarkable Men* tells of his wanderings in the East, and his meetings with outstanding men who marked his life, and helped him answer his pressing questions about the human organism and the universe.

The film opens with a solemn gathering for a musical contest, in a valley framed by majestic mountains. People from miles around, including Gurdjieff and his father, arrive to watch musicians perform before a panel of elders. The prize will be awarded to the player or singer who produces the sound with the truest vibrations. 'Only a sound of special quality can make the stones vibrate,' as Gurdjieff's father tells him. One singer makes it happen; an echo comes back from the lofty peaks. This epic yet intimate scene opens the way to the teenaged Gurdjieff's quest.

In his wanderings, after many byways and discoveries, Gurdjieff meets Father Giovanni, whose brotherhood includes people from all religious traditions. Giovanni tells the story of two of his priests, Brother Akhel and Brother Sèze.

> They go from one monastery to another, preaching. Once or twice a year, they come to us. It is always a great event. When Brother Akhel preaches, it's like hearing the birds of paradise. The speech of Brother Sèze is quite different. He mutters, you can hardly hear him. The stronger impression he makes, the faster it fades, leaving nothing behind.
>
> Brother Akhel, on the other hand, makes almost no impression, but what he says enters the heart and is written upon it.
>
> We therefore came to the conclusion that the sermons of Brother Sèze came from his intellect and worked upon our intellect, whereas those of Brother Akhel came from his being and worked upon our being.
>
> Thinking and knowledge are quite different. One must reach towards knowledge. Only that can lead to God.

These parallel and contrasted spiritual lives could almost be the profiles of two kinds of actor. One overt, lyrical, virtuosic, speaking from the mind and the agile lips to the intelligence of listeners appreciative of beauty and form. The Gielgud kind of actor, a quicksilver tenor, a bird of paradise indeed. The other digging into darkness and risking incoherence, blitzing form, speaking from the depths, from the belly through a tortured throat to the guts of spectators. The Scofield actor, a baritone with sinewy vocal cords sculpting words afresh. Brook refused to jettison one for the sake of the other, lived with the contradiction. He had loved the eloquence of Gielgud's quality of acting; he had also felt the tug of the depths and dangers of Scofield's.

In the first half of his career, Brook had seemingly been a member of the suave, tasteful theatre – the 'perfumed' theatre, as Peter Hall called it – of which Gielgud was such a figurehead, touching the intellect and the heart. At the same time Brook was always contesting this cultural, well-mannered

English theatre ritual and the kind of playing that fed it. Long before he came in touch with *The Conference of the Birds*, Brook had begun to seek the drive and apparent formlessness of a Brother Sèze, the actor who breaks all the rules and conquers the whole being. As he moved into his fifties, Brook accepted the primacy of this complete being, which encompassed the heart and the intellect.

Now in the final phase of his career, Brook found and moulded actors from a spectrum of nationalities and traditions and drew forth the spare, light and elliptical performances of *The Conference of the Birds* and the shows which followed. Initially, French critics, with their culture of laws and decorum, found many of these performers clumsy, ill-spoken, unpolished. But Brook was aiming at a bigger target, and a long and roundabout way, through obstacles and insufficiencies, had to be followed to reach it. With his filming of *Meetings*, Brook began to lift the veil on some sources of the Gurdjieffian work he had been following.

With this film he 'came out' as a Gurdjieffian, even if he could be testy about the way it was discussed. When Margaret Croyden tried to probe what Brook actually *did* as a Gurdjieff disciple, he sharply refused:

> The question put – 'Do you follow this? Do you practise this?' – isn't a serious question, because it shows a complete misunderstanding about what any-body's involvement with a search can be. On a very naive level, there are followers and disciples and adherents of different religions, of different schools, and of different ways, but that doesn't go very far, and isn't really serious. You don't get committed to somebody's methods and somebody's teaching because of some hero worship or because you think they have a panacea. It's something very different. You have your own personal search, and that becomes illuminated at certain times by certain things that you receive. I don't think that the moment you reach a deep level, you can say there is such a thing as a disciple or a follower. That's very external.

In February 2003, Brook did agree to discuss what Gurdjieff means to him. I asked him first what this 'work' was that followers of Gurdjieff use to describe what they do.

Peter Brook: Gurdjieff speaks of a 'harmonious' development of body, thought and feeling. It isn't possible for the human organism to come together without becoming, in life terms, finer. And for that reason, it isn't good or evil; it is hard, concrete fact. A chaotic individual, where all these needs and images are exploding in all directions, can perform what we call 'vile actions'. As the different parts come together, a direct moral sense emerges without being the result of ethical principles, what the French call 'crutches'.

It is natural for human beings to aspire upwards rather than downwards. The sense of upright behaviour, of an upright community, is a natural thing in a developed human organism. The taste of it is there in everyone, but it doesn't come into being naturally, by argument or persuasion or theory or philosophy. It has to be worked for, and worked for in a very special way.

That's what led me and leads me to a form of what in crude terms is called a teaching, but really is a shared search that never ends.

Michael Kustow: **When you discovered Ghika's book about proportion and 'the golden section', and then you found the same diagram of the octave in Gurdjieff, was that an exciting discovery?**

PB: When I first found this expression of abstract ideas, it was a time when ideas interested me, abstract ideas in themselves. Their fascination and their beauty appealed to me. Secondly, I wasn't convinced you could separate feeling from science, the human feeling that an artist has from the cool analysis of a scientist. Since I couldn't believe in those divisions, I thought that religion was saying something essential, but saying it wrongly. How did this all tie up? My sense of wonder and surprise was linked to a sense of questioning. I couldn't fail to observe as I worked with a designer that we were saying to each other that this is better than that, and we took it for granted that these words had a meaning.

Anybody touched by any religious idea will find that in all things, there's a high, a middle and a low. The essence of Hinduism is in these three levels. There is *satva*, which is the high; there is *rajas*, which is all the activity and turmoil of the world, and there is *tamas*, the leaden, sluggish bottom. That is the basis of almost all penetrating vision – then and now.

MK: **When you went to your teacher Jane Heap, you seemed to be a young man full of ego. You tell the story of turning up at the group in black tie for a late-night party, 'locked in my social personality' and when she put you down,**

you say you can still feel your startled ego slapped into recognising its blindness.

PB: Yes, I was full of ego. In the world of schools, universities, I had an inborn suspicion of teachers: 'Who do you think you are? What gives you the right to be running this course? Why do you think you know?' Then I found that there was a very, very ancient traditional understanding – nothing to do with 'tradition' as we understand it commonly. I was learning the two faces of tradition. Up till then, I had one idea of tradition as a lot of shit you've got to get rid of; traditional people are stiff, rigid and pompous, they impose on you a respect that you've no reason to give them. This 'tradition' means 'fossilised'.

And then suddenly, and it's more than an eye-opener, comes this real tradition. True tradition is a river that comes from a distant source, but while you acknowledge that the source comes from a long way off, you don't find yourself in something remote; when you step into that river, you're stepping into something that is moving. Not only that, but the river you're in now is adapting itself. Where you are, the river is doing movements it didn't do way back in time, and yet it's the same river.

But the entropic nature of life is such that every single religion within a very short time loses its flexibility. What are considered the traditional ideas of Christianity or Judaism, for instance, have all frozen and fossilised the great teaching that was their basis.

Things have to be interpreted and reinterpreted all the time. Gurdjieff said that through his 'meetings with remarkable men' he had found his way to an ancient teaching that had been almost lost, almost forgotten, but just kept alive orally, and that he had the role of bringing this into the West.

MK: **What did you learn from Jane Heap as a teacher?**

PB: She set out first principles for the beginner, guidelines. There are two things you must watch out for, she said. One is going and discussing it with other people before you know what you're talking about. You'll dissipate it all in words, words, words. You explain something to someone, and they say, 'That's a lot of nonsense,' and you say, 'No, it isn't nonsense, listen to me' and so on. You must find ways of avoiding such discussions.

The other thing is, you don't mix this 'work' with other things, because this isn't an advanced polytechnic, or a method of helping you to do better in life. It has nothing to do with that. This separation was absolutely rigorous, and I saw why. So I tried to avoid the real death trap, which is to say, 'I can use this teaching. I can use it, and I will do a better job as a result.'

It was almost thirty years, until *The Conference of the Birds* and *The Mahabharata*, before I could allow myself to bring the two streams together. But naturally, something that develops your vision and sensibility makes you see things in your own field which are material for development.

I showed Brook a transcript of this talk. He sat on it for a while. Then he said, 'I'll have to write this myself.' A few weeks later, he gave me back his summary in his own written words of what Gurdjieff meant to him. He had already made one attempt at this, in a collection of essays by artists, scientists and musicians, published in France in 1997.

Although firmly rooted in a very ancient, lost tradition, Gurdjieff's teaching is bitingly contemporary. It analyses the human predicament with devastating precision. It shows how men and women are conditioned from earliest childhood, how they operate according to deep-rooted programmes, living from cause to effect in an unbroken chain of reactions. These in turn produce a stream of sensations and images, which are never the reality they pretend to be; they are mere interpretations of a reality which they are doomed to mask by their constant flow.

This recalls Brook's description of his own energies in the earlier part of his life, which he later saw as an inner tug-of-war between his conquering 'warrior' energy, precociously powerful, whether in his theatre work or his sexual conquests, and his intimations of another kind of energy, patient, less self-centred, connected with others, less domineering, more relaxed, able to see his own unimportance. Gurdjieff seemed to mirror his own inner wrestling. He continues:

Every phenomenon arises from a field of energies, every thought, every feeling, every movement of the body is the manifestation of a specific energy, and in the lopsided human being one energy is constantly swelling up to swamp the other. This endless pitching and tossing between mind, feelings, and body produces a fluctuating series of impulses, each of which deceptively asserts itself as 'me': as one desire replaces another, there can be no continuity of intention, no true wish, only the chaotic pattern of contradiction, which we all live, in which the ego has the illusion of willpower and independence. Gurdjieff calls this 'the terror of the situation'.

Through half a lifetime of classes, retreats, lessons, exercises and reflections on parallel images and stories, Brook had broken out of his conditioning. He was now ready, through a film, to show the sources of whatever freedom he had attained.

'One of India's worst legacies to the world is the word "guru",' Brook said to me one day. 'I'm not a guru. Gurus take themselves too seriously.' Entering his eighties, Brook still has an air of one of Yeats' scholar-mystics, with their 'ancient glittering eyes'. But it is theatre and cinema, it is what a Zen or Sufi adept might call *the way of theatre*, with roughness as well as its holiness, its earthiness and its aspiration to heights, which keeps him firmly in this world and stops him succumbing to any universalising faith.

This is powerfully echoed in his answer to my question 'What do you believe today?'

My deepest wish would be to say with complete sincerity I believe in nothing. This is almost impossible – we believe all the time and this is a rope around our throats. Cordelia says 'Nothing, my Lord' and Lear answers 'Nothing comes of nothing'. For Cordelia nothing is the inexpressible fullness of the heart, while for Lear nothing, quite brutally, is nothing.

Like silence, like emptiness, nothing takes us beyond all that our formative thinking can grasp. All or nothing, we cannot avoid the dialectic. We are forced to analyse, to divide and choose or else we could not survive. But all is nothing, all is in nothing and nothing has its meaning on another level.

Images are treacherous, they are so beguiling. One that always touches me in ancient teaching is the image of the ladder to the sky. As one begins to climb the rungs are firm, the direction is clear. As one goes higher, the ladder begins to disappear. Then at the end one sees that the ladder one climbed with so much effort never existed at all. Beliefs are the rungs of the ladder. We need them, but as we grasp them something tells us they are not as solid as they seem. We must learn to believe without believing. Otherwise, belief is poison.

Brook wrote the screenplay for *Meetings With Remarkable Men* in close collaboration with Jeanne de Salzmann, who insisted on attending the shoot of the film. She was in her eighties in 1977, but she came to Afghanistan for the filming and endured its arduous conditions – on the first day there was a thunderstorm, followed by sandstorms, snakes, dysentery, even a minor earthquake. A commanding presence, she sat in a tent the crew had rigged up and watched each take on a video monitor.

Born in 1889 in Geneva, she trained as a dancer and was teaching eurhythmics when she met Gurdjieff in Tiflis, Georgia, in 1919, where he had fled from Moscow to avoid the upheavals of the Russian Revolution. Jeanne de Salzmann's pupils gave the first performances of Gurdjieff's 'sacred dances' and in 1922 she and her husband Alexandre travelled with Gurdjieff to France, living a spartan life in his new centre, the Institute for the Harmonious Development of Man, at Fontainebleau. After a car accident, Gurdjieff spent more time writing than working at the Institute, and passed long hours in the Café de la Paix, near the Opera, distilling his teachings into words. Photographs of him from this time show a powerful-looking man, whose indisputable magnetism was felt by that glittering generation of artists and thinkers and socialites who flocked to Paris after the First World War, making it 'the capital of modernism'. Russian émigrés, Dadaists from Zurich and Berlin, Freudians and Jungians, Theosophists and experimental poets – these were the constituents of 'the Paris jigsaw'. The surrealist writer René Daumal became a pupil at Fontainebleau; Katherine Mansfield went there seeking a cure for the disease that killed her.

When Gurdjieff died in 1949, Jeanne de Salzmann took up the reins as his agreed successor, heading the Gurdjieff Foundations until she died in 1990, overseeing the edition of his writings, and further developing his teachings.

This was the woman who trudged up hills with Brook and his crew in Afghanistan. The crew, who had come to Brook's film from making *Star Wars* at Pinewood studios, fell under her spell, and scuttled around making sure 'Madame' was happy, before they returned to eating their full English cooked breakfast in the heat. 'The whole unit was very taken with Madame de Salzmann,' says Nina Soufy, Brook's PA on the film. 'She was always the first up the hill and the last down. The crew treated her as if she were the Dalai Lama.' The film completed its shoot at Pinewood, where the grave, hypnotic movements of the sacred dances created by Gurdjieff and embodying the elusive balance of energies, made a strong impression on the crew. Back on familiar ground, they were still 'intrigued, bewildered and amazed', says Nina Soufy. 'There was nothing superfluous, she didn't waste energy on anything.'

With *Meetings With Remarkable Men*, Brook had returned to filmmaking for the first time in eight years, since *King Lear*. In the years between, an upheaval in his theatre work had taken place. Like Lear, he had 'cast off his lendings', thrown away what he knew he could do well, tested himself by starting again from scratch. He was highly aware that the cinema could not match theatre in its ability to suggest. Theatre quintessentially could convey Brook's cherished 'double image'; images on a screen were what they were, a moving mural of surfaces. But perhaps they could be pushed to secrete more than a factual account.

In the magazine of esoterica, *Parabola*, Brook asked:

How is it possible, in a form as documentary as the cinema, to show people in a certain state of inner development, masters, or people on their way to becoming masters, unless you are doing it with real people? An actor, who has within him the possibilities of being a remarkable man, can't by two or three months of rehearsals turn into one and sustain it for a year or a month; but he can sustain it for the time a given shot may take in a film; and it isn't a lie. It would be a lie if he went off and started his own esoteric group! . . . But because he's an actor, for a tiny space of time he can open in a way beyond his normal self.

Casting Gurdjieff was never going to be easy. Brook was looking for a young man, able to speak English, Slavic looking, with an intense innerness allied to an outer force. His casting director, Bojana Makavajev, showed Brook pictures of Yugoslav actors and he thought they had struck gold when he saw and met Dragan Maksimovic, who was working in a theatre in Belgrade. They had to send him to a language school in London for a year before he was ready to start work. Around him, Brook cast a range of British actors he knew for their rich temperaments and strong features – Colin Blakeley, who had been in Brook's *Oedipus*; Terence Stamp, the angel-faced hero of Pasolini's 1968 film *Theorem*; the South-African playwright Athol Fugard, a wry, charismatic actor; and, a wily choice to play Gurdjieff's father, the comic actor, Warren Mitchell.

The interviews Brook gave when the film came out in England in September 1979 betray a certain anxiety, almost a wish to guide people to view the film in the way he intended. 'I hope people will see it twice. The second time not knowing what they are going to see,' he told the *Guardian*. 'It has to be received in a very simple way. We took enormous care with both image and sound. But in the end it is just a film about a search, and how the truth can come to you at sudden, unexpected moments in your life. We wanted to create a real world, but not necessarily one that is literally true. It is the world we surely all inhabit – one which is engaged with reality yet not totally bound by it.'

When I first saw the film, on video on a small monitor, I was uncertain about it. It seemed *faux-naif*, with some overacting to convey brooding Slavic intensity or the coltish exuberance of young people. Seeing it again on the big screen of the Paris Cinémathèque, it felt quite different. The great mountains in the opening sequence really soared over the action. Magnified in full-screen close-up, the carefully chosen faces of actors playing sages and monks and masters planted themselves into the mind, showing that size and scale can become one way for the cinema to approach what lies behind surface reality.

Returning back to the Bouffes du Nord, and to his responsibility to keep the theatre fed with work, Brook now turned for the first time to Chekhov. By the time he came to do *The Cherry Orchard* in the spring of 1981, Brook knew well what a compacted battery of actors he was working with. Once again he sought to strip away the nineteenth-century interior conventions which had adhered to the play, and now, aided by the designer Chloe Obolensky, and actors capable of microscopic intensity (Natasha Parry's fragile and volatile Ranevskaya, Michel Piccoli's lovable Gayev hopelessly trying to protect his sister), he moved even further in the direction of paring down, that quality which characterises his later theatre: elimination, a simplicity with depth.

Chloe Obolensky had just published *The Russian Empire, A Portrait in Photographs*, based on her Russian husband's family photograph albums. Brook at once realised she was the ideal designer to conjure up a Russian world for *The Cherry Orchard* in the Bouffles du Nord. The affinity was so great that she became his designer for the next twenty years. Prompted by Brook, she stripped the Bouffes du Nord stage of everything, except well-worn Persian carpets cast across the floor, with their burnished colours and intricate patterns.

This *Cherry Orchard* was a kind of indoors carpet play, like the kind the group had staged in Africa. The Persian carpets were an emblem of the comforting home that Ranevskaya's estate had been, but also of the tangled relationships and emotions of Chekhov's characters. Performed without an interval at some two-and-a-quarter hours duration, *The Cherry Orchard* fairly raced along. There were no heavy pauses to milk the emotion of a scene, yet the impetus of the performance spoke of life's transience. There was one scene alone in which the tempo slowed: the love scene that might have been between Lopakhin and Varya. It left an ache of hopes unspoken and desires unrealised.

*   *   *

L'amour est un oiseau rebelle
Que nul ne peut apprivoiser
Et c'est bien en vain qu'on l'appelle
S'il lui convient de refuser
Rien n'y fait menace ou prière
L'un parle bien l'autre se tait
Et c'est l'autre que je préfère
Il n'a rien dit mais il me plait.

Love is a rebellious bird
That nobody can ever tame
Calling him's a waste of time
If all he wants is to say no

Nor threat nor prayer can change his mind
One speaks well, the other's dumb
The silent guy is the one I like.

L'amour est enfant de Bohème
Il n'a jamais jamais connu de loi
Si tu ne m'aimes pas je t'aime
Et si je t'aime prends garde à toi

Love is just a gypsy child
Who's never never obeyed a law
You may not love me, but I love you
And if I love you, better look out

La Tragédie de Carmen, which Brook opened in November 1981 and which became one of the theatre's big successes, is a foray, through the erotic nature of opera, into the power of love and sex. The love of which *Carmen* sings is sexual, passionate, obsessive, and if possessed by such love, one is possessed by death. This is the fate of Carmen and José in Bizet's opera. But nineteenth-century tradition had too often overlaid it with spectacle, making a meal out of the bullfighting and the exoticism of Spain, rather than the intimate tragedy of Carmen and José.

Brook, Jean-Claude Carrière and his composer/conductor Marius Constant set about paring away the accretions to get back to the body of the piece, as conceived in Prosper Mérimée's novella, a spare, intense piece of writing which had first awakened Bizet's musical imagination. Constant reduced the score down to an orchestra of just fifteen musicians which could fit in the wings of the Bouffes du Nord, with no conductor in view, no chorus and a cast of six.

In the opera house, *Carmen* is always performed in repertory, because its vocal demands on the singers are too great to play it nightly. But Brook wanted a straight run of performances, as if it were a play. This meant double casting for the principal roles. There were three Carmens alternating the role – Hélène Delavault, Zehava Gal and Eva Saurova – three Don Josés and two Micaëlas. When after a triumphant international tour Brook came to film the production, he insisted on filming it three times, each with a different cast of principals. It would be unfair if just one cast were filmed, he said:

> We had three casts working together in every rehearsal. One would sing, and the other would mime while the other one was singing for them – which enabled them to concentrate on the acting, on being with the character, instead of being obsessed with their vocal challenges. Every bit of action was found by the entire company. There wasn't an A and B company, a second cast. That's something which I think is without precedent in all opera history. When we opened the three casts in the same week in the Bouffes, each night the audience saw this amazing spectacle: the other Carmens in the audience getting up and applauding vigorously.

From the arresting start of Carmen, Brook created a credible, though largely invented, gypsy world of spells, fortune-telling and fatalism. Lights came up on a sand-strewn stage, with what at first seemed a heap of rags at its centre, and then became a figure hooded in blankets the colour and texture of elephant skin. Like the snout of an animal, its head turns from side to side to track Don José as he traipses back and forth in his army uniform emptying buckets of dirty water. A bony hand appears from the creature, holding out a Tarot card to the soldier, who spurns it, though he is intrigued. This is Carmen on the hunt for love. She places the card on the ground, circles it with a hank of rope, places feathers and a dried bone on the circle, sprinkles soot and then a bright orange powder, the colour of turmeric, in a wider circle. The die is cast. Like the infernal machine of a Cocteau play, it will inexorably unwind to love, and from love to death.

Halfway through the opera, which was played without an interval, Don José and Carmen consummate their love in a wattle-hut in the mountains. A stooped, shrouded gypsy (actually played by a man) encircles their tryst with the same magical ingredients as the gypsy at the start. He leaves a round loaf of bread dipped in the turmeric, which the two lovers eat, in a marriage ritual (which was approved by real gypsies). Then they make love, and are surprised by Garcia, Carmen's husband. As the two men fight, knives flashing in the firelight, Carmen deals a Tarot card and shudders: it is the skeleton card of Death.

Carmen sings her aria of fate with a thrilling dark vibrato. In the film he made of the production, Brook shoots her with an uninterrupted steady shot, tongues of flame flickering from the left-hand side of the frame up her face.

> *Mais si tu dois mourir si le mot redoubtable*
> *Est écrit par le sort*
> *Recommence vingt fois la carte impitoyable*
> *Répétera la Mort*
> *Encore Encore Toujours la Mort*
>
> But if you are fated to die if the fearful word
> Is inscribed by fate
> You can play and play again the pitiless card
> Will still repeat Death
> Again and Again and Always Death

Her husband re-enters, only to fall to the ground with José's knife in his back. José (Howard Hensel) looks like a bandit on the run, a rough country boy hopelessly in love with Carmen, while she, attracted by the toreador Escamillo, doesn't want him any more, wants him out of her life. But José's kind of love is not so easily dismissed.

And here Brook pulls off a bold, intuitive coup. After the intimacy of a duet of quiet keening by Carmen and Micaëla, the theatre explodes with the sound of a full, pre-recorded orchestra playing the Toreador song, the one everyone knows. When Brook was asked why he suddenly switched to the sound of a full symphony orchestra, after the delicate sounds of Marius Constant's fifteen musicians, he said, 'I thought it was time at this stage of the show to wake the audience up, give them a jolt.' There speaks the pragmatic showman in Brook, a side often obscured by the otherworldly image of the guru.

La Tragédie de Carmen was a runaway success, and went on touring internationally for months with continual cast changes. The popularity of Bizet's music drew mainstream opera buffs the world over, and its television version brought Brook's subtle reinterpretation to an even wider audience.

Carmen was an example of the distinction Brook makes between *mises-en-scène* – stagings of work that his theatre needs to turn over – as against *recherches*, works of theatrical research that plumb new depths of content and form and relationship to an audience. Often, as with *Carmen*, the 'bread-and-butter' work turns out to display delights of invention and ingenuity, as if some impish spirit in Brook had been set free to create old-style 'theatre magic'. But as *Carmen* seduced audiences around the world, an ambitious new *recherche théâtrale* was in development – had been so, in fact, for the best part of a decade. Brook had been working with Jean-Claude Carrière and a Sanskrit scholar called Philippe Lavastine to condense for the stage a poetic and mythical masterpiece that was widely loved and known in India and the subcontinent, but little known in Europe and the West. To conquer *The Mahabharata*, Brook would need to raise his group and the scope of his theatre to ever greater heights.

14

OF GODS AND WAR: THE MAHABHARATA 1985

7 July 1985. Dusk on a warm evening. I take a twenty-minute boat ride along the Rhône, and in the company of about a thousand theatregoers, climb a slope, walk along a plateau and look down into the bowl of a quarry, where the world première of *The Mahabharata* is about to take place, in an out-of-town venue of the Avignon Festival. A man high up on a cliff-top sounds a horn, and the performance begins. Twelve hours later, we reel back into the Avignon streets, dazed, tired, exhilarated.

The Mahabharata, fifteen times the length of the Bible, was written in Sanskrit over two thousand years ago, and developed and enlarged by successive generations of writers. It is a saga like *The Iliad*, a compendium of the marvellous like *The Arabian Nights*, a collage of action, adventures and religion like the Old Testament. It offers childlike excitements, wonders and miracles and legendary characters. Its hero Arjuna and its spellbinding god Krishna are known to all Indian children today through comic-strip versions. It is the narrative foundation for Indian thought, the source of its deepest moral philosophy. It has spread through South-East Asia, inspired Kathakali dance-dramas, and been adapted as a weekly soap watched by millions on Indian television.

At Avignon, in an arena of rock, sand, water and fire, Brook's multiracial group of actors plays out its sequence of fantastic fables, fierce battles and parables about life and death. After ten years' preparation, Brook and Jean-Claude Carrière have adapted *The Mahabharata* into three plays: *The Game of Dice*, *The Exile in the Forest* and *The War*. The titles describe the three-part action of the war between two related clans, the Kauravas (the 'sons of darkness') and their cousins the Pandavas ('the sons of light') which forms the heart of *The Mahabharata*. In the dice game, the Pandava king Yudishthira gambles away his kingdom, his family and himself. In the purging exile that follows he, his four brothers and their shared wife learn wisdom through suffering. In the culminating battle multitudes die and yet the world and its inhabitants reach towards a better order, a truer *dharma*.

What is *dharma*? Generations of scholars and interpreters have worked to define this untranslatable quality. 'A question,' wrote Brook, 'that no one can answer. But *The Mahabharata* brings back something immense, power-ful and radiant – the idea of an incessant conflict within every person and every group, in every expression in the universe; a conflict between a possibility, which is called "dharma" and the negation of that possibility.'

Vyasa, the poet and scribe of *The Mahabharata*, says at the outset of Brook's theatrical journey, that it will be 'the poetical history of mankind'. The stream of theatrical images that Brook and his troupe throw up embodies the dynamic insights of *The Mahabharata*, and perhaps of Brook's theatrical philosophy: that there is no single way, political, psychological or moral, to seize a reality which mixes illusion and truth; that we live in a plurality of worlds; that belonging or owning are transient states, or, as he said of *The Mahabharata* itself, 'It belongs not only to India, but to the universe.'

Brook's staging in the quarry conjures up flickering, flame-like apprehensions of reality. The stage lighting shrinks and expands the space; the cracked rockface and standing sheets of water are illuminated by clusters of candles and torches so that they tremble insubstantially. These are effects and devices he learned among the monumental tombs and plains of Persepolis, but now they serve a text which time and waves of writers have enriched, not a modern fantasia on mythical themes. The costumes – vivid colours and dried-out sacking, cuirasses and boots suggesting feudal Tudors and Japanese samurai, saffron and white robes against glittering sand – open out the harmonics of the story and display the national variety of the actors.

Brook turns bamboo screens, bows and arrows and chariot wheels, white scarves, curtains and rush mats, and the red earth carpeting the stage into literal story elements and at the same time symbolic emblems of the mastery of life or the imminence of death. When mud grips the wheel of the warrior Karna's chariot – one large cartwheel standing in for his whole chariot – it is 'as if the earth itself were rising up in protest'. In *The Mahabharata* Brook's theatre almost transcends the stubborn materiality of bodies and things. Dance is used, but always in the service of the story. Draupadi, the queen of the defeated Pandavas is left at the mercy of her Kaurava captors who try to unwind her sari to get at her. But her sari spools out endlessly, becoming a river of golden cloth, filling the stage as she twirls inside it, protected.

One thread guides you through *The Mahabharata*'s luxuriant forest: the making of a good king. The story of Yudishthira centres on a man passing through trials and tribulations in order to become a better monarch, of his kingdom and of himself. This personal development, from weak goodness to a strength greater for having been wrecked and remade, is like the journey of many Shakespearean monarchs – Richard II in the poetry of his destitution, the guilty usurper Henry IV, Prince Hal becoming the complex Henry V. Yudishthira treads the path of defeat leading to discovery; and here the personal is inseparable not only from the public, but from the cosmic: *The Mahabharata*'s Great Chain of Being has the reverberations which Shakespeare fully attained in his later tragedies and romances.

And then, like a cold gust from the deep, as we are watching a court entertainment, Yudishthira has a vision of the world of collapse and catastrophe in which they are living:

> It's the age of Kali, the black time. The countryside a desert, crime stalks the cities, beasts drink blood and sleep in the streets, all the waters sucked up by the sky, scalded earth scorched to dead ash. The fire rises borne by the wind, fire pierces the earth, cracks open the underground world, wind and fire calcinate the world, immense clouds gather – blue, yellow, and red – they rise like deep-sea monsters, like shattered cities. Forked with lightning, the rains fall, the rains fall and engulf the earth; twelve years of storm, the mountains split the waters, I no longer see the world.

Andrzej Seweryn's Yudishthira speaks these words with frozen fear, speaking into a void as heavy as lead. We have been in a king's court, rich with exotic colours and cloths, candles and spices, but this abrupt vision of destruction imagined two thousand years ago brushes against our worst nightmares now. Not that this *Mahabharata* tries opportunistically to plug into our fears of nuclear war, of manmade destruction: it just takes its story of fratricidal war to its ultimate outcome.

So when, in Part Three of *The Mahabharata*, the war between the Pandavas and the Kauravas breaks out in an eruption of violence, Brook uses theatre's multiple devices and doubled images to affect the audience on every level. The physical: tournament skills of swirling swords and clubs, straining bows and whizzing arrows; dervish warriors leaping, wheel formations slowly turning in a choreography of carnage – the combat display we thrill to in tattoos. The magical-mystical level: the devastating war-disc, the *pasupata*, the unbeatable weapon of mass destruction, bestowed by the god Shiva on the warrior Arjuna, exploding in a flare brighter than a thousand suns. Rivers running with fire and blood. And the cosmic level: war of the worlds, ultimate firestorm, everything consumed, as *dharma* pursues its path, as destiny demands. And in the middle of the cacophony of the screams of the killers and the cries of the dying, the blind king Dhritarashtra sits, sniffing the air to catch the battle's ebb and flow. Just as Brook set the blinded Gloucester in *King Lear* on a bare stage straining to make sense of the sounds of a distant battle.

On the eve of battle, ringed by a circle of hard-breathing soldiers weaponed to the hilt, the god Krishna deepens his lesson. His words, the *Bhagavad Gita*, separated from the narrative of a devastating war about to break out, have become the moral distillation of *The Mahabharata* and of Hindu wisdom for the West. Reintegrated here into the plot of an immense saga, with dogs of war straining at the leash, Krishna whispers his message into the ear of Arjuna, who is appalled at the massacre he will perpetrate:

Krishna: Matter is changeable, but I am all that you say, all that you think. Everything rests upon me, like pearls on a thread. I am the sweet smell of the earth and I am the heat of fire, I am appearance and disappearance, I am the trickery of tricksters, I am the gleam of whatever shines. All creatures fall into the night, and all are restored to the day. I have already defeated all these warriors; he who thinks he can kill, and he who thinks he can be killed are equally mistaken. Weapons cannot pierce this life that animates you, nor fire burn it, nor water dampen it, nor wind dry it out. Have no fear, and stand up, for I love you. Act as you must act. I myself am never without action.

The *Bhagavad Gita*, 'the embodiment of brahminical religious teachings', is reset into a dramatic action. Rather than a holy text it becomes an urgent parable of the god Krishna intervening on the battlefield. Instead of bringing everything to a halt to recite a set of precepts, Brook gives us the Kafka-esque essence of a god whispering a precious message, most of which we can't hear. The freeze-frame on the battlefield jerks back into action. The two armies tear each other limb from limb. War, briefly a metaphor for the spirit, becomes a brutal reality for torn flesh.

Offstage, the voice of Death asks, 'What is the greatest marvel?' Yudishthira replies, 'Each day death strikes around us and we live as if we were immortal beings.' A wheel whipped along by an actor to signify a chariot later becomes the wheel of life on which its rider dies, recalling Shakespeare's Lear: 'I am tied to the wheel, and I must stay the course.' The human and the inhuman melt into each other. Sounds echo around the natural amphitheatre – blare of horn and trombone, wail of reeds, reverberations of sitar, as the musicians join the actors coming back from death, surrounded by floating candles and almost imperceptible music. There have been scenes of Jacobean horror, and Chekhovian tenderness; above all, reminders of those Shakespeare parables in which cloud-capped towers dissolve and some final reality seems to be within reach.

As the fame of *The Mahabharata* spread with its international tours, first in French then in English, it met two kinds of reaction: complete ecstasy, and bitter criticism. The *Guardian* critic Michael Billington, reporting on the premiere of the English-language version at a boathouse in Zurich, was in awe: 'Our communal one-night stand began around eight o'clock on a warm summer's evening. It ended sensationally eleven hours later with the revelation that the back wall of the boathouse was like a large moveable blind which was slowly lowered to reveal a dazzling morning sun. Even Nature now appears to be directed by Peter Brook.' Another enthusiast was Michael Kurfeld, writing in the *Los Angeles Times*, when the show played a Hollywood film studio: 'The show's real magic lies in its let's-pretend theatricality. The violence of birth, the bedlam of war, a hunter's kill, a god's metamorphosis – all are suggested in light, fabric, intonation and the sparest of props, with the devious artifice of a master storyteller who knows just how to match word and gesture. Anyone plump on a diet of Spielbergian realism may need to allow time for a creaky imagination to meet the play halfway.'

The *Daily Telegraph's* Charles Osborne, on the other hand, saw the show 'in a disused granite quarry in the middle of the Australian bush' outside Perth. 'It soon became evident,' wrote Osborne, 'that this was to be little more than a comic-strip romp through a complex work of epic poetry, often played for easy and inappropriate laughs and directorial effects . . . I should be surprised if any educated persons from the sub-continent were to find this *Mahabharata* anything more than an uncomprehending foreigner's travesty of their great epic.' A more thoughtful and grounded criticism came from Gautam Dasgupta, co-publisher of the New York review *Performing Arts Journal*. '*The Mahabharata* is nothing, an empty shell, if it is read merely as a compendium of martial legends, of revenge, valour and bravura. And that, precisely, is the reading attributed to *The Mahabharata* by Carrière and Brook.'

Osborne was soon joined by a chorus of politically correct academics and cultural theorists attacking Brook's 'appropriation' of Indian 'cultural property'. The most demagogic of these was Rustom Bharucha, in an essay called 'Peter Brook's *The Mahabharata* – A View From India':

Peter Brook's *Mahabharata* exemplifies one of the most blatant (and accomplished) appropriations of Indian culture in recent years . . . The British first made us aware in India of economic appropriation on a global scale. They took our raw materials from us, transported them to factories in Manchester and Lancashire, where they were transformed into commodities which were then forcibly sold to us in India. Brook deals in a different kind of appropriation: he does not merely take our commodities and textiles and transform them into costumes and props. He has taken one of our most significant texts and decontextualized it from its history in order to 'sell' it to the West.

A different view of Brook's 'appropriations' came from Maillika Sarabhai, the only Indian actor of the troupe, who played the part of Draupadi. An Indian classical dancer, she has appeared in more than forty Indian films, and runs the Darpana Academy of Performing Arts in Ahmedabad. 'I have to say completely unequivocally, both as an Indian and as a woman,' she said, 'that had I not felt that this representation was right, had I felt at any time that there was anything of which I should be ashamed and for which I would have to apologize to Indians, then I would have left.' She stresses just how inseparable from Indian life and thought *The Mahabharata* is: 'At the same time as the kernel of *The Mahabharata* was being created, Hinduism was developing in a philosophical fashion, and was being recorded in written form for perhaps the first time. So somewhere along the way story, religion, philosophy and moral history all became wrapped into one.' And Gautam Dasgupta reminds Western spectators that *The Mahabharata* 'is not mere epic constrained by literary and narrative strategies, but a revelatory injunction, ethical and theological in purpose, that determines and defines the social and personal interactions of millions of Indians'.

Brook never replied directly to Bharucha or to the other detractors of his *Mahabharata*. What he did offer as a response seemed at first rather simple. He said the only thing that mattered was quality. By this he meant a precise and unmistakable state that can occur in the psyche of actors and audience. Giving a lecture to an audience of psychoanalysts in the aftermath of *The Mahabharata*, he tried to convey that theatrical rule of thumb every theatre worker knows, that suck-it-and-see pragmatism that produces a result that *feels right* and that *works*. Against upholders of *The Mahabharata*'s sanctity, against cultural nationalists and their ideas of authenticity, he asserted theatre as no more but no less than the arising of *quality*, quality of attention, quality of shared, almost chemically altered, silence:

> An audience comes to the theatre for one reason only, which is to live a certain experience, and an experience can only take place at the moment when it is experienced. When this is truly the case, the silence in a theatre changes its density and in every form of theatre, in all different traditions and all the different types of theatre all over the world you can see exactly the same phenomenon.

An audience is composed of people whose minds are whirling. As they watch the event, sometimes this audience is touched – again we do not really know what 'touched' means, except that it is a phenomenon. At first, the audience isn't touched – why should it be? Then all of a sudden, something touches everyone.

At the moment that they are touched an exact phenomenon occurs. What has been up till then a collection of individual experiences becomes shared, unified. At the moment when the mass of people becomes one, there is one silence and that silence you can taste on the tongue. It's a different silence from the ordinary silence that is there at the beginning of the performance. This shared recognition expresses itself through the increasing density of the same silence.

Brook's practical understanding of these phenomena of the mind, the heart and the spirit – the basis of his theatre craft – is his riposte to the charges of bad faith. He could have rested his case upon the quality of the actors Marie-Hélène Estienne had found at the four corners of the earth, as well as those who had been with the troupe from the start. The quality of their performances, their evidence and presence, the melding of the actors' native body language and traditions with the call of the story of *The Mahabharata*: for Brook this evidence experienced on the stage is what made it impossible to reduce discussion of the piece to post-imperial denunciations.

And more positively, it made him confident that he had created an ensemble of actors – 'a storyteller with twenty heads' – which was equipped to cross cultural frontiers. They were not 'translating' a 'foreign' work into the idiom and assumptions of a 'home' culture. As an international group, they shared no such homeland. Nor were they conducting 'crossovers' or 'fusions' of the kind that 'world music' was beginning to do; what they carried was more referential than music, it entailed myths, stories, theology. The result was a deliberately hybrid performance, finding its own structures and creating its own theatrical truth in the space between cultural markers and specifics they had all made. As Brook wrote:

More than ever in our work, it was clear that forms had to come last, that the true character of the performance would only emerge when a hodgepodge of styles had passed through a filter to eliminate the superfluous.

We imitated ancient techniques, knowing that we would never be able to do them well. We fought, chanted, improvised, told stories, or we introduced fragments from each of the group's widely different traditions. The path passed through chaos and muddle towards order and coherence. But time worked for us. Suddenly the day came when the whole group found that it was telling the same story.

During its world tour, Brook continued to articulate the cultural space, the local and universal meanings within which *The Mahabharata* played. 'We are trying to celebrate a work which only India could have created but which carries echoes for all mankind,' he wrote. What he had made in *The Mahabharata*, and in his whole line of work from *Timon* onwards, was intuitive, not schematic. 'When we were bringing together the group of performers,' he told Georges Banu, 'we did not set out with any schematic ideas in mind. We didn't cast in the spirit of UNESCO, saying that one country will represent such and such a thing. We worked by searching and "sifting".' By the same token, since *The Mahabharata* did and did not belong to India alone, the concept of 'cultural property' was irrelevant. Brook has a healthy hostility to what can truly be called 'cultural piracy', as he forcefully told the Australian journalist David Britton:

Cultural piracy is what the English have done without any hesitation over a hundred years in India, which is to take their objects and without paying for them put them in British museums. That is piracy.

What happened in *The Mahabharata* is that here is a very great work which all the pirates ignored because there was no cash to be made out of it. You steal a Buddha from a temple and you can resell it, as people are doing all over the place. *The Mahabharata*, one of the great works of humanity, to this day remains a name that most people in the west haven't heard, a totally unknown work, apart from a few scholars and specialists.

And yet it is a work of the greatness of the works of Shakespeare, of the greatness of the great Greek epics, a supreme religious work as well, totally unknown. Now, all the Indians with whom we have been in touch are deeply touched to find that today, after a hundred years in which every educated

Indian was forced to know the works of Shakespeare, there is a group of people from many countries who have spent a long time, with all the care and respect they can muster, to say that this is a work that belongs to mankind and should be known.

Why has nobody accused the west of cultural plundering because it reads *The Odyssey*? Why should *The Odyssey* be known and *The Mahabharata* be totally neglected? I think the Indians don't see this as stealing but as an opening.

It was the *Bhagavad Gita*, the very nub of the poem's moral meaning, that caused the most shock and dissatisfaction. Cherished by Hindus as their fundamental sacred text of moral teaching, they found it whispered by Krishna into Arjuna's ear, inaudible to the audience. 'Theatre is not a lecture, theatre is not a religious ritual, theatre is not a sermon,' Brook told David Britton. He did not want to hand his theatre piece over to the Brahmins and theologians, to stop it in its tracks for a recital of the jewels of wisdom of the *Bhagavad Gita*. He wanted it to be there, suggested, but not spelt out. Only later, in the *Mahabharata* film, did a few key lines of the *Gita* appear in a big close-up of Bruce Myers as Krishna.

Krishna speaks to Arjuna on the battlefield, but only in a whisper does he deliver the essence of his teaching about the deepest human question. 'It is the epicentre of the *Bhagavad Gita*,' Brook says to Banu. 'Should you reject and withdraw from confrontation, should you act, or what? That question "or what?" is on everyone's lips today.' That is the question, to act or not to act, and in the acting, to find out what is true action. It is too deep a matter to be sermonised from a stage. But it can be evoked.

15

DEPARTURES AND RETURNS

1989–2000

After the Himalayan effort of *The Mahabharata*, throughout the 1990s Brook pursued a variety of paths, none of them on such a gigantic scale, all of them feeding the Bouffes du Nord, or translating his theatre work into film terms. He filmed *The Mahabharata* in a six-hour version, finally shot in an expanded set in the last days of a Paris film studio, after scouring the world – India, Australia, Tunisia – for suitable locations. Mounting a distilled, chamber-version of Debussy's *Pelléas et Mélisande*, he continued to renew opera at the Bouffes du Nord, though with a work much less popular than *Carmen*, and he pursued his engagement with opera by doing *Don Giovanni* at the festival of Aix-en-Provence.

He staged Beckett's *Happy Days*, with his wife as Winnie. He constructed a theatrical collage around *Hamlet*, splicing Shakespeare's text with aphorisms from the pioneering twentieth-century directors. He wrote and spoke about Shakespeare, and staged *The Tempest* with an arresting cast. With two penetrating productions he plunged into the interior world of the human brain. He began a continuing association with black South African theatre, and its passionate connection between performance and politics. And he hunted down the heart of *Hamlet*, in an English-language production in his Paris theatre.

He opened the South African vein of work with a play devised by two black South African actors, working with a white South African writer and director. *Woza Albert!* was a product of that upsurge of drama from the

South Africa townships in the 1960s, which Brook had first encountered in a South African season at the Royal Court Theatre in 1973. Townships such as Soweto or Sophiatown had begun in the 1950s to break open their country's dominant white culture in a flood of creativity through jazz, journalism, photography, music and especially theatre. It was an ebullient return of the repressed, as black people found their voice through devised and collectively authored plays, in which white theatre-makers such as playwright/actor Athol Fugard and writer/director Barney Simon joined with actors such as John Kani and Winston Ntshona.

Brook was stirred by this eruption of energy and life in the face of oppression and deprivation. *Woza Albert!*, which opened at the Bouffes du Nord in 1989, was Brook's French staging, translated by Marie-Hélène Estienne, of a show devised by Percy Mtwa, Mbongeni Ngema and Barney Simon. It turned upon an idea which the two black author/actors had brought to Barney: that Jesus Christ makes a second coming – in apartheid South Africa today. It was a ninety-minute vaudeville of angry yet strangely gleeful tableaux, a demonstration that the victim is more generous-spirited than the oppressor. The work had the chutzpah of the African street comedian, as the two actors cut a ping-pong ball in half and each stuck a half on his nose, to play rich white people.

Micheline Rozan has said that 'Peter had a weakness – *un faible* – for African actors'. He settled down with pleasure to work on *Woza Albert!* with two of the outstanding actors of *The Mahabharata*, Mamadou Dioume and Bakary Sangaré. The 'something else' Brook found in his two actors from Africa was not just the suppleness of their bodies, the directness of their contact with an audience; it was what he called 'transparency', an openness and simplicity, the ability to slip in and out of character, a playfulness whose source was laughter, no matter how grim the story told, the circumstances revealed.

Reflecting on the work, Brook wrote:

> In the world of apartheid, the audience which the actor addressed was at one and the same time his witness and his subject. The township plays, and the actors' way of performing them, came about not because of an artistic wish to adapt a theatre form to the present day but simply because there was no other

choice . . . Plays about social injustice generally adopted a serious tone. Athol Fugard, for his part, saw that it wasn't through anger but through the cruelty of laughter that the hardship of life in the townships could best be evoked. Barney Simon continued in this path, encouraging the actors, black and white, to include as many elements of real life as possible in their work. Social reality had no need to be foregrounded, the context was so strong that it seeped into the most intimate of human situations.

Brook's South African involvement continued through the 1990s. Putting on *Le Costume* (*The Suit*) in 1999 maintained his connection with the Market Theatre, Johannesburg, where Barney Simon had mounted his and Mothobi Mutloatse's adaptation of Can Themba's short story. Themba was a legendary actor, writer, journalist and high-liver from Sophiatown, a kind of township Damon Runyon. He was one of the first and most popular writers for *Drum*, the racy photo-magazine established in the 1950s, freeing up black South African prose, so it no longer aped 'correct' English. A generation of reporters, storytellers and poets grew up around *Drum*, until the government had it closed down – at the same time as they banned the African National Congress party. The stifling both of a vibrant magazine and of organised political opposition sent a generation of writers into exile. Can Themba, uprooted and desperate, drank himself to death in Swaziland.

Brook recognised that Themba was a born storyteller; *The Suit* tells a sad story with rueful humour. It is the story of a punishment, a lifelong sentence that ends in death. A young couple, Philemon and Matilda, live in a bustling township. Philemon is madly in love with his wife but finds her in bed with another man. The lover escapes, leaving his suit behind. Philemon tells Matilda her punishment will be to take the suit into the house as if it were an honoured guest, seating it at their evening meal, treating it with respect and consideration, nailing her to the evidence of her adultery.

In a wonderful scene, Matilda, left alone, dances cheek to cheek with the suit; her hand snakes out of the sleeve of its jacket and begins to caress her back and her bottom to the sound of Hugh Masakela's trumpet. The show is full of such beautifully simple images: eating and washing up are mimed as in a children's play, a gown-rail swings around to mark out rooms and doors, a vivid shawl becomes a bedspread and a wardrobe. But gradually, as

Philemon's rage exposes her to the whole town, she begins to crack. One day, she is dead.

The Suit is about love lost. It could take place in a Cape Town penthouse just as easily as in a pinched terraced house in Sophiatown. Though the hard working conditions of the men who leave each morning for a long train journey into the city are vividly shown, there is no sermonising.

The Suit became a tremendous hit for Brook and Micheline Rozan. It toured internationally for over two years and transferred to the Paris equivalent of the West End. Marie-Hélène Estienne, having written the French version of the text and cast many of its actors, began to direct the new versions of the production. It succeeded because it was not a costly show, with just four actors and one set; but also because of the warmth of its humanity, its tough but sweet comedy.

In 2000, Brook paid tribute to two actors from South Africa, John Kani and Winston Ntshona and to Athol Fugard's dense stoic tragedy *The Island* by helping them revive the play for a British and world tour, almost thirty years after they had created it. The play tells of two black convicts on Robben Island, one of whom wants to rehearse *Antigone* for a prison concert, the other of whom is gradually giving up hope. The sight of the two visibly older actors sweating and puffing as they hump rocks in the long opening sequence was painful evidence of the scars apartheid had left.

In the 1990s, Brook, normally so objective with regard to himself, began to let into his writing and his activity glimpses of the personality who stood behind his stream of work. His little book *Evoking (And Forgetting) Shakespeare*, published in 1998 is not only his most succinct summation of what he finds remarkable about Shakespeare; it also reflects significant aspects of Peter Brook:

> Genetically speaking, Shakespeare was a phenomenon, and the bald head we have seen on so many pictures had an amazing, computer-like capacity for registering and processing a tremendously rich variety of impressions . . . Now, is it sufficient to say that he had a great memory? I don't think so.

Memory, said the ancient Greeks, was the Mother of the Muses, and here
Brook revels in its fertile and frequently indiscriminate activity, 'its permanent
state of flux; feelings, images, colours, sensory impressions, theories, thoughts
and ideas', as he was to write when trying to imagine the mind of Mozart.
Brook was similarly intrigued by his own mind, by his flood of thoughts and
words, and his strange behaviour such as not seeing the consequences of his
acts on others, and by numinous images that could take years to decipher.

This is of a piece with descriptions of the *boy genius*, the *prodigal child,*
young Master Brook with which his precocious talent was first greeted. But
'genius' is a slippery and now unfashionable, 'elitist' term.

In his Shakespeare essay, Brook goes on to say that the accumulative
power of memory is not enough to make art of Shakespeare's quality.
Memory alone would result in an undifferentiated mental rag-and-bone
shop. A processing is needed, and that process is called 'poetry'. For Brook,
the difference between a poet and the rest of us is that:

> We, at any given moment, don't have access to the whole of our lives. None of
> us is capable of penetrating below the conscious level . . . to enter into the
> entire richness of what we have absorbed over our whole life. In many of us, it
> could take a long search to dig into our past impressions. For some of us it
> would even need years with a psychiatrist to reach into those strange tunnels
> where all one's experiences are buried waiting to be revived. But a poet is
> different. The absolute characteristic of 'being a poet' is the capacity to see
> connections where, normally, connections are not obvious.

And these connections, Brook insists, are made moment by moment and
microsecond by microsecond. Brook believes that Shakespeare's plays were
written fast; another reason why Shakespeare cannot be erected on to a
pedestal of cultural grandeur, nor can his work be reduced to any over-
arching belief or ideology. What makes the totality of what we call
'Shakespeare' an irreducible phenomenon is a sense he shared with his
audience of something beyond the world of sense data:

> For Shakespeare and for his audience, and for the time in which he was living,
> with the tremendous mixture of people in transformation, with ideas explod-

ing and collapsing, there was a lack of complete security. This was a blessing because it created a very deep intuitive sense that behind this chaos there was some strange possibility of understanding, related to another sort of order, an order that had nothing to do with political order.

We can perhaps turn these words into a reflection on Brook himself, as a theatre-maker and as an individual.

Brook now turned again to Shakespeare, to *The Tempest* (*La Tempête*, *1990*), his third attempt at Shakespeare's last play. This time casting was crucial to his interpretation: Prospero and Ariel were to be played by two African actors, Sotigui Kouyaté and Bakary Sangaré, who had played lead parts in *The Mahabharata*. Sotigui, descendant of a famous family in Senegal, was a well-known African film and stage actor and a traditional *griot*.

A *griot* is a storyteller, and in West African villages, preserves and transmits oral history. A *griot* is also a praise-singer, a peacemaker in disputes, a satirist and commentator. The *griots* can trace back human ancestry to times before writing, when memories and storytelling were the repository of history and beliefs. Through his ancestry, Sotigui also had a familiarity with the world of gods and spirits. 'In other cultures,' Brook told me at the time, 'in the societies we call traditional, images of gods, magicians, sorcerers and ghosts evoke deep human realities. So an actor from such a culture can touch them without embarrassment.' Sotigui, a tall, skeletal actor, also enjoyed a commanding confidence to work an audience, learned from countless appearances telling stories to large crowds.

Bakary Sangaré, born in a village in the south of Mali, was a surprising choice for Ariel, a role traditionally envisaged as an ethereal spirit. Instead, here was a large, deep-voiced, very black actor, rooted in traditional village storytelling. He had an almost circus-like virtuosity, capable of turning the horsepower of his voice into a gleeful gurgle or pirouetting with the delicacy of a dancer. 'Mature African actors,' Brook said of them both, 'have a different quality from white actors – a kind of effortless transparency, an organic presence beyond self, mind or body such as great musicians attain when they pass beyond virtuosity.'

Caliban, traditionally played by an earthy (and often non-European) actor, was played by the diminutive David Bennent, a German actor best known in the title role in Volker Schlöndorff's film of Günter Grass's celebrated novel *The Tin Drum*. The casting flouted the then-fashionable interpretation of the noble native Caliban exploited by a colonial Prospero, showing him instead as an angry adolescent.

Chloe Obolensky's set was a Zen sandpit – 'a sand-carpet, a playing field', as Brook defined it – raked at the start into Zen patterns, but progressively marked and inscribed by the performance. The English scholar David Williams describes the effect: 'Sandcastles, footsteps and hieratic markings will disturb its surface temporarily, recording a Rorschach-like narrative itinerary, a calligraphic imprint of individual histories written by bodies in action.' When Prospero 'wipes the slate clean' with his treacherous brother and all the stories of betrayal and bitterness, the disturbed sand is raked back to its original pristine state. This erasure recalls the end of *The Empty Space*: 'The theatre always has one special characteristic. It is always possible to start again . . . In the theatre the slate is wiped clean all the time.' Here this life-reversing, life-redeeming action happens on the stage, here and now, before our very eyes.

Looking back across Brook's Shakespeare productions, certain characters seem to mirror Brook's engagement with directing. Lear trying to get everyone to follow his retirement plot eating his cake yet having it – a bad director. The Duke in *Measure for Measure* setting up a situation to test his wilful deputy, disguising himself and manipulating the action unseen – a sneaky director. Hamlet setting up a play to catch the conscience of Claudius – a director of psychodrama. Now, in this Shakespeare play Brook has visited the most, Prospero appears not just as a master *metteur-en-scène*, but, Brook recognises, as a remarkable man.

> Prospero is neither a 'director' nor a 'character', in the conventional sense of these terms: he is a 'remarkable man', in the Gurdjieffian sense. Sometimes he locates himself at one level of reality, sometimes at another – a prisoner of anger, yet free of his passions. Any attempt to explain him which stems from a psychological or historical analysis is bound to fail: there cannot really be any answers to any of the questions that one might have from these perspectives. Prospero is a 'force', an energy, a living mystery. What's the point of explaining him?

In theatre, one must always retain one's freedom in relation to reductive analyses. Everything can be conveyed by means of performance if the spirit is free, if the text is free and if the preparation rigorous and precise.

Like an underground river, Brook's meditation on the mind had been flowing for years beneath the overt surfaces of his work. When Shakespeare's Theseus asserts that 'the lunatic, the lover and the poet / Are of imagination all compact', his words chime with Brook's curiosity about the apparatus that transmits and interprets our human sense of being. He was interested in his own mind: its sideslips and recalls, its riffs and cliffhangers, its 'off-line' passages, its surges. He grew familiar with the workings of his own imagination, learning to respect its rhythms of incubation and attack. Though he had a psychoanalyst as a brother, delving into his own psyche did not attract Brook – not psychoanalytically, in any event.

But now, in two theatre-pieces, he dealt directly with the question of the hurt brain and mental illness. *The Man Who* (*L'Homme qui*), a piece inspired by the writing of the neurologist Oliver Sacks, was his first venture, in 1993. Five years later, he returned to the field in *I am a Phenomenon* (*Je Suis un phénomène*, 1998), based on the work of the Russian neurologist Alexander Luria. He then wrote a screenplay based on this piece, which has never been made. It's clearly a subject with which he had to come to terms during the 1990s, as he entered his seventh decade. He told me:

The thinking which was beginning to swell up long before *The Mahabharata* was ended was that parallel to this imagery from the past, the only field in which there could be the same effect in terms of today is science. The starting point was science; and in fact I had meetings with atomic physicists, with a mathematician, looking for an area in which we might work. I always came up against the objection, 'but it's inhuman'. Theatre has to have flesh and blood. In themselves, scientists are not remarkable, once you take away their science; or you end up doing a biographical play about Einstein or Alan Turing. We came up against the fact that science can't be dramatised, because the drama in science is in equations and thoughts.

Then Brook met Harold Pinter who enthused about Oliver Sacks' *Awakenings*. Sacks was a British-born, New York-based neurologist who had become a literary giant in 1985 with his book *The Man Who Mistook His Wife for a Hat*, a collection of neurological case-studies, written up like short stories by Chekhov. After reading it, Brook became inspired by the idea of an epic show about the brain. There was a fortuitous connection with the epic protagonists of *The Mahabharata*: in his foreword, Sacks compared his patients to the heroes of ancient epics. 'Classical fables have archetypal figures – victims, martyrs, warriors; neurological patients are all of these.' He compared their travails to those of the bold travellers of the past, and their journey through their illness as 'an odyssey'.

The meeting of Brook and Sacks was a meeting in many respects of like with like. As Sacks' memoir *Uncle Tungsten* shows, both grew up in substantial houses in the London suburbs. Sacks, eight years younger than Brook, was also despatched to a boarding school in the country to avoid German bombing. Both came from Jewish though not particularly observant families; both had clever, dynamic fathers.

Brook invited Sacks to Paris in 1988, to talk to the actors and watch the improvisations based on his book. 'We wanted him to be critical,' said Brook, 'only to find that he was so enthralled to see actors improvising his stories that he was the most uncritical audience we had ever had. He rolled around roaring with laughter.' The actors were watching the doctor in Dr Sacks as well as the patients they were improvising. This doubling of roles – actors switching from the sufferer to the 'saviour' – became a crucial element in the delicately balanced piece.

It had a hard gestation. For the final two years of *The Mahabharata* tour, they had worked at segments of Sacks' book. At this stage, Brook envisaged a large company for the piece. Jean-Claude Carrière read Sacks' book, and wrote a script from it. But it failed to pass the test for all dramatisations of medical stories: it was soap opera, focusing on the 'human interest' around the science, whereas what interested Brook was the science itself. But to use a storytelling structure led straight to melodrama. Marie-Hélène Estienne kept detailed dramaturgical notes, but as the research mounted up, a workable theatrical form seemed further and further away. They felt completely stuck, and Brook was on the point of abandoning the project.

Then Estienne suggested to Brook that the number of actors should be restricted to four – Sotigui Kouyate, Maurice Benichou, David Bennent, Yoshi Oida. Brook gathered this group and said, 'We're going to spend a couple of months in hospitals, we're going to improvise on what we've seen, as a language in itself, but we're not going to talk for at least two months about how are we going to show this. That is taboo. We're just going to absorb it. And then there will be the next phase: what can be retained which is vivid. And then that very secret thing, finding the order.'

Then Brook remembered *Tadada*. *Tadada* had been the joyful, whipped-together vaudeville performed at the Bouffes du Nord by all the actors and singers in *Carmen* at Christmas 1981. It is almost a secret, not figuring on any Brook career summaries. Yet it was to provide the theatrical model for the form which *The Man Who* was seeking. 'I had the intuition,' Brook told Michael Billington, 'that there was another sort of form based on something we'd just done at our Paris theatre, called *Tadada*, a string of music-hall songs that might have been sung in the Bouffes over the past century. We'd borrowed tables from our local café and put them in the theatre, got together some of the singers who'd been in *Carmen* and invited friends in from the local *quartier*.' This, as Billington remarks, is pure Brook: his capacity 'to see how the techniques of a free-form vaudeville can be applied to an odyssey into the human brain.'

Placing *The Man Who* in the main line of work at the Bouffes, Brook adds, 'The essential work from *Conference of the Birds* onwards is that, whatever the field is, it's more than ever become a question of trying to get something hidden to emerge by elimination. At the end of *The Man Who*, there was a hush and people felt they'd had a very special experience.' They had watched a patient who can only see one side of his face in the mirror; another who experiences his leg as an alien dead limb; one who cannot experience his body; another whose memory gave out forty years earlier; and a sufferer from Tourette's syndrome, a condition that jolts the face, the body and the tongue into a series of tics and eruptions, jerks, grunts and curses. They had seen this on a stage bare except for a table, a few chairs and a TV monitor showing beautifully coloured but mysterious maps of brain scans.

The Tourette's patient – 'the Ticker', as he came to be known – was the most spectacular creature, 'whose clownish tics, sudden scatological explosions and hyper-self-consciousness,' wrote John Lahr in the *New Yorker*, 'make Robin Williams' schizoid frenzy look lethargic.' The Ticker is paradigmatic of the theatre, as well as of the human striving to work through a broken brain and nervous system; for the tics disappear momentarily once the patient is engaged in a meaningful or even just playful activity. The Tourette's patient tells the doctor that his tic goes away when he plays ping-pong, or 'if I dance, it's my natural tempo, the tempo of my temperament'. The Ticker seizes the microphone on which he is being recorded and, wielding it like a stand-up comic – 'I can't help it. I love it. It's stronger than I am' – plays out the drive to sway an audience shared by actors and Tourette's patients. The 'lunatic, the lover and poet' are separated by the thinnest of partitions. These patients remind us of the fleeting redemption of theatre. And of the saving humour some mentally ill people can produce, like the Tourette's sufferer in this play: 'A ticker friend said to me the other day, "I can never go to an auction."'

Sacks endeared himself to Brook, as much as to his patients, by his tireless identification and commitment. 'Oliver uses all his human reactions as his instrument,' he said. 'There's a patient of his with amnesia, a man who had been a fan of the Grateful Dead in the 1960s. Oliver wanted to see whether he could increase this man's memory by relating to something he really loved; so he took him 200 miles to a rock concert. The patient had this marvellous experience, he came alive listening to the music and singing along with it. In the car coming back Oliver said: "How did you like the concert?" And the man said, "What concert?" But what's marvellous is Oliver going 200 miles full of hope!'

Brook returned to the theme of consciousness and the brain with *Je Suis un phenomène* (1998) a piece about being over-, not under-endowed. Three televisions and two tall loudspeakers surrounded a table and chairs on a sand-coloured carpet, as a clinical setting for the story – scarcely a story, more an excavation – of a man with an infallible memory. Solomon Shereshevsky is a prodigy, a phenomenon. He cannot help himself remembering. He loses his job as a journalist because, unlike his colleagues, he never takes notes when he is reporting. His prodigious memory triggers another rare faculty: synaesthesia. When he hears a word, it immediately produces an image. Or a colour, a taste, a smell, a musical texture. He makes these into a visual landscape, where they can pun or free-associate into memory and meaning. People with synaesthesia told Brook and his co-writer Marie-Hélène Estienne that their condition was at once joy and torture.

Solomon Shereshevsky's story was first published in 1965 by Alexander Luria, a predecessor of Oliver Sacks. It concerns 'a Jewish boy who, having failed as a musician and as a journalist, had become a mnemonist, a memory-man, met many prominent people, yet remained a somewhat anchorless person, living with the expectation that at any moment something particularly fine was to come his way.'

Solomon Shereshevsky says he can't bear to listen to poetry, because its richness of reference overwhelms him. Yet in the hands of the sympathetic Dr Luria (played with great tenderness by Bruce Myers), he retrieves the first three lines of Dante's *Inferno* in Italian, which he does not speak, using a dance of images to summon up the lines. The bright video images of the brain's shapeshifting, its spectacular torrent of connections, are the most theatrical thing in a deliberately damped-down evening.

In this production Brook allows theatre no more than a supporting role, elliptically creating Solomon's mind-reading performances on the stages of Russian music-halls, which he took up as a last resort. A red scarf, a follow-spot and canned applause serve to conjure up the vaudeville of 'mind-reading'. In the final section of this low-key, involving play, Brook, who remarks in *Threads of Time* on his own still unquenched need to find 'something else', imagines a reunion with the patient Solomon in an American brain research institute today, thirty after the actual date of Solomon's death. Now Solomon can see on television monitors images of his brain in action, the screen tracking the biochemistry from which his memory games are born. He is not crushed by the sight. He neither rejoices nor does he have any answer to the doctor who asks him if he thinks there is a God. He exits, holding an X-ray of his own brain segments, still in search of 'something particularly fine'.

Brook's 'brain cycle' points towards an under-layer of health and of courage, an almost imperceptible law of compensation, even for the most reduced person. These glimpses of a lost world restored, of a plenitude to be recaptured – despite the Tourette's patient's reminder that 'the blind force of the sub-cortex always wins in the end' – these are the observations of a hyperactive mind and an overflowing spirit, which Brook saw fit to realise through his cruelly confined use of theatre in these two pieces.

Brook was now approaching seventy, and the time seemed ripe for a stock-take of what he had spent his life doing: directing. After many a detour, it came to life in 1995 as *Qui est là?* a condensed version of *Hamlet* cross-cut with an anthology of quotations from pioneer directors: Gordon Craig, Stanislavski, Meyerhold, Artaud and Brecht. But *Qui est là?* was a painfully fractured theatre-piece, which didn't leave him satisfied.

It had a roundabout gestation. He had pitched the idea of such a show to Richard Eyre, director of the National Theatre in London, and had approached David Hare about researching and writing it. Hare, engaged in writing his trilogy for the National Theatre, declined. Nick Dear, who had written some ten plays, including a blistering play about William Hogarth, *The Art of Success*, and adaptations of Molière and Tirso de Molina, joined as writer. He now feels that he gave a good deal of time to the project, had an enjoyable working relationship with Brook but, as each piece of writing was turned down, never quite knew what Brook was after. In the end Brook, with the help of Marie-Hélène Estienne and Jean-Claude Carrière, put together a script himself. It is peppered with pointed quotations from the masters of modern theatre. Gordon Craig's words seemed to give Brook licence for limitless experiment and cultural iconoclasm: 'It would be good now and then to make experiments, completely preposterous attempts, no matter whether these experiments succeed or not. For example, for Shakespeare . . . we would scarcely play a quarter of the text. Nowadays, the great dramatic masterpieces are treated like the Roman Catholic church service. When an actor begins "To be or not to be" and so on and so on, it's as if he said, "Our Father which art in heaven".'

Brook mounted the patchwork in a workshop/laboratory environment, and alluded to the different traditions – Japanese, African, Asian – which the group had explored with him or brought from their country of birth. Some English critics who came across to see it were enthused. Michael Coveney reported with fulsome abstraction that 'the event becomes an extension of the play's material, not a diminution . . . and the play is finally rediscovered as a tingling compendium of states of being.' Others were less carried away.

'It was not good. It was like a Theatre In Education programme,' said one British director. Brook knew that, after this theatrical mosaic, he still had to make his assault on *Hamlet* itself.

Meanwhile, he turned to Samuel Beckett, directing *Happy Days* (*O les beaux jours*) in 1995, with his wife Natasha Parry playing the buried but incurably optimistic Winnie. The main feature of this production was Brook's realisation that Beckett, adapting his own play into French changed the tone from rough to musical, from raw to genteel, respecting the natural purity of the French language. As a result, against Chloe Obolensky's white sky, Winnie, in Brook's words, 'became a woman drawn upwards by the light, by her wish to be a bird, while her earthy nature dragged her downwards. As Beckett's third major play, it is not about man in darkness – though the husband is in the bowels of the earth – but for the first time the feminine has central place.'

But *Hamlet* still beckoned.

Tracing Brook's engagement with *Hamlet* sends us back to his childhood puppet-show in the Chiswick living-room; to his 1955 production with Scofield which elated Moscow audiences and underwhelmed London ones; to the Meyerholdian cut-up version Charles Marowitz did for Brook's 1964 *Theatre of Cruelty* experiment; and to *Qui est là?* of 1995. Like the 'old mole' working away in the earth to which Hamlet compares his father's ghost, this play has taken hold of Brook over the years.

In 2000, he mounts his latest attempt at what he calls *The Tragedy of Hamlet* – pointedly renamed to distinguish it from Shakespeare's full text, and subtitled *Adapted and Directed by Peter Brook*, just to allay any doubt. Brook's adaptation removes about twenty per cent of the text, relocating anthologised passages, and runs at two and a half hours without a break. And, in an even bolder move, Brook for the first time premiered *The Tragedy of Hamlet* in English in his French theatre.

In his Hamlet, Adrian Lester, a young black British actor who he had seen playing Rosalind in *As You Like It*, Brook had found a magnetic performer: sensuous, articulate, anguished, physical. Having an Afro-Caribbean-British leading player was, like many other things in *The Tragedy of Hamlet*, a confirmation of Brook's work since he'd been in France. He had another actor from a similar background, Jeffery Kissoon, who had been in *The*

Mahabharata, as the Ghost and as Claudius; and Shantala Shivalingappa, a classical Indian dancer from a culture in which a daughter's submission to the rule of her father was absolute, as Ophelia; the British actors Natasha Parry as Gertrude and Bruce Myers as Polonius and also as a jig-dancing Irish gravedigger; Naseeruddin Shah, an Indian Bollywood actor and Rohan Siva from England. This multi-ethnic cast was the true landscape of this *Hamlet*, not some elaborate Elsinore décor.

'There are plays that are perfect in their form,' Brook told Richard Eyre when BBC4 broadcast the film he shot of his production. 'And then there are plays – and *Hamlet* is the supreme example – which came into existence because Shakespeare as a practical dramatist was reworking somebody else's play. *Hamlet* was not Shakespeare's invention. There was a bestseller, a pot-boiler melodrama, a revenge play called *Hamlet*, and Shakespeare came in to rework this popular play. I don't think that Shakespeare's genius shone through every detail. What happened was that a fairly ordinary melodrama was totally transformed by the fact that all through it there's one character who is so amazing that the world's never got over him.'

Here is Brook's hunch that *Hamlet* is not an imperishable, long-pondered jewel, but, like most of Shakespeare's plays, something written fast, though drawn from a deep well, in response to a pragmatic need of his theatre. 'The key phrase,' Brook says to Eyre, 'comes when the Ghost says, "You must revenge," and his son says, "Yes, dad, of course." And the Ghost says, "But howsoever thou pursuest this act / Taint not your mind." That phrase blows away all the discussions – Is Hamlet a weakling? Is he indecisive? Is he confused? You say to one of your children, "Go and kill someone, but don't taint your mind." If the child is insensitive, they forget about that, and they just go and kill the person. Because what is being asked is impossible. And yet Hamlet is not shown as a pacifist. He confronts the fact that killing may be necessary.'

Brook recalled *The Mahabharata*, whose protagonist, the prince Yudishthira, faced a similar challenge to Hamlet.

> The great idealistic figure has to plunge his hands in blood and his feet in the mud to become a full human being. There is in Hamlet at first an element of the pretension of the person who wishes purity at all costs. Then there's the

Hamlet who, having inadvertently put his hands in blood by killing Polonius, now realises, with a sort of tragic, stoical sense, that this is how it is. Destiny throws him into this situation; he can't get out of it. So now he can do with an untainted mind what he's been asked to do by the Ghost, because he realises that the untainted mind is a mind that accepts.

This is the heart of the piece, in Brook's unearthing of it in 2000: the pledge to act with an untainted mind, and the new, equally strong realisation that you have to get your hands dirty, and that murdering Polonius entails going on to kill Claudius as well. The tension between these imperatives brings Hamlet to the brink of contemplating self-slaughter in 'To be or not to be', which Brook resets at the pivot of the action, after Hamlet's inadvertent murder of Polonius.

There was some demurral among English critics about the disappearance of familiar textual landmarks and characters. But many, like John Peter, rose to the extraordinary impact of the work:

> Intellectually, emotionally, psychologically, it is tense with apprehension, expectation, curiosity. The acting is honed to a simplicity that clearly comes from the most meticulous and sophisticated observation and questioning . . .
> The characters have a natural, unself-conscious immediacy about them, seemingly untouched by the necessary selfishness and skill of direction . . .
> At its most self-effacingly and perfectly integrated, as it is here, the theatre is almost identical with life.

Preparing for the final duel, Hamlet comes to accept life in its entirety and his death as imminent: 'If it be now, 'tis not to come; if it be not to come, it will be now; if it be not now, yet it will come.' In *The Mahabharata*, Arjuna, on the eve of battle, has a new perception of his life, expressed with equal riddling equilibrium: 'He who thinks he can kill and he who thinks he can be killed are both mistaken. No weapon can pierce the life that informs you; no fire can burn it; no water can drench it; no wind can make it dry.' Both protagonists have reached an acceptance, which Hamlet distils into two yielding monosyllables: 'Let be.'

This *Hamlet* looked stunning. The *Independent* critic Paul Taylor was transported by what he called 'the therapeutic power of colour'. Brook had designed the stage himself, asking Chloe Obolensky to do the costumes. 'With its green, yellow and indigo,' wrote Taylor, 'its geometrical inset rugs and its ethnic tinged costumes, has the visual charm of some out-of-time collaboration between Rothko and Matisse.' It was also like a children's playground, a joyful metaphor which allowes Brook periodically to puncture the loftiness of the story with knockabout and clowneries: the Gravedigger pole-vaulting his way in, bawling his crazed jig, and the music-hall routine which Hamlet performs for Horatio in the graveyard, sticking the skull of Yorick on to his staff to leer at us like a carrion Archie Andrews.

The first words of Shakespeare's *Hamlet, Prince of Denmark* arresting in their ordinariness, are 'Who's there?' They are also, in another radical change, the last words of *The Tragedy of Hamlet*. No entrance of Fortinbras at the head of his army, no brisk, decisive, untroubled commander come to clear up the mess left by the prince of dreams. Instead, an echo of the opening, with the advent of the Ghost. But where that apparition originally happened in midnight darkness, now 'Who's there?' is posed by Horatio, Hamlet's only trustworthy friend, the man who will carry on his spirit. Waving Horatio away, Hamlet slowly sags to his knees. He is smiling. Then his neck gives way, his head lolls and he is dead. In a brilliant crescendo of light, a resurrection: as the light mounts, all the corpses of the duel scene and all the story's dead – Ophelia, Guildenstern, Rosencrantz, Polonius – rise from the floor, casting off their parts and assuming their condition as actors.

'But look,' says Horatio, like Edgar who endures all the disasters of *King Lear*, like every newborn baby at the end of Shakespearean carnage; 'But look,' he says, as they all stand and take us in, within the shared light; 'But look, the morn in russet mantle clad / Walks o'er the dew of yon high eastern hill.' And then, in the phrase that encapsulates Hamlet's (and indeed Brook's) openness to experience and his hunger for knowledge: 'Who's there?'

16

BELIEF WITHOUT BELIEVING
2000–2004

Encouraged by his American publishers Cornelia and Michael Bessie, Brook had started to gather material towards a memoir. It appeared in English in 1998, and in French five years later. In *Threads of Time* Brook, now in his seventies, made an associative weave of 'the threads that have helped to develop my practical understanding'. But only some of the threads. It is something more than a memoir and definitely not a showbusiness autobiography. It is rather a soliloquy, an often lyrical narrative of his apprenticeship in the search for meaning, shuffling the cards of chronology to re-enact insights of his life. This biography has, on the other hand, sought to convey chronologically, and through many voices, the experience of being with, working with, changing with Peter Brook, and to measure the radical impact of his greatest work and to reveal its origins.

What remains striking about *Threads of Time* (the French title, *Oublier Le Temps*, is more drastic, casting away time) is the urgency of Brook's still unsatisfied searching, which evolves into, but is not replaced by, a more balanced acceptance. 'When I was young' he writes, 'I used to think, "It's possible to *get there* spiritually within one's lifetime"; in fact, I felt a moral obligation to accomplish an inner *getting there* before it was too late. Then as the nature of our human condition became clearer, this was replaced by the more realistic thought that "it would need several lifetimes". But bit by bit, common sense has prevailed and shows that one is no more than a fleeting particle within a humanity that is struggling, groping, rising, and falling endlessly, searching for a *there* that in the whole future course of human history it may never know.'

To his work on stage, too, he began to let in autobiographical echoes. In 1998 he returned to opera, to *Don Giovanni*, and one could detect in his programme note something of a self-portrait, the director in his early seventies conjuring up the appetite and accelerated spirit of the young man in his twenties.

> Mozart's genius alternated despair, the awareness of death, humour, joy, derision, speed of thought and the ability to see life simultaneously on a social and cosmic level. In the face of death, our feeling for life is momentarily and extraordinarily reinforced. Throughout his music, Mozart constantly comes back to a contemplation of this presence. All the elements of his works lie between two poles: a joy for life and an underlying fear of death.

Brook staged *Don Giovanni* with a young cast and his own radically abstract design: a geometry of coloured poles, reminiscent of Mondrian, but also thrown and manipulated in a Meyerholdian dance. At the invitation of Stéphane Lissner, who had taken over from Micheline Rozan at the Bouffes on her retirement, he directed it at the open-air Aix-en-Provence opera festival. He saw in Giovanni something he had watched in himself as a young man in work and in love: an all-consuming commitment to the truth of the present moment and a blindness to seeing the results of one's actions and passions on others, as he wrote in the Aix programme:

> Don Giovanni's error, his Achilles heel, is perhaps the fact that he lives the wealth and joy of the moment to excess. He is endowed with nearly every quality: charm, energy, the appeal of a free man, yet he cannot see that the present moment is inseparable from the moment which follows. In the immense kaleidoscope of his qualities, there is one essential thing lacking, the understanding that every act has its consequences . . . There is the flaw: he never foresees the terrifying consequences of his acts. He refuses even to recognise them. It is a vision of Hell.

In the finale of the opera. Brook brings Don Giovanni back from the dead. The pallid, impassive seducer moves silently and unseen among the people whose lives he has altered: Leporello, still dumbfounded by the shock of seeing his master dragged down to hell; Donna Anna in the arms of her betrothed; Zerlina embraced by her husband; Donna Elvira in black, destined to enter a convent. 'Now he sees the consequences of what he has done to each of them,' said Brook; and Don Giovanni's face shows that he is touched, not by remorse or guilt, but by a flicker of understanding, at least, about the effect he has had on them all. It is no longer a cursory coda to the demise of an evil-doer, as if to say, 'we're well rid of him', but a much more ambivalent tableau. It was Brook's steady grasp of the tension between these naked truths about the sexual life and the marvel of Mozart's music, down to its 'vibrations of the utmost delicacy' that gave his production of *Don Giovanni* what he called a 'strange joy'.

In life as in art, you start out believing you are making a new beginning. Fresh start seems to follow fresh start. Then you realise that there is no beginning, no completely new departure, only sequels, suites, flowing from some source you will never know. The past thirty years of Brook's work, and especially the twenty years since *The Mahabharata*, are in an important sense a recapitulation, a summing- and a summoning-up. This is also the way Brook handles the many traditions he has gathered in his troupe, respecting them, but also lifting and jolting them out of their origins into a new context, a culture not yet fixed and defined. Retrievals and replays abound in these late works; intertextuality, that trope so favoured in modern literary theory, is at work.

Chekhov's letters gave Brook the opportunity to re-weave long threads – of love for its author, of Russianness, of marriage, of the life of the theatre – when in 2003 he staged *Ta main dans la mienne*, based on Carol Rocamora's *I Take Your Hand in Mine*, a two-character play inspired by the letters of Chekhov and Olga Knipper. An actor and an actress evoke Chekhov ill in Yalta, Olga rehearsing *The Cherry Orchard* in Moscow, in a measured dance of love and rehearsal, writing and distance and dying. The actors, Natasha Parry and Michel Piccoli, recalled Brook's production of that same *Cherry Orchard* twenty years earlier, when she played

Lyubov Ranevskaya and he her brother Gayev. A retrieval of the life and work of Chekhov, it was also a distilled example of the moving but almost laconic restraint which was becoming a trademark of Brook's late work.

Brook staged a number of glowing miniatures at the Bouffes du Nord as the new century broke, small-scale productions which spoke about the world's violence in a voice of muted horror. In Caryl Churchill's *Far Away* (2002), the only play by a living British author he has mounted at the Bouffes du Nord, he made a cool, elegiac environment for her fable of universal discord and non-stop massacre: 'It was tiring there,' says her female protagonist, 'because everything's been recruited, there were piles of bodies and if you stopped to find out there was one killed by coffee or one killed by pins, they were killed by heroin, petrol, chainsaws, hairspray, bleach, foxgloves, the smell of smoke was where we were burning the grass that wouldn't serve.' Brook found an undemonstrative style to match Caryl Churchill's surreal, impassive account of the virus of violence and retaliation being passed on from generation to generation, species to species.

In *La Mort de Krishna* (*The Death of Krishna*, 2004), Brook, Marie-Hélène Estienne and Jean-Claude Carrière made a text for Maurice Benichou to perform as a one-man show about the death of Krishna, the god he had played in *The Mahabharata*. It too told a story of devastation, opening on the battlefield on the morning after the war. 'The sun is slowly rising over eighteen million corpses. Birds of prey drag heroes by the feet. With cruel beaks they hack at mangled faces till the last mark of recognition goes. The beauty of a man leaves no trace on the beast's jaws.' Maurice Benichou delivered the story of Krishna taking his leave of a world of disorder with grave stillness and infinitely sad poise. 'Having removed himself from his senses, his words and his spirit, he lay down on the ground.'

Gurdjieff and Grotowski played a vital role in Brook's life, and in 2001 he took an opportunity to make a reckoning and a tribute to his two mentors. Grotowski had confronted him with a spirit of challenge, of *contestation* even fiercer than his own, an intensity of spiritual search and a cultivated, widely informed set of theatrical exercises and techniques to raise the actor's ambition. Gurdjieff's teaching and 'work', to which he devoted years of energy and practice, had given him a tangible picture of what a developed human being could be, with all energies working in equilibrium, and an acute awareness of alibis and evasions, in life and in work.

Brook went on helping Grotowski after he left Poland, was fêted as a guru in America, and, troubled by ill-health, started a 'work-centre' in Italy, where he gave up making theatre for the sake of 'para-theatrical' gatherings. Brook made speeches at fundraising events for Grotowski's centre and backed him as Professor of Theatrical Anthropology at the Collège de France; Grotowski gave his inaugural lecture in the Bouffes du Nord. He died in 1999.

In November 2001 Brook seized on an invitation from the Grotowski Centre in Wrocław to try to bring together the currents of these two formative 'remarkable men' in his life, by distilling as clearly as he could one of the most intangible themes at work in him: the relation of Gurdjieff's teaching to the work of the actor. In this improvised speech, he tried to find words for what he had been doing for over three decades. His subject was *Gurdjieff and the Actor*.

Gurdjieff often spoke of how it is important for each person to be an actor, and to learn to play his role in life. But it is important to understand that Gurdjieff was not talking about theatre . . .

In the heart of Gurdjieff's teachings is one word: 'identification'. Identification means something very painful for us to recognize. Identification means that at this moment, sitting here, talking to you, I am totally convinced that the person speaking is my real self. This is not true. I am 'glued'. Glued to the part I am playing at this moment. I believe totally in the words that I am saying because I am glued to them.

Let's compare this with the situation of an actor. An actor plays a part. If he or she is really good, all of us watching believe that every fibre of that imaginary person that we are watching is 'the character'. Actors, in an extraordinary mysterious way, adapt their natural body to the body of the character they are playing . . . The actor must be in touch at each moment with every single muscle, with his thought and feeling, so that it is possible for the entire body to become a whole. Only then will the part – in both senses of the word – become completely believable.

So we come to something that is almost impossible to accept as a concept. An actor really acting his part is both so close to his role that he is completely within it and yet distant: involved and not involved at the same time. Somewhere in the organism there is space. And from this free space, this space of freedom, come the impulses that bring the character to life . . .

Nothing can change. An actor playing Oedipus has to make Oedipus's blindness to his past and the optimism with which he faces each new revelation so real that even the audience, while knowing the end of the story, is brought to believe that this time somehow the tragedy will be avoided. As a human being, the actor longs to change the course of the play. Every fibre in him wishes for there to be a way out. But yet the actor knows that he has to go on playing his role right to the end. And again tomorrow. And again the next day. And that is one further degree of removal from identification.

Gurdjieff uses the actor as a metaphor to help us to see what a fully developed man could be. This can easily be misunderstood. Being an actor in life, playing a role in life, may seem to mean pretending to be something different from what one really is. This is absurd. At each precise moment, nothing can be other than what the moment contains. The wish to change the present is a projection into the future, which blocks entirely our capacity to live fully the moment itself, in fact to live our lives. However, if one is like an actor – the difference is essential – one is not glued to the action, it unfolds in freedom. In life, I hear some terrible noise outside. I run to the window to see what it is. I run, completely absorbed by the sudden movement and the rush of feelings. Is it possible to do the same thing like an actor? That means that the person sitting quietly and hearing a cry from outside runs to the window without being a complete slave to reactions.

In English, two words help to make this clear: 'act' and 'react'. All the time, all our lives, we are reacting . . . All our lives are reaction, reaction, reaction. To be able to act is a very great aim. It is the start of a long apprenticeship. It is Work.

So when Gurdjieff used the image of an actor it was not for the purpose of making better theatre. The theatre is just a very useful field of investigation. Gurdjieff called it a 'reflector of reality'. And in the reflector we can see certain processes which can help us, as struggling human beings, to understand something more. The immediate question is of inner space. Only in this space can a free central axis exist. What can make this possible? I am tempted to believe in will-power. Try for yourself. It won't work. Something new has to come into the human organism – a finer energy. This is needed, it is essential for it to enter the field of other energies and begin to harmonize and balance their functioning.

I cannot say any more about that. Explanations are useless. Inner work is practical. It opens great living questions. This is the starting point of a search that no one can accomplish alone.

Just as there are no completely fresh starts in life, so there are no absolute departures. Your birthplace and your past remain in you. Brook dislikes thinking of himself as an exile or an expatriate, and is in reality no further away from his native land than a three-hour Eurostar train-ride. He reads the English papers; he was incensed at Mrs Thatcher's philistinism, quizzical about Tony Blair's self-righteousness, calmly ironic about the moral contortions of world politicians. He comes to London to see shows, do workshops or talks, meet old friends, often in the remaining haunts which recall his life as a young man in post-war London: the battered décor of Dino's trattoria on the Gloucester Road; Manzi's fish restaurant in Leicester Square; Olivelli's restaurant near London University.

England keeps reaching out to him. A new generation of directors and theatre-makers has crossed Brook's path since he left London in 1970. Through their eyes, one can see the legacy of the director, and his presence as a man. Declan Donnellan, director of Cheek by Jowl, one of the most immediate and involving British theatre companies, first got to know Brook when he cast Natasha as Gertrude in his *Hamlet*. Donnellan recalls the uncanny way Brook seemed to call from Paris to ask how things were going just at the times when some intractable production looked most hopeless. Donnellan admits Brook has been something of a father-figure and he has an acute understanding of some very basic things that Brook has handed on:

Peter's got a way of bringing somebody into the space that is just full of authority. He is deeply imbued with the mystery of time and space. I think one of the most wonderful things about Peter is the sacred and profane that he talked about in *The Empty Space*. It's a very profound dualism and it's absolutely true that if you lose either one of those poles as an artist, you aren't going to produce very good art. Sometimes I've listened to Mozart, and I've realised how vulgar it is, and at the same moment I've realised how profound it is. It's something quite strange: the actual moment of showmanship is the moment of profundity. It's not as if you need a bit of this and a bit of that, it's understanding that the shit and the spirit, the music-hall and the mass are one and the same thing. The thing I think is completely unique about Peter is his possession of both those poles.

Donnellan shares with Brook an outsider's distance from English culture, as an Irishman, a homosexual and a director with cosmopolitan tastes – he introduced plays by Racine, Lope de Vega, Ostrovsky, Lessing and de Musset to the English stage. Driven by the state of British theatre to leave the country, he went to live and work in Russia, making his return with spare, passionate productions of *Boris Godunov* and *The Winter's Tale*. His production of Corneille's *Le Cid* was invited by Brook to play at the Bouffes du Nord. In Brook he sees the showman and the shaman indissolubly linked, though as Brook prunes down his work to a pure essence, Donnellan longs for him to create another expansive production:

I still love that moment when he shows that he has showmanship in him. Rather than take sides in one of these fatuous polarisations – 'This one's all tits and teeth and a show queen and this one's a rather tedious searcher who has people grunting, looking at their navels' – when you see them reunified so profoundly in Peter it makes the heart leap.

David Lan is a playwright and the director of London's Young Vic theatre, to which Brook has brought *Le Costume* and *The Tragedy of Hamlet*. In his speech while presenting Brook with a lifetime achievement award in 2001, Lan seized on the phrase of Brook's which had inspired so many actors and directors with a sense of freedom and possibility, 'The Empty Space'. Then he warned against sticking to it too slavishly.

Like many students of acting in the 1970s, I found *The Empty Space* a holy text. Only theatre in improvised or 'found' spaces was true theatre. Everything

else was condemned as comforting, compromised or even dishonest. Or if you
did choose to perform on a conventional stage, it had to be with the minimum
of lamps, colours, fabrics. The poorest possible theatre, the barest man on the
barest stage was not just an idea, it was a necessity.

And so, of course, we had missed the point. We had turned an insight into a
dogma, a potential into a prescription.

An empty space as a starting place for an act of theatre needs to be genuinely
empty. When it comes to being filled, this should be with nothing but your – or
you and your colleagues' – own individual needs, desires, hunches, improvisations, spontaneities. This, I think, is the much harder lesson that Peter Brook
has been teaching all his working life.

As his producer, when Brook brought his shows to the Young Vic, Lan
was struck by two qualities, on the surface antagonistic: Brook's ordinariness and his seriousness. 'If you said to him, theatre is the last haven for myth
in our society, he would say, yes, but first you have to get bottoms on seats.
And if you said, we have to fill the house, he would say, it's worth playing
even if there's only one person there, providing the work is deep and the
experience from which it comes is deep and intense. It's very infectious when
he says things like that to you when he's with you. And hard to hold on to
them when he's not.'

Another young British director, Simon McBurney, has a different, though
equally profound, take on Brook. McBurney's Théâtre de Complicité has
staged an immense span of work over its twenty-one-year existence, ranging
from comedy improvisation influenced by McBurney's teacher, the French
mime and mask artist Jacques Lecoq, to Brecht, John Berger, Dürrenmatt,
Shakespeare and a devised show *Mnemonic*, about memory and time.
McBurney re-imagines the factors that pushed Brook into leaving England:

Brook began by working in a theatre that seemed to be addressing a
particularly narrow social band; and that social band, like the whole of
British society, was still in a kind of strange mourning and regret, as if they
hadn't got over the loss of empire. After the war, there was a glimpse of hope,
with the Labour government. In the theatre, starting in the late fifties, there
was a great shift, with the Royal Court and the arrival of Michel St Denis and

the use of improvisation. But the theatre establishment was resistant to all this: rather than realise its own 'theatre-ness,' it retreated into a kind of conservative self-preservation. This led to a feeling of disillusionment. Unless you were going to follow the status quo, or cleverly manoeuvre yourself, if you were genuinely looking for the truth of something, then England wasn't a place which was particularly yielding. And I'm not only thinking of Peter Brook, I'm also thinking of my friend John Berger, and many others, who felt that there wasn't anything for them in mean-spirited Britain. Both Berger and Brook intuitively had the foresight to see what was coming: the great disintegration of the 1970s and the arrival of Mrs Thatcher in the eighties. Both were thinking and looking ahead.

McBurney also understands what a welcoming contrast Paris and French culture offered to Brook:

Paris has always been a place of itinerant or émigré artists. And because it was the centre of the Revolution, it maintained a special atmosphere – all that insouciance and rudeness, which is really marvellous. In French culture, there's a place for the artist. In France they ask you, 'What do you do?' and you say, 'I'm an artist' and that's the end of the conversation. In England, if you say you're an artist, they say, 'Yes, but how do you earn your living?' Brook really needed to make the break from England, to cut himself off in order to begin again, because he knew that if he stayed where he was, he would never have done it.

When Simon McBurney saw *The Conference of the Birds* and *The Mahabharata*, he realised the challenge Brook was throwing down:

that in this age of film and television, theatre had to utterly declare itself. In its search to do this, his theatre dispenses with all disguise. The audience is looking only at what is there. There is no sense of hiding and producing, but rather everything is declared for the audience to see, who are reminded that this is theatre. Then, with almost nothing, the audience is transported into the essence of the piece. The way he does something and what it means are indivisible, and the singularity of the ideas comes shooting out into the heart and soul of the observer.

McBurney acknowledges the importance for him of 'Brook's carpet' – the concept, and the practice, that by simply unrolling a carpet you create a playing space, an area of acting – and you can see this, with many variations, in Complicité shows. But what moves him most in Brook's work are moments like the opening of *The Mahabharata*, which he saw at the semi-restored Tramway in Glasgow, converted from a disused transport museum, with the patina of its bared bricks and the glow of its painted plaster walls:

> Into this self-consciously created space entered the figure of the man and the boy. Everything was implied by that, everything that Brook's soul seems to yearn for, perhaps that we all yearn for: the idea of continuity, of the passing of stories from father to son, from older man to younger man, of forming part of a continuous chain. When a piece of theatre like that happens, you are made aware that this continuity is lacking in our lives.

Richard Eyre, director of the National Theatre, has lunch with Brook in Paris, after seeing *L'Homme Qui*. Having confided to his diary that he feels 'like a surrogate son' with him, he says the show is 'beautifully acted, distilled, elegant' and then is forced to ask what directors actually create. 'The show is a logical destination for Peter's work: its subject matter is how we think, feel and act, and it's as near to an 'authored' piece as he's ever done. *All* directors lean towards *auteur*ism, and the longer they go on, the more acute the leaning becomes.'

When I talked to Eyre later, he remarked that one noteworthy thing about Brook was how very few living English-language authors he had directed: *Serjeant Musgrave's Dance* by John Arden, in 1963, in French; Beckett's *O les beaux jours*, in Beckett's revealing French version in 1995; Caryl Churchill's *Far Away* in 2002; none of them premieres. When a director works with a playwright on the premiere of a play, there is, to some degree, shared authorship. Brook has not sought this since he left England. There has been modern writing, of course, but it is either adaptation (of Oliver Sacks, Colin Turnbull) or documentary material, including new writing, assembled the way a film director – the real *auteur* in the cinema – might shape a film, as in *US*. Does this mean that Brook sees directing as a kind of authorship, replacing the contemporary playwright? Declan Donnellan gives a sharp response to the accusation that Brook has failed to 'serve the writer': 'I think it's terribly dangerous to go down the path of asking has he served new writers properly. I could just as easily say, have they served him well enough?'

Brook has never said that directing is like an author writing – a 'distiller' is the closest to a definition he has come. The impression he gives is of an unruffled objectivity about what he does, as if he was constantly aware that, in the phrase of Coriolanus which he likes to quote, 'there is a world elsewhere'. This does not dilute his passion about each piece of work. But to see Brook, as his son Simon films him in the documentary *Brook par Brook*, utterly engaged in operating a glove puppet or cutting out paper animals to make a zoo for his grandson Prosper, one can imagine that same curiosity and concentration applied to travelling or toy-making.

Brook's impassivity, however, was jostled from an unexpected quarter in June 2002. David Hare, arguably Britain's most serious playwright, and of late virtually the National Theatre's house author, was invited to lecture on John Osborne at the Hay-on-Wye literary festival. He took the opportunity to lash out at Brook's evasiveness compared with Osborne's steadfastness:

> John's romantic attempt to go on throwing himself against the bars of the cage was not pretty, and it was also doomed. But John went on writing, insisting on meaning, way beyond a point where the world thanked him for it. He did not, like Peter Brook, go into exile, and set about draining plays of any specific meaning or context to a point where each became the same play – a universal hippie babbling which represents nothing but fright of commitment.

Brook was hurt by this attack. After some weeks and several drafts, he replied to Hare. It was the beginning of an exchange of letters which says much about Brook's relationship with English culture now, with its 'common-sense' dismissal of 'airy mysticism', and its theatre's drive to justify itself by being 'political'. He had noticed how many critics protectively regretted the absence of the political dimension when he cut Fortinbras in his *Tragedy of Hamlet*. Now he engaged with Hare in a serious debate, which nonetheless shows that his reasons for leaving England over thirty years ago to seek a different climate of work and ideas seemed still be valid.

14 September, 2002

Dear David,

One day, in an interview, I was rash enough to criticize one of Orson Welles' Shakespeare films. When the article appeared, Orson was rightly furious and said 'We all suffer enough from critics without needing to start criticizing one another.' I am sure your own experience confirms this.

Fair criticism is always fair, but I am also sure you would agree that the basis of honest criticism is a rigorous respect for facts.

It would be an absurd vanity on my part to expect you to know all our work over the years, but it is very reasonable to expect you to refrain from affirming what you don't know. What first-hand observation allows you to declare that what we do here and across the world is always the same play, drained of meaning?

At the time when I began to work in France, I saw that times had changed, that issues were more and more complex and confused. I no longer believed in the value of debates, pamphlets, statements and pseudo-Brechtian speeches. It seemed necessary to focus on the areas where action was and is possible. In the theatre, we had a possibility of direct action in relation to one of the most painful subjects – racism.

Since 1970 we have quietly and rigorously based our activities on the co-existence of radically different cultures, with a very wide range of races working together. As a result, we have seen that a living example – starting with the field of casting – has a far greater influence, and even action, both on audiences and on the profession than polemics that cry out 'Look at my commitment'.

But lurking behind your quip, do I sense the suspicion of any self-respecting Englishman that in this work in 'exile' there might be some 'hum-hum' suggestion that there's more to life than the rational mind can grasp? If this is hippie babbling, I'm sorry it offends you.

Perhaps you've forgotten that the first person I approached to make a vast social history of directing in the twentieth century, showing all the passionate and contradictory attempts to link the stage with the world outside was yourself. Alas, you said 'no' and as this daunting task needed a very remark-able and generous writer, I was forced to abandon it.

I think there is only one point of disagreement between us. I have always admired your work.

Peter

23 September 2002

Dear Peter,

Well, this was obviously not a good day to get your letter – the day when I hear of Joan Littlewood's death. If you're my age, then your theatre-going was partly formed by the argument between the work of the two greatest directors of your youth – you and her. I have told you before that it was your production of *King Lear* that made me want to spend my own life in the theatre.

You are right to rebuke me by saying there are critics enough, and that one artist shouldn't attack another in print. As you probably guessed it was the production of *Far Away* which goaded me into saying what I did. Bruised ego is one thing, and, believe me, I am as vulnerable to it as you are, no doubt more so, but there is also – as well you know – a profound argument here, and one in which it is likely neither you nor I are wholly in the right.

When I saw your production of Caryl's play then it seemed to me to represent, if you like, the end-point, the defining limitation of everything you have tried to do in a theatre without politics. You have deliberately taken yourself out of any specific social context. But, to me, in theatre, social context is everything. You make the sneer about pamphlets, debates and pseudo-Brecht. You accuse me of a diminishing rationalism – a strange accusation against the author of *Racing Demon*. But, on my side of the argument, there is an equally available sneer – that there is now a kind of one-size-fits-all mysticism which affects your work to drain individual plays of any specific meaning. It is as if you are so scared of saying anything crude that you forget to say anything at all. *Hamlet* without Elsinore! *Far Away* without politics!

You probably remember better than me what Ken Tynan wrote about the difference between *The Ik* and *Fanshen*. And he was right – not necessarily in which side he supported – but in his feeling that there was going to be a decisive split in the road at that moment in European theatre. You took one path – and it produced *The Mahabharata*, so I am not saying the path can be proved to be wrong. (Work of that greatness doesn't come from stupidity.) But

I do believe it is a path which leads finally to diminishing returns – because, characteristically, you have followed it to its logical conclusion.

I took the other path. The best production I have seen this year is the Al-Kasaba production of *Alive from Palestine*, which a group of us paid to bring from Ramallah to London. It was everything political theatre should be – no, it was everything *theatre* should be – a front-line report, produced by actors who live under occupation, describing; without grandstanding, without affectation, what life has been like in the last two years of the intifada. By locating their own experiences in a place that is completely specific, and describing the political circumstances under which they reached their present emotions, they achieve exactly the universality to which you or I would both hope theatre aspires. The politics was like a scaffolding under water on which these greatly moving men and women danced.

I shall be very surprised if the man who asked me to write, effectively, a history of twentieth-century theatrical ideas, does not recognize the legitimacy of each other's doubts about the course the other one has chosen. This is a historic argument, as you of all people know. If I couched my doubts about your choices in a way that offended you then I apologize. It was not my intention. If I think you are wrong, be clear: I think you are magnificently wrong.

All best wishes,

David

15 October 2002

Dear David,

Your thoughtful letter touches a real issue and I'm glad you've opened it. I think our points of view aren't really opposed to one another.

Can the theatre ever do more than to increase for a moment the quality of our awareness – and, as a consequence, of our understanding and our actions? The only question is – what tool digs the deepest? The recognizable or the unknown? The everyday or the mythic?

Ever since the time when I was doing *Oedipus* and *US* virtually back to back – and later with *The Mahabharata* followed by *Woza Albert!*, I've lived with a century-old question – figurative or non-figurative, abstract or illustrative?

In *Oedipus*, the rotten state of Thebes is not shown, it is evoked by a few vivid words. The *Lear* you mentioned seemed 'real' to us, but the Russian establishment of the day was horrified by the lack of 'realism'.

In England there is a powerful tradition – from the first GPO films to Ken Loach, from Granville Barker to Joan Littlewood – that is firmly rooted in a social context. But there are many other traditions which bring out more hidden aspects of the human experience and demand more abstract means.

In Europe, there is an aesthetic cult that is often bloodless, but the true tradition – abstract in painting – is very rigorous. It is one of 'elimination'. All we can do, whatever the theme, is to try to put a temporary accent on one or other aspect of reality, 'eliminating' what an audience doesn't need explaining for the hundredth time.

I cannot go along with you in believing that one way, one style, one tradition can ever be 'right', nor another one 'wrong'. I think our only hope is to follow respectfully each other's work and try to understand the different instruments we need, which – surprisingly – are often complementary.

Peter

A final signal from English culture came from the playwright David Edgar – a playwright very different from Hare, although he shares his social concerns, and with an academic career, as head of Birmingham University's playwriting course. His review of *Threads of Time* for the *London Review of Books* goes beyond the dispute between 'the recognisable and the unknown', as the best way of describing reality and making us aware. He understands and is sympathetic to the wager that underpins Brook's work since the move to France, the belief that in 'an intercultural situation', there can be found 'what gives a form of culture its life – not studying the culture itself but what is behind it', as Brook says in *Threads of Time*. Edgar gives Brook the benefit of the doubt, as a practical theatre-maker:

Aware of the horror with which anthropologists (and literary critics) would greet such an idea, Brook's belief is that while cultural habits go deeper than clothing, they are still only garments, to which an unknown life gives body. Stripped of these specificities, 'each race, each culture can bring its own word to a phrase which unites mankind', the moment 'to which all theatre leads'. In this Brook may be wrong, but he knows what he's saying, and he has thought through the consequences.

Edgar does not lambast this 'universal life' as some cultural theorists would do to any mention of universality. He sees that Brook's early interest in rhythm and proportion in theatre and art connect with his spiritual journey. Brook's project as a whole rests on a wager about human communication as fragile as that of Pascal on the existence of God. But in the theatre, it is a wager that can be tested in performance, and David Edgar, in his persona as a playwright and as a professor, has seen it work:

The project can be and has been accused both of presumption and pretentiousness. On the first, it must be said that it accords with what directors, writers, actors and audiences actually do more accurately and usefully than any other intellectual model of the endeavour; and the fact that actors and audiences from so many different human cultures have found that Brook's project speaks to them would suggest that some universal set of catathropic shapes, tempos and proportions might indeed cross cultures and unite them (though how they relate to the often exclusive specifics of culture is clearly a vexed question).

Edgar, like Donnellan and McBurney, sets Brook's universalism against his roots in pragmatic British showbiz, and in the fluidity, even looseness, of British culture, which enabled him to move easily from one sphere to another. Brook says of the soporific theatre he worked in during his formative years that it was his job to stop people falling asleep. Operating in 'a theatre in which Paul Scofield could go from King Lear into a West End musical and not see any essential difference between the two endeavours', Brook grew up as removed from 'continental' theory and argument about theatre as any ordinary English director. This, says Edgar, is what enabled him to avoid the trap of intellectualism, and to pose the deepest questions with a childlike intensity. The two halves of his life are complementary and indissoluble. 'Only in England,' concludes Edgar, 'could Brook have posed the question he has striven to answer in France.'

Without British theatre's capaciousness, without British culture's refusal of rigid categories, Brook could not so widely have practised the spectrum of theatre, nor brought such a range of theatrical experience to bear on his later search. But that's only part of the truth. Without Brook's innate sense of difference and distance, without the detachment his origins gave him and without the sustained work on himself over years to bring mind, body and heart into harmony, he would not, in France and in his wanderings, have pursued so intensely the questions that drove his work.

Without a kind of spiritual ruthlessness, he would not have so decisively left London ('If I'd have stayed, I would have just gone on directing one play after another,' he said to me), would not have made an empty space in himself by discarding everything he could do best, and then started from emptiness to fill that space with a renewed self. Talking to his actors at the end of their American journey, he compared being an actor with being a samurai: 'years of preparation, and then one decisive blow.' Applied to himself, his words make manifest the Shakespearean phrase with which he most identifies. 'The readiness is all.'

CODA
Brook in Barcelona, July 2004

I thought I had finished this book. After three years of close identification and critical reflection, I had built up a picture of many levels and voices, responding to Peter's challenge to match the monologue of his own memoir. Sometimes the writing had been heady, as I evoked the glow left by his productions; sometimes hard, as I struggled to grasp the sheer scale of his life and imagination. Exhilarated but also emptied out, I thought I had completed it. And then Peter came up with a new piece – which in fact he'd been nurturing for decades – and in summer 2004 I set off to Barcelona to catch it, even in its half-born state, wondering whether it would be yet another new beginning.

The drama of *Tierno Bokar*, which I saw in Barcelona's converted flower market on its way to its Paris opening, centres on a bitter dispute between rival religious factions. At stake is whether a prayer should be said eleven times instead of twelve. What begins as a doctrinal dispute is turned, with the malign intervention of the French colonial service, into a realpolitik exercise of divide-and-rule. A play on this subject written by a Voltaire or a Shaw would have been a rationalist's mockery of organised religion. In the hands of Brook, his dramatist Marie-Hélène Estienne and his multiracial cast, *Tierno Bokar* becomes an empathetic elegy for a way of living which is crushed as much by colonial domination as by its own fanaticism.

Brook found the story of Tierno Bokar in the writings of Amadou Hampaté Ba, an African writer and preserver of oral storytelling and traditions, whom he met in Paris when Hampaté Ba took up a post at UNESCO. Ba was himself the pupil of Tierno Bokar, the Koranic teacher and spiritual leader of the village of Bandiagara, in Mali. In Brook's *recherche théâtrale*, a title he prefers to 'production' or 'play', Tierno Bokar tries to reconcile the fierce antagonisms between two communities over the number of times the 'Pearl of Perfection' prayer is recited in the daily service. Tierno Bokar's community recited it twelve times, following a time-honoured tradition; in the distant village of Nioro a young holy man of the same Sufi sect obeyed a mission to restore the prayer to the true number of eleven times. Execrations, appeals to ancient authority, boycotts and curses sprang from this difference. But Tierno Bokar wants to meet the young *chérif* Hamallah of Nioro, and make up his own mind based on the quality of the meeting.

The encounter and the nightly theological debates – a haunting scene of two men circling in near-darkness, whispering just out of our earshot – convinces Tierno that the 'Hamallists', as the French authorities have labelled them, are sincere and their beliefs well-founded. He also recognises that the younger man has an even greater spirituality than himself. But this is where Tierno's troubles begin.

His own family and village turn against him, ban him from the village mosque, forbid any contact with him. Shopkeepers are forbidden to sell to him; his remaining followers have to smuggle food to him. He sits in his clay hut, his prayer-beads in his hands, having struggled to avoid a religious conflict, having failed, and now, in Ba's words, 'accepting destiny absolutely, without looking back'.

Sotigui Kouyate, one of the core actors of Brook's group, seems to sculpt Tierno Bokar with the lightness of his fine fingers and his elongated body and the steadiness of his voice, like a stream. He brings to the part of Tierno Bokar a radiant good humour, a tenderness that is never sanctimonious and a gift for pungent, direct speech. 'I pray God,' Tierno Bokar said, 'that at the moment I die I have more enemies to whom I've done nothing than friends.' Sotigui, and the four other engaging African actors playing major parts (Habib Dembélé, Abdou Ouloguem, Dorcy Rugamba and Pitcho Womba Konga), together with Brook's long-standing actors with whom he has shaped his group's style, Bruce Myers and Yoshi Oida, communicate those qualities that have so captivated Brook in African actors since *The Mahabharata*, *Woza Albert!* and *Le Costume*. Exuberance. Gravity. Elegance.

Irreverence for things of the earth. Reverence for the spirits that rule human life.

Brook designs a paradisal world, a stage soaked in the colours of honey, gold and sand – a reminder that Mali edges on to the Sahara. Glowing in bright light, Brook sets out the simplest elements – straw matting, a low platform on which coloured rugs are rolled out, coiled raffia that can become a stool or a pillow. In this shimmering surround, ten actors and two musicians – threading and shaping the action with their plucked and bowed sounds – wear ample robes of a billowing beauty, tracked down by Marie-Hélène Estienne in the *soukhs* of Fès and Marrakech. By contrast, the military uniform of the French prefects and governors looks clumsy.

When the Governor General sends the young Hamallah into distant exile because France sees him as a troublemaker and his followers as a threat to their order, the back wall of the set glides away upstage behind him, as if he is being thrust out of history, which he is; he will die, we are told, in a prison in Montluçon, in mainland France. At such moments, in a reverse-telescope effect, we glimpse 'our' European historical context: Tierno Bokar's timeless story is in fact taking place during the 1930s and 40s, and the new Governor General, we realise, is an official of Vichy France. As the Hamallists are persecuted, two pillars which have framed the life of the mosque lie fallen and askew. We also follow the high-minded oppression of French rule through the third main character, Amkoullel, Bokar's prize pupil, as he rises into the French colonial service and confronts its racism.

The *mission civilisatrice* exists to serve the interests of the conquerors, and is just as blinkered as the enraged partisans of the 'eleven-times' or the 'twelve-times' prayer paths. They recall Brook's own words, in his talk at the Grotowski centre in 2001; 'I am "glued". Glued to the part I am playing at this moment. I believe totally in the words that I am saying because I am glued to them.' French patriots singing chauvinistic anthems with their pupils in an African classroom are glued. Intemperate defenders of a faith that cannot tolerate any other faith or practice are glued. Their mission has become their fetish. But the theatre can momentarily unglue rigid beliefs, and show us that they do not span the entire horizon. And that is why Brook concludes, in a time of fundamentalisms and crusades, 'We must learn to believe without believing. Otherwise, belief is poison.' Making theatre has helped Peter Brook to be free, and we respond to his freedom.

Chronology of Plays and Films

Note: In this chronology, plays appear in the year and at the theatre in which they opened, films appear in the year in which they were shot.

1943   *Doctor Faustus*, Torch Theatre, London
1944   Film: *A Sentimental Journey*
1945   *The Infernal Machine*, Jean Cocteau; at Chanticleer Theatre Club, London
       Man and Superman, Shaw; *King John*, Shakespeare;
       The Lady from the Sea, Ibsen; at Birmingham Repertory Theatre
1946   *Love's Labour's Lost*, Shakespeare; Stratford-upon-Avon
       The Brothers Karamazov, Dostoevsky; Lyric Theatre, London
       Vicious Circle, Jean-Paul Sartre, Arts Theatre, London
1947   *Romeo and Juliet*, Shakespeare; Stratford-upon-Avon
       The Respectful P . . ., Jean-Paul Sartre; Lyric Theatre, London
1948   *La Bohème*, Puccini; Covent Garden, London
       Boris Godunov, Mussorgsky; Covent Garden, London
       The Olympians, Arthur Bliss; Covent Garden, London
       Salome, Richard Strauss; Covent Garden, London
       Le Nozze di Figaro, Mozart; Covent Garden, London
1949   *Dark of the Moon*, Howard Richardson and William Berney; Lyric Theatre
       Hammersmith, London
1950   *Ring Round the Moon*, Jean Anouilh; Globe Theatre, London
       Measure for Measure, Shakespeare; Stratford-upon-Avon
       The Little Hut, André Roussin; Lyric Theatre, London
1951   *Mort d'un commis voyageur* (*Death of a Salesman*), Arthur Miller; Théâtre
       National, Brussels
       Penny for a Song, John Whiting; Haymarket Theatre, London
       The Winter's Tale, Shakespeare; Phoenix Theatre, London
1952   *Colombe*, Jean Anouilh; New Theatre, London
       Film: *The Beggar's Opera*, John Gay
1953   *Venice Preserv'd*, Thomas Otway; Lyric Theatre, London

       Faust, Gounod; Metropolitan Opera, New York
       TV: *King Lear*, Shakespeare, CBS Television, New York
1954   *The Dark is Light Enough*, Christopher Fry; Aldwych Theatre, London
       Both Ends Meet, Arthur Macrae; Apollo, London
       House of Flowers, Harold Arlen and Truman Capote, Alvin Theater, New York
1955   *The Lark*, Jean Anouilh; Lyric, London
       Titus Andronicus, Shakespeare; Stratford-upon-Avon
       Hamlet, Shakespeare; Moscow Art Theatre, Moscow; Phoenix Theatre, London
       The Power and the Glory, Graham Greene; Phoenix Theatre, London
       The Family Reunion, T. S. Eliot; Phoenix Theatre, London
1956   *A View from the Bridge*, Arthur Miller; Comedy Theatre, London
       Chatte sur un toit brûlant (*Cat on a Hot Tin Roof*), Tennessee Williams; Théâtre Antoine, Paris
1957   *The Tempest*, Shakespeare; Stratford-upon-Avon
       Eugene Onegin, Tchaikovsky, Metropolitan Opera, New York
1958   *Vu du pont*, (*A View from the Bridge*), Arthur Miller; Théâtre Antoine, Paris
       The Visit, Friedrich Dürrenmatt; Lunt-Fontanne Theater, New York, Royalty Theatre, London
1959   *Irma la douce*, Alexandre Breffort, Julian More, Monty Norman; Lyric Theatre, London
       The Fighting Cock, Jean Anouilh; ANTA Theater, New York
1960   *Le Balcon* (*The Balcony*), Jean Genet; Théâtre du Gymnase, Paris
       Film: *Moderato cantabile*, Marguerite Duras
1961   Film: *Lord of The Flies*
1962   *King Lear*, Shakespeare; Stratford-upon-Avon, Aldwych Theatre, London, toured internationally and to New York
1963   *La Danse du Sergent Musgrave* (*Serjeant Musgrave's Dance*), John Arden; Théâtre de l'Athénée, Paris
       The Physicists, Friedrich Dürrenmatt; RSC, Aldwych Theatre, London
       Le Vicaire (*The Representative*) Rolf Hochhuth, Théâtre de l'Athénée, Paris
1964   *Theatre of Cruelty* season, LAMDA Theatre, London
       The Screens, Jean Genet; Donmar Theatre, London
       The Persecution and Assassination of Marat as Performed by the Inmates of Charenton under the Direction of the Marquis de Sade, Peter Weiss, English verse adaptation Adrian Mitchell; RSC, Aldwych Theatre, London, Martin Beck Theater, New York
1965   *The Investigation*, Peter Weiss; RSC, Aldwych Theatre, London
1966   *US*, Peter Brook, Sally Jacobs, Adrian Mitchell, Denis Cannan, Geoffrey Reeves, Albert Hunt, Michael Kustow, Michael Stott; RSC, Aldwych Theatre, London
       Film: *The Marat/Sade*
1967   Film: *Tell Me Lies*
1968   *Oedipus*, Seneca, translated by Ted Hughes; National Theatre, London
       The Tempest, Shakespeare; RSC, The Round House, London
1969   Film: *King Lear*
1970   *A Midsummer Night's Dream*, Shakespeare; Stratford-upon-Avon
       Leaves London for Paris
1971   Beginning of the International Centre for Theatre Research, Paris
       Orghast, Ted Hughes; Festival of Shiraz/Persepolis, Persia
1972   The group continues to train and experiment in Paris

1973   Journey to Africa
        Journey to USA
1974   Beginning of the International Centre for Theatre Creation in Paris and the
        opening of the Bouffes du Nord Theatre
        Timon d'Athènes (Timon of Athens), Shakespeare
1975   *Les Ik (The Ik)*, Colin Turnbull
1977   *Ubu aux Bouffes*, Alfred Jarry
        Film: *Meetings with Remarkable Men*
1978   *Antony and Cleopatra*, Shakespeare; Royal Shakespeare Theatre, Stratford-
        upon-Avon
        Mesure pour mesure, (Measure for Measure) Shakespeare
1979   *La Conférence des Oiseaux (The Conference of the Birds)*, Farid Uddin Attar,
        Festival d'Avignon
        L'Os (The Bone)
1981   *La Ceriseraie (The Cherry Orchard)*, Chekhov
        Opera: *La Tragédie de Carmen (The Tragedy of Carmen)*, Bizet, Vivian
        Beaumont Theatre, Lincoln Center, New York
1982   Film: *La Tragédie de Carmen* (3 versions)
1985   *La Mahabharata (The Mahabharata)*, adapted for the theatre by Jean-Claude
        Carrière, Festival d'Avignon
1988   Film: *The Mahabharata*
1989   *Woza Albert!* by Percy Mtwa, Mbongeni Ngema, Barney Simon
1990   *La Tempête (The Tempest)*, Shakespeare
1992   Opera: *Impressions de Pelléas (Impressions of Pelléas)*, Debussy
        L'Homme qui (The Man Who), adapted by Peter Brook and Marie-Hélène
        Estienne from a book by Oliver Sacks
1995   *Qui est là? (Who Is There?)*, theatre research by Peter Brook, after texts by
        Antonin Artaud, Bertolt Brecht, Gordon Craig, Meyerhold, Stanislavski and
        Seami
        O les beaux jours (Happy Days), Samuel Beckett, co-production with Vidy E T E
        – Lausanne
1998   *Je suis un phenomène* after *The Mind of a Mnemonist* by Alexander Luria,
        adapted by Peter Brook and Marie-Hélène Estienne
        Opera: *Don Giovanni*, Mozart; 50th Festival International d'Art Lyrique,
        Aixen-Provence
1999   *Le Costume (The Suit)*, Can Themba, adapted and translated by Marie-Hélène
        Estienne
2000   *The Tragedy of Hamlet* (in English)
2002   *Far Away*, Caryl Churchill
        TV Film: *The Tragedy of Hamlet*
        La Tragédie de Hamlet (in French)
2003   *Ta main dans la mienne* The letters of Anton Chekhov and Olga Knipper
2004   *Tierno Bokar*, Marie-Hélène Estienne, after Amadou Hampaté Ba
        La Mort de Krishna, Jean-Claude Carrière, Marie-Hélène Estienne and *Le
        Grand inquisiteur*, Dostoevsky, translated by Marie-Hélène Estienne

Notes

Introduction

Chapter 1

Chapter 2

29 **François Truffaut,** in Sacha Guitry, *Le Cinéma et moi*, Paris, Editions Ramsay, 1984
30 **Dear Brook, Doctor Sutton** This and all following quotations on this affair are reprinted by kind permission of Magdalen College, Oxford

Chapter 3

40 **A very refined** *Threads of Time*, p. 30
40 **to serve an art** Sally Beauman, *The Royal Shakespeare Company, A History of Ten Decades*, Little, Brown & Co, London, 1982, p. 167
40 **an essentially simple** ibid p. 168
41 **When I first met** Paul Scofield, this and all subsequent quotes from letters to the author, February and April 2003
42 **I feel most strongly** Letter to *The Sunday Times*, 13 January 1946
44 **You will find,** Philip Hope-Wallace, *Manchester Guardian* 27 April 1946
44 **At its close** *Observer*, 19 May 1946
44 **Brook's presentment** *The Times*, 29 April 1946
44 **It is a recipe** Philip Hope-Wallace, *Manchester Guardian*, 27 April 1946
44 **the violence, the passion** *Observer*, 9 April 1947
45 **I first saw it** Peter Hall, in conversation with the author, March 2002
46 **Ideally, each sentence** J. C. Trewin, *Peter Brook – A Biography*, London Macdonald, 1971, p. 29
49 **Brook's,** Peter Hall, ibid
49 **This play, one must** Ivor Brown, *Observer*, 7 April 1947
49 **How To Conserve Shakespeare** Peter Ustinov, *New Theatre*, May 1947
50 **Not much liked** Clive Barnes, *New York Times*, 18 January 2001
50 **first-class musical mind** Norman Lebrecht, *Covent Garden – The Untold Story*, London, Simon & Schuster, 2001, p. 102
51 **It is essential** Peter Brook, *The Times*, 6 May 1947
51 **numbers and sumptuousness** Charles Stuart, *Observer*, 16 May 1948
51 **that was able** Peter Brook, *The Times*, 6 May 1947
51 **He ran up against** Lebrecht, ibid p. 102
52 **Strauss' music** *Theatre News Letter*, 11 November 1949
53 **I was as close to death** Peter Brook, interview with the author, February 2003
53 **The preposterous** *Salome Observer*, 21 November 1949
54 **Of the production** *The Sunday Times*, 20 November 1949
54 **Those who booed** *Sunday Graphic*, 13 November 1949
54 **the revolution has shown** Robert Muller, *Daily Mail*, 12 November 1949
54 **Why should we** *Observer*, 4 December 1949
54 **His meteoric rise** *Musical Opinion*, June 1950
55 **It is said that** Peter Brook. *New Theatre*, Summer 1950
55 **One must remember** ibid
56 **Craig loved Henry** Peter Brook, *New Theatre*, 1956.
56 **He retired to Italy** Peter Brook, *New Theatre*, Summer 1950

Chapter 4

58 **Sexual energy** Peter Brook, interview with the author, July 2002
58 **The morality was** ibid

58 I defended Don Giovanni Peter Brook, interview with the author, August 2002
59 Jean was married Peter Brook, in conversation with the author, October 2003
60 My mother was furious ibid
61 Love? I've been Peter Brook to Robert Facey, 10 September 1950
62 Pretty figure; small Quoted in *Brook par Brook*, a film by Simon Brook, 2002
62 Yesterday Peter rang Read out by Brook in Simon Brook's film, *Brook par Brook*
63 It was a real Natasha Parry, in conversation with the author, June 2002.
64 I have a little Peter Brook, *Encore* magazine, July/August 1961
64 Until I came across In *Brook par Brook*, a film by Simon Brook, 2002
64 I managed to Peter Brook to Robert Facey, 4 January 1968
65 Disputes between us *Threads of Time*, p. 92
65 it became a crazily Kenneth Tynan, *Evening Standard*, 10 May 1949
65 is complete wedding cake ibid
66 Gielgud as Angelo *The Times*, 10 March 1950
66 To these crippled Harold Hobson, *The Sunday Times*, 19 March 1950
66 a long prickly moment Kenneth Tynan, *Observer*, 16 March 1950
67 leaves out Peter Ivor Brown, *Observer*, 19 March 1950
68 the most literate John Osborne on *Heaven and Earth* (ITV) by Peter Brook and Denis Cannan, *Evening Standard*, 7 March 1957
69 *Saint's Day* may well be Peter Brook an Tyrone Guthrie, letter to *The Times*, 12 September 1951
69 The newest and overwhelming Letter from Peter Brook to Robert Facey, August 1951
70 I came across Peter Brook, interview with the author, February 2003
71 He was referring Peter Brook, *Threads of Time*, p. 65
71 I was being asked ibid, p. 68
72 the reality of a Henri Corbin, *Spiritual Body and Celestial Earth*, 1977, p. vii
72 My first impressions Peter Brook, letter to Professor Holly Baggot, 1997

Chapter 5

75 astonishing range of speed C. A. Lejeune, *Observer*, 7 June 1953
75 when you flop Interview with Maurice Hatton and Richard de la Mare, *Guardian*, 29 November 1962
76 The brilliant, unabashed theatricality In *I Lost It At The Movies*, 1994, pp. 117–18
77 the champion of ibid
77 A director has A text written by Denis Cannan especially for this book, April 2003
78 'In John,' wrote Peter Brook, *The Shifting Point*, 1988, p. 80.
78 A prodigy has been *A View of the English Stage*, Kenneth Tynan, 1975, pp. 133–4
79 He was the best Peter Brook, interview with the author, September 2002
81 Hitchcock rang up Peter Brook, interview with the author, May 2003
82 the first day J. C. Trewin, *Peter Brook – The Biography, p. 76*
82 within a few weeks Sleeve-notes for *House of Flowers*, Columbia Masterworks CD, 2003 (SK 86857)
82 you people ibid
82 We have to create ibid
83 one of the stupidest T.S. Eliot, in introduction to *Titus Andronicus*, Arden edition, 1964, p. xvii
84 This is tragedy Kenneth Tynan, *Curtains*, London, Longmans, p. 103

84 As Lavinia, Vivien Leigh ibid, p. 104
84 inducted into its Peter Shaffer, interview with the author, August 2003
84 *Titus Andronicus* is already Jan Kott, *Shakespeare our Contemporary*, pp. 282–8
85 This was the moment Peter Brook, *The Sunday Times*, 18 December 1955
85 The Russian sees ibid
86 One would expect ibid
86 The old works ibid
87 The panels in the Peter Brook, '*Hamlet* Fat and *Hamlet* Lean', ibid
87 They were fascinated ibid
88 Valya – Valentin Plouchek Peter Brook, interview with the author, June 2003
89 The Scofield–Brook *Hamlet Gielgud's Letters*, London, Weidenfeld & Nicolson, 2004, p 192
89 Give Peter Brook *Observer*, January 1956
89 I fell headfirst Peter Brook, interview with the author, March 2003
89 Occasionally, things go terribly Peter Hall, interview with the author, February 2002
90 And when he did Arthur Miller, *Timebends*, London, Methuen, 1987, pp. 429–30
90 Doesn't a grocer's son ibid
91 The families oohed ibid
91 Peter Brook has not forgotten *New Statesman*, 20 June 1957
91 Mr Brook is *Spectator*, 15 December 1957
92 The romantic quality Peter Brook, *New York Times*, 27 October 1957
92 You expected to *Combat*, 12 February 1958
93 macabre parable Patrick Bowles, introduction to *The Visit*, 1962
93 an audience of uncles Peter Brook, *The Shifting Point*, p. 36
94 From Orly Airport *Threads of Time*, p. 84.
94 Like a Svengali Diana Rigg, interview with the author, 1962
94 Now my experience Peter Brook, *Threads of Time*, pp. 69–70
95 The new Lunt-Fontanne Walter Kerr, *New York Herald Tribune*, May 1958
95 The Brecht theatre Peter Brook, *The Shifting Point*, pp. 42–3
96 Expecting, no doubt Bernard Levin, *Daily Express*, June 1960
96 When I first entered John Osborne, *Tribune*, 27 March 1959

Chapter 6

102 He said, 'Boys Julian More, interview with the author, June 2002
102 She turned out ibid
103 We opened in Bournemouth ibid
104 It is a play Harold Hobson, *The Sunday Times*, 20 July 1958
104 Peter came in Elizabeth Seal, in conversation with the author, July 2003
105 I went on ahead ibid
106 I was astonished Peter Brook, *Threads of Time*, p. 104
107 A conspiracy of *Le Canard enchaîné*, 13 April 1960
107 wore large hats Peter Brook, *Threads of Time*, pp. 104–5
108 The work in improvisation *Threads of Time*, ibid
108 Would you like Peter Brook, *Threads of Time*, p. 105.
108 What Mr Brook Harold Hobson, *The Sunday Times*, 20 May 1960
108 I was very far Peter Brook, *Threads of Time*, p. 104
108 With its red velvet *Observateur Littéraire*, 15 May 1960

109 **the sharp scent** Peter Brook, *Threads of Time*, pp. 59–60.
109 **He went to his group** Interview by Richard de la Mare and Maurice Hatton in the *Guardian*, 29 November 1962
110 **You can't say** Peter Brook, *The Shifting Point*, p. 201
110 **There is this completely** *Films and Filming*, July 1961
111 **Jeanne Moreau works like** Peter Brook, *The Shifting Point*, p. 201
111 **I have sympathy** *Le Monde*, 25 May 1960
111 **We were prepared** John Russell Taylor, *Sight and Sound*, Spring 1967, p. 80
112 **Shakespeare would have** Peter Brook, *The Shifting Point*, p. 202
113 **to do good things** Sally Beauman, *The Royal Shakespeare Company: A History of Ten Decades*, p. 243
113 **The unfortunate players** Harold Hobson, *The Sunday Times*, 6 April 1960.
113 **a confederacy of individuals** *The Royal Shakespeare Company: A History of Ten Decades*, p. 244
114 **In every production** Conversation with Michael Billington, Theatre Museum video, May 2001
115 **The actors who are** Peter Brook, *Encore*, November 1960
115 **I'm interested in why** ibid
116 **in or about December** Virginia Woolf, 'Mr Bennett and Mrs Brown', 1924

Chapter 7

117 **fed up with theatre** In *Brook par Brook*, a film by Simon Brook, 2001
117 **Spiegel's first fifty years** Philip French, *Observer*, 25 June 2003
118 **a dictator** with quotes from David Lean, Gore Vidal and Billy Wilder, in Natasha Fraser – Carassoni, Little, Brown, 2003
118 **All I wanted** Peter Brook, *The Shifting Point*, p. 193
118 **We followed that up** Peter Shaffer, interview with the author, October 2003
118 **Shaffer wrote a remarkable** Peter Brook, interview with the author, June 2003
118 **I recall him** This and all quotes from Peter Shaffer in this chapter from conversation and correspondence with the author 2003–4
119 **the beauty of Natasha** Peter Shaffer, interview with the author, October 2003
120 **We had spent** Peter Brook, *The Shifting Point*, p. 195.
120 **I believed that the reason** ibid, p. 197.
121 **It had always** ibid, p. 196.
121 **Peter gave me** Gerry Feil, interview with the author 2003
122 **Stumbling along the strand** Jonathen Miller, *New Yorker*, 31 August 1963
122 **specific, not straining** ibid
122 **It is an** Penelope Gilliatt, *Observer*, 2 August 1964
123 **Alas, you can't** Interview by Sheila More, *Guardian*, 16 September 1952
124 **I came to King Lear** Peter Brook, interview with the author, February 2003
124 **Another, older RSC** 'Lear Log', *Encore*, November 1962, p. 15
124 **On Lear's cue** ibid
125 **never more effective** Tom Stoppard, *Scene*, 15 October 1962
125 **Let me not** *King Lear*, Act I, scene 5, line 46
126 **This production brings me** Kenneth Tynan, *Observer*, 11 November 1962
126 **Gloucester is left** Tom Stoppard, *Scene*, 15 October 1962
126 **stylized and detached** Irving Wardle, *Plays and Players*, November 1962
127 **The outline is fixed** Kenneth Tynan, *Observer* 13 January 1963

128 **It will come** *King Lear* Act IV, scene 2, lines 47–9
128 **These are expressions** Irving Wardle, Foreword to *Peter Brook – A Theatrical Casebook*, compiled by David Williams, 1991, p. xix
129 **Hall suffered a variety** Stephen Fay, *Power Play: The Life of Peter Hall*, p. 158
129 **In 1963, the Royal** Peter Hall, interview with the author, May 2002
130 **Beckett at his finest** Peter Brook *Encore*, January 1962
130 **Certainly this is a play** Peter Brook *Encore*, September 1962
131 **We were sitting** Julian More, interview with author, July 2002. All quotes from Julian More come from this interview
132 **A little shoulder** Interview with Peter and Irina Brook, *The Sunday Times*, 14 May 1989
134 **This is spell-binding** Michael Billington, *Guardian*, 20 October 1963
134 **another dreadful ordeal** *Sunday Times*, 21 October 1963
134 **The demonstration that** Peter Brook, *The Empty Space*, pp. 70–71
134 **Black is for death** John Arden, *Encore*, October 1959
135 **put Musgrave firmly back** Albert Hunt and Geoffrey Reeves, *Peter Brook*, London, Cambridge University Press, 1995, p. 63
135 **M. Jean-Jacques Gautier** Harold Hobson, *The Sunday Times*, 12 June 1966
136 **It acts on the mind** Bertrand Poirot Delpech, *Le Monde*, 18 December 1963

Chapter 8

137 **When I was** Interview with Michael Billington, Theatre Museum collection, London, May 2002.
138 **to break through** Antoin Artaud, *The Theatre and Its Double*, New York, Grove Press, 1958
138 **Our object was** Peter Feldman, Joe Chaikin letter (undated)
139 **Either we restore** Peter Brook, *Encore*, January 1964, p. 13
139 **work that cancels itself** Susan Sontag, *Under The Sign of Saturn*, New York, Farrar, Straus and Giroux, 1980, p. 67
139 **One had to,** Glenda Jackson, interview with the author, April 2003
140 **I was already** Sally Jacobs, interview with the author, June 2003.
140 **Very quickly** ibid, p. 92.
140 **An actor sits** Peter Brook, *The Empty Space*, p. 49.
141 **to mint a new** ibid, p. 51
142 **the total involvement** Martin Esslin, *Encore*, June 1964.
142 **He was given** Glenda Jackson, interview with the author, May 2003
143 **stripped, merciless** Jack Kroll, *Newsweek*, 1 June 1964
143 **I couldn't disguise** Charles Marowitz in *Peter Brook – A Theatrical Casebook*, p. 21.
144 **an Academician, a Soldier** Albert Hunt, in Hunt and Reeves, *Peter Brook*, p. 82
144 **series of shattering,** Tom Milne, *Encore*, June 1964
145 **the author seems** in the collection of the Lord Chamberlain, play-licensing documents, British Library
145 **Its breadth, its totality** Bernard Levin, *Daily Mail*, 21 August 1964
146 **Starting with its title** Introduction to Peter Weiss, *The Persecution and Assassination of Marat as Performed by the Inmates of the Asylum of Charenton under the Direction of the Marquis de Sade*, London, John Calder Books, 1965
147 **I thought, this man** Adrian Mitchell, interview with the author, May 2002
149 **I do think** Letter to *The Times* from Terence Rattigan, 22 August 1964

149 **Brook's direction** Alan Brien, *Spectator*, 4 September 1964
149 **What Peter Weiss has** A. L. Alvarez, *New Statesman*, 4 September 1964
150 **One way to** *Burnt Bridges*, p. 96
150 **it surges, opens** Stanley Kauffman, *New York Times*, January 1966
151 **The untormented faces** *Herald Tribune*, 29 December 1966
151 **all the lovely** Harold Klurman, *Nation*, January 1966
151 **The author had** *Herald Tribune*, 12 January 1967
151 **keeping as close** *The Shifting Point*, p. 189
152 **With three, sometimes four** *The Shifting Point*, p. 189–90
153 **The difference between** ibid, p. 190
154 **a nightmare of vast** Peter Brook, *The Empty Space*, p. 17
154 **The actor must** ibid, p. 136
155 **When a performance** ibid, p. 139.
155 **anyone who refuses,** ibid, p. 139
155 **it takes yesterday's action** ibid, p. 139
156 **This is where** ibid, p. 140
157 **It's the Germans** Programme note for *The Investigation*, 19 October 1965

Chapter 9

159 **There are times** Introduction to *US – The Book of the Royal Shakespeare Theatre Production*/US/Vietnam/US/Experiment/Politics/Full Text/Rehearsal/Reactions/Sources/Peter Brook/Denis Cannan/Albert Hunt/Geoffrey Reeves/Sally Jacobs/Michael Kustow/Adrian Mitchell/Richard Peaslee/Do it Yourself, John Calder Books, London, 1966
161 **Mike Williams suddenly** ibid, p. 20
162 **July 6, 1966** Joseph Chaikin letter to Jean-Claude van Itallie.
162 **Would he fight? . . .** *US*, p. 24
163 **The shock of** Peter Brook, Introduction to *Towards A Poor Theatre* by Jerzy Grotowski, London, Simon & Schuster, 1968.
164 **He runs a laboratory** ibid
165 **we non-established playwrights Hunt** and Reeves, *Peter Brook – Directors in Perspective*, p. 116
165 **to show the people** Adrian Mitchell, interview with the author, July 2003
165 **so you end** *US*, London, Calder playscript, 1966
168 ***The Soldiers* is all** Kenneth Tynan, *Letters*, Weidenfeld & Nicolson, 1994, p. 366
169 **If democracy means** *Threads of Time*, pp. 140–41
169 **involves its participants** Bishop of Woolwich, *Listener*, 15 May 1966
170 **If no act** Peter Brook, *Threads of Time*, p. 141

Chapter 10

173 **He would only** *Peter Brook – From Oxford to Orghast*, edited by Richard Helfer and Glenn Loney, Australia Harwood Academic Publishers, 1998, p. 163
173 **John knew that** *The Shifting Point*, p. 83
174 **he was raging** Ted Hughes, in A.C.H. Smith, London, *Orghast at Persepolis*, 1972
175 **it got quite** Colin Blakeley, in *From Oxford to Orghast*, p. 173
176 **I've erased or** Michael Birkett, interview with the author, winter 2002

176 **Birth, bed, womb** British Sound Archive, May 1968
176 **What in Grotowski** Charles Marowitz, *Village Voice*, May 1968
178 **It is one** David Sylvester, *About Modern Art*, Pimlico, London, 2002, p. 57
180 **I haven't yet** This and all subsequent unattributed Brook quotes in this chapter are from Peter Brook's letter to Robert Facey, 4 January 1968
183 **These bodies had** *Threads of Time*, p. 143
184 **considered to be** Yashi Oidan , *An Actor Adrift*, London, Methuen, 1992, p. 12
184 **I was less impressed** *Threads of Time*, p. 147
185 **I had experienced** ibid, p. 145
185 **the old man** ibid, p. 147
185 **a non-stop marathon** ibid, p. 145
186 **not a literal interpretation** *Lunatics, Lovers and Poets*, London, McGrant Hill, 1974, p. 256
187 **There are plays** Peter Brook, interview with Richard Eyre, BBC Television, March 2003
187 **If your job is to bring** *Peter Brook – From Oxford to Orghast*, edited by Richard Helfer and Glenn Loney, p. 180
193 **It is not only** Irving Wardle, foreword Peter Brook: *Theatrical Casebook*, London, Methuen, 1988
194 **Once is a while** Clive Barnes, New York Post, 1971

Chapter 11

197 **In the hall** Peter Brook, *Sunday Times*, 23 September 1962
198 **was far ahead** ibid
199 **The world's theatre** October 1969 document, CIRT (International Centre for Theatre Research)
200 **The problem today** ibid
202 **Through her own unremitting** *Threads of Time*, p. 123
203 **the pre-expressive substrata** David Williams, *Peter Brook and the International Centre for Theatre Research*, p. 46
205 **Our job is to** This and other quotes on this page, A.C.H. Smith, *Orghast at Persepolis*, London, Methuen, 1972, p. 32
207 **What you hear** Ted Hughes, interview with Tom stoppard, *Times Literary Supplement*, 10 October 1971
207 *Orghast* **aims to be** ibid
208 **We are not making** Peter Brook quoted in A.C.H. Smith, *Orghast at Persepolis*, p. 108
208 **It would be complete** *From Oxford to Orghast*, p. 160
208 **Iran is not** In *Conversations with Peter Brook*, Margaret Croyden, New York, Faber & Faber, 2003, p. 48
210 **Despite their talents** Geoffrey Reeves, 'The Persepolis Follies of 1971', *Performance* magazine, December 1971
210 **He told them** A.C.H. Smith, *Orghast at Persepolis*, pp. 135–6
211 **Inside the group** In 'The Persepolis Follies of 1971', *Performance* magazine, December 1971
213 **The focus changes** Irving Wardle, *The Times*, 14 September 1971
214 **What we saw** Richard Findlater, *Observer* 12 September 1971
215 **When from the darkness** Andrew Porter, *Financial Times*, 28 August 1971
215 **Book would call** John Heilpern, *Conference of the Birds*, London, Faber, 1977 p.

215 **See the camp** ibid, pp. 112–3; 115
216 **at times it was as if** ibid, p. 133–4
216 **It was as if** ibid, p. 144
217 **An old man** Tony Harrison, interview with the author, December 2003
218 **Living, pulsating** Quoted in *Sessions in the USA*, Michael Wilson, duplicated report for CIRT, 1973, p. 12
220 **The Simorgh became** In *Sessions in the USA*, Michael Wilson, duplicated report for CIRT, 1973, p. 15
222 **We have a-situation** ibid, p. 15.
223 **The training of an actor** ibid, p. 16.
223 **rough theatre, vulgar, comic** ibid, p. 42
223 **If we had touched** ibid, p. 43

Chapter 12

225 **I was immediately certain** Peter Brook, in *The Open Circle*, by Jean-Guy Lecat and Andrew Todd, London, Faber & Faber, 2003, p. 6
226 **Otherwise we'd be** Peter Brook, interview with the author, 2003
226 **The designer Georges** Peter Brook, interview with the author, June 2003
227 **We want to do these** *Conversations with Peter Brook*, Margaret Croyden, p. 184
228 **A journalist asked** Peter Jean-Claude Carrière, interview with the author, March 2003
228 **look like crows** In *Peter Brook – A Theatrical Casebook*, London, Methuen, 1991, p. 245
229 **she changes her** Peter Brook, interview with the author, 2003
230 *Timon* itself Elizabeth Hardwick, *New York Review of Books*, 12 December, 1974
231 **never locked within** *Peter Brook – A Theatrical Casebook*, p. 250
231 **Timon is a romantic** Elizabeth Hardwick, *New York Review of Books*, 12 December 1974
232 **I'm going toward** *Conversations with Peter Brook*, Margaret Croyden, pp. 171–172
232 **Listening to the applause** Albert Hunt, *New Society*, 20 February 1975
233 **Brook believes** *Peter Brook – A Theatrical Casebook*, p. 259
233 **a form of myth** ibid, pp. 259–60
236 **Between scenes supporting** Nina Soufy, interview with the author, 2003
236 **We'd done the film** Glenda Jackson, interview with the author, March 2002
238 **The whole company** Robert Cushman, *Observer*, October 1978
238 **In France, there are** Jean-Claude Carrière, interview with the author, April 2003
239 **The tree presented** *The Open Circle*, p. 69
239 **an ordinary-extraordinary** ibid, p. 73
241 **The double image** In *Conversations with Peter Brook*, Margaret Croyden, p. 175
242 **For the actor** Peter Brook, afterword to *The Conference of the Birds*, 1979
242 **Our point of departure** ibid

Chapter 13

245 **In his wanderings** Screenplay for *Meetings With Remarkable Men*, by Peter Brook and Jeanne de Salzmann
246 **The question put** *Conversations with Peter Brook*, Margaret Croyden, p. 117

249 **Although firmly rooted** In *Gurdjieff: The Secret Dimension*, London, New York, Continuum Books, 1998, p. 94
249 **Every phenomenon arises** In *Gurdjieff: The Secret Dimension*, p. 96
250 **One of India's** Peter Brook, interview with the author, 2003
250 **My deepest wish** Peter Brook, letter to the author, summer 2004
251 **The whole unit** Nina Soufy, interview with the author, 2003
252 **How is it possible** Peter Brook in *Parabola: The Magazine of Myth and Tradition*, vol. IV, no. 2
253 **I hope people will** Peter Brook, *Guardian*, 8 September 1979
256 **We had three casts** Peter Brook, interview with the author, June 2004
257 **I thought it** Peter Brook, interview with the author, 2003

Chapter 14

260 **A question that no one** *The Shifting Point*, pp. 163–4
261 **as if the earth** Maria Shevtsova in *Peter Brook and The Mahabharata: A Casebook*, London, Methuen, 1987, p. 213
261 **It's the age** this and all other quotes from the playscript, *The Mahabharata*, (adapted by Jean-Claude Carrière, translated by Peter Brook), London, Methuen, 1987
263 **the embodiment of** ibid, p. 208
263 **Our communal one-night stand** Michael Billington, *Guardian*, 18 August 1987
264 **The show's real magic** Michael Kurfield, *Los Angeles Times*, 28 August 1987
264 **It soon became evident** Charles Osborne, *Daily Telegraph*, 21 March 1988
264 *The Mahabharata* **is nothing** Gautam Dasgupta, *Performing Arts Journal*, no. 30, 10 (3) 1987, p. 263
265 **The British first made us** *Peter Brook's Mahabharata: A View from India*, Framework, no. 35, 1988, pp. 34
265 **I have to say completely** In *Peter Brook and The Mahabharata*, edited David Williams, p. 103
265 **Peter Brooks Mahabharata**
265 **At the same time** ibid p. 99.
265 **is not mere epic** Gautam Dasgupta, *Performing Arts Journal*, no. 30, 10 (3) 1987, p. 263
265 **An audience comes** *Can Nothing Come From Nothing?* The Ernest Jones Lecture given by Brook on 13 June 1994 at University College, London
267 **More than ever** *Threads of Time*, pp. 218–9
267 **We are trying to celebrate** Foreword to *The Mahabharata*, London, Mathuen, 1987, p. xvi
267 **When we were bringing** In *Peter Brook and The Mahabharata*, ed. David Williams, p. 58
267 **Cultural piracy is** ibid, p. 58
268 **It is the epicentre** ibid, p. 51

Chapter 15

270 **Peter had a weakness** Micheline Rozan, interview with the author, 2003
270 **In the world of apartheid** Preface to *South Africa, the Theatre of the Townships*, CICT, 1989

272 **Evoking** *(And Forgetting) Shakespeare* First published in French as *Avec Shake-speare* in 1998; originated as a lecture in Berlin

272 **Genetically speaking** *Evoking (And Forgetting) Shakespeare*, Nick Hern Books, 2000, p. 8

273 **its permanent state of flux** Programme note for Aix-en-Provence festival, June–July 2002

273 **We, at any given moment** *Evoking (And Forgetting) Shakespeare*, p. 10

274 **For Shakespeare and** *Evoking (and Forgetting) Shakespeare*, pp. 18–19

275 **Sandcastles, footsteps** *Peter Brook – A Theatrical Casebook*, p. 414

275 **The theatre always** Peter Brook, *The Empty Space*, p. 157

275 **Prospero is neither a 'director'** *Peter Brook – A Theatrical Casebook*, p. 432

276 **The thinking which** Peter Brook, interview with the author, June 2004

277 **classical fables have** Oliver Sacks, preface to *The Man who Mistook His Wife for a Hat*, London, Duckworth, 1985

277 **We wanted him** Peter Brook, interview with the author, 2003

277 **We're going to spend** ibid

278 **I had the intuition** Peter Brook, interview with Michael Billington, *Guardian*, 27 February 1994

279 **whose clownish tics** John Lahr, *New Yorker*

279 **Oliver uses all his human** 'Mind Games' by John Cornwell, *The Sunday Times*, 13 February 1994

281 **It would be good** Gordon Craig, in Peter Brook, 'The Art of the Director', *New Theatre*, Summer 1950

281 **the event becomes** Michael Coveney, *Observer*, 14 January 1996

282 **became a woman drawn** Peter Brook, interview with the author, July 2004

283 **There are plays that are** Peter Brook to Richard Eyre, BBC4, January 2003

284 **Intellectually, emotionally** John Peter in *The Sunday Times*, 10 December 2000

285 **the therapeutic power** Paul Taylor, *Independent*, 7 December 2000

Chapter 16

286 **The threads that** *Threads of Time*, pp. 2

286 **When I was young** ibid, pp. 226–7

287 **Don Giovanni's Error** *Entretien avec Peter Brook* in Festival brochure, 54th Festival d'Aix-en-Provence, 2002

288 **Now he sees** Peter Brook, interview with the author, summer 2002

289 **It was tiring** Caryl Churchill, *Far Away*, London, Nick Hern Brooks, 2001, p. 37

290 **Gurdjieff often spoke** Peter Brook, text of lecture, Grotowski Centre, Wroclaw, November 2001

292 **Peter's got a way** Declan Donnellan, interview with the author, autumn 2003

293 **I still love that** ibid

293 **Like many students** David Lan, interview with the author, autumn 2003

294 **If you said to him** ibid

294 **Brook began by** Simon McBurney, interview with the author, autumn 2003

295 **Paris has always been** ibid

296 **Into this self-consciously** ibid

296 **feels like a surrogate** Richard Eyre, *National Service*, London, 2003, p. 187

297 **John's romantic attempt** David Hare, lecture on John Osborne at the Hay Literary

Festival June 2002, reprinted as 'Theatre's Great Malcontent' in the *Guardian*, 8 June 2002

298 **14 September 2002, Dear David** unpublished correspondence between Peter Brook and David Hare, reprinted by permission of the authors

301 **an intercultural situation** David Edgar, *London Review of Books*, 12 November 1998

301 **Aware of the horror** ibid

302 **The project can be** ibid

302 **A theatre in which** ibid

302 **Only in England** ibid

303 **If I'd have stayed** Peter Brook, interview with the author, autumn 2003

Select Bibliography

1. By and About Peter Brook

Banu, Georges *Peter Brook – De Timon d'Athènes à Hamlet*, Paris, Flammarion, 2001

Brook, Peter *The Empty Space*, London, MacGibbon & Kee, 1968

Brook, Peter *The Shifting Point*, London, Methuen, 1988

Brook, Peter *There Are No Secrets*, London, Methuen, 1993

Brook, Peter *Threads of Time*, London, Methuen, 1998

Brook, Peter *Evoking Shakespeare*, London, Nick Hern Books, 1999

Croyden, Margaret *Conversations with Peter Brook 1970–2000*, New York, Faber & Faber, Inc, 2003

Heilpern, John *Conference of the Birds, The Story of Peter Brook in Africa*, London, Faber & Faber, 1977

Helfer, Richard, and Glenn Loney (eds.) *Peter Brook: From Oxford to Orghast*, Australia, Harwood Academic Publishers, 1998

Hunt, Albert, and Geoffrey Reeves *Peter Brook – Directors in Perspective*, Cambridge, Cambridge University Press, 1995

Lecat, Jean-Guy, and Andrew Todd *The Open Circle: Peter Brook's Theatrical Environments*, London, Faber & Faber, 2003

Smith, A. C. H., *Orghast At Persepolis, An Account of the Experiment in Theatre Directed by Peter Brook and Written by Ted Hughes* London, Methuen, 1972

Trewin, J. C., *Peter Brook – A Biography*, London, Macdonald, 1971

Williams, David (ed.) *Peter Brook – A Theatrical Casebook*, London, Methuen, 1988

Williams, David (ed.) *Peter Brook and The Mahabharata: Critical Perspectives*, London, Routledge/Taylor & Francis Books, Inc., 1991

2. Playscripts

Le Théâtre des Bouffes du Nord has published, in French, playscripts of all of Brook's productions there, with introductions or afterwords by Brook. The series begins with *Timon d'Athènes* and includes *Le Mahabharata* and *La Tempête*. They can be ordered from Le Théâtre des Bouffes du Nord, 37bis, Boulevard de la Chapelle, 75010 Paris, France.

The Man Who, Peter Brook and Marie-Hélène Estienne, London, Methuen, 2002
L'Homme Qui, Je Suis Un Phénomène, de Peter Brook et Marie-Hélène Estienne, Paris, Actes Sud, 1999
The Mahabharata by Jean-Claude Carrière, translated from the French by Peter Brook, London, Methuen, 1987
Conference of the Birds, adapted by Jean-Claude Carrière, translated by Peter Brook, New York, Drama Bookshop, 1991
Afrique du Sud, Théâtre des Townships (The Island, Sizwe Banzi est mort, Le Costume) de Collectif, traduit par Marie-Hélène Estienne, Paris, Actes Sud, 1999

3. On Gurdjieff

Gurdjieff, Georges, *All and Everything: An objectively Impartial Criticism of the Life of Man, or Beelzebub's Tales to His Grandson*, London, Routledge & Kegan Paul, 1950
Gurdjieff, Georges, *Meetings with Remarkable Men*, London, Picador, 1978
Ouspensky, P. D. *In Search of the Miraculous*, London, Routledge and Kegan Paul, 1964

4. Website

There is a well informed website, created in France by Laurent Perron, at www.peter-brook.net/brookFR/PB.html

Index

A NOTE ON THE AUTHOR

Michael Kustow has been at the cutting edges of innovation
in theatre, performing arts, film and television for four decades,
working at the RSC, the ICA and the National Theatre, and for
eight years as Channel 4's first Commissioning Edior for Arts.
His first book, *The Book of US* (1968), was a detailed account
of Peter Brook's controversial Vietnam theatre show. He is the
author of three other books, *Tank* (1975), an autobiographical
novel, *One in Four* (1987), an account of his time at Channel 4
and *theatre@risk* (2000), an impassioned plea for live theatre.
A writer and producer, he lives in London.

A NOTE ON THE TYPE

The text of this book is set in Linotype Sabon, named after the type founder, Jacques Sabon. It was designed by Jan Tschichold and jointly developed by Linotype, Monotype and Stempel, in response to a need for a typeface to be available in identical form for mechanical hot metal composition and hand composition using foundry type.

Tschichold based his design for Sabon roman on a font engraved by Garamond, and Sabon italic on a font by Granjon. It was first used in 1966 and has proved an enduring modern classic.